A Resource Guide
for Secondary
School Teaching

A Resource Guide for Secondary School Teaching

Planning for Competence

5th EDITION

Eugene C. Kim
Richard D. Kellough

California State University, Sacramento

MACMILLAN PUBLISHING COMPANY

NEW YORK

COLLIER MACMILLAN CANADA

TORONTO

Editor: Robert Miller
Production Supervisor: Linda Greenberg
Production Manager: Valerie Sawyer
Text and Cover Designer: Jane Edelstein
Cover illustration: Viqui Maggio

This book was set in New Baskerville by Waldman Graphics, Inc., and printed and bound by Semline. The cover was printed by Lehigh Press.

Macmillan Publishing Company
866 Third Avenue, New York, New York 10022

Collier Macmillan Canada, Inc.
1200 Eglinton Avenue, East, Suite 200
Don Mills, Ontario, M3C 3N1

Library of Congress Cataloging-in-Publication Data

Kim, Eugene C.
    A resource guide for secondary school teaching: planning for competence / Eugene C. Kim, Richard D. Kellough.—5th ed.
        p. cm.
    Includes bibliographical references.
    ISBN 0-02-363860-5
    1. High school teaching. 2. Curriculum planning. I. Kellough, Richard D. (Richard Dean) II. Title.
    LB1737.A3K53 1991   89-28188
    373.19—dc20   CIP

Printing: 1 2 3 4 5 6 7   Year: 1 2 3 4 5 6 7

We Are One

Truth, love, peace, and beauty,
We have sought apart
        but will find within, as our
Moods—explored, shared,
        questioned, and accepted—
Together become one and all

Through life my friends
We can travel together,
for we now know
each could go it alone.

To assimilate our efforts into one,
While growing in accepting,
and trusting, and sharing the
        individuality of the other,
Is truly to enjoy God's greatest gift—
Feeling—knowing love and compassion.

Through life my friends
We are together,
for we must know
we are one.

—R. D. Kellough

Preface

New educational technology, current activities regarding cultural diversity in schools, recent research findings, the middle school movement, and actions resulting from the educational reform movement of the 1980s have prompted us to make major changes in this edition of our resource guide. Revisions to this fifth edition have been accurately incorporated in appropriate locations throughout: in essence, the text has been rewritten. However, we continue in our desire to provide a practical and concise guide for

- Students who are in a secondary methods course in teacher education.
- Students who are in their field component of teacher education.
- Veteran teachers who wish to continue developing their teaching competencies.
- Administrators who wish to have available for reference a current and useful resource guide about secondary school teaching.

We continue in our belief that learning should be active, pleasant, fun, and productive. Consequently, with each edition of this resource guide we have been persistent in our effort to prepare it in an enthusiastic, cognitive-humanistic way that is helpful to its users. Let us explain further our beliefs and how we have incorporated those into this fifth edition.

We believe teaching competencies can be learned. As in medicine, where there are skills and knowledge to be learned and developed before the student physician is licensed to practice with "live" patients; as in law, where there are knowledge and skills to be learned and developed before the law student is licensed to practice an actual legal case; so it is in teacher education: *There are knowledge and skills to be learned and developed before the teacher candidate is licensed to practice the art and skills of teaching with active, responsive learners.* As we have said in previous editions, and continue to believe, we would never consider allowing a person "off the street" to treat our own child's illness or to defend us in a legal case; the professional education of teachers is no less important. Receiving professional education in how to teach is absolutely necessary, and certain aspects of that education must precede any interaction with alert, lively young people if we are to become truly competent and professional.

We believe there are developmental elements involved in becoming a competent, professional secondary school teacher. This resource guide continues to be organized around four developmental elements: *what, why, how, and how well.* The teacher needs to know what is to be taught, and why; Parts I and II are devoted to these elements. For this fifth edition, all four chapters of Part I were revised to make the reading clearer and to reflect accurately what we know about secondary-school teaching in this final decade of this century. For example, information about cultural diversity and multicultural education has been included in appropriate chapters, namely, Chapters 1, 9, and 11. Teacher competencies have been rewritten and clearly explained in Chapter 4, and as in previous editions, revisited many times in the book, reflecting our desire to reinforce and facilitate the development of your teaching competencies.

Part II, Planning for Instruction in a Secondary Classroom, has been revised with the addition of important information about student textbooks (Chapter 6) and the introduction of "seven-step planning" (Chapter 8). Related to planning for instruction are relevant sequential exercises that lead the user through steps from preparing a course outline (Chapter 6), instructional objectives (Chapter 7), a course syllabus and instructional plans (Chapter 8), and student assignments (Part III, Chapter 11) to grade determination procedures (Part V, Chapter 16).

We believe that the "how" component of professional teacher preparation is essential to becoming a competent teacher. The "how" component continues to be reflected in a major portion of this resource guide, but especially in Parts III and IV. Although it remains difficult to anticipate the twenty-first century, particularly to predict what specifically the young people of today will need to know when they are in the work force of that century, we do believe that they will need to know how to learn, how to read, and how to reason and to think critically, and to enjoy doing these things. We continue in our belief that secondary-school students need skills in acquiring knowledge, in processing information, and in learning experiences that will utilize their fullest potentiality for thinking; they need skills that foster effective communication and productive, cooperative behaviors. We want students to feel good about themselves, about others, about their learning, and about their schools. For reaching these goals we continue in our belief that the best teaching strategies are those that incorporate thoughtful planning, acceptance of all, honesty, trusting, sharing, risking, communicating, and cooperating. Furthermore, we believe students best learn these skills and values from teachers who model the same. This resource guide is dedicated to that hope and to that end. In this edition we have increased the number of active exercises that are designed to encourage users to think about their own thinking and to analyze and to plan their own skill development.

Part III has been updated and includes current descriptions of teacher facilitating behaviors (Chapter 10), the latest from research about the use of specific teaching strategies (Chapter 11), and about the use of modern technology and resources available to the classroom teacher (Chapter 12).

Part IV continues to provide a balanced description of approaches and guidelines for classroom management, while Part V focuses attention on the fourth and final element, the element of *how well* the teacher and the students are doing. As with previous editions, Part VI is a guide for the student-teaching component of teacher preparation and provides updated information and guidelines for obtaining a teaching position.

We continue to respond to the many reviewers and users of this resource guide and have made changes as a result of their feedback. Reviewers who have provided in-depth suggestions for which we are deeply grateful are Kenneth Ahrendt of Oregon State University; Dolly S. Baldwin of Bluefield State College; Leigh Chiarelott of Bowling Green State University; Nora M. Evers of Kalamazoo College; Robert P. Green, Jr., of Clemson University; J. Vernon Hoyle, Jr., of the University of North Carolina at Charlotte; Edward S. Jenkins of SUNY–Buffalo; and Allan R. Miller of Fort Hays State University.

We have rewritten nearly all exercises and added a sizable number of new ones. Nearly all "Questions for Class Discussion" at the end of the chapters have been revised and lists of "Suggested Readings" are current. A glossary has been added, and the index and contents are thorough for ease of cross-reference and aid to the user. Preparation of this fifth edition has involved a major rewrite; we hope you find it useful now and throughout your professional career.

As before, we continue to appreciate the help we receive from former students who forgave us our trespasses; teachers and colleagues who continue to share their ideas and successes and have permitted us to include their names in this book; authors and publishers who graciously granted their permissions to reprint materials; and manuscript reviewers who have helped us improve each edition, although, as always, we assume full responsibility for its shortcomings. The education of teachers is an ever-increasingly complex enterprise, and no single book can possibly tell you everything you will need to know. We hope that with this resource guide we have penetrated the surface enough to facilitate your feeling comfortable and on the road to competency as a secondary-classroom teacher.

We express continued admiration and appreciation to the efficacious people at Macmillan.

To Sue Kim and to Noreen Kellough, both competent teachers in their own right, we thank you for sharing your ideas and allowing us the alone time to write. Indeed, we are indebted to and grateful for all the people in our lives, now and in the past, who have interacted with us and reinforced that which we have always known: Teaching is the most rewarding profession we know.

E. C. K.
R. D. K.

Contents

PART I ORIENTATION TO SECONDARY SCHOOL TEACHING   **1**

1 What Do I Need to Know About Today's Secondary Schools?   **3**

  A. About Orientation and Schedules   4
     Orientation Meetings   *4*
     Teacher Schedules   *5*
  B. About Students   6
     Understanding the General Characteristics of Special-Needs Students   *7*
     Cultural Diversity and Multicultural Education   *8*
  C. About Meeting My Students   9
     Exercise 1.1: Getting Acquainted with My Students   *11*
  D. About Teachers   13
  E. About Administrators   13
  F. About the Overall Picture   14
     Exercise 1.2: Reflecting Upon My Own High School Experiences   *17*
     Exercise 1.3: Returning to a Secondary School Classroom   *19*
     Exercise 1.4: Interviewing High School Students   *21*
     Exercise 1.5: Interviewing Junior High or Middle School Students   *23*
     Exercise 1.6: Returning to an "Open House" at a Secondary School   *25*
     Exercise 1.7: Attending a Parent–Teacher Organization Meeting   *27*
     Exercise 1.8: Interviewing a Teacher Candidate   *29*
     Exercise 1.9: Interviewing a Teacher   *31*
     Exercise 1.10: Interviewing a School Administrator   *33*
  Questions for Class Discussion   35
  Suggested Readings for Chapter 1   36

2 What Are the Expectations of a Secondary School Teacher?   **39**

  A. About the Code of Ethics   39
     Code of Ethics of the Education Profession   *39*
  B. About Instructional Responsibilities   41
     What Are Some of the Instructional Responsibilities I Will Meet?   *41*
  C. About Noninstructional Responsibilities   42
     What Are Some of the Noninstructional Responsibilities I Will Meet?   *42*
  D. Summarizing the Expectations of a Secondary School Teacher   43
     Exercise 2.1: The Life of a Teacher   *45*

Questions for Class Discussion   47
Suggested Readings for Chapter 2   47

3   How Do I Develop a Teaching Style?   49

A.   Descriptions of Two Teaching Styles   49
B.   The Theoretical Origins of Teaching Styles   50
C.   Research Contributions Toward the Development of Teaching Style   50
Learning Environment   51
Lesson Planning   51
Teacher Behaviors   51
Learner and Learning   52
Exercise 3.1: Developing a Profile and a Statement About My Own Teaching Style   *55*
Exercise 3.2: Analyzing One Teacher, One Style   *59*
Exercise 3.3: Analyzing Advance Organizers As Used by a Teacher   *61*
Questions for Class Discussion   63
Suggested Readings for Chapter 3   63

4   What Are My Current Competency Levels?   65

A.   Twenty-two Characteristics of the Competent Secondary School Teacher   65
B.   Identifying My Own Competencies   68
Exercise 4.1: Teaching Competencies: My First Self-Evaluation   *69*
Exercise 4.2: My First Self-Evaluation: How Can It Help Me?   *71*
C.   Resources Available for Developing My Competencies   73
Data from Students   73
Comments from Administrators   73
Comments from the University Supervisor   73
Other Resources   76
Questions for Class Discussion   76
Suggested Readings for Chapter 4   77

PART II   PLANNING FOR INSTRUCTION IN A SECONDARY CLASSROOM   79

5   Why Should I Plan and How Do I Select Content?   81

A.   Rationale for Planning   81
B.   Components of a Complete Plan   82
Exercise 5.1: A Pre-Planning Check   *83*
Exercise 5.2: Lesson Planning Pretest   *85*
Exercise 5.3: Examining Teacher Instructional Plans   *87*
C.   Instructional Theory into Practice   89
Questions for Class Discussion   90
Suggested Readings for Chapter 5   90

6   How Do I Know What to Teach?   93

A.   Documents That Provide Guidance for Content Selection   93

Exercise 6.1: Examining State Curriculum Frameworks   *95*
Exercise 6.2: Examining Curriculum Guides   *97*
B.   About Student Textbooks   99
Exercise 6.3: Examining Teacher's Manuals and Student Texts   *101*
Exercise 6.4: Textbook Selection Checklist   *103*
Exercise 6.5: Determining Textbook Reading Level   *105*
C.   Beginning Preparation for a Course   107
Exercise 6.6: Preparing a Tentative Course Outline   *109*
D.   Dealing with Controversial Issues   111
Exercise 6.7: Teaching About Controversial Issues   *113*
Questions for Class Discussion   115
Suggested Readings for Chapter 6   115

7   What Are Instructional Objectives?   117

A.   How to Write Instructional Objectives in Behavioral Terms   118
Audience   118
Anticipated Measurable Performance   118
Condition   119
Performance Level   119
Exercise 7.1: Recognizing Behavioral Objectives: Diagnostic Test 1   *120*
B.   How to Classify Instructional Objectives   121
Cognitive Domain Hierarchies   122
Psychomotor Domain Hierarchies   124
Affective Domain Hierarchies   125
Exercise 7.2: How Knowledgeable Am I About Behavioral Objectives?
   Diagnostic Test 2   *126*
C.   How to Judge Whether Instructional Objectives Are Worth the Time   128
D.   How to Select Verbs for Stating Specific Learning Objectives   128
Exercise 7.3: Writing My Own Behavioral Objectives   *131*
E.   A Danger in Overobjectivity   133
Questions for Class Discussion   133
Suggested Readings for Chapter 7   134

8   How Do I Prepare an Instructional Plan?   135

A.   Guidelines for Planning: The Seven-Step Plan   135
B.   The Course Syllabus   136
Its Value and Purposes   136
What It Includes   136
Exercise 8.1: Preparation of My Course Syllabus   *139*
C.   Preparing Lessons for Class Meetings   141
The Set   141
The Closure   142
The Lesson Body   142
Exercise 8.2: Analysis of a Lesson That Failed   *143*
Model Lesson Plan   145
Exercise 8.3: Preparing a Lesson: A Generic Lesson Plan Format   *153*
Exercise 8.4: Evaluation of My Lesson Plan   *155*
D.   Preparation of a Teaching Unit   157

Exercise 8.5: Writing My Teaching Unit   *159*
Exercise 8.6: Evaluation of My Teaching Unit   *161*
E.   Unit Plan and Daily Plan: Samples   163
Sample 1: Art   163
Sample 2: Biology   165
Sample 3: Typing   170
Sample 4: Home Economics   171
Sample 5: English   173
Sample 6: Music   175
Sample 7: Physical Education   177
Sample 8: Social Studies   179
Sample 9: Spanish   181
A Model for a Unit Plan Contract   183
Questions for Class Discussion   185
Suggested Readings for Chapter 8   185

9   How Can I Individualize the Learning Experience for Students?   187

The S.I.P.   187
A.   Identifying the Students' Needs in Your Classroom   188
Teaching to Different Needs at the Same Time   189
Teaching Students Who Do Not Receive Special Services   190
Teaching Slow Learners, Recalcitrant Learners, Gifted Learners, Bilingual Learners,
*   and a Class That Is Mixed   190*
Guidelines for Teaching the Slow Students Who Indicate Willingness to Try   191
Guidelines for Teaching the Recalcitrant Learners   191
Guidelines for Teaching Gifted and Talented Students   193
Guidelines for Teaching Students Who Have Limited English Proficiency   193
Working With a Class That Is Mixed   194
B.   Multicultural Education and What a Teacher Can Do   194
Activities for Multicultural Education   196
C.   Developing the Self-Instructional Package   204
Exercise 9.1: Preparing a Self-Instructional Package   *204*
Questions for Class Discussion   217
Suggested Readings for Chapter 9   217

PART III   CHOOSING AND IMPLEMENTING INSTRUCTIONAL STRATEGIES IN THE SECONDARY CLASSROOM   219

10   What Are the Basic Teacher Behaviors That Facilitate Student Learning?   221

A.   Fundamental Teacher Classroom Behaviors   222
Structuring   222
Accountability   222
Withitness and Overlapping   222
Variation and Challenging   223
Modeling   223
Data Facilitation   223

Acceptance   224
Clarifying   224
Silence   224
Questioning   224
    Exercise 10.1: Facilitating Behaviors: My First Self-Analysis   *226*
    Exercise 10.2: Facilitating Behaviors: My Personal Plan for Skill Development   *227*
B. About the Use of Questioning   228
    Guidelines for the Use of Questioning   228
    Cognitive Levels of Questions   229
    Exercise 10.3: Identifying the Cognitive Levels of Questions:
        A Self-Diagnostic Test   *231*
    Exercise 10.4: Observing the Cognitive Levels of Classroom Verbal
        Interaction   *232*
    Exercise 10.5: Raising Questions to Higher Levels   *233*
    Exercise 10.6: Creating Cognitive Questions   *235*
    Exercise 10.7: Analyzing the Level of Questions in Textbooks   *237*
    Exercise 10.8: Micro Peer Teaching 1: The Use of Questioning   *239*
    Exercise 10.9: Identifying Basic Teacher Behaviors in Classroom Interaction   *241*
Questions for Class Discussion   244
Suggested Readings for Chapter 10   244

**11 What Are the Guidelines for the Use of Lectures and Other Discretionary
Instructional Strategies?   245**

A. First Decision in Strategy Selection: The Delivery or the Access Mode?   245
        A Listing of Instructional Strategies   247
    Rule in Planning   247
B. Using the Lecture: Twenty Important Guidelines   248
    Exercise 11.1: Micro Peer Teaching 2: Planning and Implementing
        a Lecture   *251*
C. Using Inquiry and Discovery: The Difference   253
    Inquiry Versus Discovery   253
        Levels of Inquiry   253
        Inquiry Cycle   254
    The Processes   254
    Promoting Inquiry   255
    Mystery Island: An Inquiry Lesson   255
D. Using Classroom Discussions   258
    Exercise 11.2: Discussion as a Strategy: What Do I Already Know?   *259*
    Exercise 11.3: Guidelines for Using Discussions   *261*
    Equal Time to All Students   263
    Exercise 11.4: Teacher Interaction with Students According to Student
        Gender   *265*
    Advice for a Teacher-Led Discussion   267
E. Using Demonstrations   267
    Purposes for a Demonstration   267
    Guidelines for Using a Demonstration   268
F. Using the Textbook   268
G. Using Assignments   270
    Values in Using Assignments   270

Guidelines for Using Assignments   *270*

Exercise 11.5: Planning Course Assignments   *273*

Exercise 11.6: Analysis of a Teaching Episode   *275*

H. Using Term Papers and Student Oral Reports   277

Form for Evaluating Written and Oral Report   278

I. Using Games   278

Why Are Games Used?   *278*

What Are Games? A Classification   *279*

Sources of Educational Games   *280*

Exercise 11.7: Creating My Own Instructional Game   *281*

A Sampling of "Homemade" Games   *283*

Game 1: Living Tic Tac Toe   283

Game 2: Oral Communication   283

Game 3: Cooperation Square Game   284

Game 4: Lunar Survival Game   285

Game 5: Musical Bingo   286

Additional Sources of Games   *288*

Questions for Class Discussion   289

Selected Readings for Chapter 11   289

12   What Other Aids and Resources Are Available to the Secondary-School Teacher?   291

A. General Guidelines for Selection of Aids and Resources: The Learning Experiences Ladder   291

B. Aids and Resources for Direct and Simulated Experiences   293

C. Aids and Resources for Vicarious Experiences   293

Computers   *293*

Why Use Computers?   *294*

Selecting Computer Software   *296*

The Eric Information Network   *298*

Exercise 12.1: Conversion of an Abstract Learning Experience   *299*

D. Aids and Resources for Visual and Verbal Experiences   301

The Writing Board   *301*

The Overhead and Opaque Projectors   *301*

Guidelines for Using the Overhead Projector   *302*

Sources of Overhead Transparencies   303

Exercise 12.2: Using the Overhead Projector   *305*

Charts, Drawings, Globes, Graphs, Maps, and Other Visuals   *307*

Objects   *307*

Audio and Video Tapes, Computer Programs, Films, Filmstrips, Laser Videodiscs, and Slides   *307*

Sample Videodisc Titles and Publishers for Secondary Use   308

Resources for Free and Inexpensive Teaching Materials   311

Community Resources   *312*

Copying Machines   *312*

Guidelines for Use of Copyrighted Materials   *313*

E. Professional Periodicals and Resources   315

Exercise 12.3: Identifying Professional Journals   *317*

Exercise 12.4: Beginning My Resource File   *319*

Questions for Class Discussion 320
Suggested Readings for Chapter 12 320

13 What Are Some Motivational Strategies? An Annotated List of More Than 200 Possibilities 323

A. General Ideas for Motivation 324
B. Expressing Encouragement as a Motivator 325
C. Motivational Ideas Specific to Subject Areas 326
   Art 326
   Business Education 327
   English (including ESL, Speech, Drama, Journalism) 328
   Foreign Languages 330
   Home Economics 330
   Mathematics 331
   Music 332
   Physical Education 334
   Science 334
   Social Science 336
   Exercise 13.1: Selecting and Experimenting With a Motivational Technique *339*
Questions for Class Discussion 341
Suggested Readings for Chapter 13 341

PART IV CLASSROOM MANAGEMENT, DISCIPLINE, AND LEGAL GUIDELINES 343

14 What Do I Need to Know to Cope with the Daily Challenges of Secondary-School Teaching? 345

A. Beginning the School Year 346
   Establishing Classroom Behavior Rules 346
B. Surveying the Physical Environment of the Classroom 349
   Exercise 14.1: What Should I Do to Maintain the Physical Environment of My Classroom? *351*
C. Achieving Routine Maintenance 353
   Exercise 14.2: How Can I Maintain Efficiency in Responding to Routines and Clerical Responsibilities? *355*
   Exercise 14.3: Writing a Positive Note to a Parent/Guardian *357*
D. Legal Guidelines That Support Your Teaching Rights and the Rights of Secondary-School Students 359
   Exercise 14.4: What Legal Guidelines Are Available to Me? *361*
   Exercise 14.5: What Do I Know About Legal Guidelines in My State for the Secondary-School Teacher? *363*
Your Teaching Contract and Tenure 366
   Liability Insurance 366
Questions for Class Discussion 366
Suggested Readings for Chapter 14 367

15   What Do Some Authorities Suggest as Approaches to Classroom Control?   369

A.   The Meaning of Classroom Control   369
B.   Student Responses to Questions About Management and Discipline   370
   Symptoms of Drug Abuse   372
C.   Today's Effective Classroom Management Systems   372
D.   Guidelines for Establishing an Effective Classroom Management System   374
   Resources for Teachers Working with Children Affected by Divorce   375
   Exercise 15.1: Case Studies for Class Discussion   376
   Exercise 15.2: How to Work with a Difficult Student: Brainstorming Ideas   381
Questions for Class Discussion   383
Suggested Readings for Chapter 15   383

PART V   EVALUATION OF TEACHER PERFORMANCE AND STUDENT ACHIEVEMENT   385

16   How Do I Evaluate and Report Student Achievement?   387

A.   Purposes of the Assessment Component   387
B.   Guidelines That Permeate the Assessment Component   388
C.   Evaluating Student Achievement   389
   Evaluating a Student's Verbal and Nonverbal Behaviors   389
   Guidelines for Evaluating What the Learner Does and Says   389
   Evaluating a Student's Written Behaviors   392
   Guidelines for Evaluating What the Student Writes   392
D.   Recording My Observations and Judgments: A Word of Caution About the Anecdotes I Write   393
   Exercise 16.1: An Evaluation of Written Teacher Comments   394
E.   Maintaining Records of Student Achievement   395
F.   Grading Student Achievement   395
   Criterion-referenced Versus Norm-referenced Grading   395
   Arriving at Grades   396
G.   Testing for Student Achievement   398
   Purposes for Testing   398
   When and How Often to Test   398
   Administering Tests   398
   About Cheating   399
   Time Needed for a Test   399
H.   Preparing Test Items: Twelve Types   400
   General Guidelines for Test Item Preparation   400
   1. Arrangement Type   400
   2. Completion Drawing Type   401
   3. Completion Statement Type   401
   4. Correction Type   401
   5. Essay Type   401
   6. Grouping Type   403
   7. Identification Type   404

8. *Matching Type* *404*
9. *Multiple-Choice Type* *405*
10. *Performance Type* *407*
11. *Short Explanation Type* *407*
12. *True-False Type* *408*
Exercise 16.2: Preparing Test Items *409*
Exercise 16.3: My Grade Determination Procedure *411*
I. Conferencing with an Angry Student *413*
J. Reporting a Student's Achievement *413*
Suggestions for Preparing Report Cards *414*
K. Conferencing with a Parent *414*
Guidelines for Parent–Teacher Meetings *414*
Questions for Class Discussion *416*
Suggested Readings for Chapter 16 *416*

17 How Can I Continue to Evaluate My Developing Competency? 417

A. A Look at My Pre-employment Competency Development:
Micro Peer Teaching 3 *417*
Exercise 17.1: Micro Peer Teaching 3: Putting It All Together *418*
Exercise 17.1: Micro Peer Teaching 3 Form A: MPT Preparation *419*
Exercise 17.1: Micro Peer Teaching 3 Form B: Peer Evaluation *421*
What to Look for in Video Playback Session for Your Self-Evaluation *423*
Exercise 17.1: MPT 3 Form C: Instructor's Evaluation *425*
Exercise 17.2: How Can I Further Analyze My Verbal Interactions with
Students? *427*
B. Another Look: My Secondary Teachalogue, with Twenty Teaching
Suggestions *428*
C. Still Another Look: Secondary Student-Teaching Evaluation Form and
Competency Descriptions *430*
Exercise 17.3: Secondary Student-Teaching: What Does My Second
Self-Evaluation Tell Me? *433*
D. Looking Ahead: Sample Forms Used to Evaluate Teacher Effectiveness *434*
Teacher Self-Evaluation *434*
Exercise 17.4: Self-Improvement Plan *439*
Teacher Evaluation by Classroom Visitation: Sample Long Form *441*
Teacher Evaluation by Classroom Visitation: Sample Short Form 1 *446*
Teacher Evaluation by Classroom Visitation: Sample Short Form 2 *448*
Questions for Class Discussion *450*
Suggested Readings for Chapter 17 *450*

**PART VI WHAT SHOULD I KNOW ABOUT THE STUDENT-TEACHING
EXPERIENCE AND BEYOND? 451**

18 What Should I Know About the Student-Teaching Experience? 453

A. The Paraprofessional Experience *454*
Exercise 18.1: Classroom Paraprofessional Duties: Self-Evaluation *455*

B. The Student-Teaching Experience   459
  Will My Student-Teaching Be the "Real Thing?"   *459*
  How Can I Best Get Ready for My Student-Teaching?   *459*
C. The Student-Teaching Experience from the Cooperating Teacher's
  Point of View   459
D. The Student-Teaching Experience from the Principal's Point of View   461
  Exercise 18.2: The Student-Teaching Experience from the Student
    Teacher's Point of View: How Can I Continue My Self-Evaluation
    as a Secondary-School Teacher?   *465*
Question for Class Discussion   467
Suggested Readings for Chapter 18   467

19 What Do I Need to Know That May Help Me in Getting a Teaching Job?   469

A. Guidelines to Help Me Get a Teaching Job   469
  Resources for Locating a Teaching Position   *469*
  The Professional Résumé and Its Accompanying Application Letter   *470*
  Exercise 19.1: Preparing a Résumé and Application Cover Letter   *471*
  The Personal Interview   *472*
B. Information Sources About Credential Requirements State by State   473
C. Professional Associations in the United States of Interest to
  Secondary-School Teachers   476
  Exercise 19.2: My Final Self-Evaluation of Competencies as Reviewed
    Through *A Resource Guide for Secondary School Teaching: Planning
    for Competence*   *479*
Questions for Class Discussion   485
Suggested Readings for Chapter 19   486

Epilogue   **487**

Glossary   **489**

Index   **493**

A Resource Guide
for Secondary
School Teaching

PART I

Orientation to Secondary School Teaching

Part I deals with your perceptions

- About secondary school teaching.
- About students, teachers, and administrators.
- About the kind of secondary teacher you would like to be.
- And your proposed goals for the development of your teaching style.

Personally I am always ready to learn,
although I do not always like being taught.
—Sir Winston Churchill

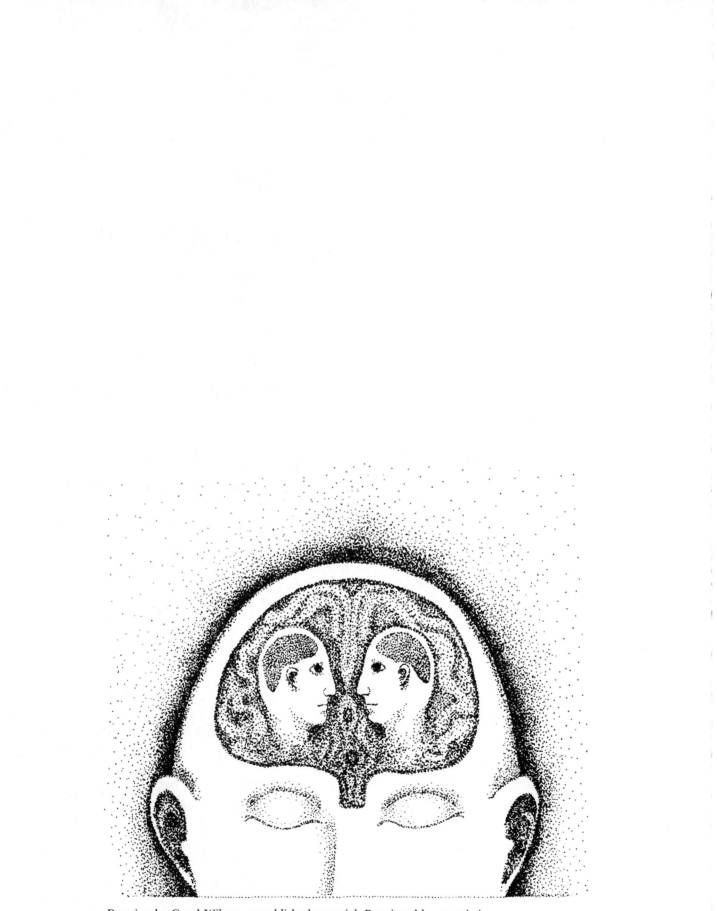

Drawing by Carol Wilson, unpublished material. Reprinted by permission.

1

What Do I Need to Know About Today's Secondary Schools?

One day soon you will likely be offered your first teaching contract, and what an exciting moment that will be for you! But after the initial excitement wears off and you have time to reflect, many questions will begin to take shape in your mind. Which school will I be assigned to? Will it be a high school, a junior high, or a middle school?[1] Will it be a regular secondary school, or will it be a "magnet" school, or will it be a "fundamentals" school? Will it be a school that has its start in the fall, as is traditional, or will it be a year-round school? Which subjects will I be assigned to teach? Specifically, what grade levels will I have? How many different preparations will I have? What supervision responsibilities might I have? What are the students like? the faculty? What textbooks will I use, and when can I expect to see them? How should I prepare? How *can* I prepare when there are so many unanswered questions? What school district policies are there that I need to learn about now? What support services can I expect? Will my teaching assignment be split between departments? Will the department chairperson like me? How extensive are the school's rules and regulations? Will there be an orientation for new and beginning teachers? How can I prepare for students I know nothing about?

Those questions, and many others, are often the focus of long, concentrated moments of thought by beginning secondary school teachers. To guide you through this initial experience the following informative paragraphs about school organization, about secondary school students, and about teachers and administrators offer a glimpse into the world of secondary education. This bright, active, ever-changing world is so complex that few authors can say all the words that need to be said to every reader. However, you will realize the necessity in starting *somewhere,* and so we begin with certain aspects of school organization.

---

[1]"Middle schools" are schools that have been planned for students ranging in age from 9 through 14. Middle schools generally include grades five through eight (with grades six through eight being the most popular organization), although many varied patterns exist. For example, a school might include grades seven and eight and still be called a middle school. Although middle schools vary considerably in organization, generally the fifth and sixth grades are each self-contained (each class has one teacher for all or most of the day), while seventh and eighth grades are departmentalized, i.e., students in these grades may meet each day for a homebase class, then go to other rooms and teachers for other subjects.

A. ABOUT ORIENTATION AND SCHEDULES

Orientation Meetings

As a beginning teacher, you will no doubt be invited to participate in an orientation meeting. Some school districts begin their academic year with a district-wide orientation for beginning and new teachers, whereas others schedule on-site orientations at each secondary school. Many school districts do both, with perhaps a district-wide meeting in a morning followed by the beginning of on-site meetings that afternoon. Of course, the ways the orientation meetings are scheduled and planned are going to vary, district by district and school by school. However, the objectives for each orientation meeting should be quite similar. District personnel will encourage the beginning teacher to:

- Meet other teachers and establish the start of new collegial friendships.
- Become familiar with the policies of the school district. These policies are many and will cover a wide range, e.g., policies for procedures relating to students involved in accidents while at school, for procedures involving student medications, for finding dangerous weapons or drugs, for class conduct, for school programs, for off-campus field trips, for parties in the classroom, for students out of the classroom during the school day, grading policies, procedures for completing attendance and tardy forms, for sending students to the office of the vice-principal or to the counselor, and for chaperoning and sponsoring student activities. And those samples are just the beginning!
- Become familiar with courses of study, curriculum guides, resource units, teacher's manuals, student textbooks, and supplementary materials.
- Become familiar with available audiovisual resources and equipment, and procedures for reserving and using them, and to prepare materials for the classroom.
- Become familiar with the school library/resource center, its personnel and procedures.
- Meet district personnel and become familiar with the many services that support you in your classroom.

As a teacher candidate in a secondary teacher education program, you may be asked to participate in an orientation meeting at your college or university. Perhaps this meeting will be a function of one of your college or university courses. You will receive your secondary school assignment (a junior or senior high school, a middle school, an intermediate school, or perhaps some combination of these), the date (with time and specific location) when you should report to your assignment, the name of your cooperating teacher (the experienced teacher who has volunteered or been assigned to work with you), the grade level, the subject(s), the names of the school and the school district, and perhaps the name of your college or university supervisor. You will probably be encouraged to follow the objectives listed at the beginning of this section, meet other teacher candidates and district teachers, become familiar with school and district policies, review the required curriculum materials for your teaching assignment, plan for needed audiovisual materials, and learn what to do in emergencies!

When you arrive at your assigned secondary school and the proper introductions have been made, you should begin to get acquainted with the school campus and the way the school is organized. Know where your classroom is and locate the nearest restrooms, for students and for faculty. Become familiar with the location of such areas as the teachers' workroom, the faculty room (a large comprehensive high school may have more than one), and the faculty lunch room. Determine where the students eat their lunches. Where is the auditorium for student assemblies? Is there a nurse's room? Where are the nearest first-aid supplies? the fire extinguishing equipment? How do you notify maintenance personnel quickly? What is the fire-drill plan? Where is it? Where are the various administrative offices? Where is the library? the media center? the resource room? Where are textbooks stored? How are they checked out and distributed? Where is the attendance office? Are there offices for resource specialists? Have you met your department chairperson? Do you know where he or she can be found at various times during the school day? Where are student records maintained? What access do you have to them? Where are teaching supplies kept, and how do you check them out? Have you located your own faculty mailbox and the place to sign in/sign out? What procedures do you follow if you are absent because of your own illness, or when you are going to be late to school because your alarm failed to awaken you, or your car failed to start, or the local transit authority went on strike? Do you have the necessary phone numbers? And, not least in importance, if you drive to school where do you park? Otherwise, what is the best local transportation available to you to get to school each day?

After you have become acquainted with the campus and have answers to some of your more urgent questions, you will want to focus your attention on the school schedule.

Teacher Schedules

Teacher schedules vary from state to state, from district to district, and from school to school. Middle and junior high school teaching schedules may vary slightly from those of high school teachers, perhaps being slightly shorter each day. The school year for secondary schools will likely begin in late August or early September, and continue through late May or mid-June. Some schools operate a year-round schedule, a practice that began in some schools a number of years ago but is only now beginning to catch on. With year-round operation, a teacher might teach for three quarters followed by one quarter off, or, work in a 45/15 program, which is nine weeks (45 days) of school followed by three weeks off. Most secondary schools operate five days a week, although some are open for just four days. The school year, recently lengthened in many states and/or districts, still approximates 180 days.

The school day will begin around 8:00 a.m. and last until around 3:00 or 4:00 p.m. in the many secondary schools that have recently lengthened the school day. In some of these latter schools, the first or last period is optional for students and teachers. For most secondary school teachers the school day consists of six periods, each period lasting 50–60 minutes. One of these periods will be a preparation period, sometimes referred to as the "free" period.

Besides the conventional schedule, some secondary schools have designed a "modular schedule" where each module is usually 15–22 minutes. On a given day you might meet one of your classes for only one or two modules, whereas on another day you might meet the same class for several modules. In the late 1950s and through the 1960s many variations of modular scheduling were tried, and some schools continue the practice today. Having students sometimes for a block of time longer than the usual 50–60 minutes is attractive, particularly to teachers of science, art, home economics, and industrial arts. Teachers in other areas (such as mathematics and foreign languages) often prefer to meet their students for regular periods of time each day for daily drill and practice. Occasionally you may find that a secondary school has successfully combined modular and traditional schedules within the curriculum, thus satisfying the wishes of teachers who prefer modular scheduling as well as those who prefer the traditional schedule.

A typical schedule for a secondary school teacher includes meeting three or four classes before lunch and two or three following lunch. When the teacher's "free" or "prep" period falls during the first or during the final period of the day, or just before or just after lunch, the teacher is still expected to be present on the school campus during that "free" period. Most teachers are quite busy during their preparation periods, reading and grading student papers, preparing materials, conferencing, or checking audiovisual equipment. It is also a time when you sometimes may prefer to sit and relax over a cup of tea or coffee, perhaps in the pleasant surroundings of the faculty room. Teachers need "think time" too!

In addition to the expectation that you be "on duty" throughout the school day, teachers in most districts are expected to be available on campus for a period of time (usually 15–30 minutes) before and after school, a time when students and parents as well as administrators may wish to contact and/or conference with you. You may be expected to sign in upon arrival and sign out upon departure, which is a policy that ensures that the school staff knows you are on duty.

Some secondary schools stagger the start and end of each day so that some teachers (and students) arrive and leave earlier than others. This is a common practice in crowded schools. Some schools even stagger their class times so that each day begins with a different period, a practice common in high schools during final examination week.

Whatever your schedule, you will be busy and your lunch time will seem much too brief for proper rest and digestion. Eat a good breakfast before you leave home in the morning!

It is difficult to generalize about secondary school teachers' schedules, but perhaps we have given you sufficient information to arouse your curiosity about the many variations that can and do exist within America's public secondary schools. Later in this chapter (Exercise 1.3) you will visit a school and learn more at first hand about teacher schedules. For now, let us turn to a discussion about secondary school students.

B. ABOUT STUDENTS

The bell rings for first period to begin and the students enter your classroom— 28 of them, "a kaleidoscope of personalities, all unique, each a bundle of idiosyncracies, different strengths, different attitudes and aptitudes, different needs."[1]

[1]Mary Hatwood Futrell, *Education Week,* April 3, 1985, p. 10.

What a challenge to you this is!—to understand and to teach 28 unique individuals all at once, and to do it four more times that day, five days a week, 180 days a year. You must be prepared not only to teach your subject but to do it effectively with students of different cultural backgrounds, of diverse linguistic abilities, of different learning styles, and with certain students who have been identified as having "special needs." Indeed, what a challenge!

What a wealth of information abounds about these young people! And, as a secondary school teacher you are expected to know it all! Certain facts you have learned and accumulated along the way will lodge in your mind. While concerned with the student's cognitive development, you are simultaneously concerned about the student's attitude and value development, social adjustment, emotional health, and physical well-being.

You will be sensitive and understanding about the disadvantaged youth. You will attempt to learn as much as possible about each youngster, aware of who has difficulties in adjusting or developing at school because of socioeconomic and multicultural factors (racial insensitivities, or language-minority characteristics). Your need for background knowledge is increased further because handicapped students are to be educated with their peers in the regular classroom when possible. You will need information and skills unique to teaching any special learners in your classroom.

In 1975, Public Law 94-142 (the Education for All Handicapped Children Act) was passed. P.L. 94-142 created certain requirements relative to meeting the educational needs of exceptional children in the regular classroom. The *exceptional child* is defined as a child who deviates from the average or normal child (1) in mental characteristics, (2) in sensory abilities, (3) in neuromotor or physical characteristics, (4) in social behavior, (5) in communication abilities, or (6) in multiple handicaps.

The general purpose of P.L. 94-142 was to encourage educators to place these special students in the least restrictive and most appropriate environment possible, in an environment as close to normal as possible. In some instances, this placement is the regular classroom (and is popularly called "mainstreaming"); in others, it is not. P.L. 94-142 made other significant provisions also important to every classroom teacher, including that all public school students are entitled to a free and appropriate education, and that all students are entitled to nonbiased testing.

As a regular classroom teacher, you should keep this important fact in mind: When a student with special needs is placed in your classroom, your objective should *not* be to "make the student normal," but, rather, to deal directly with the differences between this student and other students in your classroom.

In order to deal directly with these differences, you should: Develop an understanding of the general characteristics of different types of special-needs students; attempt to identify and meet the student's unique needs relative to *your* classroom, and design lesson plans that teach to different needs at the same time, as much as possible.

Understanding the General Characteristics of Special-Needs Students

In a regular classroom, there may be students already identified as having specific special needs. These students, when identified, are placed in a particular category, based on their *primary* area of exceptionality. These areas of exceptionality may include the following: the gifted and talented, the developmentally disabled, the behavior disordered (also known as emotionally handicapped or EH), the learning disabled (LD), the sensory impaired, the speech and language disordered, the physically handicapped, and students with chronic health problems.

Having been categorized according to one of these specific areas does not necessarily mean that the student will not have strengths and weaknesses in another area. For example, a student identified as gifted and talented could have some difficulties in speech, or could be visually impaired; a student identified as hearing impaired could be academically gifted. The category of exceptionality under which a student is identified simply means that it appears to be the primary area of special need, not the only one.

Students who are identified as exceptional may be placed in the regular classroom for either the majority of the school day, or only for designated periods. Students mainstreamed into the regular classroom only for designated periods will have more specialized needs. As the regular classroom teacher, you should expect the special education teacher working with the student to assist you in providing appropriate instruction for that student for those periods of time when the student is in the regular classroom.

Cultural Diversity and Multicultural Education

Historically, the United States has always been a "melting pot" of immigrants, but only recently have educators recognized the importance of our cultural diversity, of accepting students who are culturally different, and the concept of "multicultural education." The goals of multicultural education are to:[1]

1. Recognize the strength and value of cultural diversity
2. Develop human rights and respect for cultural diversity
3. Legitimate alternate life choices for people
4. Provide social justice and equal opportunity for all
5. Equally distribute power among members of all ethnic groups.

A teaching credential authorizes you to teach in any public school throughout a state, and for many states today, that means teaching in a school that is ethnically, culturally, linguistically and socioeconomically diverse. A teacher whose preparation occurs exclusively among students who are similar to that teacher may not be well prepared to teach in a classroom of such diversity. In order to be compatible with, and able to teach, students who are different from you, you need to develop skills in

1. establishing a classroom climate where all students feel welcome.
2. providing a classroom environment where all students feel they can learn.
3. involving students in democratic decision-making.
4. building upon students' learning styles.
5. adapting to students' skills levels.
6. using techniques that emphasize cooperative learning and that deemphasize competitive learning.

[1]Source: C. Sleeter and C. Grant, "An analysis of multicultural education in the United States," *Harvard Educational Review* 57(4): 421–444 (1987).

C. ABOUT MEETING MY STUDENTS

When those 28 students walk into your classroom for the first time, what will you have planned to do? A major contributor to effective classroom management during the school year is the manner by which you *begin* the year: a proper beginning will make your life easier for the entire school year. Consider these *guidelines for getting the year off to a good beginning.*

1. Before the school year begins, spend time getting your classroom organized (if you have your own room), finding out where equipment and materials are and will be kept, and preparing your teaching plans.
2. As soon as you receive your class lists (lists of names of students in your classes), practice pronouncing the students' names.
3. Prepare a seating chart to begin the year, and have students sit in their assigned seats so as to expedite your learning their names. The sound of your own name is one of the most beautiful sounds in the world, and students' awareness that you know them by name will greatly benefit the early establishment of rapport with your classes.
4. Teach your students your CBRs (classroom behavior rules) early, keeping the list of rules brief and enforceable. Among other matters, these might include:
   a. How to correctly obtain your attention and help.
   b. How to properly enter and leave the room.
   c. Tardy and absentee rules.
   d. Procedures for seatwork, for using a pencil sharpener and wastebasket.
   e. How to maintain papers, books, and other class materials in order.
   f. Your policy regarding late assignments, missed tests, and extra credit work.
   g. Your academic and social (school citizenship) grading procedure.
5. As the beginning of the year proceeds, monitor student behavior and respond quickly when necessary, establishing early your expectations and the consequences the students may expect. Remember, your good modeling behavior counts!
6. Use strong communication skills, such as giving directions clearly, listening actively, smiling appropriately, and establishing eye contact with every student in the classroom on the average of about *once every 45–60 seconds* when addressing the entire class. Be mobile in the classroom. A good teacher is usually tired at day's end because of being so physically active during the school day.
7. Plan carefully what it is you will do on that very first day of class.

One teacher begins with a get-acquainted activity such as going around the room asking each student to answer three or four questions, thus having each member of the class tell a little about his or her self—questions such as "What name would you like to be called by?" "Do you have a job?" "Where did you attend school last year?" "Do you have brothers or sisters?" "What is your favorite hobby?"

Another teacher prefers to start the first day of class by telling students about the course—description, objectives, study hints, assignment expectations, grading procedures—and distributes books, then starts immediately into subject content.

Yet another secondary-school teacher begins the first day with interest-oriented activities such as games or a laboratory investigation, preferring to build students' motivations on the subject itself and leave get-acquainted and/or "housekeeping" activities to a later date. In some secondary schools there are so many student class changes during the first week of school that teachers prefer to neither distribute textbooks nor cover much content until class change has settled down.

What *you* plan to do the first day and the first week of school will be guided by the nature of your school, your students, your subject, and by your own philosophy of education (discussed in Chapter 3). We ask that you consider the guidelines we have set forth, then plan accordingly.

The get-acquainted activity mentioned at the start of Guideline 7 might be especially valuable if you are teaching first-year junior high school students, who may be particularly anxious about their new school experience. Another get-acquainted activity is to provide magazines, newspapers, and catalogs, scissors and paste, and ask each student to prepare a "Get Acquainted Collage," having selected cut-outs of items that mean something to him or her, perhaps with the student's name in the center of the collage. The collages are then shared with the rest of the class. The teacher makes his or her own collage—modeling counts!

Do you like the idea of a get-acquainted session to start the year in your subject field? Can you think of or find other creative "get-acquainted" activities, and share them with members of your class? That is the purpose of the first exercise in this chapter, Exercise 1.1.

EXERCISE 1.1: GETTING ACQUAINTED WITH MY STUDENTS

What are some "getting-acquainted" activities you could plan for secondary students? Your educational purpose for this exercise is to select a grade level of your choice and record at least one activity you might use that would enable you and the students to become better acquainted during the first week of school. Share your activity with other teacher candidates.

Subject and grade level: _____

Description of getting-acquainted activity: _____

_____

_____

_____

_____

_____

_____

_____

_____

_____

_____

_____

Notes to myself regarding ideas I received when sharing my activity with other teacher candidates:

_____

_____

_____

_____

_____

_____

_____

_____

_____

D. ABOUT TEACHERS

Secondary school teachers are unique and independent, and represent myriad individual personalities—perhaps impossible to generalize about. Indeed, it is much easier to generalize about mediocre teachers, as they exhibit many more traits in common than do competent teachers, who seem to exhibit much more diversity among themselves. But let us suppose that a teaching colleague mentions that Mr. Wonderful in Room 17 is a "great teacher," "one of the best we have," "super," and "terrific." What might be some of the characteristics you would expect to see in Mr. Wonderful's teaching behaviors? Generally speaking we can expect Mr. Wonderful to "run a tight ship," to be organized, to present stimulating lessons, to be verbally facile, and to know what he is talking about.

Throughout this resource guide we return to this topic of teacher behavior, but for now let us look at the chief administrator in charge of everything, the building principal.

E. ABOUT ADMINISTRATORS

One person significantly responsible for the success of a school is the principal of that school. What are the characteristics of an effective secondary school principal? An effective principal

- Is an advocate for teachers and students.
- Places an importance on making everyone feel like a winner.
- Tries to catch teachers and students doing things right.
- Admonishes behaviors, not personalities.
- Encourages people, when they have made a mistake, to say "I'm sorry," rather than making them feel compelled to cover their mistakes.
- Runs a school of problem-solvers, not of blamers and faultfinders.
- Promptly follows up recommendations, concerns, or complaints.
- Makes sure that basic school policies and rules are closely defined and clearly communicated.
- Keeps everyone well informed of events.
- Spends time each day with students.
- Is positive.
- Encourages mastery learning, as opposed to "bell curve" learning.
- Makes sure staff and students receive proper recognition for accomplishments.
- Fosters professional growth and development for faculty, with opportunities for intervisitations, demonstrations, conferences, workshops, and projects.

Yes, the building principal has the ultimate responsibility for everything that happens on the secondary school campus, although he or she will have staff vice principals with delegated authority in various school activity areas. Department chairpersons may also serve administrative functions. As a new teacher, or as a student teacher, one of your tasks is to become familiar with the chain of command within your school and district.

What kind of administrative support should you expect during your beginning year? You should expect support through informal discussions, teachers' meetings, a faculty handbook, and school memos. The principal and the administrative staff will share information with you about many topics:

1. *Records you are expected to keep.* There are lesson plans, audiovisual forms, supply forms, conference forms, anecdotal records, students' grade report forms, budget request forms, classroom inventory forms, field trip forms, and attendance record forms.
2. *Policies that regulate the school and the district.* There are policies about student conduct, field trips, school assemblies, class parties, before- and after-school activities, and planned school events scheduled during the year.
3. *Opportunities for professional growth and development.* Professional growth and development opportunities will vary from district to district; however, many of these opportunities include: (1) district in-service workshops, classes, and meetings; (2) professional organization workshops and conferences; (3) nearby college or university courses; (4) curriculum improvement committee participation; (5) demonstration teaching for your district; and (6) later in your career, serving as a host teacher for a teacher candidate in a teacher education program. Some of these opportunities may be tied to an increased salary plan in your district. Find out what your district's policies are.
4. *Help from other educators.* Some principals will introduce you to selected resource people and to curriculum coordinators. Other principals will assign one of their teachers as a "big brother" or "big sister," to work with you during this first year—sometimes these teachers have been designated as "mentor" teachers. Still other principals and the department chair will begin some scheduled (or unscheduled) visits to your classroom; these visits are followed up with get-togethers afterwards. The visits are to be expected and you should not be frightened because they are for your professional growth. Often, conferences with your principal can be scheduled so you can ask all of those questions you have.

F. ABOUT THE OVERALL PICTURE

In the early 1980s no one facet of education received more attention from the media, caused more concern among parents and teachers, or got bigger headlines than that of a decline (factual or fanciful) in students' achievement in the public schools, namely the secondary schools and higher education. Curiously, elementary school education seemed to escape most of that attention. In any case, reports were issued, polls taken, debates organized, dialogues established, and blue-ribbon panels formed. Indeed, the year 1983 may be recorded by historians as "The Year of the Educational Reports." Within a six-month period in that year no less than eight reports or studies of national significance gained public attention. What initiated this attention? We are not sure, but it has never been matched in its political interest and participation. Perhaps never before have so many critical reports about education been published in such a short period of time. Consider this list:

- *Academic Preparation for College: What Students Need to Know and Be Able to Do.* New York: The College Board, 1983.
- *Action for Excellence.* James B. Hunt, Jr. (Chairman), Task Force on Education for Economic Growth, 1983. 1066 Lincoln, #300, Denver, CO 80295.
- Adler, Mortimer J. *Paideia: Problems and Possibilities.* New York: Macmillan, 1983.
- *A Nation at Risk.* National Commission on Excellence in Education. Washington, DC: United States Office of Education, 1983.
- Boyer, Ernest L. *High School: A Report on Secondary Education in America.* New York: Harper & Row, 1983.
- *Educating Americans for the 21st Century.* Washington, DC: National Science Board, 1983.
- Feistritzer, Emily. *The Conditions of Teaching: A State-by-State Analysis.* Princeton, NJ: Princeton University Press, 1983.
- Goodlad, John I. *A Place Called School.* New York: McGraw-Hill, 1984.
- Graubard, Stephen R., ed. "The Arts and Humanities in American Schools," *Daedalus,* 112:3 (Summer 1983).
- *Making the Grade.* Twentieth Century Fund, 41 E. 70th St., New York, NY 10021. (1983).
- Sizer, Theodore R. *Horace's Compromise: The Dilemma of the American High School.* Boston: Houghton Mifflin, 1984.

A 1983 Gallup Poll indicated that most Americans believed that our schools were not working hard enough, that more "basics" should be taught. But that's not all! The poll indicated that the majority of Americans also want the schools to provide information and instruction about Communism, computers, driver education, and parenting. They also want the students to be aware of the dangers of alcohol, drug abuse, and nuclear waste. Needless to say, the poll did not give national, state, or local educators a clear indication of priorities in the desired curriculum changes. So, countless regional, state, and local committees were established and a national reform movement in education was under way.

The educational reform movement became centered around two areas of concern: the teacher shortage, and a movement toward increasing standards, both for public school student achievement and for the professional education of teachers. A discussion of possible solutions to the dilemma is beyond the limits of this text, but many of the potential solutions appear on the surface to be mutually antagonistic. Consider these items. During the last half of the 1980s actions in the educational reform movement included:

- State commitments to upgrade the teaching force.
- Tougher teacher-certification standards.
- Teacher-competency testing.
- Higher salaries for beginning teachers.
- Pay raises for continuing teachers.
- Higher pay for master teachers or mentors.
- Merit pay for schools and teachers (salary tied to performance as indicated by student achievement).
- Extension of the school day and the school year.
- Stricter disciplinary standards for both students and teachers.
- Achievement and competency testing for students.

- Tougher course requirements for high school graduation.
- Tougher course requirements for college entrance.
- New "basics" required for a high school diploma.
- Increasing the number of periods taught daily by each teacher.
- Higher scholastic average and satisfactory marks in citizenship in order to establish and maintain eligibility for cocurricular participation.
- Increasing the amount and quality of homework required of each student.
- Computer classes for students from kindergarten through high school.
- Merit pay for administrators (or for schools) where money received is tied to student scores on standardized achievement tests.

By 1985 it was clear that a crisis was developing as too few college students were indicating a desire to assume teaching as a career, and in 1986 the U.S. Education Department projected that by 1993 elementary and secondary schools would need 211,000 new teachers each year but that schools of education will be graduating only 133,000 teacher candidates, a shortfall of about 37 percent. The problems are further compounded by the fact that as the number of minority students increases, the scarcity of minority teachers is acute. And, as the number of potential at-risk students increases, the number of qualified teachers seems also to be at-risk.[1]

Another critical problem facing public schools is the scarcity of funds needed to operate quality programs. For example, an increasingly larger percentage of the voting public, those people who vote when bond issues for improving school funding are on ballots, are less likely to vote for such tax increases because they are older people on fixed incomes and without school-age children.

By the end of the 1980s major issues in public education included:

- Reduction of the urban dropout rate. Despite the national tendency toward improved mean performance of students on standardized tests, the dropout rate in urban areas is approximately 40 percent.
- How to best train teachers to work effectively with students who are culturally different.
- The scarcity of minority teachers.
- The requirement of teachers and teacher candidates to pass competency tests.
- A shortage of qualified teachers. Approximately 20 percent of the nation's teachers are teaching in fields for which they are not qualified.
- Scarcity of funds needed to operate quality schools.

What other issues confront the nation's secondary schools today? The exercises that follow will assist you in your effort to come closer to the reality of secondary school teaching today.

[1]Source: *Education Week*, May 14, 1986, p. 28.

EXERCISE 1.2: REFLECTING UPON MY OWN HIGH SCHOOL EXPERIENCES

Instructions: The purpose of this exercise is to share with others your reflections on that experience.

1. What high school did you attend, where and when? _____
   _____
   _____

2. What do you remember most about your teachers? _____
   _____
   _____

3. What do you remember most about other students? _____
   _____
   _____

4. What do you remember most about high school life? _____
   _____
   _____

5. What class do you specifically recall with fondness? Why? _____
   _____
   _____

6. What class would you particularly like to forget? Why? _____
   _____
   _____

7. While a high school student, did you receive academic or personal counseling? Describe the nature and quality of that counseling experience. _____
   _____
   _____
   _____

8. How do your current aspirations compare with those you had as a high school student?
   _____
   _____
   _____
   _____

9. What do you recall about peer and parental pressures? _____

_____

_____

10. Is there any other aspect of your attendance at a high school you wish to share with others?

_____

_____

_____

EXERCISE 1.3: RETURNING TO A SECONDARY SCHOOL CLASSROOM

What will it be like to return to a classroom as a teacher? In most teacher education programs the teacher candidate is expected to visit schools to observe the school plant, the classrooms, the support services, the teaching styles, and the students and their behaviors. Often, the teacher candidate is assigned to participate in the classroom to perform a variety of instructional and noninstructional tasks as part of the teacher education program. (See Chapter 18, Section A for this paraprofessional experience.) If your teacher education program does not require an initial school visit, this exercise provides an opportunity to observe at a school site.

Your educational purpose is to schedule an observational visit to a nearby secondary school. Of course, you may wish to visit more than one, perhaps a junior high school, a middle school, and a high school, for comparison. Professional courtesy is expected in all of your relationships with school personnel. On the day of your visit, arrive early and check in at the administrative office. If you drove to the school, you should inquire whether you parked properly. A school employee, or perhaps a student, may escort you to the proper classroom or provide you with a map of the campus. Professional courtesy continues as you enter the classroom in a quiet, unobtrusive manner. Please wait until the teacher recognizes you, for the teacher may be in the midst of "that teachable moment."

As an integral part of your observational visit, you may want to complete Exercises 1.4, 1.5, 1.9, and 1.10. Plan to share with other teacher candidates the comments of your visits, your observations, and the likes and dislikes mentioned by the secondary school students from the schools you visited.

A gracious "thank you" is appropriate when you leave the classroom at the completion of your visit, and as you stop by the administrative office to notify the staff that you are leaving the campus. Some teacher candidates extend their professional courtesy still further—within the following week, they write brief thank-you notes to the principal and the classroom teacher.

Since time you could spend in length of school day, and in length of class time, varies by state law and/or district policy, compare your observations with the discussion of schedules as presented earlier in this chapter. How similar were they? How different?

EXERCISE 1.4: INTERVIEWING HIGH SCHOOL STUDENTS

Instructions: The purpose of this exercise is, while visiting a high school campus, to interview one or more students (videotape?), using the question format that follows. Share with others the results of your interviews.

1. Name and location of school: _____

   _____

2. Date of visitation: _____

3. How old are you (optional)? male or female? ethnicity? _____

   _____

4. What do you like most about your teachers? the least? _____

   _____

   _____

5. What do you like most about other students? the least? _____

   _____

   _____

6. What do you like most about high school life? the least? _____

   _____

   _____

7. What class have you most enjoyed? Why? _____

   _____

   _____

8. What class have you most disliked? Why? _____

   _____

   _____

9. While in high school, have you received academic or personal counseling? Can you describe the nature and quality of that experience? _____

   _____

   _____

10. What are your career aspirations? _____

    _____

11. With what student activities have you been involved? _____

   _____

   _____

12. Is there anything else that you can add that would help me understand your experiences and feelings about being a high school student? _____

   _____

   _____

EXERCISE 1.5: INTERVIEWING JUNIOR HIGH OR MIDDLE SCHOOL STUDENTS

Instructions: The purpose of this exercise is to visit a junior high or middle school campus and interview one or more students (videotape?), using the question format that follows. Share with others the results of your interviews.

1. Name and location of school: _____

2. Date of visitation: _____

3. How old are you (optional)? male or female? ethnicity? _____

4. What do you like most about your teachers? the least? _____

5. What do you like most about other students? the least? _____

6. What do you like most about junior high (or middle) school life? the least? _____

7. What class have you most enjoyed? Why? _____

8. What class have you most disliked? Why? _____

9. While in junior high (or middle) school, have you received academic or personal counseling? Can you describe the nature and quality of that experience? _____

10. What are your career aspirations? _____

_____

11. With what student activities have you been involved? _____

_____

_____

12. Is there anything else that you can add that would help me understand your experiences
and feelings about being a junior high (or middle) school student? _____

_____

_____

EXERCISE 1.6: RETURNING TO AN "OPEN HOUSE" AT A SECONDARY SCHOOL

What happens at "Open House" or "Back-to-School Night" in a secondary school? As part of your experiences in a teacher education program, you may be expected to participate with your cooperating teacher in the "Open House" activities of your assigned school. This activity will provide an opportunity to observe educational and community-related activities as prepared for this special event.

Your educational purpose is to schedule an observational visit to a secondary school during its "Open House" night. Of course, if you want to observe this activity in more than one school (perhaps a middle school and a senior high school for comparison), make arrangements to do so. Some schools within the same district schedule their "Open House" activities on different evenings, for the convenience of parents with children enrolled in different schools. You will be attending as an interested school supporter. Record your observational notes on the form that follows.

What school(s) did you visit? _____

_____

What is the total population of the school? _____

What is the average daily attendance (ADA)? _____

If there is a discrepancy between the population and the ADA, how large is it, and how is it explained? _____

_____

What grades and subject classes did you visit? _____

_____

Are (Were) you the student-teacher of this class? _____

What exhibits did you see? _____

_____

What speeches or presentations did you hear? Who delivered them? Describe each presentation in terms of effectiveness and assess the audience's reaction. _____

_____

_____

What student work did you see? _____

_____

Whom did you meet? Principal? Vice Principal? Teachers? Parents? _____

_____

_____

What types of questions did parents ask of the teacher? _____

_____

_____

How did the teacher and parents respond to one another? _____

_____

What evidence was there that teachers and students worked together to prepare for this event? _____

_____

_____

Did the educators demonstrate self-confidence, clarity in school expectations, and did they describe their programs and goals so the parents understood? _____

_____

Would you like to have been a student in this school? _____

_____

Would you like to be a teacher in this school? _____

_____

Would you be satisfied if your own child were a student in this school? _____

_____

What other observations about this visit would you like to share? _____

_____

_____

EXERCISE 1.7: ATTENDING A PARENT-TEACHER ORGANIZATION MEETING

Parents and teachers are supportive of one another and are linked together by their common interests in youth, in the academic achievements of students, and in the total development—social, physical, emotional, and intellectual growth—of each boy and girl. To demonstrate this support and interest, teachers and parents join together. You will find that each school has a parent-teacher association, organization, or parent's club. Attend one meeting as an interested teacher candidate, and observe (1) the membership; (2) the number of parents attending the meeting; (3) the number of teachers attending the meeting, and what disciplines they are from; (4) the agenda; (5) the interests related to the school; (6) any educational issues; (7) the attitudes of participants; and (8) fund-raising projects.

Record your notes about the meeting here. Share and discuss with other teacher candidates.

EXERCISE 1.8: INTERVIEWING A TEACHER CANDIDATE

Let's explore why other teacher candidates have selected secondary school teaching as a career goal. Select one teacher candidate (preferably one who is not in your class) and record that person's responses as you ask the following questions.

1. What motivated you to select secondary school teaching as a career? _____
_____

2. Even though you indicate secondary school teaching as a goal, do you have a preference as to what level, middle, junior, senior high school, or even elementary? _____

3. What specifically are you preparing to teach? _____

4. Are you looking forward to being free during summer months? Or would you be willing to contract with a year-round school? _____

5. Would you be interested in teaching in a "fundamentals" school, or in a "magnet" school?
_____

6. Do you know that a nine-month teaching salary is often divided into twelve salary warrants? _____
_____

7. How will you plan to spend your vacation months? _____
_____

8. Would you like to be an administrator or counselor at some future date? _____
_____

9. Are there any other teachers in your family? _____
_____

10. What experiences with young people have you had prior to entering this teacher education program? _____

11. In what way did the experiences help or hinder your teaching secondary school youth?
_____
_____

12. In a brief statement, how do you really feel right now about secondary school teaching?
_____

13. What subjects in your discipline do you look forward to teaching? Which ones worry you the most? _____

EXERCISE 1.9: INTERVIEWING A TEACHER

For this exercise you are to interview one (or more) secondary school teachers. You may decide to interview a junior high school teacher who is in his or her first year of teaching, or one who has been teaching for ten or more years; or, you may choose to interview a high school teacher who is in his or her first year, or who has been teaching ten or more years. Your instructor may give further guidance for this exercise, but we suggest the following questions to guide the interview(s).

1. What subject(s) and grade levels do you teach? _____

   _____

   _____

2. Why are you teaching at this level? _____

3. What training did you have for teaching this subject and this grade level? _____

   _____

4. How many years have you been teaching? _____

5. About how many hours a week do you spend on school-related matters? _____

   _____

6. What do you like most about teaching secondary school students? the least? _____

   _____

   _____

   _____

7. What advice can you give me with respect to my own preparation? _____

   _____

8. Is classroom management a problem for you? Why or why not? _____

   _____

   _____

   _____

9. Do you have any advice for me with respect to professional organizations? _____

   _____

10. What kinds of student teaching experience did you have? What advice would you give

    to student teachers? _____

    _____

    _____

EXERCISE 1.10: INTERVIEWING A SCHOOL ADMINISTRATOR

Instructions: The purpose of this exercise is, while visiting a school campus (Exercise 1.3), to interview one or more administrators, using the question format that follows. Appointments should be prearranged. Follow-up thank-you letters are in order. Share with your colleagues the results of your interviews.

1. Name and location of school: _____

2. Date of visitation: _____

3. Male or female? ethnicity? _____

4. What is your administrative title? Your functions? Where do you fit in the chain of command, and how did you get this job? _____

5. Is this your first administrative experience? How many years have you been working in the schools, and in what capacities? _____

6. What is your academic preparation? Were you adequately prepared to administer? _____

7. Is this where you intend to remain for your career? _____

8. What do you like most about your job? the least? _____

9. What are your school's most serious problems? _____

10. What advice can you give with respect to my own preparation to teach at this level? _____

In beginning to plan for developing your teaching competencies, you have read an overview of today's secondary schools, considered how you will get acquainted with your students, recorded your thoughts about your own secondary school experiences, returned to a classroom, visited an "Open House," attended a meeting of a parent-teacher organization, interviewed secondary school students, another teacher candidate, an experienced teacher, and a school administrator. All of these experiences will be useful in your assimilation of the content of the next chapter, "What Are the Expectations of a Secondary School Teacher?" But before proceeding to that chapter, you and your class may wish to study and discuss the following questions related to topics in this chapter.

QUESTIONS FOR CLASS DISCUSSION

1. Do you recall the teacher who influenced you most during your secondary school years? Why do you suppose that teacher had an influence on you? Were the teacher's behaviors similar to or different from those of Mr. Wonderful as discussed earlier in this chapter?
2. What recent societal influences have affected today's secondary schools and students? What have been the results?
3. Of the many activities offered in our secondary schools, which may have the strongest positive influence on students?
4. What evidence have you seen to indicate that a longer school day or year results in better student achievements?
5. What do you see as the main goals of our secondary schools today? Did you observe any indication that the school you visited was working successfully toward these goals?
6. Do you support the point of view that junior high school students should be required to pass a basic competency test before they are promoted to a senior high school? What subjects should be included in a basic competency test if such a test were given to students? What grade levels should be tested? What are the current competency test requirements in your state?
7. Reviewing the teaching behaviors that seem to be important for effective teaching, what evidence do you have that some of these teaching behaviors were occurring during your classroom visit?
8. Recalling the points that may guide a principal toward success with a staff, how would you rate a selected, anonymous principal of your choice? Why?
9. Nobody decides to become a teacher in order to become wealthy; however, salaries for teachers in this country have increased approximately 100 percent during the past decade. Have salaries for teachers kept pace with inflation? What salary can you expect as a beginning teacher in your state?
10. The following is quoted from a major task-force report: "Until we pay teachers at least as well as the middle echelon of executives, we cannot expect the profession to attract its full share of the available range of talents. Salaries must be raised immediately and substantially." Does that strong recommendation sound familiar? It came from the Rockefeller Brothers Fund report of 1958, *The Pursuit of Excellence: Education and the Future of America.* Discuss any feelings this leaves you with, with your classmates.

11. Does your teacher education program require any portion of your experience be completed in an elementary school, even though your training is as a secondary single-subject teacher? What is your feeling on this kind of requirement? Why do you suppose in some teacher education programs this is the case?

12. Can you find any research evidence to indicate that your subject *should* be taught in secondary schools? Is it absolutely necessary that your subject be taught in a secondary school? Why?

13. District school boards have been considering whether to admit or exclude students with AIDS. For some districts that admit AIDS students, there will be employee training in the hygiene techniques and procedures for safe handling of blood and blood-contaminated items (perhaps a negotiable item in collective bargaining). For school boards that exclude students, the district policy will refer, in some way, to the interest of protecting the student and the concern about the possible transmission of the disease to others. Enrollment of a student with AIDS has been met with considerable protest from certain communities and their members. Identify a nearby district and determine the district's policy. Discuss with others in your class. What is your opinion about proposed employee training in hygiene techniques as a negotiable item for the teacher's union and their collective bargaining talks?

SUGGESTED READINGS FOR CHAPTER 1

Adler, M. J. *Paideia: Problems and Possibilities.* New York: Macmillan, 1983.

———. *The Paideia Proposal: An Educational Manifesto.* New York: Macmillan, 1982.

Alexander, W. M. "The middle school: What? Why? How? How well? *Journal for Supervision and Curriculum Development* 2(3):6–13 (Spring/Summer 1989).

Banks, J. A. *Teaching Strategies for Ethnic Studies.* 3d ed. Needham Heights, MA: Allyn & Bacon, 1984.

Banks, J. A., and Banks, C. A. M. *Multicultural Education: Issues and Perspectives.* Needham Heights, MA: Allyn & Bacon, 1989.

Boyer, E. L. *High School: A Report on Secondary Education in America.* New York: Harper & Row, 1983.

Brooks, D. M. "The teacher's communicative competence: The first day of school." *Theory Into Practice* 24(1):63–70 (Winter 1985).

Carnegie Task Force on Teaching as a Profession. *A Nation Prepared: Teaching in the 21st Century.* New York: Carnegie Forum on Education and the Economy, 1986.

Clark, B. R. "The high school and the university: What went wrong in America, Part 2." *Phi Delta Kappan* 66(7):472–475 (March 1985).

Csikszentmihalyi, M., and McCormack, J. "The influence of teachers." *Phi Delta Kappan* 67(6):415–419 (February 1986).

Doyle, D. P., and Levine M. "Magnet schools: Choice and quality in public education." *Phi Delta Kappan* 66(4):265–270 (December 1984).

Emmer, E. T., et al. *Classroom Management for Secondary Teachers.* 2d ed. Englewood Cliffs, NJ: Prentice Hall, 1989.

Fantini, M.D. *Regaining Excellence in Education.* Columbus, OH: Merrill, 1986.

Goodlad, J. I. *A Place Called School: Promise for the Future.* New York: McGraw-Hill, 1984.

Hirsh, E. D., Jr. *Cultural Literacy: What Every American Needs to Know.* Boston: Houghton Mifflin, 1987.

Kane, P. R. "Public or Independent Schools: Does Where You Teach Make a Difference?" *Phi Delta Kappan* 69(4):286–289 (Dec. 1987).

Litt, M. D., and Turk, D. C. "Sources of stress and dissatisfaction in experienced high school teachers." *Journal of Educational Research* 78(3): 178–185 (March 1980).

Ornstein, A., and Levine, D. U. *Foundations of Education.* 4th ed. Boston: Houghton Mifflin, 1989.

Sizer, T. R. *Horace's Compromise: The Dilemma of the American High School.* Boston: Houghton Mifflin, 1984.

Slavin, R. E., and Madden, N. A. *Effective Programs for Students at Risk.* Needham Heights, MA: Allyn & Bacon, 1989.

Slavin, R. E., et al. *Learning to Cooperate, Cooperating to Learn.* New York: Plenum, 1985.

Sleeter, C. E., and Grant, C. A. *Making Choices for Multicultural Education: Five Approaches to Race, Class and Gender.* Columbus, OH: Merrill, 1988.

Stedman, L. C., and Kaestle, C. F. "The Test Score Decline is Over: Now What?" *Phi Delta Kappan* 67(3):204–210 (Nov. 1985).

Wheelock, A., and Dorman, G. *Before It's Too Late: Dropout Prevention in the Middle Grades.* Chapel Hill, NC: Center for Early Adolescence, University of North Carolina, 1988.

2

What Are the Expectations
of a Secondary School Teacher?

As a secondary school teacher your professional responsibilities extend beyond those important ones of working in the classroom from 8:00 a.m. until 3:00 p.m. In this chapter we guide you through the reality of those responsibilities as they exist today.

A. ABOUT THE CODE OF ETHICS

What do the words "to follow the code of ethics" or "to be ethical" mean? Do they mean to be honorable in your professional actions? virtuous? moral? decent, equitable, and just? Some educators consider the words to mean to portray, as closely as possible, an ideal educator, or to practice certain moral principles inherent in educational pursuits. Others see the terms as meaning to conform to professional standards of conduct. Still others believe they are a way to describe an educator's relationship to action—or performance.

You will see that all of these aspects—the aspects of portrayal, of professionalism, and of performance—stand out in the following code of ethics for the education profession, a code often printed on the reverse side of a teaching credential. The two sections of the code guide your pledge to the students and to the profession.

Code of Ethics of the Education Profession[1]

Preamble

The educator, believing in the worth and dignity of each human being, recognizes the supreme importance of the pursuit of truth, devotion to excellence, and the nurture of democratic principles. Essential to these goals is the protection of freedom to learn and to teach and the guarantee of equal educational opportunity

---

[1]Code of Ethics of the Education Profession, National Education Association, 1975. Reprinted by permission.

for all. The educator accepts the responsibility to adhere to the highest ethical standards.

The educator recognizes the magnitude of the responsibility inherent in the teaching process. The desire for the respect and confidence of one's colleagues, of students, of parents, and of the members of the community provides the incentive to attain and maintain the highest possible degree of ethical conduct. The Code of Ethics of the Education Profession indicates the aspiration of all educators and provides standards by which to judge conduct.

The remedies specified by the NEA (National Education Association) and/or its affiliates for the violation of any provision of this Code shall be exclusive and no such provision shall be enforceable in any form other than one specifically designated by the NEA or its affiliates.

Principle I—Commitment to the Student

The educator stives to help each student realize his or her potential as a worthy and effective member of society. The educator therefore works to stimulate the spirit of inquiry, the acquisition of knowledge and understanding, and the thoughtful formulation of worthy goals.

In fulfillment of the obligation to the student, the educator—

1. Shall not unreasonably restrain the student from independent action in the pursuit of learning.
2. Shall not unreasonably deny the student access to varying points of view.
3. Shall not deliberately suppress or distort subject matter relevant to the student's progress.
4. Shall make reasonable effort to protect the student from conditions harmful to learning or to health and safety.
5. Shall not intentionally expose the student to embarrassment or disparagement.
6. Shall not on the basis of race, color, creed, sex, national origin, marital status, political or religious beliefs, family, social or cultural background, or sexual orientation, unfairly:
   a. Exclude any student from participation in any program;
   b. Deny benefits to any student;
   c. Grant any advantage to any student.
7. Shall not use professional relationships with students for private advantage.
8. Shall not disclose information about students obtained in the course of professional service, unless disclosure serves a compelling professional purpose or is required by law.

Principle II—Commitment to the Profession

The education profession is vested by the public with a trust and responsibility requiring the highest ideals of professional service.

In the belief that the quality of the services of the education profession directly influences the nation and its citizens, the educator shall exert every effort to raise professional standards, to promote a climate that encourages the exercise of professional judgment, to achieve conditions which attract persons worthy of the trust to careers in education, and to assist in preventing the practice of the profession by unqualified persons.

In fulfillment of the obligation to the profession, the educator—

1. Shall not in an application for a professional position deliberately make a false statement or fail to disclose a material fact related to competency and qualifications.
2. Shall not misrepresent his or her professional qualifications.
3. Shall not assist entry into the profession of a person known to be unqualified in respect to character, education, or other relevant attribute.
4. Shall not knowingly make a false statement concerning the qualifications of a candidate for a professional position.
5. Shall not assist a noneducator in the unauthorized practice of teaching.
6. Shall not disclose information about colleagues obtained in the course of professional service unless disclosure serves a compelling professional purpose or is required by law.
7. Shall not knowingly make false or malicious statements about a colleague.
8. Shall not accept any gratuity, gift, or favor that might impair or appear to influence professional decisions or actions.

B. ABOUT INSTRUCTIONAL RESPONSIBILITIES

The aspects of portrayal, of professionalism, and of performance take on a very real shape when you consider the instructional related and the noninstructional related responsibilities in secondary teaching.

What Are Some of the Instructional Responsibilities I Will Meet?

The following checklist of questions introduces you to the instructional responsibilities you will have as a secondary teacher. Ask yourself these questions:

1. Have I allotted time each day for planning the daily lessons that are needed?
2. Have I allotted time for reading and evaluating papers?
3. Have I allotted time to record grades in my record book?
4. Do I realize the importance of preparing my classroom for instruction?
5. Do I acknowledge the actual time I spend in classroom instruction?
6. Am I aware of the time I need to devote to professional growth and development to help improve my instruction?
7. Have I arranged time to prepare all the materials I will need for my lessons?
8. Have I incorporated my philosophy of education into a "firm but fair" classroom management system?
9. Have I prepared long-range plans as well as short-term lesson plans?
10. Have I developed my classroom policies?
11. Have I considered how I will work with students who are different than I, socioeconomically, ethnically, linguistically, in learning styles, or in any other way?

12. Am I familiar with the developmental characteristics of this age level?
13. Am I familiar with the background of youngsters with behavior or personality problems, and who may cause concerns in the classroom?

C. ABOUT NONINSTRUCTIONAL RESPONSIBILITIES

What Are Some of the Noninstructional Responsibilities I Will Meet?

The following questions will focus your thoughts on the many noninstructional responsibilities you will meet during your first year of teaching. Ask yourself these questions:

1. Am I familiar with the school building and the campus?
2. Do I take the time to become acquainted with the teaching staff and with the nonteaching staff?
3. Am I aware of school and district policies?
4. Am I knowledgeable about the background of all my students?
5. Am I familiar with the community that is served by the school?
6. Am I knowledgeable about such routine procedures as
   a. before-and-after-school events?
   b. restroom regulations?
   c. distribution and collection of school materials and books?
   d. dismissal procedures?
   e. ordering supplies?
   f. established fire-drill routines?
   g. recording daily attendance, tardiness, and absences?
   h. procedures during assemblies?
   i. school and district policies regarding classroom conduct?
7. Have I thought about classroom duties?
   a. Do I maintain a cheerful, pleasant overall classroom environment?
   b. Do I open and close classroom windows as needed?
   c. Do I prepare or locate needed materials and/or supplies for each lesson for each day?
   d. Do I keep the teaching supplies orderly?
   e. Do I clean the chalkboard during the day, as needed?
8. Do I anticipate the many conferences that will be needed, such as between
   a. teacher and teacher?
   b. teacher and student?
   c. teacher and parent?
   d. teacher and administrator?
9. Have I acknowledged the hours needed for professional meetings, such as
   a. faculty meetings?
   b. other school meetings or committee meetings?
   c. parent-teacher meetings?
   d. meetings, conferences, and workshops sponsored by the local, regional, state, and federal professional organizations?

Now that you have reviewed these checklists of questions, turn your attention to the total role of a first-year teacher.

A major continuing role of the teacher is maintaining an awareness of the quality of the interaction within the classroom. Regardless of technological developments of the past 50 years the teacher is still the director of learning, and that learning is dependent upon the quality of classroom interactions. Many times in this resource guide we focus on various aspects of that interaction.

D. SUMMARIZING THE EXPECTATIONS OF A SECONDARY-SCHOOL TEACHER

The following list of instructional and noninstructional responsibilities is by no means exhaustive; it does represent the kinds of activities that can exhaust a teacher. Many of these tasks are unavoidable and absolutely necessary for each teacher to perform; others are negotiable. The beginning teacher must first concentrate on the classroom instruction, then move cautiously into those other necessary but more or less optional kinds of activities. Study the list, then proceed with Exercise 2.1, which follows.

A. Responsibilities related to *housekeeping* functions:
  1. Attendance checking and reporting.
  2. Preparation of budget and schedules.
  3. Ordering, using, and maintaining audiovisual materials and equipment.
  4. Ordering, using, and maintaining textbook and curriculum materials and supplies.
B. Responsibilities related to *advising, supervision, and sponsorship.*
  5. Supervision of halls, cafeteria, and student assemblies.
  6. Supervision of homerooms and/or activity periods.
  7. Supervision of intramural contests.
  8. Advising and sponsoring student clubs.
  9. Advising and sponsoring plays, concerts, graduation exercises, and other events and productions.
  10. Advising and sponsoring student government.
  11. Support of the athletic program (e.g., ticket seller or ticket taker, scorer, supervision of stands at ball game, record keeper).
  12. Sponsoring and arranging for guest speaker and campus visitors.
  13. Advising, guiding, and counseling of students.
  14. Responsibility for student safety.
  15. Chaperoning student dances, bus trips, and other student activities.
C. Responsibilities related to *school-community* activities:
  16. Attendance and participation at parent-teacher association meetings.
  17. Attendance and participation in community events.
  18. Support of local bond issues.
  19. Parent conferences.
  20. Representing the school at social gatherings
  21. Establishing rapport with other adults (e.g., administrators, teachers, para-professionals, clerical and custodial staff).

D. Responsibilities related to *professional* activities:
   22. School and district-wide committee work.
   23. Continued study and development in your field.
   24. Support of professional associations—local, state, and national.
   25. Responsibility to professional Code of Ethics.
E. Responsibilities related to *instructional* activities:
   26. Preparation for daily instruction (e.g., long-range planning, daily lesson planning).
   27. Reading and evaluating student work.
   28. Preparing classroom for daily instruction.
   29. Giving your own "think time" about individual students in your classes.
   30. Private consultation time with individual students (e.g., before or after school hours).

EXERCISE 2.1: THE LIFE OF A TEACHER

The educational purpose of this exercise is to assist you in furthering your understanding that teaching is a full-time job. One 24-hour day in the life of a teacher can be safely divided into four categories: time spent in actual classroom instruction; time spent in reading papers, preparing lessons, and generally readying for classes; time spent in myriad noninstructional responsibilities; time spent in your own personal life functions.

Instructions: Have your class divide into small groups and ask each group to discuss and predict how much of a *beginning teacher's* time is spent in each of the items listed in the chart that follows. Compare your group's predictions with those of the other groups. Visit some teachers and ask them to estimate the time spent in each of the areas; then compare what they say with your group predictions. How similar, how different?

Chart for Exercise 2.1

Estimated Number of Hours Spent in One Seven-Day Week

A. *Time spent in clerical and maintenance functions*

   1. attendance checking and reporting............ _____

   2. preparation of budgets and schedules .... _____

   3. ordering, using, and maintaining AV materials and equipment .... _____

   4. ordering, using, and maintaining textbook and curriculum materials and supplies .... _____

 4a. other (specify)................................... _____

B. *Time spent advising, supervising, sponsoring*

   5. supervision of halls, cafeteria, assemblies..... _____

   6. supervision of homerooms and activity periods .... _____

   7. supervision of intramural contests............ _____

   8. advising and sponsoring plays, concerts, other events and productions.................. _____

   9. advising and sponsoring student government .... _____

 10. support of athletic program (e.g., ticket taker, supervision, serving as scorer).......... _____

 11. sponsoring and arranging for guest speakers and campus visitors .... _____

 12. advising, guiding, and counseling of students .... _____

 13. responsibility for student safety .... _____

 14. chaperoning student dances and bus trips ... _____

 15. other (specify)................................... _____

C. *Time spent in school-community activities*

16. attendance-participation at PTA .... _____
17. attendance-participation in community
    events.. _____
18. supporting local bond issues .... _____
19. parent conferences............................... _____
20. representing the school at social gatherings _____
21. establishing rapport with other adults (e.g.,
    administrators, teachers, paraprofessionals,
    clerical and custodial staff) .... _____
21a. other (specify)................................... _____

D. *Time spent in professional activities*

22. school and district-wide committee work ..... _____
23. continued study and development in your
    field .... _____
24. support of professional associations—local,
    state, and national .... _____
25. responsibility to professional Code of Ethics _____
25a. other (specify)................................... _____

E. *Time spent in instructional activities*

26. preparation *and implementation* of daily
    instruction .... _____
27. reading and grading student work............ _____
28. preparing classroom .... _____
29. giving time for individual students outside
    of regular class time .... _____
29a. other (specify)................................... _____

Total hours per week = _____

We estimate an approximate average of 52 hours per week. How do your averages compare?

In this chapter, you reviewed the instructional related and noninstructional related responsibilities facing a beginning secondary-school teacher. In the next chapter we focus on the identification of teaching styles.

QUESTIONS FOR CLASS DISCUSSION

1. How do you now feel about being a secondary-school teacher—motivated, excited, enthusiastic, befuddled, confused, depressed? Explain and discuss your current feelings with your classmates. Sort out common concerns or anxieties, and design avenues for correcting any negative attitudes or feelings you might have.
2. Which instructional responsibilities excite you the most? Which concern you most?
3. Which noninstructional responsibilities interest you most? Which frighten you most?
4. A quarter of a century ago a publication entitled *Six Areas of Teacher Competence*[1] detailed six roles of the teacher: director of learning, counselor and guidance worker, mediator of the culture, link with the community, member of the school staff, and member of the profession. Are all of these of equal importance for the secondary school teacher of today?
5. Teaching involves interaction between teacher and students, but most research studies in this area have been limited to observations of the teacher while working with the entire class. Teachers frequently work with individuals or small groups of students. What research can you find that has studied the interaction of the teacher with individual students or with students in small groups?
6. How possibly can failure be viewed by a student as positive feedback?
7. Is it possible for a teacher to be sending two separate and contradictory messages to a student? If so, what are the ramifications for teacher education?
8. When should and can "controlled silence" be used by a teacher?
9. Teachers' use of strong praise to an individual within a group should be used sparingly and for specific content-related matters. Why do you suppose this is the case?
10. What other questions would you like to have discussed? How might answers be found?

SUGGESTED READINGS FOR CHAPTER 2

Good, T. L., and Brophy, J. E. *Looking in Classrooms.* 4th ed. New York: Harper & Row, 1987.

Hightshue, D. et al. "Writing in Junior and Senior High Schools." *Phi Delta Kappan* 69(10):725–728 (June 1988).

[1]California Teachers Association, "Six Areas of Teacher Competencies." Burlingame, CA, 1964.

Segal, J. W.; Chipman, S. F.; and Glaser, R. eds. *Thinking and Learning Skills, Volume I: Relating Instruction to Research.* Hillsdale, NJ: Lawrence Erlbaum Associates, 1985.

Silvernail, D. L. *Teaching Styles as Related to Student Achievement.* 2d. ed. Washington, DC: National Education Association, 1986.

Smith, H. A. "The marking of transitions by more and less effective teachers." *Theory Into Practice* 24(1):57–62 (Winter 1985).

3

How Do I Develop a Teaching Style?

Teaching style is defined as *the way instructors teach, their distinctive mannerisms complemented by their choices of teaching behaviors and strategies*. Style is determined by (1) the teacher's personal characteristics, (2) the instructor's own experiences as a student, and (3) by research studies.

A. DESCRIPTIONS OF TWO TEACHING STYLES

One way to describe teaching styles is from observations of classroom interactions of teachers with students. Traditionally, a teacher is an information giver, a "sage-on-the-stage," while in a more modern style the teacher facilitates student learning, taking less of a center-stage role, is a "guide-on-the-side." *This is not to imply that one is always better*, but simply to distinguish two style types. While today's secondary school teacher is likely eclectic in style, utilizing the best from each, the following descriptions characterize those two styles.

	Traditional Style	Facilitating Style
Teacher is	autocratic	democratic
	formal	informal
	direct	indirect
	dominative	interactive
	prescriptive	reflective
	informative	inquiring
	confrontive	supportive
	judgmental	nonjudgmental
Classroom is	teacher-centered	student-centered
	linear (seats facing front of room)	grouped or circular seating
	barren, nondecorative	stimulating
Instructional modes	abstract learning	concrete learning
	teacher-centered discussions	discussions
	lectures	peer coaching
	competitive learning	cooperative learning
	some problem solving	problem solving
	demonstrations by teacher	student inquiry

B. THE THEORETICAL ORIGINS OF TEACHING STYLES

Teaching styles are deeply rooted by certain theoretical assumptions about learners and their development, and although beyond the scope of intent for this resource guide to explore deeply into those assumptions, there are three major theoretical positions and recent research findings that may help you understand the basis of your own emerging teaching style. Each of the three positions is based upon certain philosophical and psychological assumptions that suggest different ways of working with learners. The theoretical positions are:

1. The learner's mind is neutral-passive to good-active and the main focus in teaching should be the addition of new ideas to a subconscious store of old ones (tied to the theoretical positions of *Romanticism-Maturationism*).

    Key persons include Jean J. Rousseau and Sigmund Freud.

    Key instructional strategies include classic lecturing with rote memorization.

2. The learner's mind is neutral-passive with innate reflexes and needs, and the main focus in teaching should be on the successive, systematic changes in the learner's environment to increase the possibilities of desired behavioral responses (tied to the theoretical position of *Behaviorism*).

    Key persons include John Locke, B. F. Skinner, A. H. Thorndike, and John Watson.

    Key instructional strategies include practice and reinforcement as epitomized in programmed instruction.

3. The learner is a neutral-interactive purposive individual in simultaneous interaction with the physical and biological environments, and the main focus in teaching should be on facilitating the learner's gain of new perceptions that lead to desired behavioral changes that ultimately lead to a more fully functioning individual (tied to the theoretical position of *Cognitive-Experimentalism*).

    Key persons are John Dewey, Jerome Bruner, Jean Piaget, and Arthur W. Combs.

    Key instructional strategies include discovery and inquiry learning.

If our hypothesis is correct that a competent teacher assumes a combination of thoughts from these three theoretical positions, then indeed that teacher's style is eclectic. We think that with a diversity of students, to be competent a teacher *must* be eclectic, utilizing at appropriate intervals the best of strategies and knowledgeable instructor behaviors, regardless of whether individually they can be classified within any style dichotomy, such as "traditional or facilitating," "direct or indirect," "formal or informal," or "didactic or progressive." Our own bias as we have taught and as we have prepared this resource guide is to provide an eclectic approach with a bent toward Cognitive-Experimentalism because of its emphasis on divergence in learning.

Exercise 3.1 is designed to help you develop a profile of your own philosophical position.

C. RESEARCH CONTRIBUTIONS TOWARD THE DEVELOPMENT OF TEACHING STYLE

The preceding section presented three theoretical positions that have had an historical bearing upon the development of teaching styles. Also affecting teaching style are variables that have been shown to have a relationship between instruction and learning. These variables are: the learning environment, lesson planning, teacher behaviors, and the nature of the learner and learning. With each variable there are actions that have positive effects upon student learning.

Learning Environment

The classroom environment in which learning takes place is crucial; optimum learning takes place when the student

- Feels welcomed to the classroom.
- As a person feels accepted by the teacher.
- Clearly understands course expectations.
- Is personally involved in the learning activities.
- Can maintain some control over the pace of the learning.
- Perceives the teacher as being approachable.
- Feels that although the course is demanding the rewards are within reach.
- Develops a better understanding of his or her own learning/thinking style.

Lesson Planning

Within the category of lesson planning, research tells us that the following teacher actions contribute positively to student learning. The teacher provides

- Lessons that are thoughtfully prepared (and students can tell).
- Specific and clearly stated learning expectations (that are understood by the students).
- Interesting and motivating lesson introductions.
- Frequent learning practice and comprehension checks.
- Lessons of student-perceived content relevancy.
- Content links between what the students already know and what they are going to learn.

Teacher Behaviors

Research indicates the following teacher behaviors as being positive contributors to student learning. The teacher

- Poses thoughtfully prepared, and carefully worded, questions that are clearly understood by the students.
- Uses questioning frequently, and allows for student response time.
- Appreciates the importance of and allows for student "think time."
- Uses a variety of types of questions that are designed to lead students to higher levels of cognition.
- Demonstrates enthusiasm for teaching and learning.
- Uses meaningful gestures and body language.
- Uses variations in voice inflections.
- Is businesslike, but with a sense of humor.

- Is approachable.
- Initiates sincere but low-keyed praise for individual student achievement.
- Uses a variety of teaching-learning strategies.
- Adjusts his or her teaching style according to student learning styles and activities.
- Is constantly monitoring student activity.
- Is able, in class, to attend to more than one thing at a time.

Learner and Learning

A fourth and final variable is the nature of the learner and of learning. Interesting educational research is coming from several, but perhaps related, areas: student learning and thinking styles, hemispheric brain research, and learning modalities. While it appears that some learners have left-hemispheric brain preference (i.e., verbal learning; prefer deductive reasoning, logical and rational thinking) and others have right-hemispheric preference (i.e., think in pictures, prefer inductive reasoning, intuitive thinking), traditional education in the United States historically has shown a bias toward the left side of the brain. While some teachers may tend to teach the way they were taught, or in the way in which they themselves learn best, students in the class may have learning modalities (verbal, visual, or kinesthetic) different from that of the teacher. Instruction that uses a singular approach, such as verbal (e.g., lecturing), cheats students who learn better another way. This difference can effect student achievement. Furthermore, if a teacher's verbal communication conflicts with his or her nonverbal messages, students can become confused, and this too can affect their learning. And, "if there is incongruity between the verbal and the nonverbal, the nonverbal will win hands down.[1]

Research in those areas may lend support to the hypothesis that a teacher's best teaching style choice is eclectic, at least until the day arrives when students of certain thinking styles are matched to teachers with particular teaching styles. Future research will undoubtedly shed additional light on the relationships among pedagogy, pedagogical styles, and student learning. Until that research is available, we can turn to the information we now have about learning style assessment. Several sources have added to our knowledge and are in the list that follows.

[1]Patrick W. Miller, *Nonverbal Communication*, Washington, DC: National Education Association, 1986, pp. 6–7.

SAMPLE SOURCES OF LEARNING STYLE ASSESSMENT INSTRUMENTS

Cognitive Style Interest Inventory, by Joseph Hill. In *Personalized Education Programs Utilizing Cognitive Style Mapping*. Bloomfield Hills, Mich.: Oakland Community College, 1971.

Dunn, R. S.; Dunn, K. J.; and Price, G. E. "Identifying individual learning styles." In J. W. Keefe (Ed.), *Student Learning Styles: Diagnosing and Prescribing*. Reston, VA: National Association of Secondary School Principals, 1979, pp. 39–54.

"Find your modality strengths," by Walter Barbe. In *Instructor* (January 1980).

Kolb, D. A. *Learning Style Inventory Technical Manual*. Boston: McBer and Company, 1976.

Learning Strategies Questionnaire, by Norman Kagan and David R. Krathwohl. In *Studies in Human Interaction*. Washington, DC: HEW/USOE Bureau of Research, 1967.

Learning Style Identification Scale, by Paul Malcom, William Lutz, Mary Gerken, and Gary Hoeltke. Publishers Test Service (CTB/McGraw-Hill), 2500 Garden Road, Monterey, CA, 93940, 1981.

Learning Styles Inventory, by Albert A. Canfield and Judith S. Canfield. Humanics Media, (Liberty Drawer) 7970, Ann Arbor, Mich., 48107, 1976.

Myers-Briggs Type Indicator, by Isabel Briggs Myers and Katherine C. Briggs. Consulting Psychologists Press, Inc., 577 College Avenue, Palo Alto, CA. 94306, 1976.

Productivity Environmental Preference Survey, by Rita Dunn, Kenneth Dunn, and Gary E. Price. Price Systems, Box 3271, Lawrence, KS, 66044.

Short Inventory of Approaches to Studying, by Noel Entwistle. In *Styles of Learning and Teaching*. New York: John Wiley and Sons, 1981.

SRI Student Perceiver Interview Guide. Selection Research, Inc., 2546 South 48th Plaza, P.O. Box 6438, Lincoln, Neb. 68506, 1978.

Student Learning Styles Questionnaire, by Anthony F. Grasha and Sheryl W. Riechmann. Institute for Research and Training in Higher Education, University of Cincinnati, Cincinnati, OH, 45221, 1974.

Swassing-Barbe Modality Index, by Walter Barbe and Raymond Swassing. Columbus, OH: Zaner-Bloser, 1979.

Transaction Ability Inventory, by Anthony F. Gregorc. Department of Secondary Education, University of Connecticut, Box U-33, Storrs, CN, 06268.

Your Style of Learning and Thinking, Forms A and B, by E. Paul Torrance, Cecil R. Reynolds, T. R. Riegel, and O. E. Ball. *Gifted Child Quarter 2* (1977):563–573.

EXERCISE 3.1: DEVELOPING A PROFILE AND A STATEMENT ABOUT MY OWN TEACHING STYLE

Instructions: The purpose of this exercise is to help you clarify and to articulate your own assumptions about teaching and learning. You will develop a profile of your emerging teaching style, and from that, a statement representative of your current thinking about teaching and learning. Proceed with the following five steps.

Step 1. Read each of the 50 statements and rate your feeling about each, giving a *1* to those with which you strongly agree, a *2* for those for which you are neutral, and a *3* for those with which you strongly disagree.[1]

Remember: 1 = agree; 2 = neutral; 3 = disagree

___ 1. Most of what students learn, they learn on their own.
___ 2. Students should be concerned about other students' reactions to their work in the classroom.
___ 3. An important part of schooling is learning to work with others.
___ 4. Students learn more by working on their own than by working with other students.
___ 5. Students should be given opportunities to actively participate in class planning and implementation.
___ 6. In an effective learning environment grades are inappropriate.
___ 7. Students enjoy working in a class that has clearly defined learning objectives and evaluative criteria.
___ 8. I favor classroom methods that maximize student independence to learn from their own experiences.
___ 9. Most of what students learn is learned from other students.
___ 10. Students should be concerned with getting good grades.
___ 11. An important part of class should be to learn how to work independently.
___ 12. A teacher should not be contradicted by a student in the classroom.
___ 13. Interchanges between students and a teacher can provide ideas about content better than those found in a textbook.
___ 14. For students to get the most out of a class, they must be aware of the primary concerns and biases of the teacher.
___ 15. Students should not be given high grades unless clearly earned.
___ 16. Learning should help a student to become an independent thinker.
___ 17. Most of what students learn is learned from their teachers.
___ 18. A teacher who makes students do things they don't want to do is an ineffective teacher.
___ 19. Learning takes place most effectively under conditions in which students are in competition with one another.
___ 20. A teacher should try to persuade students that particular ideas are valid and exciting.
___ 21. To do well in school students must be assertive.
___ 22. Facts in textbooks are usually accurate.
___ 23. I favor the use of classroom methods that maximize student and teacher interaction.

[1]Adapted from William H. Berquist and Steven R. Phillips, *A Handbook for Faculty Development* (Washington, D.C.: The Council for Independent Colleges, June, 1975), pp. 25–27. By permission.

___ 24. Most of what students learn is learned from books.

___ 25. A teacher who lets students do whatever they want is ineffective.

___ 26. Students can learn more by working with an enthusiastic teacher than by working alone.

___ 27. I favor the use of classroom methods that maximize student learning of basic content.

___ 28. Ideas of other students are useful for helping a student understand class material.

___ 29. A student should study what the teacher says is important and not necessarily what is important to that student.

___ 30. A teacher who does not motivate student interest in subject matter is ineffective.

___ 31. An important part of education is learning how to perform under testing and evaluation conditions.

___ 32. Students can learn more by sharing their ideas than by keeping their ideas to themselves.

___ 33. Teachers give students too many trivial assignments.

___ 34. Ideas contained in the textbook should be the primary source of content in a class.

___ 35. Students should be given high grades as a means of motivating them and increasing their self-esteem.

___ 36. The ideas a student brings into a class are useful for helping the student to understand material.

___ 37. Students should study what is important to them and not necessarily what the teacher claims to be important.

___ 38. Learning takes place most effectively under conditions in which students are working independently of one another.

___ 39. Teachers often give students too much freedom of choice.

___ 40. Teachers should clearly explain what it is they expect from students.

___ 41. Student ideas about content are often better than those ideas found in textbooks.

___ 42. I have found that classroom discussions are beneficial learning experiences.

___ 43. A student's education should help the student to become a successful member of society.

___ 44. Learning takes place most effectively under conditions in which students are working cooperatively with one another.

___ 45. Teachers often are too personal with their students.

___ 46. A teacher should encourage students to disagree with that teacher in the classroom.

___ 47. Students have to be able to work effectively with other people to do well in school.

___ 48. For students to get the most out of school, they must assume at least part of the responsibility for their learning.

___ 49. Students seem to enjoy discussing their ideas about learning with the teacher and other students.

___ 50. A student's education should help the student to become a more sensitive human being.

Step 2. From the list of 50 items write the following items in two columns, those with which you strongly agreed in the left column, and those with which you strongly disagreed in the right column. Ignore those items that you ranked 2 (neutral).

Strongly agreed   **Strongly disagreed**

Step 3. In groups of three or four, discuss your lists (in Step 2) with your colleagues. From the discussion you may rerank any items you wish.

Step 4. You now have a finalized list of those items with which you were in agreement, and those with which you disagreed. On the basis of those two lists, write a paragraph (on separate paper) that summarizes your present philosophy about teaching and learning. It should be no longer than one page in length. That statement is a theoretical representation of your present teaching philosophy.

Step 5. Compare your philosophical statement with the theoretical positions as discussed earlier in this chapter. Can you clearly identify your position? Name it: What is your rationale?

At the completion of this course, you may wish to revisit your philosophical statement, perhaps even to make revisions to it. It will be useful to have your philosophy firmly implanted in your memory for teaching-job interviews at a later date.

EXERCISE 3.2: ANALYZING ONE TEACHER, ONE STYLE[1]

Instructions: The purpose of this exercise is to visit a secondary school class to observe and identify the instructional style. Be certain to obtain permission and to explain to the host teacher that you are observing, not evaluating, for teaching style. The host teacher may be interested in discussing with you your observations. A follow-up thank-you letter is appropriate.

Class and School Visited:
Date of Visitation:

From the start of your classroom observation observe at one-minute intervals for a period of ten minutes what the teacher is doing at that very moment and tabulate the appropriate item on the following chart. Continue for entire class meeting.

minute	1	2	3	4	5	6	7	8	9	10	etc.	Totals
Traditional Teacher Behaviors 1. Prescribing: giving advice, directions, being critical, evaluative, offering judgments.												
2. Informing: giving information, lecturing, interpreting.												
3. Confronting: directly challenging students.												
										Traditional Behaviors Total _____ .		
Facilitating Teacher Behaviors 4. Cathartic: releasing tension, using humor.												
5. Mediating: asking for information, being reflective, encouraging self-directed problem-solving.												
6. Supporting: approving, confirming, validating, listening.												
										Facilitating Behaviors Total _____ .		

Total traditional behaviors ÷ total facilitating behaviors = T/F Ratio = _____

Your conclusion about the host teacher's style on this day:

Did you discuss your observations with the host teacher?

[1]Adapted from J. Heron, *Six Category Intervention Analysis* (Mimeo, Guildford: Centre of Adult Education, University of Surrey, England, 1975).

EXERCISE 3.3: ANALYZING ADVANCE ORGANIZERS AS USED BY A TEACHER

Advance organizers are the links a teacher makes between material that students already know and that they are about to learn—techniques for introducing new material and helping students learn it either by arranging the material and providing key concepts and terms (an *expository organizer*), or by helping students see similarities and differences between what they already know and what they are about to learn (a *comparative organizer*).

Your educational purpose in this exercise is to observe a teacher and how that teacher introduces new material. Record the advance organizer used and identify whether it was an expository organizer or a comparative organizer.

Share your observations with students in your class who are in the same discipline area.

Grade level and subject I visited: _____

Advance organizer(s) observed and type(s): _____

_____

_____

_____

_____

_____

_____

_____

_____

_____

_____

_____

_____

_____

_____

_____

_____

_____

_____

_____

_____

_____

_____

In this chapter teaching style has been defined as the way teachers teach, their distinctive mannerisms complemented by their choices of teaching behaviors and strategies. Style develops from tradition, from experience, and from research findings. Many variables affect a teacher's style, some of which we know very little about, but what is believed about the reciprocal process of teaching and learning is that to effectively reach the highest percentage of students the competent teacher must utilize a style that is eclectic.

Chapter four helps you identify your own teaching skills and weaknesses, an important first step in the development of a teaching style.

QUESTIONS FOR CLASS DISCUSSION

1. If a certain teaching style correlates with student achievement, can you conclude that this teaching style causes an increase in student achievement?
2. Which environmental factors can instructors manipulate in order to improve their teaching effectiveness?
3. What research can you find to add to your knowledge base about hemispheric preferences? about modality strengths and preferences? about thinking styles?
4. Is hemisphericity more, or less, important to teaching-learning in your specific academic field?
5. Identify a teacher who you consider to be very competent, and compare what you recall about that teacher's classroom with the variables listed in this chapter.
6. Can a lecture effectively reach students with dominant visual or kinesthetic learning modalities? How?
7. Do you believe most teachers understand the philosophical and psychological assumptions that underlie their behaviors and strategies? or should they? why or why not?
8. What evidence can you find that indicates thinking-learning patterns differ from one discipline to another?
9. Do you believe that a secondary school teacher can and should help students to develop their awareness and selection of their own learning processes (metacognition)?
10. What questions do you have about the content of this chapter? How might answers be found?

SUGGESTED READINGS FOR CHAPTER 3

Baddeley, A. *Your Memory: A User's Guide*. New York: Macmillan, 1982.

Barbe, W. B., and Milone, M. N., Jr. "What we know about modality strengths." *Educational Leadership* 38(5):372–375 (Feb. 1981).

Belenky, M. et al. *Women's Ways of Knowing*. New York: Basic Books, 1986.

Chapman, S. F.; Segal, J.; and Glaser, R., eds. *Thinking and Learning Skills: Vol. 2: Research and Open Questions*. Hillsdale, NJ: Lawrence Erlbaum Associates, 1985.

Claxton, C. S., and Murrell, P. H. *Learning Styles: Implications for Educational Practices*. ASHE-ERIC *Higher Education Reports*. Washington, DC: Association for the Study of Higher Education, 1987.

Davis, D. S., and Chasson, P. "Style—A manner of thinking." *Educational Leadership* 8(5):376–377 (Feb. 1981).

Dunn, R., and Griggs, S. A. *Learning Styles: Quiet Revolution in Secondary Schools.* Reston, VA: National Association of Secondary School Principals, 1988.

Gardner, H. *Frames of Mind: The Theory of Multiple Intelligences.* New York: Basic Books, 1983.

Haglund, E. "A closer look at the brain as related to teachers and learners." *Peabody Journal of Education* 58(4):225–234 (July 1981).

Halpern, D. F. *Thought and Knowledge: An Introduction to Critical Thinking.* Hillsdale, NJ: Lawrence Erlbaum Associates, 1984.

Hand, J. "Brain function during learning," D. Jonassen, ed., in *The Technology of Text.* Englewood Cliffs, NJ: Educational Technology Publication, 1982.

Hart, L. *Human Brain, Human Learning.* White Plains, NY: Longman, 1983.

Johnson, V. R. "Myelin and maturation: A fresh look at Piaget." *The Science Teacher* 49(3):41–49 (March 1982).

Jones, M. G., and Wheatley, J. "Factors influencing the entry of women into science and related fields." *Science Education* 72(2):127–142 (April 1988).

Kane, M. "Cognitive styles of thinking and learning: Part one." *Academic Therapy* 19(5):527–536 (May 1984).

Kuhn, D. et al. *The Development of Scientific Thinking Skills.* San Diego, CA: Academic Press, 1988.

Maxwell, W. ed. *Thinking: The Expanding Frontier.* Philadelphia: The Franklin Institute Press, 1983.

Moore, W. E.; McCann, H.; and McCann, J. *Creative and Critical Thinking.* 2d ed. Boston: Houghton Mifflin, 1985.

Mosston, M., and Ashworth, S. *The Spectrum of Teaching Styles.* White Plains, NY: Longman, 1989.

Myers, J. T. "Hemisphericity research: An overview with some implications for problem solving." *Journal of Creative Behavior* 16(3):197–211 (Third Quarter 1982).

Nisbet, J. and Shucksmith, J. *The Seventh Sense.* Edinburgh: Scottish Council for Research in Education, 1984.

Resnick, L. B., and L. E. Klopfer, eds. *Toward the Thinking Curriculum: Current Cognitive Research.* 1989 ASCD Yearbook. Alexandria, VA: Association for Supervision and Curriculum Development, 1989.

Segal, J. W.; Chipman, S. F.; and Glaser, R., eds. *Thinking and Learning Skills, Vol. 1: Relating Instruction to Research.* Hillsdale, NJ: Lawrence Erlbaum Associates, 1985.

Springer, S., and Deutsch, G. *Left Brain, Right Brain.* New York: W. H. Freeman, 1985.

Sylwester, R. et al. "Symposium: Educational implications of recent brain research." *Educational Leadership* 39(1):6–15 (Oct. 1981).

4

What Are My Current Competency Levels?

The overall purpose of this resource guide is to assist you in identifying and building upon your instructional competencies. In order to do that we need a starting place and this chapter is it, beginning with the presentation of a list of specific competencies, followed by a self analysis of your own skills and weaknesses with respect to those competencies.

A. TWENTY-TWO CHARACTERISTICS OF THE COMPETENT SECONDARY SCHOOL TEACHER[1]

No teacher expertly models all the characteristics that follow; they represent an ideal to strive for. If a teacher is perfect, then that teacher belongs not on a school faculty but in heaven.

1. *The teacher is knowledgeable about the subject matter.* "Knowledge of subject" means that the teacher has both historical understanding and current knowledge of the structure of the subject matter, and of the facts, principles, concepts, and skills needed for that subject. This doesn't mean the teacher knows everything about the subject, but more than he or she is likely to teach.
2. *The teacher is an active member of professional organizations, reads professional journals, maintaining currency in the field.* We have known teachers who have become professionally inactive, who no longer read the latest writings in their field, and who have almost simultaneously become ineffective as teachers.
3. *The teacher understands the processes of learning.* The teacher assures that students understand course objectives and the teacher's expectations, that students feel welcomed in the classroom and involved in the learning activities, and that they have some control over the pacing of their own learning. Furthermore, the teacher's lessons include consideration of the life experiences of the learners, present content in reasonably small doses, and in a logical and coherent sequence, while

---

[1]The list of 22 competencies may be substituted by a list of teacher competencies from your own local district, college, university, or state department of education.

utilizing visual, verbal, and kinesthetic learning activities, with opportunities for student practice and reinforcement, and frequent comprehension checks to assure that students are learning.

4. *The teacher is an "educational broker."* The teacher knows where and how to discover information about the subject. The teacher cannot know everything there is to know about the subject, but should be knowledgeable about where and how to best research it, and how to assist students in developing some of those same skills. Among other things, this means that for the twenty-first century the teacher must be computer literate.

5. *The teacher uses effective modeling behaviors.* The teacher's own behaviors are consistent with those expected of students. If, for example, the teacher desires students to demonstrate inquiring minds, to behave cooperatively, to be attentive to recitations of others, to suspend judgments until sufficient data are in, to demonstrate skills in critical thinking, and to use proper communication skills, then the teacher does likewise, modeling those same behaviors and attitudes for students.

6. *The teacher is open to change, willing to take risks and to be held accountable.* If there were no difference between what is and what can be then formal education would be of little value. A competent teacher knows not only of historical and traditional values and knowledge, but also of the value of change, and is willing to carefully plan and to experiment, to transcend between that which is known and that which is not. Realizing that little of value is ever achieved without a certain amount of risk taking, and because of personal strength of convictions, the competent teacher stands ready to be held accountable for assuming such risks.

7. *The teacher is unbiased and nonprejudiced toward gender, sexual preference, ethnicity, skin color, religion, physical handicaps, learning disabilities, or national origin.* Among other things, this means no sexual innuendos, religious jokes, or racial slurs. It means being cognizant of how teachers, male and female, knowingly or unknowingly, historically have mistreated female students, and of how to avoid those same errors in your own teaching. It means learning about the needs of special students in your classes. For example, a physically handicapped student might need more time for writing an essay exam.

8. *The teacher organizes the course and plans lessons carefully.* Course outlines and lesson plans are prepared well in advance, thought about, revised, and competently implemented with creative, motivating, and effective strategies.

9. *The teacher is an effective communicator.* The teacher uses thoughtfully selected words, carefully planned questions, expressive voice inflections, useful pauses, meaningful gestures, and productive and expressive body language.

10. *The teacher is constantly striving to further develop a repertoire of teaching strategies.* Competent teachers are good students, continuing their own learning by evaluating their own work, attending workshops, studying the work of others, and conferencing with students and colleagues.

11. *The teacher demonstrates concern for the safety and health of students.* The teacher strives to maintain an ideal room temperature with proper ventilation, and to prevent safety hazards in the classroom. Students who are ill are encouraged to stay home and to get well. Teachers of laboratory courses maintain currency about laboratory safety standards, consistently modeling safety procedures, and assuring precautions necessary to protect the health and safety of students.

12. *The teacher demonstrates optimism, while providing a constructive and positive environment for student learning.* Students enjoy and learn better from a teacher who is positive, encouraging, happy, and optimistic, than from a teacher who is pessimistic, discouraging, and grumpy.

13. *The teacher demonstrates confidence in students' abilities.* For a student nothing at school is any more satisfying than to be taught by a teacher who demonstrates confidence in that student's abilities. Each of us can recall with admiration a teacher (or other significant person) who showed confidence in our ability to accomplish seemingly formidable tasks.

14. *The teacher is skillful and fair in the assessment of student learning.* A useful phrase is that a teacher should be "firm, fair, and friendly." The competent teacher is knowledgeable about implementation of learning assessment tools, and avoids abusing power afforded by the evaluation process.

15. *The teacher is skillful in working with parents, colleagues, administrators, and the classified staff, maintaining and nurturing friendly and ethical professional relationships.* Faculty, administrators, and classified staff are all present for one purpose, that they share with parents, which is to serve the education of students. They best serve students when they do it cooperatively.

16. *The teacher demonstrates continuing interest in professional responsibilities and opportunities.* The competent teacher assumes an active interest in total school life, knowing that ultimately each and every activity has an effect upon the classes. The purpose of the school is to serve the education of students, and the classroom is the primary but not sole place where this occurs. Every committee meeting, every athletic and music event, every faculty meeting, every board meeting, every office, program, and any other planned function on the campus shares in the ultimate purpose of better serving the education of students.

17. *The teacher demonstrates a wide range of interests.* This includes interests in the activities of students and the many aspects of the school and surrounding community. The competent teacher is interesting because of his or her interests; a teacher with varied interests more often motivates and captures the attention of more students.

18. *The teacher shares a healthy and enjoyable sense of humor.* Because humor releases tension and anxiety, students appreciate and learn more from a teacher who shares a sense of humor, as long as that humor is not self-deprecating or disrespectful of others.

19. *The teacher is quick to recognize a student who may be in need of special student service.* A competent teacher is alert to recognize a student showing behaviors indicating a need for special attention, such as counseling, and knows how and where to refer that student, doing so with minimal class disruption or embarrassment to the student.

20. *The teacher makes special and frequent efforts to demonstrate how the subject may be related to the lives of students.* A potentially dry and boring subject is made significant and "alive" when taught by a competent teacher. Regardless of subject, somewhere there are competent teachers teaching that subject, and one of the significant characteristics of their effectiveness is that they make their subject alive and relevant to their students.

21. *The teacher is knowledgeable about career opportunities for students in the subject field, and invokes student awareness of those opportunities.* Because students are exploring

career and job opportunities, a competent teacher makes frequent special efforts to provide students with knowledge about career and employment opportunities in fields related to the subject.

22. *The teacher is reliable.* The competent teacher is prompt for class meetings, and can be relied on to fulfill promises and commitments. A teacher who cannot be relied upon is quick to lose credibility with the students. An unreliable teacher is an incompetent teacher. Furthermore, a teacher who persistently fails to assume school and district-wide committee responsibilities will most likely soon be looking for other employment, or should be.

B. IDENTIFYING MY OWN COMPETENCIES

As this resource guide is prepared to assist you in identifying and developing your competencies as a secondary school teacher, it is important that you now do a personal assessment. Later you will complete a second assessment, comparing it with this first one, to analyze the progress in building your own teaching competencies. Not only does continuing self-evaluation help you become an effective teacher; it also helps you better understand your students, your collegial relationships, and will prepare you for teaching-job interviews.

EXERCISE 4.1 TEACHING COMPETENCIES: MY FIRST SELF-EVALUATION

Instructions: Before proceeding you may wish to duplicate unmarked copies of this exercise; see Step 4 of Exercise 4.2. Read the following list of competencies (referring to the preceding section for full descriptions) and indicate by circling the letter for each what you perceive to be your own current skill level.

List your subject teaching field(s):

G = good, I have nearly achieved perfection.
F = fair, I need minor improvements.
W = weak, I need major improvement.

The Competency	Current Level		
1. Knowledgeable in subject field	G	F	W
2. Professionally active	G	F	W
3. Understanding of the processes of learning	G	F	W
4. Knowledgeable educational broker	G	F	W
5. Can use effective modeling behaviors	G	F	W
6. Open to change, risk taker, accountable	G	F	W
7. Unbiased, unprejudiced, accepting of all students	G	F	W
8. Can plan effectively	G	F	W
9. An effective communicator	G	F	W
10. Continuing to learn new ways	G	F	W
11. Knowledgeable and concerned about safety and health	G	F	W
12. Optimistic	G	F	W
13. Confident in students' abilities	G	F	W
14. Skillful in evaluation of student learning	G	F	W
15. Skillful in working with staff	G	F	W
16. Interested in professional opportunities	G	F	W
17. Wide range of interests	G	F	W
18. Good sense of humor	G	F	W
19. Knowledgeable about students with special needs	G	F	W
20. Can help students see relevancy	G	F	W
21. Knowledgeable about related career opportunities	G	F	W
22. Reliable	G	F	W

EXERCISE 4.2: MY FIRST SELF-EVALUATION: HOW CAN IT HELP ME?

Instructions: Before proceeding, see the following Step 4. Now that you have completed evaluating your competency levels (Exercise 4.1),

Your first self-evaluation will assist you in discussing competencies.

Step 1: Share that evaluation with your colleagues.

Your first self-evaluation will provide information about your competency development.

Step 2: After sharing your evaluation with others, reread all the statements you marked with a *G*. Then take a few minutes to generalize your thoughts about those statements and write your generalizations in a brief paragraph. This paragraph will reflect your most competent areas. Now return to the list and reread all the statements you marked with a *W* or an *F*. Form your thoughts into a second paragraph, one that indicates what you may need to work on during your time in this course.

First paragraph, *G:* _____

_____

_____

_____

Second paragraph, *W* or *F:* _____

_____

_____

_____

Your first self-evaluation will assist in planning your agenda.

Step 3: From Exercise 4.1, identify the skills you marked with a *W*. Select one. Do you believe you will be able to develop this competency? Or do you believe that it is an innate one? If it is one that you believe you will be able to develop, what activities would you suggest to assist you in developing the competency?

_____

_____

_____

_____

Your first self-evaluation will assist you in future evaluations.

Step 4: Duplicate several copies of unmarked Exercises 4.1 and 4.2. Select calendar dates at mid-semester and during the final week, and mark the competencies again. Compare these later self-evaluations with this first self-evaluation. What growth have you made in the competencies?

C. RESOURCES AVAILABLE FOR DEVELOPING MY COMPETENCIES

The bad news is that most of us are not born with innate teaching skills; the good news is that *teaching skills can be learned.* Teachers who wish to improve their teaching can do so, and (other than this resource guide) there are many resources that can help. If you are already teaching, then certainly one source of data for improvement is student data.

Data From Students

Some secondary school teachers obtain student input about the course in the form of *formal* feedback collected via student evaluations of the course, usually during the final class meeting. In addition, many teachers collect student feedback opinions around mid-semester so that students might benefit from their own suggestions. In either case, teacher decisions about what to do with student opinions is the most important aspect of collecting those opinions. The teacher must make decisions about the relevancy of the opinions, and whether and how to act on them. Filing feedback data without review and action is unprofessional and indicates no commitment to excellence. Our suggestion is that you ask a colleague to review the data and to provide interpretations as to their meanings.

Informal student data are available throughout the year, by observing the attentiveness of students in class, from informal discussions with students outside of class, and from the quality of student work on assignments and exams. Having a colleague, cooperating teacher, or your university or college supervisor review samples of your students' work and discussing with that person your own observations will provide insights for improving your teaching. Through such discussions you probably will discover that your own teaching problems are not unique to you, and you can learn how other teachers have resolved similar problems.

Comments From Administrators

In addition, you will receive comments from the principal or his or her designee. Recommendations for improvement result from administrator evaluations of one or more visitations to your class. You may or may not know when administrator visitations are going to occur; consequently, the best way to forestall unfortunate events during a visitation is to plan for each and every class as if you were going to be visited and evaluated. You should be aware that one of the problems that can occur as a result of an administrator's observation (or when a college supervisor observes a student teacher) is when the evaluator's perceptions of a teacher's effectiveness are clouded by their own learning modalities (discussed in Chapter 3).

Comments From the University Supervisor

When is the supervisor coming? Is the supervisor going to be here today? Do you see a university or a college supervisor's observation of your student teaching as a pleasant experience or a painful one? Do you realize that classroom observations of your teaching continue during your beginning years of teaching? Being observed and evaluated doesn't have to be a painful, nerve-racking experience for you. And no—you don't have to become a bundle of raw nerve endings when you realize the supervisor is coming to see you. Some professional suggestions may help you turn an evaluating observation into a useful, professionally satisfying experience.

What to Do Before an Observation

"Successful teachers," writes Helen C. Lee, "seem to be able to ameliorate tension and get through an evaluation with skill and tact." Lee suggests that a teacher who is about to be formally evaluated prepare for an evaluator's visit in these ways:

- Decide what you do well in the classroom and plan to demonstrate your best skills.
- Select your best skills to discuss first with the evaluator; let your perceived weaknesses be your second targets.
- Decorate your room and bulletin boards. Display student work.
- Make sure your desk is neat (this shows good organization).[1]

Is your supervisor coming to see you? If so, read the previous list, and if you decide that the list makes sense, then plan to accomplish every single task on it. As a teacher-candidate, you realize that you can present a good, organized appearance, perhaps assume the responsibility of preparing a display table, a chart, or bulletin board in the classroom, and with your host teacher's cooperation, select an academic aspect of the teaching day that demonstrates some of your best teaching skills. If your university supervisor has targeted some of your weak areas, plan to demonstrate growth in those teaching abilities. With all this done, you wait for the supervisor. The hands of the clock turn slowly yet relentlessly around and around until the time of the visit arrives.

What to Do During an Observation

Some supervisors and administrators choose to preannounce their visits. This is certainly true with the practice of *clinical supervision*. Clinical supervision is supervision that is based on shared decision-making, between the supervisor and teacher, focusing on improving, rather than evaluating, teaching behaviors.[2] With the use of clinical supervision, you know when the supervisor or administrator is coming, and you will probably look forward to the visit because of the rapport that has been established among members of your triad (in student teaching situations, your triad is comprised of you, your cooperating teacher, and your university or college supervisor).

Sometimes your supervisor or administrator may drop in unannounced. When that happens we recommend you take a deep breath, count to ten (quietly), and then proceed with your lesson. You wll undoubtedly do just fine if you have been following our guidelines. Additional guidelines for a classroom observation of your teaching are as follows.

[1]Helen C. Lee, "Evaluation Without Tears," *Educational Horizon* 61(4):200–201 (Summer 1983). Bloomington, IN: Pi Lambda Theta.
[2]K. A. Acheson and M. D. Gall, *Techniques in the Clinical Supervision of Teachers,* 2d ed. (New York: Longman, 1987).

GUIDELINES FOR OBSERVATION OF YOUR TEACHING

- Allow the observer to sit wherever he or she wishes.
- Do not interrupt your teaching to introduce the observer, unless the observer requests it, but *do* prepare your students in advance by letting them know who may be visiting and why.
- Do not place the observer on the spot by suddenly involving the observer in the lesson, but *do* try and discern in advance the level of participation desired by the observer.[1]
- Without "missing a beat" in your lesson you may walk over and quietly hand the observer a copy of the textbook (or of any other materials being used), opened to the appropriate page.

Soon after the observational visit, there should be a conference where observations are discussed in a *nonevaluative* atmosphere. It might be necessary for you to assure that such a conference is scheduled. This means you need to make prior arrangements so you can leave the class for this conference. The purpose of this postobservation conference is for you and the observer(s) to discuss, rather than to evaluate, your teaching, and for you to exit the conference with agreements about areas for improvement and *how* to make those improvements.

What to Do During an Observation Conference

Some university supervisors will arrange to have a conference with you to discuss the classroom observation and to begin to resolve any classroom teaching problems. As a teacher or teacher-candidate, you should be quite professional during this conference. For instance, one student teacher asks for additional help by requesting resources. Another takes notes and suggests developing a cooperative plan with the supervisor to improve teaching competencies. Still another discusses visiting other classrooms to observe certificated teachers.

During other conferences, student teachers may ask for assistance in scheduling other meetings with the supervisor. At these, the teacher (or teacher-candidate) views films of selected teaching styles or methods, listens to audiotapes, or visits an outside educational consultant or nearby resource center.

Almost all supervisors conclude their conferences by leaving something in writing with the teacher or teacher-candidate. This written record usually includes (a) a summary of teaching strengths or weaknesses, with a review of classroom management;

---

[1]If you have been assigned to a secondary-school classroom for a teacher-candidate field experience, your university supervisor will meet with you and explain some of the tasks you should attend to when the supervisor visits your class. These tasks may be variations of Lee's list. For instance, some supervisors prefer to walk into the classroom quietly and not interrupt the learning activities. Some supervisors prefer not to be introduced to the class or to participate in the activities. Some supervisors are already well known by the students and teaching staff members from the supervisor's visits to the school during a previous semester or year. Other supervisors may give you a special form to be completed before the supervisor arrives for the visit. Often this form resembles a lesson plan procedure and includes space for your objectives, your lesson procedures, your motivational strategies, your related activities, and your method of evaluating how well the students learned from the lesson. Remember, keep the line of communication open with your supervisor so you have a clear understanding of what is expected of you when the supervisor visits your classroom.

(b) the supervisor's recommendations; and (c) perhaps steps in an overall plan for the teacher's (or student teacher's) professional growth and development.

What to Do After the Supervisor Leaves

In addition to observing the classes of other teachers, attending workshops, signing up for conferences, and conferencing with college and university authorities, Lee[1] suggests the following ways to implement your plan for improvement:

- Do what you and the observer have agreed on. Document your activities with a record or diary with dated entries.
- Get help if you need it. Ask colleagues you trust to help you by visiting your classroom.
- Write comments to parents or guardians about students' progress, and leave a space for a return message from the adult. Keep positive responses from adults and present them at your next evaluation conference.
- If your problem is classroom management or organization, seek information on class management skills from others and from articles in the professional literature.
- Sometimes the answer lies simply in more self-discipline and hard work; sometimes *smart* work is better than hard work.
- Many beginning teachers are unaware that they need to debug their lesson plans by walking through them in advance.

Other Resources

There are many other resources for building your competencies as a beginning and as a continuing secondary school teacher, such as

- Reading professional texts, journals, and other publications.
- Attending professional workshops, seminars, and conferences.
- Attending school, district, and county faculty development workshops.
- Observing classes of other teachers.

This completes Part I of our resource guide, which has provided an overview about secondary school teaching. You will now proceed to Part II, which provides the important aspects of specific planning for your classroom instruction.

QUESTIONS FOR CLASS DISCUSSION

1. What teacher behaviors seem easy for you? Difficult?
2. What can you do to ensure that an administrator or a supervisor's classroom visit is a positive experience for you?

---

[1]Lee, *op cit*, p. 201. By permission.

3. What can you do to reduce friction if you do not get along with or respect your supervisor?
4. Do secondary school students know the difference between effective and ineffective teachers?
5. From a single observation of your class, can a principal (or his or her designee) really evaluate your teaching effectiveness? Why or why not?
6. Many teachers feel quite alone in their work. Talk with experienced teachers to find out how often and who visits their classes to give them constructive feedback about their teaching.
7. Do you believe that teachers should be tenured? Why or why not? In your state, when is a teacher granted tenure, and on what basis is it granted?
8. Begin thinking about and preparing your classroom behavior rules (CBRs) that, as a teacher, you will present to your students, probably at the first class meetings, and share your rules with others in your class.
9. Obtain information for teachers in your state about guidelines and requirements for student safety in the classroom.
10. What questions do you have about the content of this chapter? How might answers be found?

SUGGESTED READINGS FOR CHAPTER 4

Acheson, K. A., and M. D. Gall. *Techniques in the Clinical Supervision of Teachers.* 2d. ed. White Plains, NY: Longman, 1987.

Mandeville, G. K. and Rivers, J. "Is the Hunter Model a Recipe for Supervision?" *Educational Leadership* 46(8):39–43 (May 1989).

Ryan, K., and Cooper, J. M. *Those Who Can, Teach.* 5th ed. Boston: Houghton Mifflin, 1988.

PART II

Planning for Instruction in a Secondary Classroom

Part II responds to your needs about

- Why you should plan.
- What you should plan.
- How to select textbooks.
- How to prepare instructional objectives.
- How to prepare unit and lesson plans.
- How to individualize the learning experience.
- How to work with special students.

The art of teaching is the art of assisting discovery.
—Mark Van Doren

5

Why Should I Plan and How Do I Select Content?

Competent teachers begin careful planning of their instruction months before meeting their students for the first time. Their daily lessons are parts of a larger picture of their long-range goals for the year. A teacher who ignores this broader context, or who does not take into account where the students have been or where they are going, is doing a disservice to students. The students deserve better. Administrators, parents, and students expect better. The rationale for careful planning and the components of that planning are the topics of this chapter.

A. RATIONALE FOR PLANNING

The primary reason for planning is *to provide program coherence.* Periodic lesson plans are an integral part of a larger plan represented by course goals and objectives. Students' learning experiences are thoughtfully planned in sequence, and then orchestrated by a teacher who understands the rationale for their respective positions in the curriculum, not precluding, of course, an occasional diversion from planned activities.

There are other reasons teachers must plan. These are:

1. *To provide a mechanism for vertical (K–12) scope and sequence curriculum articulation.* Unless your course stands alone, following nothing, and leading to nothing (which is unlikely), there are prerequisites to what you want your students to learn, and there are subsequent learning objectives that follow and build on this learning.
2. *To prepare for individual differences.* The diversity of students in secondary schools demands that the teacher give planning considerations to those individual differences—whether it is consideration for student cultural experiences, learning styles, varying reading abilities, students with special needs, or any other concerns.
3. *To assure efficient and effective teaching with a minimum of classroom-control problems.* After deciding *what* content to teach follows the difficult and important task of deciding *how* that content is best taught. To assure efficient use of instructional time, two important goals of a teacher should be: (1) to not waste anyone's time and (2) to select effective strategies that assure student learning.

4. *To insure program continuation.* In your absence, in case of the need for a substitute, the program must continue.
5. *To serve as a criterion for teacher self-evaluation.* After an activity and at the end of a school year a competent teacher evaluates what was done and its effect upon student achievement.
6. *To evaluate your teaching.* Your plans represent a criterion recognized and evaluated by administrators. With those experienced in such matters, it is clear that inadequate attention to planning is usually a precursor to incompetent teaching (demonstrated later, in Exercise 8.2).

B. COMPONENTS OF A COMPLETE PLAN

A complete instructional plan has seven components. These are:

1. A *philosophy* about how students learn. (Referred to in Chapter 3).
2. An *appreciation for the cultural plurality of the nation and of the school, with a corresponding perception of the needs of society, its learners, and of the functions served by the school.* (Referred to in Chapter 1.)
3. A *goals* and *objectives* statement that is consistent with the philosophy and appreciations. (Referred to in Chapter 7.)
4. A curriculum that is *articulated vertically* (K–12) *and horizontally* (integrated with the total school curriculum.) (Referred to in Chapter 6.)
5. An organized collection of *sequentially planned learning activities* appropriate for the subject, and for the age and diversity of the learners. (Referred to in Chapters 8–10.)
6. A listing of *resources,* such as books, speakers, field trips, materials needed and where located. (Referred to in Chapter 12.)
7. An *assessment* strategy, to evaluate teacher effectiveness and student achievement. (Referred to in Chapter 16.)

EXERCISE 5.1: A PRE-PLANNING CHECK

Instructions: Let us review this chapter by completing the following.

1. List at least four reasons you should plan carefully what you are going to do.

   Reason 1 _____

   Reason 2 _____

   Reason 3 _____

   Reason 4 _____

   Reason 5 _____

   Reason 6 _____

   Reason 7 _____

2. Identify the seven components of a total curricular plan.

   Component 1 _____

   Component 2 _____

   Component 3 _____

   Component 4 _____

   Component 5 _____

   Component 6 _____

   Component 7 _____

EXERCISE 5.2: LESSON PLANNING PRETEST

Instructions: Without looking ahead to subsequent chapters, list five major components of a daily lesson plan.

1. ____________________
2. ____________________
3. ____________________
4. ____________________
5. ____________________

Now look at the suggested inclusions inverted at the bottom of this page. How did you do? The chapters that follow will aid you in planning for your teaching. But before you can plan, you need to know how one decides what to teach. Chapter 6 will provide this information.

objectives
set
procedures- lesson content
w/time planning
closure
materials & AV

Did you include the following? objectives; set induction; lesson content procedure with time planning; closure; materials and audiovisual needs.

EXERCISE 5.3: EXAMINING TEACHER INSTRUCTIONAL PLANS

Instructions: The purpose of this exercise is to examine selected instructional plans, ones you borrowed from your favorite middle, junior, or senior high school teachers, or that are supplied by your course instructor. If the plan is borrowed from a teacher, please inform the cooperating teacher that the purpose of the review is not to judge the plan but to *observe the scope of inclusions and the way the plan is organized.* Study the plan by completing the following; then share it with others in your class. (Note: this exercise is a transition for what is to come; therefore it is possible that some terms may be new to you, and if so, please locate them by referring to the index or glossary of this resource guide.)

1. Grade level and academic topic(s) content of plan studied: _____

_____

2. For what time duration is the plan? _____

3. Inclusions (give examples): _____

    3.1. specific or general objectives? _____

    _____

    _____

    3.2. set motivators at beginning of lessons? _____

    _____

    _____

    3.3. lesson content procedures? _____

        3.3a. with a time plan? _____

        _____

        3.3b. transitions? _____

        _____

        3.3c. key questions? _____

        _____

        _____

        3.3d. specific activities for teacher? _____

        _____

        _____

        _____

3.3e. lecture notes? _____

outlined or in prose? _____

3.3f. specific activities for students? _____

_____

_____

_____

3.3g. other? (identify) _____

_____

4. Is a closure accounted for? _____

_____

5. Is there a listing of materials and audiovisual needs? _____

_____

_____

C. INSTRUCTIONAL THEORY INTO PRACTICE

In reviewing a lesson plan, you may be introduced to the Madeline Hunter model of planning. Hunter's advocates claim that while the program has not been extensively evaluated, the principles on which it is based are supported by research findings.[1] Hunter's model includes elements in a lesson called anticipatory set, objectives, checking for understanding, guided practice, independent practice, and closure. The model also features activating a student's prior knowledge, teaching for transfer, and using cognitive strategies. This model is backed by educational and psychological theory and is often called Instructional Theory Into Practice (ITIP) and is discussed in Hunter's book, *Teach More—Faster* (El Segundo, CA: TIP Publications, 1980).

Hunter's critics ask questions: "Does it work?" "Do students taught by teachers who use Hunter's model learn more and learn faster?" "Does this model affect students' scores on standardized or criterion-referenced tests?" "Has the ITIP model been evaluated?"

In the preceding paragraph, the answer to the last question is yes, the model has been evaluated. In a three-year experimental-control study by Stallings[2], the ITIP model was evaluated. Subjects were from a single school in Napa, California. Results indicated some small achievement gains by both the experimental and control groups in the first two years but no gains in the third year. Certainly, other questions could be asked about these results: "Was the model implemented as rigorously the third year as in the first two years?" "Were the teachers the same ones or new to the staff?" If new to the staff, were the teachers appropriately trained?"

A second study also evaluated the model. In South Carolina, the model was incorporated into the Program for Effective Teaching (PET) and teachers were trained in Hunter's methods in 87 percent of the districts.[3] An evaluation of the achievement effects of the program over a three-year period indicated that: After controlling for prior achievement and for social-economic status (SES), there were *no* differences in achievement between students of PET-trained teachers and students of the other teachers; in classes where teachers had been trained in PET, two to three years before the posttesting, their students scored slightly *worse* than did the students of untrained teachers; achievement scores of students of PET-trained teachers were not significantly related to any of the following: (1) the amount or quality of the coaching; (2) their attitude toward PET; (3) self-reported teacher use of PET concepts and lesson plans; and (4) motivation for training.

Additionally, Donovan, Sousa, and Walberg[4] reported an evaluation of the programs for grades 3, 6, 9, and 11. In West Orange, New Jersey, ITIP-trained (35) and untrained (29) teachers participated in the model. Results indicated that adjusted achievement scores for the students of both groups of teachers were nearly identical.

[1]Robert E. Slavin, "PET and the Pendulum: Faddism in Education and How to Stop It," *Phi Delta Kappan* 70(10):753–758 (June 1989).

[2]Jane Stallings. "A Study of Implementation of Madeline Hunter's Model and Its Effects on Students," *Journal of Educational Research* 78(6):325–337 (July/August 1985).

[3]John D. Tudor, "Background for the South Carolina Implementation of the PET Inservice Teacher Training Program." Paper presented at the annual meeting of the American Educational Research Association, New Orleans (April 1988).

[4]James F. Donovan, David A. Sousa, and Herbert J. Walberg, "The Impact of Staff Development on Implementation and Student Achievement," *Journal of Educational Research* 80(6):348–351 (July/August 1987).

Considered together, all of the findings of these discussed studies indicate that the Hunter model has *not* resulted in significant improvement in student achievement. As of this writing, there is still a need for additional evidence that the program affects student achievement in a positive way.

QUESTIONS FOR CLASS DISCUSSION

1. Which characteristics of students have an effect on curricular planning? Describe the effects.
2. How do you discover which books are appropriate for a particular group of students? What characteristics define a book as appropriate, or as inappropriate?
3. Describe the difference between vertical and horizontal curriculum articulation. How important is each in your subject field?
4. Distinguish between what is curriculum and what is instruction.
5. Share an example of how a teacher's lack of careful planning affected a classroom situation.
6. When, if ever, should a secondary school teacher divert from the planned lesson?
7. For a course you intend to teach what are the advantages and disadvantages of using a single textbook?
8. What specifically do schools in your geographic area require of teachers with respect to lesson planning?
9. In case of extended absence, do secondary schools in your geographic area hire substitutes? If so, how are substitutes selected?
10. What freedom do secondary school teachers have with respect to textbook selection, and particularly for multiple section courses taught by more than one teacher?
11. When selecting a textbook and other required student materials, should the school teacher consider prices students will have to pay, or are textbooks and materials in your state supplied by the schools?
12. "Historically in this country schools focused on broadly stated aims (principally committees of the National Education Association in 1893, 1899, and in 1913; and the Educational Policies Commission in 1938 and again in 1961), but today the focus seems more on student achievement of specific competencies." Do you agree with this statement? What is the evidence to support or to reject the statement? If you agree, how do you explain this shift?
13. What questions do you have about the content of this chapter? How might you find answers?

SUGGESTED READINGS FOR CHAPTER 5

Borich, G. D. *Effective Teaching Methods.* Columbus, OH: Merrill, 1988.

Resnick, L. B., and Klopfer, L. E. *Toward the Thinking Curriculum: Current Cognitive Research.* 1989 ASCD Yearbook. Alexandria, VA: Association for Supervision and Curriculum Development, 1989.

Slavin, R. E. "PET and the Pendulum: Faddism in Education and How to Stop It." *Phi Delta Kappan* 70(10):753–758 (June 1989).

Stallings, J. "A Study of Implementation of Madeline Hunter's Model and its Effects on Students." *Journal of Educational Research* 78(6):325–337 (July/August, 1985).

Tudor, J. D. "Background for the South Carolina Implementation of the PET In-service Teacher Training Program." Paper presented at the annual meeting of the American Educational Research Association, New Orleans, April, 1988.

Wulf, K. M., and Schane, B. *Curriculum Design.* Glenview, IL: Scott, Foresman, 1984.

6

How Do I Know What to Teach?

Secondary teachers have some freedom of choice about course content, although the content of that selection is subject to peer, administrative, and community curriculum committee reviews and must adhere to the description as published in the course of study. How does the instructor select course content? That is the topic of this chapter.

Three general sources help you discover what to teach: documents, colleagues, and your own convictions about content.

- You examine school and other public resource documents for mandates and guidelines.
- You talk with colleagues and learn of common expectations.
- You probe, analyze, and translate your own convictions, knowledge, and skills into behaviors that foster the academic development of your students.

This chapter examines the first source, the resource documents.

A. DOCUMENTS THAT PROVIDE GUIDANCE FOR CONTENT SELECTION

State department of education curricular publications, district courses of study, and school-adopted textbooks are the sources you will now examine, with the guidance of the accompanying exercises.

For accreditation (normally every three–five years), high schools[1] are reviewed, and prior to the visitation of an accreditation team, campuses prepare self-study reports, for which each department reviews and updates curriculum courses of study (curriculum guides) for courses taught in that department. Those documents provide information about expected objectives and content for each course offering.

---

[1]Junior high schools are not usually required to go through periodic accreditations although in some states those schools can volunteer to be reviewed for improvement.

EXERCISE 6.1: EXAMINING STATE CURRICULUM FRAMEWORKS

Instructions: Find whether your State Department of Education publishes a curricular framework. Addresses of State Departments of Education are provided in the final chapter of this text. State frameworks can provide valuable information pertaining to content and process, and teachers need to be aware of these documents. Frameworks for the State of California, for example, are:

California Curriculum Framework: A Handbook
English Language Framework
Foreign Language Framework
Health Instruction Framework
History–Social Science Framework
Mathematics Framework
Physical Education Framework
Reading Framework
Science Framework
Visual and Performing Arts Framework
Program Descriptions for Bilingual-Bicultural and ESL Instructional Materials
Guide for Multicultural Education
Nutrition Education—Choose Well, Be Well: A Resource Manual for Secondary Teachers

QUESTIONS FOR CLASS DISCUSSION FOR EXERCISE 6.1

1. Is there a state curricular document available to teachers for your state in your subject field? _____ If so, what is its title? _____

2. If so, is it free to teachers, or how much does it cost? _____

3. Is the document specific as to subject-matter content, showing a scope and sequence articulation for various grade levels? _____

4. Does the document offer specific process strategies? _____

5. Does the document distinguish between what you *shall* teach and what you *can* teach?

   _____

6. Does the document offer suggestions for specific resources, such as supplementary books, films, microcomputer programs? _____

7. Does the document offer suggestions to the teacher for dealing with students with special needs? _____

8. Does the document offer suggestions or guidelines for dealing with controversial topics?

   _____

EXERCISE 6.2: EXAMINING CURRICULUM GUIDES

A primary resource for what to teach is referred to as the *curriculum guide,* or the *course of study.* Samples may be available in your university library or in a local district resource center. Examine how closely these documents follow the components listed in Chapter 5, Section B. An analysis of several documents will give you a good picture of expectations. Compare documents from several school districts, using the format that follows.

Title of document _____

District or school _____

Date of document _____

I. Does the document contain the following components?

	Yes	No
1. Statement of philosophy	( )	( )
2. Evidence of preassessment (regarding needs)	( )	( )
3. Goals and objectives	( )	( )
4. Scope and sequence (vertical and horizontal articulation)	( )	( )
5. Recommended procedures (learning activities)	( )	( )
6. Recommended resource materials	( )	( )
7. Evaluation procedures (assessment strategy)	( )	( )

II. Answer the following questions regarding your document, then share with members of your class.

1. Does the document list expected learning outcomes? _____

2. Does the document contain detailed unit plans? _____

3. Does it contain initiating activities? _____

    Does it contain learning activities? _____

    Does it contain enrichment activities? _____

    Does it contain culminating activities? _____

    Does it contain evaluating activities? _____

    Does it provide activities for learners with special needs? _____

4. Does it provide bibliographic entries for:

    the teacher? _____

    the students? _____

5. Does it list audiovisual and other materials needed? _____

6. Does it provide information regarding resource ideas? _____

7. Does the document clearly help you understand what you are expected to teach?

   _____

   How to do it? _____

8. Are there questions you have that are not answered by your examination of this document?

   List them for class discussion. _____

   _____

   _____

   _____

   _____

B. ABOUT STUDENT TEXTBOOKS

As much as two thirds of a secondary student's class time is spent using textbooks and related written materials. Considerable national attention is currently being given to ways of improving the quality of student textbooks, with particular attention to the need to better develop student critical thinking skills. There has been a gap between what is needed in textbooks and what has been available for student use in many classrooms. Many school districts have for several years been experiencing bad economic times, and have not been able to maintain current textbooks or a variety of books to better address the different needs and varying reading levels of students within individual classes. The textbooks you will be using may be several years old, and there may be an inadequate number of textbooks available for the number of students you will have.

Some states have statewide textbook adoption policies; others rely on local committees; yet others have a statewide process that provides a list from which local committees or a teacher make the final selection. In some high schools, the teacher can make the initial decision as to what book is to be used; that decision is then approved by others, perhaps beginning with the department chairperson, then the principal, and finally, perhaps, a district textbook approval committee, which may be comprised of laypersons from the community as well as teachers and administrators from the district. Whichever the case, textbooks represent the *de facto* curriculum in many schools, and the books used may be outdated and in short supply, in which case you will need to provide supplementary and current material to the students.

In Exercises that follow, you will become familiar with textbooks you will likely be using. Later, in Section F of Chapter 11, we provide guidelines for textbook use.

EXERCISE 6.3: EXAMINING TEACHER'S MANUALS AND STUDENT TEXTS

Textbooks are usually accompanied by a teacher's edition, which will contain specific objectives, teaching techniques, learning activities, test items, and suggested resources. Again, your university library or local schools may be your source for locating these.

Instructions: Select a textbook that is accompanied by a teacher's edition and examine the contents using the following format. *If there are no standard textbooks available for your teaching field (e.g., music, physical education, art), then select a field in which there is a possibility you might teach. Beginning teachers are often assigned to teach in more than a single field.*

Title of book: _____

Author(s): _____

Publisher: _____

Date of publication: _____

	Yes	No
I. Does the teacher's manual contain the following elements?		
1. Goals that are consistent with those of local guides and/or state guides?	( )	( )
2. Specific objectives for each lesson?	( )	( )
3. Units and lessons sequentially developed with suggested time allotments?	( )	( )
4. Suggested provisions for individual differences? Reading levels, learners with special needs?	( )	( )
5. Specific techniques and strategies?	( )	( )
6. Listings of helpful aids, materials, and resources?	( )	( )
7. Suggestions for extension activities?	( )	( )
8. Specific guidelines for assessment of student learning?	( )	( )
II. Analyze the student textbook as follows:		
1. Does it treat the content in adequate depth?	( )	( )
2. Does the book treat ethnic minorities and women in a fair manner?	( )	( )
3. Is the format attractive?	( )	( )
4. Does the book have good quality binding with suitable type size?	( )	( )
5. Are illustrations and visuals attractive and useful?	( )	( )
6. Is the reading level clear and appropriate? (See Exercise 6.5)	( )	( )

III. Would you like to use this textbook? Give reasons.

_____

_____

_____

_____

_____

IV. Share your book and this analysis with your class members.

EXERCISE 6.4: TEXTBOOK SELECTION CHECKLIST

Instructions: The purpose of this exercise is to provide a form for your textbook selection process. Locate several textbooks used in a secondary course you intend to teach, and review the textbooks as follows. (You will want to duplicate this form so you have a copy for each book reviewed.)

	Excellent 5	Good 4	Adequate 3	Problems 2	Poor 1	NA 0
A: Textbook						
1. Author(s) are respected in field.						
2. Published by a respected company.						
3. Table of contents logically sequenced.						
4. Teacher's manual available						
5. Testing materials available.						
6. Binding will hold up to use.						
7. Font (print) size for ease of reading.						
8. Page headers for quick reference.						
9. Free from excessive printing errors.						
10. Photographs (and other graphics) current.						
11. Graphics well displayed.						
12. References current and thorough.						
13. Relevant exercises provided.						
14. Latest edition has recent copyright.						
15. Clear and interesting writing style.						
B: Format						
16. Important ideas are explained and defined.						
17. Difficult ideas are visually represented.						
18. Chapter objectives are provided.						
19. Chapter summaries are provided.						
20. Relevant resources are provided.						

21. Useful research projects are suggested.
22. Useful and complete index is provided.
23. Useful glossary is provided.

C: Content

24. Content is logical and complete.
25. Meets course objectives.
26. Concepts presented accurately.
27. Footnotes (if any) are useful to reader.
28. Proper mix of cognitive question types.

D: Reading

29. Appropriate readability level. (see Ex. 6.5)
30. Levels of abstraction appropriate.
31. Material presented in an interesting way.
32. Stereotypes are avoided.
33. Sexist and racist language are avoided.
34. Concrete examples of abstract concepts.

SUBTOTALS _____

Textbook _____ TOTAL SCORE = _____

Author(s) _____

Publisher _____

Most Recent Copyright Date _____

Printing (first number of series inside front cover) (circle): 1. 2. 3. 4. 5. 6. 7. 8. 9

Year of printing (first number of series adjacent to printing): 1, 2, 3, 4, 5, 6, 7, 8, 9, 0

Date of review _____ Reviewer _____

EXERCISE 6.5: DETERMINING TEXTBOOK READING LEVEL[1]

Instructions: The purpose of this exercise is to provide a method and practice for determining the reading grade level of textbooks being considered for use in your teaching. Select several textbooks and determine their reading levels using the procedure that follows. (Duplicate blank exercise forms for each book reviewed.)

1. Select a 150-word passage.
2. Count the number of one-syllable words in that passage.
3. Use the following formula to determine reading grade level (RGL).
   20 − (Number of one-syllable words ÷ 10) = RGL
4. Repeat steps 1–3 for ten passages from various locations in the textbook, then average the RGLs to obtain the average reading grade level for the textbook.

Textbook evaluated:

Author(s):

Date of publication:

Publisher:

Date of evaluation: Reviewer:

	RGL	Page of passage	calculations
1 =	_____	_____	20 − (number ÷ 10) = RGL
2 =	_____	_____	
3 =	_____	_____	
4 =	_____	_____	
5 =	_____	_____	
6 =	_____	_____	
7 =	_____	_____	
8 =	_____	_____	
9 =	_____	_____	
10 =	_____	_____	

sum _____ ÷ 10 = _____   (the RGL for the text)

[1]A frequent concern of secondary school teachers is the reading level of their students. Although many well-known readability formulas exist, perhaps more important than which formula is used is that the same formula is applied to similar passages of different textbooks. The FORECAST formula presented for this exercise is easy to use and is satisfactory for that purpose (Source for the FORECAST formula: Novella M. Ross, "Assessing Readability of Instructional Materials," *VocEd*, vol. 54, no. 2 (Feb. 1979), pp. 10–11.)

As you review current textbooks available for secondary school students in your subject field you will undoubtedly find most of them well organized and quite useful. Textbooks may be accompanied by sequentially designed *resource units* from which you will select and build your specific *teaching units.* A resource unit usually consists of an extensive list of objectives, a large number and variety of kinds of activities, suggested materials, and extensive bibliographies for teacher and students, from which the teacher will select those that best suit his or her needs to build an actual teaching unit.

As you may have discovered from your work with Exercise 6.2, some curriculum guides consist of actual teaching units that have been prepared by teachers from a particular school district. An important question asked by most student teachers is: How closely must the student teacher follow the school's curriculum guide, whether it is a textbook or a curriculum written by teachers within that school or district? *It is a question you need to have an answer to before you begin teaching.*

In summary, your final decisions as to what content to teach will be guided (perhaps even dictated) by all of the following:

- Discussions with other teachers.
- State curricular documents.
- Local school courses of study.
- Your personal convictions, knowledge, and skills acquired in teacher education.
- The cultural backgrounds, interests, and abilities of your students.

After discovering what you will teach comes the process of preparing the plans. The remaining chapters of this part of the text will guide you through the planning process. Teacher's textbook editions and curriculum guides make the process easier *but should never substitute for your own specific planning.*

C. BEGINNING PREPARATION FOR A COURSE

You have reviewed courses of study, and while doing so undoubtedly you reflected on your own biases regarding content that you believe should be included in a course. In addition, you reviewed textbooks and you have had discussions with instructors. Now it is time to prepare a course that you intend to teach.

While some authors believe the first step in preparing a course is to write the course objectives it is our contention that a more logical first step is to prepare a sequential topic outline, the objective of the following exercise, then from that outline you will write the objectives, the purpose of the next chapter.

EXERCISE 6.6: PREPARING A TENTATIVE COURSE OUTLINE

Instructions: The purpose of this exercise is to organize your ideas about course content and the sequencing of that content.

With *three levels of headings* (as exemplified by the Contents pages at the beginning of this resource guide), prepare a sequential topic outline for a course you intend to teach. Identify the course by title, and clearly state for whom the course is intended, including any prerequisites. This outline is of topic content only, and does *not* need to include student activities associated with the learning of that content (such as laboratory exercises, assignments, or exams).

Share your outline to obtain feedback from your colleagues, or with instructors whom you have come to know. As course outlines are never to be "set in concrete," make adjustments to your outline whenever appropriate.

Content outline evaluation guidelines include:

- Does the outline follow a logical sequence, with each topic logically leading to the next?
- Does the content assume prerequisite knowledge?
- Is the outline content inclusive, and to the depth appropriate?
- Are there any serious content omissions?

D. DEALING WITH CONTROVERSIAL ISSUES

Controversial issues (usually involving matters of religion, politics, and/or sex) abound in certain disciplines, particularly English (e.g., controversial books), social studies (e.g., political issues), and biology (e.g., origin of life, evolution). Within your teaching career, particularly if you teach in any of these disciplines, you undoubtedly will have to make a decision regarding what you will do in your own teaching with respect to a particular controversial subject. Here are our guidelines for your consideration.

- *To the student teacher:* Maintain a perspective with respect to your own personal objective, which is to complete your credential so that you can then go out and obtain your first paid teaching assignment. Student teaching is *not* the time for you to "make waves," to get yourself involved in a situation that could lead to a lot of embitterment. If you maintain close communication with your cooperating teacher and your college or university supervisor, you should be able to prevent any major problems dealing with controversial issues. Sometimes, during normal discussion in the classroom, a controversial subject will emerge spontaneously, perhaps from the students asking you a question. When this occurs, *think before you say anything!* You may wish to postpone further discussion until you have a chance to talk over the issue with your supervisors, including the department chairperson. Controversial issues can seem to come from nowhere for *any* teacher, and that is perfectly normal while teaching secondary school students. These students are developing their own moral and value systems and they *need* to know how adults, particularly adults they hold in esteem, feel about things important to them.
- *To the inservice teacher:* We believe that secondary school students need discussions about issues that are important to society, and we see absolutely nothing wrong with dealing with those issues so long as the following guidelines are established:
  1. Students should learn about all sides of an issue (an *issue* differs from a problem in that *a problem generally has a solution, whereas an issue has many opinions and several alternative solutions*).
  2. Like all lesson plans, one dealing with a controversial issue should be well thought out ahead of time. Problems are most likely to occur when the plan has been underprepared. Potential problem areas, and resources must be carefully considered in advance.
  3. All involved have a right to input—parents, students, community leaders, other faculty members, and so forth. Parents and students should have the right to nonparticipation without academic penalty.
  4. We see nothing wrong with students knowing how you, the teacher, feel about an issue *as long as you make it clear that students may certainly disagree without reprisal or academic penalty*, but your opinions should perhaps be reserved until after students have had full opportunity to study other sources.

In our opinion, what makes this country so great is the freedom members of society have to speak out on issues, to express their opinions. That freedom should not be omitted from the classrooms of our public schools. Teachers and students should be allowed to express their feelings and attitudes about the great issues of today, encouraged to *study* the issues, to collect data, to form reasoned opinions after suspending judgment. *Teachers must understand the difference between teaching truth, values, and morality, and teaching* about *truth, values, and morality.*

To you, the teacher candidate, who may still be taking college or university courses in your subject field, it is not unusual in those classes to have experienced a professor who *pontificates* on a certain controversial issue—perhaps on the right-to-life issue, or on the liberation movement of a specific group of individuals in our society, or on the position of our government in Central America, or on the use of live animals in medical research, or on the issue of safety of nuclear power plants, or on "arms buildup," or on any other of the long list of important issues in society today—*but as a teacher in a secondary school you do not necessarily have the same academic freedom* and it is important that you understand this difference. The students with whom you will be working are not yet adults and they must be protected from dogmatism while allowed the freedom to learn and to develop without coercion from those who have power over their lives.

Now that we have expressed our opinion and offered our guildelines, what do you think about this topic, which will be quite important to you as a teacher? For this development and expression of your opinion we offer Exercise 6.7.

EXERCISE 6.7: TEACHING ABOUT CONTROVERSIAL ISSUES

The educational purpose of this exercise is for you to discover *before* teaching what some of the possibilities are for controversial issues in your subject field, and for you to consider what you can and will do with the issues. This exercise should first be completed by you, then shared with members of your class who share your discipline interest.

1. Your subject (discipline) field: _____

2. Spend some time in the library studying current periodicals in your subject field, and also talk with your colleagues in the schools, and list two or three potential controversial issues that are likely to come up during your teaching.

Issue	*Source*
_____	_____
_____	_____
_____	_____

3. Take one of these issues and identify "sides" and "current resources."

_____

_____

_____

4. Identify your own position on this issue with a statement of your rationale.

_____

_____

_____

5. How accepting can you be of students who take an opposing position?

_____

_____

6. Share the above with other teacher candidates from your subject field. Note any comments of theirs that you find helpful or enlightening.

_____

_____

_____

_____

QUESTIONS FOR CLASS DISCUSSION

1. Do the psychologies of Piaget, Bruner, Gagné, or others, show up in the curricular documents you have examined? Which and how?
2. Reading seems to be more effective when it has a purpose. In what ways can you make your students' content reading more purposeful?
3. Can you define and describe the differences among these terms: resource unit, textbook unit, teaching unit?
4. How will *you* really decide what to teach? How will you know if it is the proper content to be taught?
5. When we have sought original lessons and/or teaching units from experienced secondary school teachers, they frequently reply that they do not write them. Why do you believe this is the case when, in fact, we will be teaching *you* how to write lesson and unit plans?
6. Ask experienced teachers if they like the books they are using. Share their replies with others from your class. Are the majority of teachers happy with their textbooks?
7. Are the textbooks being used in your subject field too hard, too easy, or about right?
8. What distinguishes a good student textbook from a bad one?
9. Specifically how does a teacher attend to the individual differences of all the students?
10. Would you have any personal conflict using any of the documents you have examined?
11. What would be some of your options if you had to use a student textbook that you did not like?
12. Do you have a question you would like to introduce for class discussion? How might the answer be found?

SUGGESTED READINGS FOR CHAPTER 6

Brandt, R. S., ed. *Content of the Curriculum.* 1988 ASCD Yearbook. Alexandria, VA: Association for Supervision and Curriculum Development, 1988.

Mayer, W. V., and Barufaldi, J. T. *Textbook Chooser's Guide.* Berkeley, CA: National Center for Science Education, 1988.

Tyson-Bernstein, H. *A Conspiracy of Good Intention: America's Textbook Fiasco.* Washington, DC: Council for Basic Education, 1988.

7

What Are Instructional Objectives?

Now that you have prepared your course content outline (Exercise 6.6), you are ready to prepare specific instructional objectives, known also as behavioral or performance objectives—*statements that describe what the student will be able to do upon completion of the instructional experience.* In this chapter you learn how to write instructional objectives in behavioral terms, because

- Learning is commonly defined as being an observable and desired change in behavior; that is, you can tell that learning has occurred when you observe an expected change in the learner's behavior.
- For courses of study, teachers are expected to write course objectives in behavioral terms.
- Objectives stated in behavioral terms more clearly communicate to students the course expectations.
- Evaluative items (test questions) can then be written which are congruent with the stated objectives.

Instructional objectives are not the same as "instructor goals," which tell what the instructor intends to do, nor the same as "course goals," which are general statements telling about the course (as found in course catalog descriptions). Instructional objectives, when written in behavioral terms, are much more specific and are student-centered. Too frequently, that which a teacher *states* as goals, and that which the same teacher *does* (implementation of tests and implied objectives) are two separate matters, thus presenting an unwanted dichotomy that confuses students. *Matching objectives to goals, then stating the objectives clearly and in behavioral terms, while measuring student learning against those objectives, facilitates teaching effectiveness and student learning.* To students, your objectives and test questions are the clearest indicators of your real goals.

Although time-consuming to write objectives in behavioral terms, and for reasons discussed later in this chapter you may choose to not try and cover all content with behaviorally stated objectives, attempting to do so helps organize the learning for your students. And that is important because your job is to help students to learn, not to confuse them. We have known far too many teachers who engaged students in a guessing game, where the students' task was to guess what it was the teacher expected them to learn; students who got the better grades were those who guessed best.

A. HOW TO WRITE INSTRUCTIONAL OBJECTIVES IN BEHAVIORAL TERMS

When preparing behavioral objectives you should ask yourself: "How is the learner to demonstrate that the objective has been achieved?" For example, although the following might be an appropriate course goal, it is *not* a behaviorally stated objective: "The student will develop an appreciation for art." It is too ambiguous. Although "will develop an appreciation" is a student-centered phrase, it does not state how the intended learning is to be demonstrated. The objective should include a behavior that will demonstrate the intended appreciation, such as follows: "The student will demonstrate an appreciation for art by volunteering to guide visitors at a local art gallery." We *assume* that volunteering to serve as a gallery guide is indicative of the expected achievement of appreciation.

The previous example represents a "responding" objective in the affective domain (see next section). For evaluation, objectives of that domain are complicated because they represent behaviors involving attitudes, values, and feelings, which are difficult to measure objectively. Examples for each domain will follow, but first let's consider the key ingredients of a behaviorally stated objective.

A completely stated behavioral objective has four key ingredients. Referred to as the ABCDs of writing behavioral objectives, the key ingredients are

1. The *audience* (the student for whom the objective is intended).
2. The terminal *behavior* (the anticipated measurable performance).
3. The observable *conditions* (the setting in which the behavior is to be demonstrated and observed).
4. The *degree* of proficiency (the performance level, primarily for the purpose of evaluation, and frequently omitted). For exercises that follow you may ignore this ingredient, as we assume a mastery (100 percent) performance level expectation.

Audience

In educational settings, behavioral objectives are usually written with a beginning phrase such as "The student will be able to . . . " In order to eliminate needless repetitious writing we suggest that when preparing objectives you introduce all the objectives with this sentence written once: "Upon completion (of this course or lesson) you will be able to . . . ," then proceed to list each behavioral objective by its anticipated measurable performance, thus eliminating needless repetition of the phrase "You will be able to." An alternative is to begin each objective with the abbreviated YWBAT, followed by the anticipated performance. Also, especially for the course syllabus, we prefer the personalization provided by the use of "*You* will be able to . . . ," rather than "*The student* will be able to . . . "

Anticipated Measurable Performance

Success with writing behavioral objectives rests with the selection of performance words that are measurable, that is, action verbs. The primary ingredient of a well-stated instructional objective is the anticipated measurable performance. When writing behavioral objectives, there are verbs to avoid, verbs that are too vague, ambiguous, and that are not clearly measurable.

VERBS TO AVOID WHEN WRITING INSTRUCTIONAL OBJECTIVES

appreciate	indicate
believe	know
comprehend	learn
enjoy	like
familiarize	realize
grasp	understand

Conditions

Another ingredient is the conditions, or setting, in which the performance is to be demonstrated and observed. Returning to our earlier example about the student demonstrating an appreciation for art, to include the condition, we write as follows: "From a list of options, the student will demonstrate an appreciation of art by volunteering to serve as a gallery guide." The condition is the "list of options," one of which is assumed by the instructor to best indicate achievement of that objective.

Performance Level

The fourth and final ingredient of a completely stated behavioral objective is the degree or level of expected performance. For one or more reasons, this ingredient is frequently omitted. In the previous example, because the expected performance is 100 percent, the level is omitted (as it is understood).

Using another example, in another domain, suppose a mathematics instructor's *goal* is to teach students to solve quadratic equations. A behavioral *objective* could read as follows: "When given ten quadratic equations (*the condition*), the student will solve them (*the measurable behavioral performance*), with 80 percent accuracy (*the performance level*)."

Performance level is used to evaluate student achievement, and sometimes it is used to evaluate teacher effectiveness. Student grades might be based on performance levels; evaluation of teacher effectiveness might be based on student performance levels. As schools move ever closer to competency-based (or performance-based) instruction, teachers' knowledge of how to write behavioral objectives is becoming significantly more important.

Now, with Exercise 7.1, try your skill at recognizing behavioral objectives.

EXERCISE 7.1: RECOGNIZING BEHAVIORAL OBJECTIVES: DIAGNOSTIC TEST 1

Instructions: Place an *X* before each that is a measurable instructional student-centered objective. Although conditions and performance levels may be absent, ask yourself, "Is it a student-centered and measurable objective, indicating what the student will be able to do upon completion of the instructional experience?"

_____ 1. To develop critical thinking.
_____ 2. To identify those celestial bodies that are known planets.
_____ 3. To provide worthwhile experiences for the students.
_____ 4. To recognize subject and verb in a sentence.
_____ 5. To focus the microscope without damaging the objective lens.
_____ 6. To write a summary of the factors that led to World War II.
_____ 7. To fully appreciate the value of art.
_____ 8. To prepare a critical comparison of the two major political parties in the United States.
_____ 9. To illustrate an awareness of the importance of balanced ecology by supplying relevant newspaper articles.
_____ 10. To know all the rules of spelling and grammar.

Check your answers with this key:

2, 4, 5, 6, 8, 9

How did you do? If you scored 100 percent correct, please disregard what follows and go on to Section B. Numbers 1, 3, 7, and 10 of the exercise are inadequate because of their ambiguity. Number 3 is not even a student objective; it is a teacher goal. "To develop," "to fully appreciate," and "to know," are open to too many interpretations.

With correctly worded objectives, it is easy to see how the teacher can tell if the objective has been reached. When writing instructional objectives, verbs that are vague, ambiguous, and not measurable should be avoided. (See Section D for acceptable verbs.)

Although the conditions are not present, numbers 2, 4, 5, 6, and 8 are clearly measurable. The teacher would have no difficulty knowing if the learner had reached these objectives, whereas in number 9, which is in the affective domain, our "trust assumption" must be put to work. Discussions with your classmates and instructor should alleviate any further difficulty you may have had with this exercise. Read on when ready.

B. HOW TO CLASSIFY INSTRUCTIONAL OBJECTIVES

Useful for planning are three domains used in classifying learning objectives. These are

- *Cognitive domain*—involving mental operations from the lowest level of simple recall of information to high level and complex evaluative processes.
- *Psychomotor domain*—involving low level, simple manipulation of materials, to higher level communication of ideas, and finally to the highest level of creative performance.
- *Affective domain*—involving feelings, attitudes, and values, from lower levels of acquisition to the highest levels of internalization.

Many objectives written by teachers seem to fall within the cognitive domain, but when you look at the instructional goals of those same instructors, there seems to be additional interest in psychomotor and affective learning. Perhaps too frequently teacher attention is directed to the cognitive while only assuming that the psychomotor and affective will take care of themselves. Some argue the reverse; that is, when the affective is directly attended, the psychomotor and cognitive develop. Leaving this argument for the learning theorists, we shall say simply that teachers should direct their planning so that students are guided from the lowest to highest levels of operation, and that simultaneous attention is given to student development within all three domains.

Undoubtedly, from your own education, you can recall classes where instructor expectations went no further than the lowest cognitive level—the simple recall of isolated facts. Effective learning extends beyond mere memorization of facts. Indeed, to develop student skills in reasoning and in critical thinking, such must be the case. Competent teachers provide educational objectives and experiences designed to raise the level of student thinking and behaving. While later exercises are designed to help you learn how to do that, your attention now is directed to the hierarchies of levels of operation within each of the three domains.

Important: Operation at each level requires the ability to perform at each preceding level.

COGNITIVE DOMAIN HIERARCHIES[1]

Level Sample	Required Illustrative Verbs
1. *Knowledge*	Remembering and recalling

The student will recall those countries that were World War II allies.

> choose, complete, define, describe, identify, indicate, label, list, locate, match, name, recall, select, state

2. *Comprehension*	Understanding beyond recall

The student will generalize Supreme Court decisions of the last ten years about equal rights.

> classify, convert, defend, derive, describe, estimate, expand, explain, express, extrapolate, generalize, infer, interpolate, paraphrase, predict, recognize, summarize, translate

3. *Application*	Applying to new situation

The student will predict the probable physical change when oxygen is removed.

> apply, compute, construct, demonstrate, differentiate, discover, discuss, modify, operate, participate, perform, plan, predict, prepare, relate, show, use

4. *Analysis*	Converting into components; drawing conclusions; determining evidence

The student will detect discrepancies between advertising claims and actual product quality.

> analyze, debate, deduce, design, diagram, differentiate, discriminate, identify, generalize, illustrate, infer, organize, relate, select

5. *Synthesis*	Making predictions; bringing together parts to form a whole

From ideas generated during clustering, the student will compose a short story.

> arrange, categorize, combine, compile, compose, construct, create, design, develop, devise, generate, organize, plan, produce, relate, reconstruct, reorganize, summarize, synthesize, write

6. *Evaluation*	Offering opinions; value judging

The student will write a critical evaluation of a journal article about the use of public money for AIDS prevention and treatment.

> appraise, compare, conclude, contrast, criticize, decide, evaluate, interpret, justify, relate, summarize, support

[1]Adapted from Benjamin S. Bloom, ed., *Taxonomy of Educational Objectives, Book I: Cognitive Domain.* (White Plains, NY: Longman, 1984).

Whereas identification and classification within the cognitive domain is generally agreed upon,[1] classifications of the psychomotor and affective domains demonstrate less consistency, and for those domains, other authors may illustrate variations from the classifications shown here. *For a secondary school teacher, it is less important that an objective be absolutely classified than it is for the instructor to be cognizant of hierarchies of levels of thinking and to understand the importance of attending to student development from lower to higher levels of operation, in all three domains.*

[1]Rather than an orderly progression from simple to complex mental operations as illustrated in this resource guide, you should know that some instructional researchers prefer an identification of a hierarchy of cognitive abilities that range from simple information storage and retrieval, through a higher level of discrimination and concept learning, and to the highest cognitive ability to recognize and to solve problems, as organized by Robert M. Gagné, Leslie Briggs, and Walter Wager, *Principles of Instructional Design*, 3rd ed., New York: Holt, Rinehart and Winston, 1988.

PSYCHOMOTOR DOMAIN HIERARCHIES[1]

Level	Required
Sample	Illustrative Verbs

---

1. *Movement* — Coordination

The student will demonstrate catching and passing the ball without error.

adjust, carry, clean, locate, obtain, walk

---

2. *Manipulating* — Finer coordination

The student will rebuild a carburetor.

assemble, build, calibrate, connect, thread

---

3. *Communicating* — Communication of ideas and feelings

The student will indicate ability to listen to what others are saying.

ask, analyze, describe, draw, explain, write

---

4. *Creating* — Coordination of all skills in all domains

The student will create and perform a composition.

create, design, invent

---

[1]Adapted from David R. Krathwohl, et al., *Taxonomy of Educational Objectives, Handbook II: Affective Domain,* New York: David McKay, 1964.

AFFECTIVE DOMAIN HIERARCHIES[1]

Level	Required
Sample	Illustrative Verbs

---

1. *Attending (receiving)*   Attentiveness, awareness, willingness to receive

The student will demonstrate awareness of the importance of nuclear power plants by collecting relevant newspaper articles.

ask, attend, choose, discriminate, find, identify, listen

---

2. *Responding*   Responding

Taking a particular position about nuclear power plants, the student will voluntarily write a letter to the editor of a local newspaper.

answer, perform, read, write

---

3. *Valuing*   Internalization of values

The student will demonstrate a continuing desire to learn about nuclear power plants by selecting that topic for a term project.

argue, commit, report, work

---

4. *Value Development*   Behaviors are consistent with the internalized values

The student will freely express an opinion about nuclear power and nuclear waste disposal policies.

act, display, influence, practice, propose, revise, verify

---

[1]Adapted from A. J. Harrow, *Taxonomy of the Psychomotor Domain,* New York: Longman, 1977.

EXERCISE 7.2: HOW KNOWLEDGEABLE AM I ABOUT BEHAVIORAL OBJECTIVES? DIAGNOSTIC TEST 2

Instructions: Take this test; then check your answers at the end (don't peek!). Discuss disagreements with your colleagues.

I. Place an *X* before each of the following objectives that is a student learning objective stated in acceptable behavioral terms; that is, it is measurable although conditions and performance levels might be absent.

____ 1. The student will learn the major parts of speech.
____ 2. The student will appreciate the significance of the Gettysburg Address.
____ 3. The student will be able to construct an isosceles triangle with a protractor.
____ 4. Given a model of a hypothetical cell, the student will identify the cellular structures.
____ 5. The student will read and understand the chapter on civil rights.
____ 6. The unit on chemical oxidation-reduction reactions will be reviewed.
____ 7. The student will write an essay that develops an argument for or against family planning.
____ 8. The student will volunteer to visit a preschool program.
____ 9. The student will become aware of the significance of supermarket shelving practice.
____ 10. The students will translate the song "Hey Jude" into Spanish.
____ 11. The student will correctly operate the duplicating machine.
____ 12. From a list of ten substances, the student will identify those that are compounds and those that are mixtures.
____ 13. The student will write the Spanish alphabet from memory.
____ 14. The student will know the Mendelian laws.
____ 15. The learner will show an appreciation of outdoor sports.
____ 16. The learner will list the major causes of the Civil War.
____ 17. Given three hypothetical situations, the student will decide which one best represents the posture of the Republican Party.
____ 18. The student will learn to recognize differences between the music of Beethoven and of Bach.
____ 19. The student will learn ten French verbs.
____ 20. The student will create in miniature a model environment for an imaginary animal.

II. Classify each of the following objectives by writing the correct letter in the blank provided according to the following domains: Cognitive (C); Affective (A); or Psychomotor (P).

____ 1. The student will correctly focus the microscope.
____ 2. The student can summarize the histories of the origin of the two major political parties.
____ 3. The student will identify from a list those items that are Spanish cognates.
____ 4. The student will anonymously indicate in writing that this course has improved his or her confidence.
____ 5. The student will volunteer to remain after class to help clean up the classroom.
____ 6. The student will be able to identify the respective poets after reading and analyzing several poems.
____ 7. The student will translate a French poem into English.
____ 8. The student will accurately predict the results of combining equal quantities of any paired combination of secondary colors.
____ 9. The student will voluntarily read outside material related to current events.
____ 10. The student will make a goal in basketball a minimum of seven times in ten attempts.

III. For the following cognitive objectives, identify by the appropriate letter(s) the highest level within that domain (one subdomain which will be the highest within a given objective): Knowledge (K); Comprehension (C); Application (Ap); Analysis (An); Synthesis (S); Evaluation (E).

____ 1. When given a new poem, the student will recognize it as one of Shelley's.
____ 2. The student will underline from a list those words that are spelled correctly.
____ 3. The student will read a pattern and correctly select the amount of material and equipment necessary to make a dress.
____ 4. The student will create a poem using the style that is designated.
____ 5. The students will write critical appraisals of their essays on capital punishment.

Part III: (1) C, (2) K, (3) Ap, (4) S, (5) E.
Part II: (1) P, (2) C, (3) C, (4) A, (5) A, (6) C, (7) C, (8) C, (9) A, (10) P.
and 20.
Part I: The following objectives should be marked X: 3, 4, 7, 8, 10, 11, 12, 13, 16, 17,

C. HOW TO JUDGE WHETHER INSTRUCTIONAL OBJECTIVES ARE WORTH THE TIME

It is clear from surveys that often teachers do not schedule the time (nor trouble their busy hours) to write specific objectives for all the learning activities they plan. But it is also clear from research studies that, when teachers do prepare specific objectives (by writing them themselves, or by borrowing them from other sources), and teach toward those objectives, their teaching is more effective. Some school districts require their teachers to use objectives that are quite specific. There is no question that clearly written instructional objectives are worth the time, especially when the teacher evaluates students' progress against them. It is not imperative that you write all the instructional objectives that you will need. As a matter of fact, they are usually already available in the textbooks teachers use, and in other places as well.[1]

D. HOW TO SELECT VERBS FOR STATING SPECIFIC LEARNING OBJECTIVES

Arranged according to disciplines, here is a list of performance verbs recommended for use in writing instructional objectives.[2]

1. "Creative" Behaviors

Alter	Generalize	Question	Regroup	Rephrase	Rewrite
Ask	Modify	Rearrange	Rename	Restate	Simplify
Change	Paraphrase	Recombine	Reorder	Restructure	Synthesize
Design	Predict	Reconstruct	Reorganize	Retell	Systematize

2. Complex, Logical, Judgmental Behaviors

Analyze	Combine	Contrast	Designate	Formulate	Plan
Appraise	Compare	Criticize	Determine	Generate	Structure
Assess	Conclude	Deduce	Discover	Induce	Substitute
		Defend	Evaluate	Infer	Suggest

3. General Discriminative Behaviors

Choose	Describe	Discriminate	Indicate	Match	Place
Collect	Detect	Distinguish	Isolate	Omit	Point
Define	Differentiate	Identify	List	Order	Select
				Pick	Separate

[1]One such source is described in *Phi Delta Kappan*, Vol. 52, No. 3 (1970), pp. 174–175.
[2]Calvin K. Claus, National College of Education, Evanston, IL. From revision (1983) of text of paper read at February 10, 1968 meeting of National Council on Measurement in Education, in Chicago. Reprinted by permission of Calvin K. Claus.

4. Social Behaviors

Accept	Answer	Cooperate	Forgive	Laugh	Reply
Admit	Argue	Dance	Greet	Meet	Smile
Agree	Communicate	Disagree	Help	Participate	Talk
Aid	Compliment	Discuss	Interact	Permit	Thank
Allow	Contribute	Excuse	Invite	Praise	Visit
			Join	React	Volunteer

5. Language Behaviors

Abbreviate	Call	Indent	Punctuate	Speak	Tell
Accent	Capitalize	Outline	Read	Spell	Translate
Alphabetize	Edit	Print	Recite	State	Verbalize
Articulate	Hyphenate	Pronounce	Say	Summarize	Whisper
			Sign	Syllabicate	Write

6. "Study" Behaviors

Arrange	Cite	Diagram	Itemize	Mark	Record
Categorize	Classify	Find	Label	Name	Reproduce
Chart	Compile	Follow	Locate	Note	Search
Circle	Copy	Gather	Look	Organize	Sort
			Map	Quote	Underline

7. Music Behaviors

Blow	Clap	Finger	Hum	Pluck	Strum
Bow	Compose	Harmonize	Mute	Practice	Tap
			Play	Sing	Whistle

8. Physical Behaviors

Arch	Climb	Hit	March	Ski	Swim
Bat	Face	Hop	Pitch	Skip	Swing
Bend	Float	Jump	Pull	Somersault	Throw
Carry	Grab	Kick	Push	Stand	Toss
Catch	Grasp	Knock	Run	Step	Walk
Chase	Grip	Lift	Skate	Stretch	

9. Arts Behaviors

Assemble	Cut	Frame	Mold	Roll	Stamp
Blend	Dab	Hammer	Nail	Rub	Stick
Brush	Dot	Handle	Paint	Saw	Stir
Build	Draw	Heat	Paste	Sculpt	Trace
Carve	Drill	Illustrate	Pat	Send	Trim
Color	Fold	Melt	Polish	Shake	Varnish
Construct	Form	Mix	Pour	Sketch	Wipe
			Press	Smooth	Wrap

10. Drama Behaviors

Act	Direct	Enter	Imitate	Pantomime	Respond
Clasp	Display	Exit	Leave	Pass	Show
Cross	Emit	Express	Move	Perform	Sit
				Proceed	Turn

11. Mathematical Behaviors

Add	Compute	Estimate	Integrate	Plot	Subtract
Bisect	Count	Extract	Interpolate	Prove	Sum
Calculate	Cumulate	Extrapolate	Measure	Reduce	Tabulate
Check	Derive	Graph	Multiply	Solve	Tally
Circumscribe	Divide	Group	Number	Square	Verify

12. Laboratory Science Behaviors

Align	Conduct	Dissect	Keep	Plant	Set
Apply	Connect	Feed	Lengthen	Prepare	Specify
Attach	Convert	Grow	Limit	Remove	Straighten
Balance	Decrease	Increase	Manipulate	Replace	Time
Calibrate	Demonstrate	Insert	Operate	Report	Transfer
				Reset	Weigh

13. General Appearance, Health, and Safety Behaviors

Button	Comb	Eat	Fill	Taste	Unzip
Clean	Cover	Eliminate	Go	Tie	Wait
Clear	Dress	Empty	Lace	Unbutton	Wash
Close	Drink	Fasten	Stack	Uncover	Wear
			Stop	Untie	Zip

14. Miscellaneous

Aim	Erase	Hunt	Peel	Scratch	Store
Attempt	Expand	Include	Pin	Send	Strike
Attend	Extend	Inform	Position	Serve	Supply
Begin	Feel	Kneel	Present	Sew	Support
Bring	Finish	Lay	Produce	Share	Switch
Buy	Fit	Lead	Propose	Sharpen	Take
Come	Fix	Lend	Provide	Shoot	Tear
Complete	Flip	Let	Put	Shorten	Touch
Correct	Get	Light	Raise	Shovel	Try
Crease	Give	Make	Relate	Shut	Twist
Crush	Grind	Mend	Repair	Signify	Type
Develop	Guide	Miss	Repeat	Slide	Use
Distribute	Hand	Offer	Return	Slip	Vote
Do	Hang	Open	Ride	Spread	Watch
Drop	Hold	Pack	Rip	Stake	Weave
End	Hook	Pay	Save	Start	Work

EXERCISE 7.3: WRITING MY OWN BEHAVIORAL OBJECTIVES

Instructions: For the subject you intend to teach (your outline prepared for Exercise 6.6), write twelve specific behavioral objectives for that subject. Audience, conditions, and performance level may be excluded. Exchange completed exercises with your colleagues; discuss and make corrections where necessary. Subject =

1. Cognitive knowledge:

2. Cognitive comprehension:

3. Cognitive application:

4. Cognitive analysis:

5. Cognitive synthesis:

6. Cognitive evaluation:

7. Psychomotor (low level):

8. Psychomotor (high level):

9. Affective attend:

10. Affective respond:

11. Affective value:

12. Affective value development:

E. A DANGER IN OVEROBJECTIVITY

Once again, let us make it clear that it is expected that you will plan well and specifically that which you intend to teach; to convey your specific expectations to your students, and to *evaluate their learning against that specificity*. But there is a danger inherent in such performance-based teaching, and that is, because it is highly objective, it could become overobjective, and overobjectivity can have negative consequences.

The danger is if students are treated as objects, when the relationship between teacher and learner is impersonal and counterproductive to real learning. Highly specific and impersonal teaching can discourage serendipity, creativity, and an excitement for real discovery. With performance-based instruction (known also as competency-based instruction), the source for student motivation is largely extrinsic; instructor expectations, grades, society, and peer pressures are examples of extrinsic sources. To be an effective secondary school teacher, your challenge is to use performance-based criteria, but simultaneously with a teaching style that encourages the development of intrinsic sources of student motivation, and that allows for, provides for, and encourages learning beyond what might be considered as immediately measurable and minimal expectations.

This concludes this chapter about preparing instructional objectives; with your course outline and course objectives in hand, you are now ready for preparation of detailed instructional plans, the next chapter.

QUESTIONS FOR CLASS DISCUSSION

1. Discuss with secondary school teachers how they feel about writing instructional objectives, and whether they write all or any in behavioral terms.
2. Are there sources for obtaining behavioral objectives in your field, or must you create all of your own? If there are sources in your field, name them.
3. In your own teaching, do you believe you will place a greater emphasis on any particular domain? If so, which one? Why?
4. What caution do you need to remember about "highly specific" teaching?
5. Do you understand what performance level is expected when an instructor teaches for mastery learning?
6. Is performance-based (competency-based) instruction of equal value in all discipline areas?
7. Some would say it is easier to write behavioral objectives after a lesson has been taught. What is the significance of this thought?
8. Critically analyze the advantages and disadvantages of mastery learning.
9. Can you clearly distinguish among the following terms: instructional objectives; teacher goals; teacher intentions; course description; course goals; performance objectives; terminal objectives; behavioral objectives? Some of the terms are synonymous. Which?
10. What questions do you have about the content of this chapter? How might answers be found?

SUGGESTED READINGS FOR CHAPTER 7

Bloom, B. S., ed. *Taxonomy of Educational Objectives, Handbook I: Cognitive Domain.* White Plains, NY: Longman, 1984.

Bloom, B. S. *Human Characteristics and School Learning.* New York: McGraw-Hill, 1976.

Duchastel, P. C., and Merrill, P. F. "The effects of behavioral objectives on learning: A review of empirical studies." *Review of Educational Research* 43(1):53–69 (Winter 1973).

Gagné, R. M. *Instructional Technology: Foundations.* Hillsdale, NJ: Lawrence Erlbaum, 1987.

Gronlund, N. E. *Stating Objectives for Classroom Instruction.* 3rd ed. New York: Macmillan, 1985.

Harrow, A. J. *Taxonomy of the Psychomotor Domain.* White Plains, NY: Longman, 1977.

Krathwohl, D. R.; Bloom, B. S.; and Masia, B. B. *Taxonomy of Educational Objectives: Handbook II: Affective Domain.* New York: David McKay, 1964.

Mager, R. F. *Preparing Instructional Objectives.* Rev. 2d ed. Belmont, CA: Davis S. Lake, 1984.

8

How Do I Prepare
an Instructional Plan?

As stated earlier in this resource guide, teacher's manuals and resource materials will expedite your planning but should not substitute for it. You need to know how to create a good plan for teaching. Having prepared a course content outline (Exercise 6.6) you have already initiated development of your instructional plan. Using that outline, in this chapter you will proceed with development of a complete instructional plan.

A. GUIDELINES FOR PLANNING: THE SEVEN-STEP PLAN

Certain of the following guidelines have previously been addressed, and are included here for review and to consider where they fit in the seven-step plan.

1. *Course and school goals:* Consider and understand your course goals and their relationship to the purposes, goals, and functions of the school. Your course is not isolated as if being taught on the moon, but has a relationship to the total school curriculum.
2. *Expectations:* Consider topics that you are "expected" to teach, such as may be found in the course of study. (Refer to Chapter 6).
3. *Quarter plan:* You need to consider where you wish the class to be months from now. So, working from your tentative course outline, and with the school calendar in hand, begin by deciding how much class time should be devoted to each topic, penciling those times onto the course outline.
4. *Course schedule:* This schedule becomes a part of the course syllabus presented to students at the first class meeting. However, the course schedule must remain flexible to allow for the unexpected, such as a cancellation or interruption of a class meeting, or an unpredictable extended study of a particular topic.
5. *Class meeting lessons:* Working from the course schedule, you now prepare lessons for each class meeting, keeping in mind the abilities and interests of your students while making decisions about appropriate strategies and learning experiences (Part III of this text).

Preparation of lessons takes considerable time, and continues throughout the semester, as you arrange and prepare

- Lecture notes.
- Demonstrations.
- Discussion questions.
- Laboratory exercises.
- For guest speakers.
- To use audiovisual equipment and materials.
- For field trips.
- Examinations.

And, because one class meeting is often determined by accomplishments of the preceding meeting, your lessons are never "set in concrete," but need constant rechecking and evaluation by you.

6. *Instructional objectives:* With the finalized course schedule you can complete preparation of the instructional objectives (begun in Chapter 7).
7. *Evaluation:* The final step of the plan is to decide how assessment of student achievement will be accomplished. Included in this component are your decisions about assignments, examinations, and grade determination procedures.

Those are the steps in planning. Don't fret—we proceed step-by-step.

B. THE COURSE SYLLABUS

Its Value and Purposes

The course syllabus is the written information presented to students, usually at the first class meeting. A well-prepared course syllabus serves several useful purposes.

- It helps students organize their learning.
- It provides important information to students.
- It demonstrates to students that the teacher cares about them as well as about the course.
- For students, it models writing and organizational skills.
- It prevents misunderstandings, such as would otherwise occur about grading procedures, assignments, and classroom behavior expectations.
- It causes the teacher to give careful thought to seemingly minor details that could otherwise later develop into items of significant importance to students and to the teacher.
- It provides information useful to administrators and to parents.

What It Includes

It is important the syllabus be inclusive but succinct, and organized for easy reading and quick location of information. Caution against being too wordy, as students are less likely to read a lengthy syllabus—two to three pages should be sufficient. Recommended for inclusion in the course syllabus are the following items.

1. Teacher's name with *course title and brief description, class period and room number.* This information can be the heading at the top of the first page.
2. (optional) Identification of *for whom the course is intended.*
3. Identification of *prerequisites*, or state "no prerequisites."
4. Identification of *textbook;* include the identification of any other materials the student needs, such as notebook and laboratory materials.
5. Statement of *general goals.* Keep it brief!
6. List of *behavioral objectives.* Not all, but perhaps ten major objectives.
7. Class meetings schedule *with topic outline, quizzes* and *examinations.*
8. *Assignments and other expectations of students* (reading and other, with due dates). If you grade on a point system, you may wish to include point values for tests and assignments. Many instructors use a four-column outline with meeting dates on the left side column, topics in the adjacent column, and reading and written assignments in the third and fourth columns.

   Note: Items 7 and 8, the course schedule, are often placed on a page separate from the other syllabus items, since the schedule may need to be revised several times during a semester.

9. Clear statement about *grading* procedure.
10. *Other particulars,* such as your office location and phone number, free period, attendance expectations, classroom behavior rules, policies regarding late assignments, missed tests, and any other information that should be conveyed to students in writing at this time.

EXERCISE 8.1: PREPARATION OF MY COURSE SYLLABUS

Instructions: The purpose of this exercise is to prepare your course syllabus. Prepare the syllabus for a course you intend to teach, including the 10 items described in this section. Share your syllabus with your colleagues, then make appropriate revisions.

C. PREPARING LESSONS FOR CLASS MEETINGS

As described in Section A of this chapter, Step 5 of the seven-step plan is the preparation for class meetings. The process of designing a lesson is important in getting you to think the lesson through so the result is the most effective learning experience for the students. In planning lessons you should always consider these three key ingredients:

1. How the lesson is introduced—the *set*.
2. The content and methods of teaching that content—the *lesson body*.
3. How the lesson is closed—the *closure*.

As you prepare each lesson, attend to each of these ingredients as carefully as if you were an attorney preparing for a court trial, or as if an administrator were going to be visiting your class.

The Set

It is important for you to remember that students come to your class from other places, classes, and activities, and that to be mentally ready for your class they need to disassociate their minds from those immediately preceding mental occupations. You must have their attention before you can teach; your lesson plan can be designed to establish the desired mind set, capturing student attention, readying students for your instruction. There are several ways to do this. Consider the following.

An *orientation set* that provides a framework for the ensuing lesson, capturing student interest and attention for that lesson. An orientation set might be as long as an entire class meeting, as, for example, with use of students role-playing a situation that they are going to be studying about for the next several meetings, or as brief as only a few minutes, as when a teacher clarifies for students the objectives of the lesson. An effective orientation set might even be noncontent related, as when a teacher captures student attention with a friendly greeting as they arrive, or begins the lesson with a joke or a personal story or a recent experience, perhaps related to the topic.

A *transition set* that provides a smooth transition from what the students have learned, to what is to be covered in this lesson, relying on instructor use of examples and analogies. An effective transition set is also an orientation set.

An *evaluation set* that evaluates student learning prior to the introduction of new material. Instructors are using this type of set when using a questioning review of material from the previous lesson. We know a high school world history teacher who at the beginning of each lesson calls upon a student to stand and to present from memory an oral résumé of the content of the previous lesson, and the student is graded on that presentation. Because the students never know who will be called upon next, the exercise creates not only anxiety but encourages students to review material prior to each class meeting. Although we are not judging that teaching method, it does have positive learning results for that teacher's classes. An effective evaluation set can contain ingredients of all three set types; that is, it orients student thinking, it evaluates student comprehension, and it provides transition.

The Closure

Complementary to the way a teacher initiates a class meeting is the form of closure of the meeting. A lesson may be closed with a summary review, a transfer (as when students practice the new material), or by a natural crescendo. Whichever the case, while planning a lesson the teacher attends to the manner by which the lesson is to be closed.

A secondary school teacher should effectively plan her or his lessons so that the entire class period is utilized for student learning. In particular, the beginning of a class period and the last few minutes of a class period should not be wasted time, nor should students be allowed to meander toward the exit in anticipation of the class change bell.

The Lesson Body

The body of the lesson is that which occurs between the set and the closure and, of course, is of paramount importance to effective lesson implementation. When planning the body of the lesson, you need to consider each of the following.

1. The *content,* from your course outline.
2. The *strategies* used to deliver the content.
3. *Transitions* from one idea to the next, from one activity to the next.
4. *Stimulus variation* techniques, which include the teacher's use of body movements, gestures, voice inflections, pauses, interaction strategies, and sense stimulation variations.
5. *Resource materials* needed.

Before proceeding with development of your first lesson plan, consider a "Lesson That Failed" (Exercise 8.2), and following that, a "Model Lesson Plan."

EXERCISE 8.2: ANALYSIS OF A LESSON THAT FAILED

Instructions: The planning and structure of a lesson can be a predictor of the success of its implementation. The purpose of this exercise is to read the following report of an actual lesson implementation and to use the report as a basis for class discussion about its outcome.
The setting: 9th grade biology class; 1:12–2:07 p.m., spring semester.
Actual events as they took place:

1:12.	Bell rings
1:12–1:21.	Teacher directs students to read from their text, while he takes attendance.
1:21–1:31.	Teacher lectures on "parts of a flower," showing pictures on flower parts by holding up pages from a college botany text.
1:31–1:37.	Teacher distributes to each student a ditto; students are to now "label the parts of a flower."
1:37–1:39.	Teacher verbally gives instructions for working on a real flower, for example: compare with ditto; can use microscopes if they wish.
1:39–1:45.	Teacher walks around room, distributing to each student a real flower.
1:45.	Too much chaos. Teacher, writing referrals, sends two students to the office. Much confusion, students wandering around, throwing flower parts at each other, etc.
1:45–2:07.	Teacher flustered, directs students to spend remainder of period reading text. Another referral written during this time.
2:07.	End of period (much to the delight of the teacher).

QUESTIONS FOR DISCUSSION

1. Do you believe this teacher had a prepared lesson plan? If it appears so, what (if any) were the good points of it? the problems with it?
    Good:
    Problems:
2. From what you can infer from the scenario, and from what you can infer about this lesson plan, was the chaos predictable? Why or why not?
3. How might the lesson plan have been prepared to more likely avoid the chaos?
4. Choosing to use this "traditional" lesson plan format, what behaviors could the teacher have performed that might have avoided the chaos?
5. Within this 55-minute period, students were being expected to operate high on the Learning Experiences Ladder (see Chapter 12). Consider this: 9 minutes of reading; 10 minutes of hearing; 6 minutes of reading and labeling; 2 minutes of hearing; 6 minutes of action (the only direct experience); and 22 minutes of reading. In all, about 49 minutes of abstract verbal and visual symbolization. Is that a problem?

MODEL LESSON PLAN

Subject: _____ Geometry _____ Teacher: _____ Janice Wong _____

Lesson Topic: _____ Geometry theorems pertaining to alternate interior angles, corresponding _____

_____ angles, and interior angles on the same side of the transversal.[1] _____

Preassessment Strategies: Short quiz after going over questions on previous night's homework assignment on identifying interior, exterior, alternate interior, alternate exterior, and corresponding angles.

Quiz: Use the picture at the right to identify the following angles as

1. alternate interior angles

2. exterior angles

3. corresponding angles

4. interior angles

5. alternate exterior angles

Quizzes are corrected in class and collected. The purpose of the quiz is to check to see if the students have a solid background in identifying types of angles before moving on to today's lesson on theorems pertaining to these angles.

Behavioral Objectives

1. Given two parallel lines crossed by a transversal, students will identify two out of three congruent angles and state which theorem justifies that the angles are congruent.

2. Given two parallel lines crossed by a transversal, students will identify two out of three supplementary angles and state which theorem justifies that the angles are supplementary.

3. Given the degree measures of specific angles in a figure, students will find the measures of at least four out of seven angles.

4. Given specific conditions, 50 percent of the students will successfully apply the theorems about vertical, supplementary/complementary, alternate interior, interior, alternate exterior, exterior, and corresponding angles to prove that specific angles are congruent (or supplementary/complementary).

[1]Janice Wong, unpublished material. Reprinted by permission.

MODEL LESSON PLAN *(Continued)*

Type of Set

1. *Evaluation set:* Quiz to evaluate previously learned material.

2. *Orientation set:* Group work allows students to visualize the content of the presentation (lecture).

3. *Transition set:* Groups report back to the entire class the "rules" or theorems they have discovered; class as a whole decides which theorems actually work; lecture on applying these theorems to solve for missing angles and to write formal proofs.

Lesson Body

Activity	Stimulus Variation	Classroom Control Techniques
1. Quiz		frequent quizzes immediate, specific feedback to all students
2. Group Work	*Kinesic Variation* (I walk around and visit groups) *Shifting Interaction* (Students go from independent to group learning) *Shifting Senses* (Hands-on type of activity)	discovery learning ad hoc small group cluster chairs facing the center high content participation and practice change my position in the room periodically induce total group participation and effort
3. Lecture	*Shifting Interaction* (Students go from group learning to independent learning) *Pausing* (Use of silence to maintain control) *Focusing*	give clear advance organizers followed by relevant examples desks auditorium-style during lecture name-dropping and eye contact change voice volume for content effects vary voice pitch look at all students as lesson goes on point to lesson object move continually and constantly during lesson ask question, wait, call on volunteer, wait ask higher level questions on content identify source of error, ask again use name dropping/use target student's name

Type of Closure

1. *Review Closure:* Recapitulate main points of lecture.

2. *Transfer Closure:* Homework assignment will permit students to practice what they have learned.

MODEL LESSON PLAN *(Continued)*

Evaluative Items

Behavioral Objectives 1 and 2

Use the Figure (lines T, L, M) to answer the following questions:

A. Fill in the blank with the letter of the correct answer.
B. Write the theorem that justifies why the angles are supplementary (or congruent).

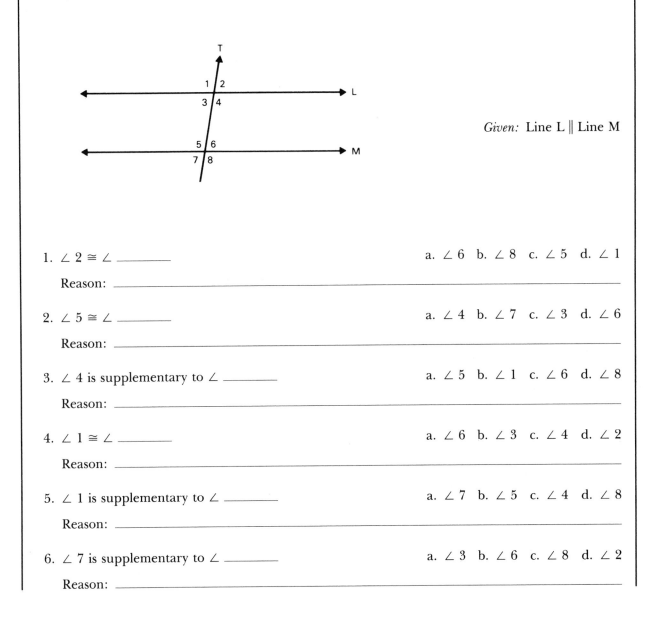

Given: Line L ∥ Line M

1. ∠ 2 ≅ ∠ _____   a. ∠ 6   b. ∠ 8   c. ∠ 5   d. ∠ 1

   Reason: _____

2. ∠ 5 ≅ ∠ _____   a. ∠ 4   b. ∠ 7   c. ∠ 3   d. ∠ 6

   Reason: _____

3. ∠ 4 is supplementary to ∠ _____   a. ∠ 5   b. ∠ 1   c. ∠ 6   d. ∠ 8

   Reason: _____

4. ∠ 1 ≅ ∠ _____   a. ∠ 6   b. ∠ 3   c. ∠ 4   d. ∠ 2

   Reason: _____

5. ∠ 1 is supplementary to ∠ _____   a. ∠ 7   b. ∠ 5   c. ∠ 4   d. ∠ 8

   Reason: _____

6. ∠ 7 is supplementary to ∠ _____   a. ∠ 3   b. ∠ 6   c. ∠ 8   d. ∠ 2

   Reason: _____

MODEL LESSON PLAN *(Continued)*

Behavioral Objective 3

Use the figure at the right to answer the following questions.

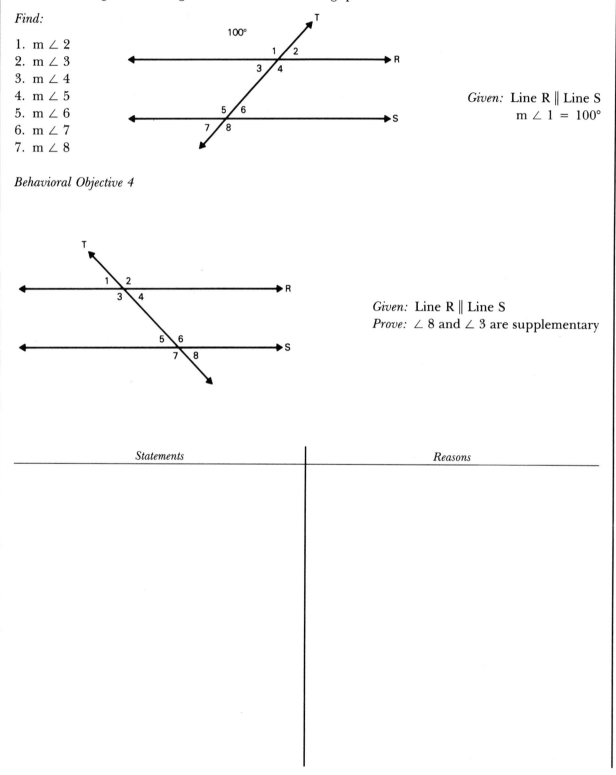

Find:

1. m ∠ 2
2. m ∠ 3
3. m ∠ 4
4. m ∠ 5
5. m ∠ 6
6. m ∠ 7
7. m ∠ 8

Given: Line R ∥ Line S

m ∠ 1 = 100°

Behavioral Objective 4

Given: Line R ∥ Line S

Prove: ∠ 8 and ∠ 3 are supplementary

Statements	Reasons

MODEL LESSON PLAN *(Continued)*

Group Work

1. Break up into groups of four.
2. Work individually when you measure the angles for Problems 1–4 and compare your answers with others in your group before proceeding to the next step. Remeasure if there are any disagreements!
3. Answer (a)–(e) for Problems 1–4; then compare your answers with those of others in your group. Everyone should agree on the answers before you proceed to the next step!
4. Discuss with others in your group about generalizations you can make from your answers to Problems 1–4 and complete a "group theorem" for each generalization. Be ready to share your theorems with the rest of the class when we regroup.
5. HAVE FUN!!!!!!!

Name _____

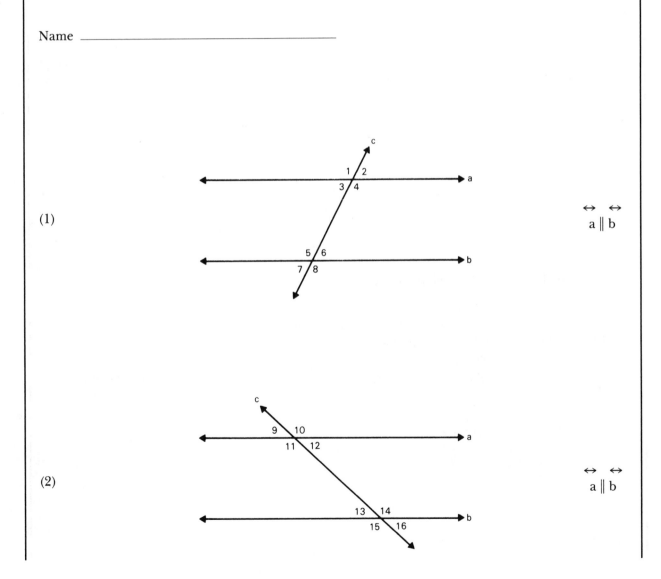

(1) $\overleftrightarrow{a} \parallel \overleftrightarrow{b}$

(2) $\overleftrightarrow{a} \parallel \overleftrightarrow{b}$

MODEL LESSON PLAN *(Continued)*

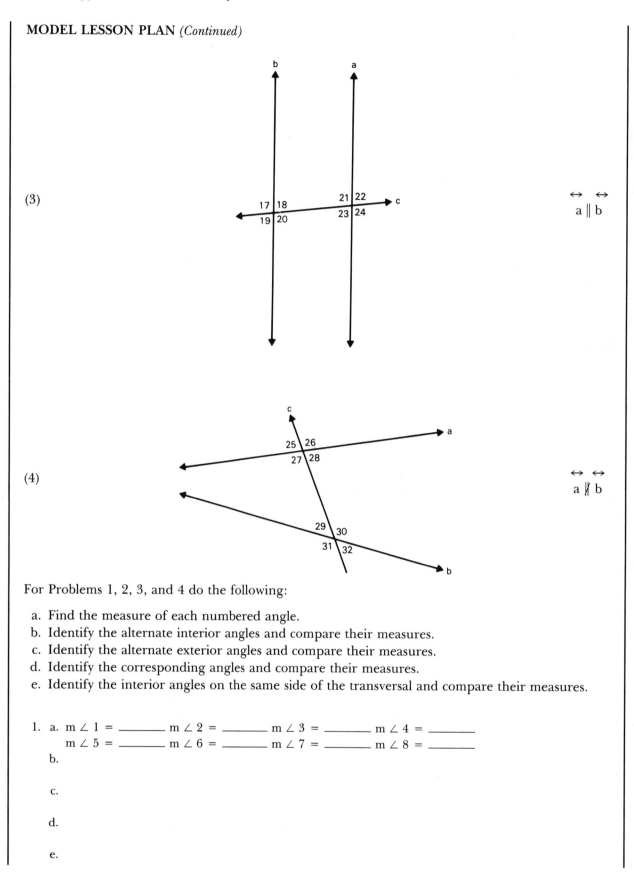

(3) $\overset{\leftrightarrow}{a} \parallel \overset{\leftrightarrow}{b}$

(4) $\overset{\leftrightarrow}{a} \nparallel \overset{\leftrightarrow}{b}$

For Problems 1, 2, 3, and 4 do the following:

a. Find the measure of each numbered angle.
b. Identify the alternate interior angles and compare their measures.
c. Identify the alternate exterior angles and compare their measures.
d. Identify the corresponding angles and compare their measures.
e. Identify the interior angles on the same side of the transversal and compare their measures.

1. a. m ∠ 1 = _____ m ∠ 2 = _____ m ∠ 3 = _____ m ∠ 4 = _____
   m ∠ 5 = _____ m ∠ 6 = _____ m ∠ 7 = _____ m ∠ 8 = _____
   b.

   c.

   d.

   e.

MODEL LESSON PLAN *(Continued)*

2. a. m ∠ 9 = _____   m ∠ 10 = _____   m ∠ 11 = _____   m ∠ 12 = _____
        m ∠ 13 = _____   m ∠ 14 = _____   m ∠ 15 = _____   m ∠ 16 = _____
    b.

    c.

    d.

    e.

3. a. m ∠ 17 = _____   m ∠ 18 = _____   m ∠ 19 = _____   m ∠ 20 = _____
        m ∠ 21 = _____   m ∠ 22 = _____   m ∠ 23 = _____   m ∠ 24 = _____
    b.

    c.

    d.

    e.

4. a. m ∠ 25 = _____   m ∠ 26 = _____   m ∠ 27 = _____   m ∠ 28 = _____
        m ∠ 29 = _____   m ∠ 30 = _____   m ∠ 31 = _____   m ∠ 32 = _____
    b.

    c.

    d.

    e.

From the above answers, make a generalization about the following:

1. alternate interior angles.

   _____

2. alternate exterior angles.

   _____

3. corresponding angles.

   _____

4. interior angles on the same side of the transversal.

   _____

MODEL LESSON PLAN (*Continued*)

5. Do your lines have to be parallel in order for your generalizations to work?

   _____

6. Write a theorem in "if-then" form for each generalization.

   _____

Lecture

1. Allow each group to report about their findings.
2. Read the actual theorem in the textbook.

Theorem: If two parallel lines are cut by a transversal, then the alternate interior angles are congruent.

Theorem: If two parallel lines are cut by a transversal, then the alternate exterior angles are congruent.

Theorem: If two parallel lines are cut by a transversal, then the corresponding angles are congruent.

Theorem: If two parallel lines are cut by a transversal, then the interior angles on the same side of the transversal are supplementary.

   Stress that the lines have to be parallel in order to use these theorems!

3. Do an example on the board applying these theorems to find the measures of missing angles.

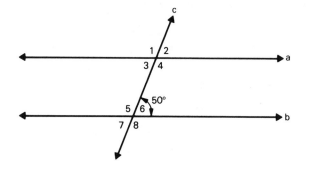

Given: Line a ‖ Line b

   m ∠ 6 = 50°

Find: m ∠ 1, m ∠ 2, m ∠ 3, m ∠ 4,

   m ∠ 5, m ∠ 7, m ∠ 8

4. Do an example of a formal proof applying these theorems, using student input.

Statement	Reason
1. Line a ‖ Line b	1. Given
2. m ∠ 1 = m ∠ 5	2. Corresponding angles are ≅ if lines are ‖
3. m ∠ 5 = m ∠ 8	3. Vertical angles are ≅
4. m ∠ 1 = m ∠ 8	4. Transitive property of equality

Given: Line a ‖ Line b

Prove: ∠ 1 ≅ ∠ 8 (without using the alternate exterior angle theorem)

5. Go over oral exercises with class.

EXERCISE 8.3: PREPARING A LESSON: A GENERIC LESSON PLAN FORMAT

Instructions: The purpose of this exercise is to prepare your first lesson for implementation. Your instructor may provide a variation from the format suggested here, depending upon subject content, learning activities, and the nature of your students. You may wish to now review the sample daily plans that follow in the next section. A guideline that should permeate the development and evaluation of any lesson plan is the question: "Is the plan detailed enough that a substitute teacher could follow it?"

From your course outline (Exercise 6.6), select a topic that fits into a *fifty-minute lesson*. On separate paper, prepare your lesson using the following format. Include probable time line for items 4–6, incorporating planned time for activities within the lesson body (item 5).

1. *Subject and grade level:*

2. *Lesson topic:*

3. *Specific behavioral objectives* (cognitive, psychomotor, and affective) for this lesson:

4. *Set:*

5. *Lesson body:*
   Detailing content, strategies, transitions, and stimulus variation techniques; recognition of student individual differences, with separate time lines for *each step* of the lesson body.

6. *Closure:*

7. *Materials and resources* needed:

8. *Comprehension checks:*
   Detailing how you will evaluate how well students *are learning* (e.g., monitoring their work during the lesson with the use of guided practice and questioning), and *have learned* (e.g., assigning independent practice at completion) the lesson.

When it is completed, have your plan evaluated by your colleagues (using Exercise 8.4); then make appropriate modifications.

EXERCISE 8.4: EVALUATION OF MY LESSON PLAN

Instructions: This exercise provides the form to be used by you and your colleagues to evaluate your lesson plans. Duplicate copies of this form should be made available so that your lesson plan can be evaluated by at least three colleagues, by placing an *X* in the appropriate boxes, followed by useful comments.

	Good	Weak	None
1. Is it clear for what subject, grade level, and topic the plan is designed?			
2. Are behavioral objectives clearly stated?			
3. Does the plan include an effective set? Is it clear how much time is planned for it?			
4. Are content and procedures spelled out clearly enough that a substitute teacher could follow the plan? Does the lesson body detail a time plan?			
5. Have transitions been clearly identified and are they appropriate? Is there adequate variety to the lesson?			
6. Is it clear what materials and resources are needed, and where they can be obtained? Are student individual differences considered?			
7. Is an effective closure planned? Has time been allowed for the closure?			
8. Have learning comprehension checks been built into the lesson, and are they appropriate?			
9. Does the procedure clearly lead to attainment of the objectives?			
10. Overall summary of the lesson plan? Is it well thought out? Is it appropriate and interesting for this subject and grade level?			

Comments and suggestions:

D. PREPARATION OF A TEACHING UNIT

Having prepared your course outline, and learned about the components of a daily lesson, you are now ready to prepare your first instructional unit plan for a grade level and subject topic you are likely to teach, and that you perhaps may be able to implement during your practice teaching. The purpose of instructional units is to arrange a course into organized and sequential blocks of content and learning activities. Each teaching unit consists of a number of daily lessons designed to achieve the broader goals of the unit. There are two general points that we should emphasize regarding the preparation of a teaching unit:

1. There is *no single best format for a teaching unit* that works best for all teaching fields. Particular formats may be best for specific disciplines or topics, and for that reason we include in this chapter sample units for nine disciplines—art, business, English, foreign language, home economics, music, physical education, science, and social studies. Although we have not included a unit plan for mathematics, we did include as our model of a complete lesson plan one in mathematics.

2. There is *no set time duration for a unit plan,* although for specific units curriculum guides will indicate suggested time durations. Units may extend for a minimum of several days or for several weeks, depending on the subject, interest, and abilities of the students. As a general rule, teaching units lose their effectiveness as recognizable units of learning when they last for much longer than three weeks. We suggest that your unit plan (for Exercise 8.5) be written for a two-week duration. Your instructor may alter the guidelines for that exercise and for its evaluation (Exercise 8.6).

EXERCISE 8.5: WRITING MY TEACHING UNIT

Instructions: The purpose of this exercise is for you to prepare a two-week unit plan for a grade level, subject, and topic you are likely to teach. Use a format that is reasonable, comfortable, and common to your discipline, but be sure to include each of the items that follows; then have your plan evaluated using Exercise 8.6.

1. Identify the
   a. grade level and subject
   b. topic
   c. time duration.
2. State the *general goal*(s) of the unit.
3. List the specific *instructional objectives* (these should be listed for each daily lesson). A two-week unit plan should include objectives from all three domains—cognitive, affective, and psychomotor.
4. List the *materials and resources* needed (and where obtained).
5. Include each *daily lesson plan,* ten in all (prepared as learned in Exercise 8.3).
6. Include *evaluation* items that will be used to assess student learning. Include all test items to be used, with each item coded to its related instructional objective.
7. Include provisions for *individual differences.* State how you will attend to varying reading levels, cultural backgrounds, students with special needs.

EXERCISE 8.6: EVALUATION OF MY TEACHING UNIT

Instructions: This exercise provides a form to be used by you and your classmates to evaluate your teaching units. The blank form should be duplicated so each teacher candidate's unit plan is evaluated by at least three other members of the class. Place an *X* on the line from 3 (high) to 1 (low).

CRITERIA	3	2	1
1. IDENTIFICATION FOR WHOM	(clearly identified)		(weakness)
2. GENERAL GOAL(S)	(clearly stated)		(ambiguous)
3. INSTRUCTIONAL OBJECTIVES	(well stated)		(weakness)
4. MATERIALS AND RESOURCES	(clearly identified)		(weakness)
5. DAILY LESSON PLANS	(well designed and written)		(problems)
6. EVALUATION	(well planned)		(problems)
7. INDIVIDUAL DIFFERENCES	(carefully planned for)		(weakness)

Evaluator's comments:

Make appropriate revisions in your unit plan and turn it in for your instructor's evaluation before implementation.

E. UNIT PLAN AND DAILY PLAN: SAMPLES

Included in this section are sample unit plans and their corresponding representative daily lesson plans (one for each unit) to serve as guidelines for your lesson planning. Sample plans are arranged in the following order: art, biology, business education, consumer education, English, music, physical education, social studies, Spanish, and a sample Contract Plan for biology.

UNIT AND DAILY LESSON PLAN—Sample 1

Grade: _____ 6–8 _____ Subject: _____ Art (ceramics) _____

Unit Topic: _____ Forming clay—hand building[1] _____ Duration: _____ three weeks _____

1. *Introduction:* The purpose of this unit is to acquaint the students with the methods of forming clay through hand-building techniques.

2. *Behavioral Objectives:* Upon completion of this unit the student will be able to:
   a. Name five different techniques for forming clay with the hands.
   b. Demonstrate forming clay over objects to create an interior form.
   c. Demonstrate forming clay inside objects to create an exterior form.
   d. Demonstrate creating a form using hand-rolled clay coils.
   f. Demonstrate creating a form using clay slabs.

3. *Content Outline*
   a. Using objects to create a form with clay (1st week)
      (1) Forming clay over objects (2 sessions).
      (2) Forming clay inside objects (2 sessions).
      (3) Pushing objects into clay (2 sessions).
   b. Coil technique of handbuilding (2nd week): rolling coils; making small pots; making large objects.
   c. Slab technique of handbuilding (3rd week): making slabs; making small boxes; making larger objects.

4. *Procedures and Activities*
   Informal lecture combined with demonstration by teacher;
   Studio experiences working in classroom studio or home studio;
   Studio demonstration.

5. *Materials and Equipment*
   clay, objects, sticks, rocks, molds, equipment, wheel, kiln, glazes, wedging table.

6. *Evaluation*
   a. Each student will show a representative sample of each technique in forming clay, rolling coils, and making slabs.
   b. Each student will demonstrate at least one other technique.

---

[1]John Meeks, unpublished material. Reprinted by permission.

UNIT AND DAILY LESSON PLAN—Sample 1 (*Continued*)

Daily Lesson Plan

Class: _____ Art Grades 6–8 _____ Topic: _____ Handbuilt Coil Pots _____

1. *Objective:* The student will make a small pot using hand-rolled clay coils.
   Skills to be learned: how to determine clay consistencies; to roll coils; to adhere clay coils to make pot shapes; to score clay coils for strengthening pot; to burnish clay for a surface.

2. *Teaching points:* Teacher will demonstrate and give an informal lecture about each step of construction. Students will then recreate sequences with individual help from teacher.

3. *Materials needed:* Each student will need:
   1 lb. of clay, fork for scoring, sponge for dampening;
   smooth block of wood for burnishing.

UNIT AND DAILY LESSON PLAN—Sample 2

Unit Plan

Subject: _____ Biology _____ Teacher: _____ D. Grobman _____

Unit Topic: _____ Microorganisms—Viruses and Bacteria[1] _____

Text: _____ Biological Science, An Inquiry Into Life _____

Topics	*Time Estimates in Periods*	*Learning Activities*
A. Viruses		
1. Discovery	$\frac{2}{5}$	T lectures
2. Electron Microscope	$\frac{3}{5}$	Ss read Chapter 9 in class and complete at home.
3. Structure	1	Lab—Inquiry 9-1 Microbiological techniques.
4. Life Cycle	1	Lab—Inquiry 9-2 A disease of bacteria.
5. Diseases	$\frac{3}{5}$	Oral participation, Q/A on previous labs.
	$\frac{2}{5}$	T goes over Quiz questions for tomorrow, Ss read and study for Quiz.
6. Review	$\frac{3}{5}$	Written Quiz.
	$\frac{2}{5}$	Ss Oral Q/A at end of Chapter 9. Ss to read Chapter 10 at home.
7. Epidemic—Bubonic Plague	$\frac{1}{10}$	T explains approach and assigns groups.
Occurrence Today	$\frac{1}{10}$	Role-playing by students. T conducts Q/A on results.
B. Bacteria		
1. Discovery	$\frac{1}{5}$	T lectures on Chapter 10.
	$\frac{1}{10}$	T introduces Lab—Inquiry 10-1. Distribution of Microorganisms.
	$\frac{7}{10}$	Ss work on lab.

[1]Deborah Grobman, unpublished material. Reprinted by permission.

UNIT AND DAILY LESSON PLAN—Sample 2 (*Continued*)

Topics	Time Estimates in Periods	Learning Activities
2. Structure		
3. Shapes		
4. Reproduction Growth, Colonies	1	Ss do lab—Inquiry 10-2. Staining and observing Bacterial cells.
5. Cultures	$\frac{9}{10}$	Ss work on Labs—11-1.
6. Diseases		Descendents of a single cell and Inquiry 11-2, War on Bacteria.
	$\frac{1}{10}$	Q/A on quiz tomorrow.
7. Evaluation	1	Written quiz.

OBJECTIVES AND SAMPLE TEST ITEMS

Instructional Objectives	Test Item
A. *Viruses*	
1. Describe the discovery.	What is the piece of equipment that made it possible to study viruses?
2. State evidence for the hypothesis that viruses are similar to the earliest forms of life.	Propose a theory explaining why viruses could not have been the first life on earth.
3. Identify the structure of a virus.	Draw and label the parts representing a typical virus.
4. Diagram the reproductive cycle of a virus.	Draw and label the stages in reproductive cycle of a virus.
5. Explain how a virus infects and affects another living cell.	Predict what would happen when a virus enters a healthy cell.
6. Identify equipment used in dealing with microorganisms.	Given various pieces of lab equipment: microscope, Petri dish, agar, inoculating loop, etc., identify each item and state its use.
7. List aseptic techniques in handling and growing microorganisms.	List aseptic techniques in handling and growing microorganisms.
8. State diseases caused by viruses, their prevention, and cure.	What are some of the diseases caused by viruses? Do these have cures? How can you be protected against them?

UNIT AND DAILY LESSON PLAN—Sample 2 (*Continued*)

Instructional Objectives	*Test Item*
9. Postulate the occurrence of a viral epidemic happening today.	See Lesson Plan that follows.
10. Describe the discovery of bacteria.	List several conditions under which bacteria survive. What helps them survive these conditions?
11. Identify the structure of a generalized bacterium.	Given a diagram of a generalized bacterium, label the parts.
12. Identify 3 bacterial shapes.	Shown various bacteria, classify each according to correct shape.
13. List the principal steps of the Lederberg-Tactum experiments of the effects of X-rays on bacteria.	List the principal steps of the Lederberg-Tactum experiments of the effects of X-rays on bacteria.
14. Explain the transforming principle.	Fill in the partially completed chart on transduction in bacteria.
15. Explain Koch's postulates.	State Koch's postulates in your own terms.
16. List ways bacteria benefit us.	Name several ways man benefits from bacteria.

UNIT AND DAILY LESSON PLAN—Sample 2 (*Continued*)

A Daily Lesson

Unit Topic—*Microorganisms, Viruses, and Bacteria*
Topic for this lesson—*Plague today, A reality?*
Class/Period—Biology 10, Period 4

Instructional Objectives

1. Postulate the occurrence of a viral epidemic happening today.
2. Identify the steps leading to the identification of the disease.
3. Explain the difference between bubonic and pneumonic plague.
4. State the animal vectors of the disease.
5. Recall and state symptoms of the plague.
6. List the defense systems of the body.
7. Trace the spread of the epidemic.
8. Propose the procedures for containment and elimination of the plague.
9. Criticize the public's reaction to the epidemic.

			Routines		
			1. Take attendance via seating chart as students enter.		

| | | | Feedback Strategies | | |
Content Item	Special Material or Equipment	Instructional Strategies	Get	Give	Time Est.
Recall concept of viruses, pathogens		T reviews Chapter 9 and conducts Q/A on viruses and diseases. "How many cases of Bubonic Plague were there in U.S. this year, 10 years ago, 50 years ago, and 100 years ago?" "Can viral diseases be controlled?"		Ss raise hands to answer. T calls on several to confirm replies.	5 min.
Bubonic Plague is thought to be a disease of the past. Is this a true statement?		T explains that the class will be simulating an outbreak of Bubonic Plague in New York City. T breaks Ss up into groups and assigns each for role-playing.			
	Prepared profiles on specific roles: 1. Initial single plague victim. 2. Police found victim and try to trace where it was contracted.	T hands out character sketches to each group and asks for questions.	T takes straw vote to confirm understanding of assignment.	Ss break into groups and ask questions.	5 min.

UNIT AND DAILY LESSON PLAN—Sample 2 (*Continued*)

Content Item	Special Material or Equipment	Instructional Strategies	Feedback Strategies Get	Give	Time Est.
Role-playing cont.	3. Health Dept. and Disease prevention and control. 4. People victims contacted. 5. Nurses and Doctors associated with the case. Try to trace victim's contacts. 6. Government officials: Mayor, etc.		Tour and look for errors. Answers Qs.	Ss start working in groups and try to solve their particular problem.	30-40 min.
Comparing results and generalizing in their cases.		T leads Q/A on class results. T asks for class agreement of proposed actions of the various groups. T shares group progress with class.	T writes results on board. T takes straw vote.	Ss respond and vote on feasibility of each group's conclusions.	5 min.
Relating a similar model.		T relates the theory proposed by Gwyneth Cravens and John S. Marr in *The Black Death*, a novel.	T asks Ss to list the similarities and differences and to justify their theory.	Ss discuses the results. T confirms correct proposals. T praises thoughtful responses.	5 min.
Look ahead		T instructs Ss to work on the write-up of the results of their group's and the class' activity.	Compliment class on good work of today (to extent this proves true).	Ss write their parts and bring to class the next day.	5 min.

If the role-playing part of the lesson takes longer than the time allotted, the remainder of the lesson plan can be carried over to the next class period and finished then.

UNIT AND DAILY LESSON PLAN—Sample 3

Subject: _____Business Education_____ Teacher: _____Christy Scofield_____

Unit Topic: ___Typing—Modified Block[1]___ Duration: _____5 days_____

1. *Introduction:* Relate business letter to personal letter which students have already written. Show similarities and differences. Talk about the importance of proper form in a business letter.

2. *Instructional Objectives:* Given a business letter in an unorganized form, the student will produce it in the proper form in 20 minutes.

3. *Unit Content:* Introduction of the 60-space line; use of the bell cue; proper spacing in the rest of the letter; use of typist's initials.

4. *Procedures and Activities*
   a. Show example of proper format in book.
   b. Review by drawing letter and format on chalkboard.
   c. Give practice by doing letters in typing book.
   d. Have papers turned in for suggestions and corrections.
   e. Work with individuals as necessary.

Lesson Plan—Daily

Subject: ___Business Education (Typing I)___ Date: _____

Teacher: _____Christy Scofield_____ Duration: _____55 minutes_____

1. *Warm-up:* Conditioning practice, p. 86, 55A.

2. *Topic for This Lesson:* Business letter in modified block form.

3. *Instructional Objective:* The student will produce two letters with proper format by the end of the period.

4. *Skills to Be Learned:* Correct form of a business letter; correct setting of right margin by listening for bell cue.

5. *Specific Teaching Points*
   Review bell cue;
   Review use of typist's initials;
   Review centering and use of 60-space line.

6. *Assignment:* Type letter problems 1 and 2 on page 87.

7. *Evaluation:* The letters completed and turned in at the end of the period should have the proper format; maximum errors, 12.

---

[1]Christy Scofield, unpublished material. Reprinted by permission.

UNIT AND DAILY LESSON PLAN—Sample 4

Course and Subject: _____ Home Economics—Consumer Education _____

Grade: _____ 12 _____

Unit Topic: _____ Coping with a Cashless Society _____

Unit Duration: _____ 10 days _____

1. *Introduction:* The purpose of this unit is to acquaint the student with checking accounts, usage of credit, and current Electronic Funds Transfer systems (EFT).

2. *Instructional Objectives:* Upon completion of this unit the student will
   a. explain in his or her own words how a checking account works,
   b. demonstrate the process of writing, entering, and balancing a checking account,
   c. explain in his or her own words a brief history of credit,
   d. demonstrate the ability to fill out a credit application,
   e. state what the EFT system is,
   f. identify the possible effects the EFT system will have on the consumer.

3. *Unit Content*
   a. Introduction of the computer revolution (1 session)—forerunners of EFT system: courtesy cards, credit, checking accounts
   b. Checking accounts (2 sessions)—writing, entering, and balancing a checking account
   c. Credit (2 sessions)—brief history, how to select credit appropriate for you, basic laws concerning billing and applying for credit, the effects of credit on consumer behavior
   d. Perspectives on EFT systems (2 sessions)—the components of EFTs, EFT issues, implications of EFT
   e. EFT and the consumer (1 sesssion)—legal issues

4. *Procedures and Activities*
   Informal lecture on each of the above topics and discussion will follow based on:
   a. Charts to be made: timetable of technological revolution, enlarged check book and balance statement
   b. Transparencies to be used: the student will be able to follow the route at which information travels in an EFT system (customer-seller-local bank-central switchboard—yes/no switchboard)
   c. Dittos to be used: How a Checking Account Works, Filling Out a Credit Application, Benefits and Problems of the EFT Systems, You Are the Computer (directions to game), What Do You Think? (preliminary to classroom discussion)
   d. Game: You Are the Computer

5. *Instructional Aids and Resources*
   Overhead projector, dittos, game

6. *Evaluation*
   Participation in classroom discussion, quiz on checking account, unit test, dittos to be handed in

UNIT AND DAILY LESSON PLAN—Sample 4 *(Continued)*

Daily Lesson Plan

Class: _____12_____ Topic: _____ Coping with a Cashless Society _____

Theme for the Day: _____ What Do You Think? _____ Time: _____1 hour_____

Objective

The student will be able to explain his or her own feelings about the effects of EFT on society and on himself or herself. The student will demonstrate the ability to participate in group discussion and decision making.

Motivation

A statement, "You don't need cash in your life."

Discussion

Key Question 1: What do you think about a cashless society?
   a. How do you feel about a computer handling your money?
   b. What are some good reasons for having a checking account?
   c. When would it be difficult to use cash?

Key Question 2: How do you think the EFT will change consumer behavior?
   a. How will people budget their money?
   b. What changes will take place in buying habits?
   c. Why will they take place?

Key Question 3: Where do you think EFT systems will have the greatest impact?
   a. How will it affect banks and stores?
   b. Will it increase or decrease the possibility of errors?
   c. Will it increase or decrease the possibility of getting credit?

UNIT AND DAILY LESSON PLAN—Sample 5

Grade: _____7th_____ Course: _____English_____ Teacher: _____Ms. Sue Morgan_____

Unit Topic: _____How to Correctly Punctuate with Commas[1]_____

Duration: _____Three weeks; two sessions each week_____

Introduction: The purpose of this unit is to introduce the correct use of the comma through student application of the comma use rules found in the grammar text to practice sentence exercises, assigned literature readings, and most importantly, to their own writing.

2. *Instructional Objectives:* Upon completion of this unit the students will
   a. correctly punctuate with commas in test exercises and passages with at least 70 percent accuracy.
   b. correctly punctuate with commas in their own writing compositions with at least 80 percent accuracy.
   c. recognize the value of correct comma use to produce clear and comprehensible writing.

3. *Unit Content Concepts*
   a. Comma use in specific occasions (Rules 1–6). Two class sessions.
   b. Comma use to separate works in direct address (Rules 7–10). One class session.
   c. Comma use to separate appositives (Rule 11). One class session.
   d. Comma use in compound and complex sentences (Rules 13–15). Two class sessions.

4. *Procedures*
   a. Students complete pretest of ten sentences (Grammar text, p. 19).
   b. Students write descriptive compositions, letters, narrative paragraphs, and a dialogue.
   c. Informal lectures introducing comma use rules.
   d. Students practice sentence and paragraph exercises orally and in writing.
   e. Students edit classmates' compositions.
   f. Class discussion of application of comma rules to the practice exercises and to student compositions.

5. *Aids*
   a. Text: Dawson, Elwell, Johnson, and Zollinger, *Language for Daily Use,* Silver Level (New York: Harcourt Brace Jovanovich, 1973).
   b. Students' compositions.
   c. Dittos of sentence and paragraph exercises.
   d. Overhead projector.

6. *Evaluation:* Three objective tests and three student compositions
   a. Pretest: Ten test sentences; one student-written letter.
   b. Midterm: Review of comma use skills, Rules 1–10.
   c. Final: Review of comma use skills, Rules 1–15.
   d. Writing: Narrative paragraph, descriptive paragraph, and Dialogue.

[1]Sue Morgan, unpublished material. Reprinted by permission.

UNIT AND DAILY LESSON PLAN—Sample 5 *(Continued)*

Lesson Plan—Daily

Subject: _____English_____ Unit Topic: _____Correct Comma Use_____

Lesson Topic: _____How to Use Commas to Separate Words or Phrases Within a Series_____

1. *Instructional Objectives*
   a. Students will apply the comma use skill requiring the separation of items in a series by commas to their classmates' descriptive paragraphs.
   b. From the above editing activity, the students will recognize the need for proper comma use to achieve sentence clarity in their own writing.

2. *Contents*
   a. Teacher explanation of the comma rule.
   b. Examples.
   c. Practice application of rule with sentence exercises.
   d. Application of rule to student writing.
   e. Group review for correction.

3. *Motivation*
   Reading and editing their classmates' writing will stimulate the students' interest and appreciation for the value of this lesson.

4. *Procedure:* Teacher will:
   a. Give short lecture introducing grammar rule regarding comma use within a series of words or phrases.
   b. Lecture using test examples and exercises displayed on the overhead projector.
   c. Assign ditto of three student paragraphs and request the class to edit the paragraphs for proper comma use within items of a series. Paragraphs done day before.
   d. Lead class discussion of the correct answers to Exercise D. Stress to the class that commas are necessary to produce clear, easily understood sentences.

5. *Instructional Aids and Materials*
   a. Overhead projector.
   b. Copy of grammar text for each student.
   c. Student copies of classmates' descriptive paragraphs.

6. *Evaluation:* Objective Test
   Given two descriptive passages from two already assigned short stories, in which the commas between series of items have been removed. Students will correctly punctuate with commas with at least 70 percent accuracy.

UNIT PLAN—Sample 6

Grade: _____6–8_____ Subject: _____Music_____ Teacher: _____John Skorich[1]_____

Unit Topic: _____Music for Fun_____ Duration: _____2 Months_____

1. *Introduction:* This unit will help students to get acquainted with basic concepts of music reading, singing, and instrument playing.

2. *Instructional Objectives:* Students will:
   a. Read basic rhythmic patterns using quarter and eighth note values with their rests.
   b. Recognize differences in sound—high, low, loud, soft, short, long—and its movement up and down by step or skip.
   c. Learn basic techniques of singing.
   d. Recognize different instruments by sight and sound.

3. *Procedures/Activities/Methods*
   Singing, instrument playing, body movements, clapping, reading, game playing.

4. *Instructional Aids or Resources*
   Basic collection of percussion instruments, records, record player, overhead projector, piano or resonator bells, guitar or autoharp.
   Text: Eunice Boardman, *Exploring Music* (New York: Holt, Rinehart and Winston, 1976).

5. *Evaluation:* Everyday performance. See following page.

[1]John Skorich, unpublished material. Reprinted by permission.

UNIT PLAN—Sample 6 (*Continued*)

UNIT TOPIC: MUSIC FOR FUN
EVALUATION

Date:

Musical Learning	Listening Selection or Song	Teaching Procedures	Materials	Evaluation
Rhythm: Long/Short		1. a. Echo clapping: T claps, Ss repeat.		Clapping accurately?
		b. Rotate some of the examples.		
	Text: *Exploring Music*, p. 38	2. a. Sing "Scotland's Burning." b. Rhythm read:	Text Guitar	Reading accurately?
Duration: Short/Long Form: Round Harmony: Round		c. Rhythm read as a round (divide class in half). d. Sing as a round (divide class in half).		Sing in the round?
Timbre Melody High/Low Sound		3. a. Introduce violin as a member of string family—demonstrate different parts & play. b. Play high/low sounds and let students identify by raising their hand.	Violin	Recognize violin by sight and hearing? Recognize high/low sounds by raising their hands?
Dynamics: Soft/Loud (*p*) (*f*)		4. Clap the following using dynamic levels as indicated.	None	Different dynamic levels?

UNIT AND DAILY LESSON PLAN—Sample 7

Grade: _____9_____ Subject: _____Physical Education_____

Unit Topic: _____Beginning Track and Field[1]_____ Duration: _____2 weeks; 55 minutes/day_____

1. *General Objective:* For students to realize and experience an increased level of cardiovascular efficiency through skill instructions and drills in the track and field unit.

2. *Specific Objectives:* The student will be able to:
   a. Demonstrate proper techniques in each of the following areas: springs, long jump, high jump, distance runs.
   b. Observe the proper safety procedures during class while pursuing the objectives above.

3. *Unit Content:* See master calendar that follows.

4. *Evaluation:* Written test and skill demonstrations.

5. *Equipment:* (for 32 students) three sets of high jump standards; three cross bars; two 18-lb. shots; two 12-lb. shots; four flights of hurdles.

MASTER CALENDAR

Monday	Tuesday	Wednesday	Thursday	Friday
		First Week		
Introduction to unit and class procedures WU: stretch and jog SI: running form SD: form running CA: 20-yd sprints	WU: stretch and jog SI: sprint start SD: start CA: 10-yd sprints	WU: Astronaut drill SI: relay techniques SD: hand-offs CA: relay race 100 yd 4 × 25	WU: stretch and jog SI: long jump SD: pop-ups CA: group jump relay	WU: stretch and form running SI: review with station work SD: stations 1. start 2. hand-offs 3. long jump 4. form running

[1]David Shipp, unpublished material. Reprinted by permission.

UNIT AND DAILY LESSON PLAN—Sample 7 (*Continued*)

MASTER CALENDAR (*continued*)

Monday	Tuesday	Wednesday	Thursday	Friday
		Second Week		
WU: astronaut drill	WU: stretch	WU: stretch and short jog	WU: upper body stretching	WU: upper body stretching
SI: distance running	SI: high jump	SI: high jump	SI: shot put	SI: discus
SD: 100-yd runs with correct form	SD: approach and take-offs	SD: jump and landing	SD: circle moves; put itself	SD: circle moves throw
CA: 1320 run for time	CA: low jump	CA: jump for maximum height	CA: group relay	CA: group relay

KEY: WU: warm up   SI: skill instructions   SD: skill drills   CA: culminating activity

Daily Lesson Plan

Class: _____ Physical Education _____   Topic: _____ Beginning Track and Field—day 1 _____

Objectives
1. Students will demonstrate correct arm movement while running.
2. Students will demonstrate correct leg action while running.

Procedure	Time	Formation	Teaching Points
1. Introduce unit and class procedures.	5 min.	x x x x x x x x x x x x x x x x	1. Listen attentively to teacher; follow instruction.
2. Warm up.	5 min.	x x x x x x x x	2. Static stretching.
3. Gather students and demonstrate form running	4 min.	same	3. Arms moving up and down. High knee action. Push off toes.
4. Have students find a place and practice form running.	3 min.	same	4. High knee action. Arms moving up and down.
5. Have students line up in 8 lines and stride out.	5 min.	x x x x x x x x x x x x x x x x x x x x x x x x x x x x x x x x x x x x x x x x	5. High knees. Point out students with this and up and down arm motion.
6. Remain in same formation and bound out 10 yds.	5 min.	same	6. Exaggerate points in Step 5.

UNIT AND DAILY LESSON PLAN—Sample 8

Grade: _____8th_____ Course/Subject: _____Social Studies_____ Teacher: _____Therese Feeney_____

Unit Topic: _____The Energy Crisis and Your Environment[1]_____ Unit Duration: _____5 days_____

Introduction

Americans today are realizing that the nation has been facing an environmental and energy problem since the 1950s. To combat these problems, several measures have been implemented. With these in mind, this five-day unit will focus on the following:

a. The students will identify the general nature of the energy crisis and how it has influenced their world.
b. The students will compare and contrast personal ideas and opinions about the energy crisis with classmates, the teacher, and the guest speaker.
c. The students will initiate and evaluate the energy-saving device that they set up in their homes.

Day 1: Objectives and Activities

a. The students are asked to define the term energy crisis in their own words (content).
b. Students will tell the class what they have heard and/or know about energy crisis (content).
c. The students are asked to list ten terms they might use to describe oil companies, and place a plus sign next to each term which has a positive connotation, a minus sign next to each negative term, and a zero next to each term that is neutral. The results are tabulated on the chalkboard totaling the plus, minus, and zero symbols. They are then asked to analyze their results and write a paragraph explaining what the exercise reveals about their own attitudes toward oil companies (inquiry).

Day 2: Objectives and Activities

a. The students will openly discuss the ways in which energy is used in their homes (content).
b. The students will decide on an appropriate energy-saving device for their homes (decision making).
c. Students will decide in their own minds what energy-saving devices that they like and might use in their future in their community (inquiry).

[1]Therese A. Feeney, unpublished material. Reprinted by permission.

UNIT AND DAILY LESSON PLAN—Sample 8 (*Continued*)

Day 3: Objectives and Activities

a. The class will have the opportunity to hear about the need for conservation from a state official, a guest speaker (content).

b. The students will ask questions about the energy crisis and other areas of concern that the guest speaker is able to answer and explain (inquiry).

Day 4: Objectives and Activities

a. The students will critique and apply the lecture presented by the guest speaker to what they are studying in class and at home while carrying out an energy-saving program (content).

b. The students will evaluate the information and experience the guest speaker shared with the class. They will also make suggestions that they can use in their home projects and in their future contacts in the real world (inquiry).

c. Through the use of the simulation game (Recycling the Resources) the students will express their own feelings, emotions, and values when placed in the various roles within the context of the game (valuing).

Day 5: Objectives and Activities

a. The students will listen carefully to their fellow classmates when they explain and discuss their home energy-saving devices (content).

b. Students will do the follow-up exercise which essentially involves the comparison of history with the energy crisis and conservation (inquiry).

Reading Assignments

1. Go to the library and consult the book reviews of the following books: *Silent Spring* by Rachel Carson and *The Quiet Crisis* by Stuart L. Udall.

   After reading the reviews you are asked to decide if the book would be worth your while to read. Does it appear to relate to our topic of discussion this week?

   or

2. Review the section in your textbook about the Native Americans. Then tell me if you think they had an "energy crisis" in their time.

Evaluation

1. The homework from Day 1 (10 percent of your grade).

2. Group participation and sportsmanship (15 percent of your grade). It will basically measure how well you work with your fellow classmates and how cooperative you are within the group setting.

3. The Home Energy-Saving Project (50 percent of your grade). This is based on the fact that you decide on a certain project and then set it up within your home environment. Lastly, you will be asked to explain your project to the class and turn in a brief summary.

4. The follow-up exercise (25 percent of your grade).

UNIT AND DAILY LESSON PLAN—Sample 9

Subject: _____ Spanish 4 _____ Teacher: _____ Gloria Rodriguez _____

Unit Topic: _____ The Uses of *Ser* and *Estar*[1] _____ Unit Duration: _____ 8 days _____

1. *Introduction:* *Ser* and *estar* are verbs which both mean "to be." These two verbs, however, are widely different in their concepts, and they can never be interchanged without a basic change of meaning. It is important that a student automatically know when to use these two verbs, considering the frequency with which they are used in the language. This unit is designed as an extensive review of the uses of these two verbs.

2. *Instructional Objectives*
   The student will:
   a. Identify the rules governing the uses of *ser* and *estar*.
   b. Complete substitution and fill-in oral and written drills involving the uses of the two verbs.
   c. Translate correctly the English sentences containing forms of "to be" into their Spanish equivalents.
   d. Spell correctly the vocabulary words presented in the chapter.
   e. Compose short oral presentation correctly using the new vocabulary and using the correct forms of *ser* and *estar*.

3. *Content Outline*
   a. Read and discuss the *Enfoque* at the beginning of the chapter (3 days).
      1. New vocabulary words (*Estudio de vocabulario*).
      2. Topic for discussion (the law).
   b. *Estructura* (3 days).
      1. General view of *ser* and *estar*.
      2. *Ser* and *estar* with adjectives.
      3. Other uses of *ser* and *estar*.
   c. Read and give presentations on *"Creación"* to reinforce vocabulary words and grammatical concepts (2 days).

4. *Procedures/Activities*
   a. Read and discuss *"Enfoque—Usted y la ley."*
   b. Handouts on vocabulary words to be learned and *ser* and *estar* drills.
   c. Have students prepare short oral presentations about their opinions and solutions to the situations given in the *"Creación."*

5. *Instructional Aids or Resources*
   a. Zenia Sacks da Silva, *On with Spanish*, Harper & Row.
   b. Handouts on *ser/estar* drill.

---

[1]Gloria Rodriguez, unpublished material. Reprinted by permission.

UNIT AND DAILY LESSON PLAN—Sample 9 (*Continued*)

6. *Evaluation*
   a. Students' answers to oral and written homework drills.
   b. Content of students' oral presentation.
   c. Vocabulary quiz.
   d. Unit test.

Daily Lesson Plan

Grade: _____12_____ Subject: _____Spanish 4_____

Unit Topic: ___The Uses of *Ser* and *Estar*___ Topic for This Lesson: ___Other Uses of *Estar*___

1. *Instructional Objectives*
   The student will:
   a. Complete the exercises, both oral and written, on the uses of *ser* and *estar* with a minimum of teacher help.
   b. Identify circumstances other than those already studied in which the verb *estar* is used.

2. *Assignment*
   Finish worksheet. Read *"Creación"* on pp. 148–149 and be prepared to discuss in class.

3. *Procedure*
   a. Review previously learned uses of *ser* and especially *estar*.
   b. Review homework on "Other uses of *ser*."
   c. Explain other uses of *ser*.
   d. Give oral drills, including Ejercicio 1 (drill on other uses of *ser*).
   e. Have class work on worksheet in class.

4. *Instructional Materials*
   On with Spanish text, ditto.

5. *Evaluation*
   Student answers to homework, performance on drills and on worksheet.

A MODEL FOR A UNIT PLAN CONTRACT

Growing in popularity in recent years has been the use of "teacher-learner contracts." Here is a sample Unit Plan Contract.

Biology: Photosynthesis[1]

Read through the following items and check those you would like to do. Then decide what grade you would like to contract for. Grades will be given as follows:

D—The starred items plus one more from each group
C—The starred items plus two more from each group
B—The starred items plus three more from each group
A—The starred items plus four more from each group

Discuss your choice with your teacher and then sign your name in the proper place on the other side of this sheet.

★ Prepare a title page for the section on photosynthesis in your notebook.
★ Introduce your unit with a brief description of the energy conversion process that takes place during photosynthesis.
★ Write a paragraph explaining why photosynthesis is a vital process in regard to life on earth.

Group I

★ Diagram a "typical" chloroplast and identify its organelles and components.

1. Explain why a high percentage of photosynthesis occurs in the ocean. State what organisms make this possible.

2. Read about Van Niel's experiment with photosynthetic bacteria. Explain where the liberated O_2 comes from during photosynthesis.

3. Set up an experiment to show how different wavelengths of light affect the rate of photosynthesis.

4. Examine *Spirogyra, Mougeotia,* and *Zygnema* under the light microscope. Locate the chloroplast in each and make a drawing of it.

Group II

★ State the probable origin of the chloroplast in the higher plants.

1. Identify the "process" that replenishes the CO_2 content of the atmosphere.

2. Explain why Ruben used $^{18}O_2$ (a stable isotope of oxygen) in his famous experiment in 1941. Write a chemical equation showing the reaction Ruben proved.

3. Extract and separate by paper chromatography the photosynthetic pigments from fresh spinach leaves. Identify the pigments on the chromatogram.

4. Examine *Mougeotia* under a microscope. Move a bright light source around the microscope in different positions and write down what you observe about the chloroplast.

---

[1]Targe Lindsay, Jr., unpublished material. Reprinted by permission.

A MODEL FOR A UNIT PLAN CONTRACT (*Continued*)

★ Explain the role of chlorophyll in photosynthesis.

1. Tell how stomatal activity and CO_2 concentrations are related to photosynthesis.

2. Make a collection of leaves from different plants. Examine the stomatiferous areas of the leaves. Try to draw some conclusions regarding the size, number, and location of stomata on the different leaves.

3. Identify five accessory pigments and explain their role in photosynthesis.

4. Explain the manometric method of detecting photosynthesis.

Date   Pupil's Signature

Grade Contracted   Teacher's Signature

QUESTIONS FOR CLASS DISCUSSION

1. Think of the classroom as a stage, and you, the teacher, are an actor on that stage. Thinking about that, where on the stage do you think you can "perform" best: front center, front right, front left, etc.? Is your location in the classroom an important consideration when planning and implementing lessons?
2. Continuing to think of the classroom as a stage, how should you position your body for your best "performance": standing straight with shoulders back; slouched; sitting on corner of desk top; hand in pocket; seated at desk, etc.? Is body position important for you to consider when planning and implementing lessons?
3. Do you fully understand the meaning of developing your teaching plan from the concrete to the abstract?
4. Identify at least ten ways you can individualize your instruction when you have a class of 28 students of varying reading abilities, cultural backgrounds, etc.
5. What dangers are inherent in using an unmodified lesson plan year after year?
6. Have you ever been a substitute teacher? If so, how useful were the lesson plans left for you by the regular teacher?
7. How many reasons can you give why both a student teacher and a first-year teacher need to prepare detailed lesson and unit plans.
8. Why should you need to know how to prepare detailed plans if the textbook program you are using provides them?
9. Do you think when preparing unit and lesson plans for your subject field a teacher needs to give consideration for student safety?
10. What questions do you have about the content of this chapter? How might answers be found?

SELECTED READINGS FOR CHAPTER 8

Eggen, P. D., and Kauchak, D. P. *Strategies for Teachers.* Englewood Cliffs, NJ: Prentice Hall, 1988.

Heinich, R., et al. *Instructional Media* 3d ed. New York: Macmillan, 1989.

Hunter, M. *Mastery Teaching.* El Segundo, CA: TIP Publications, 1982.

9

How Can I Individualize the Learning Experience for Students?

Learning is an individual experience. Teaching, unfortunately, is one of the few professions where the practitioner is expected to effectively work with "clients" on other than an individual basis—more likely thirty to one. Much has been written of the importance of individualizing the instruction. We know of the individuality of the learning experience, and that while some students are verbal learners, others are better visual or kinesthetic learners, but the teacher is in the difficult position of simultaneously "treating" thirty students who are separate and individual learners. It seems an impossible expectation, and if occasionally you do succeed, we applaud you. This chapter will help you to maximize your efforts, and to minimize your failures.

It is aphoristic that student achievement in learning is related to the quality and length of time and attention given to learning tasks. In 1968, Benjamin Bloom,[1] reinforcing a model developed earlier by John Carroll,[2] developed the concept of individualized instruction called "mastery learning," saying that students need sufficient time-on-task to master content before moving on to new content. From that concept Fred Keller developed an instructional plan (the Keller Plan or Personalized System of Instruction—PSI) that by the early 1970s enjoyed popular use and success in community and a few four-year colleges. The Keller Plan involves student learning from printed modules of instruction that allow the student absolute control over the learning pace, and is mastery oriented; that is, the student demonstrates mastery of one module before proceeding to the next.

The S.I.P.

A modification of PSI, developed about the same time (early 1970s), and one that is popular with teachers, is the self-instructional technique developed by Rita and Stuart Johnson, and called the "self-instructional package" (S.I.P.).[3] The S.I.P. is a learning package specifically designed for an individual student, using small sequential steps, with frequent and immediate learning feedback to the student, and

---

[1]Benjamin Bloom, *Human Characteristics and School Learning* (New York: McGraw-Hill, 1976).
[2]John Carroll, "A Model of School Learning," *Teachers College Record*, vol. 64, no. 8 (May 1963), pp. 723–733.
[3]Rita Johnson and Stuart Johnson, *Assuring Learning with Self-Instructional Packages* (Chapel Hill, NC: Self-Instructional Packages, 1971).

designed to teach a relatively small amount of material, at the mastery level, requiring about one hour of learning time. Exercise 9.1 is a self-instructional package designed to lead you through the process of writing your first S.I.P.

While the self-instructional package is a technique for individualizing and of assuring that learning occurs, there are other less sophisticated things you can do to individualize your instruction. Consider the following.

- Allow variations in assignments that depend upon student abilities.
- Insure that your presentations use techniques that are not only verbal, but also visual and kinesthetic.
- Encourage cooperative learning, such as with the use of peer tutoring and small group learning.
- Provide a structured course schedule, as you learned in preparation of your course syllabus, so students know what to expect.
- Provide clearly stated assignments and other requirements so the students know what is expected.
- Teach in a step-by-step sequence from concrete to the more abstract.
- Provide frequent comprehension checks to assure that the students are learning.
- Provide for overlearning. Instructional pacing is difficult to master. It helps to constantly remind yourself to slow down and to execute frequent learning comprehension checks.
- Encourage the use of observation and generalization skills.
- Provide a mix of activities that are less preferred by students with those that are more preferred.
- Encourage students who are having difficulty, and even those who are not, to meet with you individually, or in groups of two.
- Utilize interactive computer programs designed for use by individual students.
- Identify individual student needs and teach to those needs.

A. IDENTIFYING THE STUDENTS' NEEDS IN YOUR CLASSROOM

We can learn more about how to individualize as we pay particular attention to the techniques used for attending to the learning of "mainstreamed" students (see Chapter 1). Each student identified as exceptional will have an individualized educational plan (IEP) which provides the regular classroom teacher with the overall goals and objectives for that student, based on an assessment of that student's performance. These goals and objectives are helpful in planning for both the strengths and weaknesses of this student. However, the recognized needs of exceptional students are further affected by the specific classrooms in which the student is placed. As a regular classroom teacher of a secondary single subject field, you will consider the student's performance as it relates to your class. Such a system of consideration is approached by asking the following:

1. Do I teach my class mostly through visual or auditory channels?
2. Do I require students to complete work most often in a visual or an auditory way?

3. Do I allow modifications of assignments, such as:
   a. amount of work (5 instead of 25 math facts)?
   b. way of responding (underlining answers rather than writing out)?
4. Do I have a system of peer tutoring established?
5. Do I provide a structured classroom schedule, so students know *what* to expect?
6. Do I provide clear assignments and requirements so that students know what *is expected* of them?
7. Do I teach in a step-by-step sequence from simple to more difficult?
8. Do I provide for overlearning of skills?
9. Do I teach observation and generalization skills in order to attend to skills that are not learned incidentally?
10. Do I positively attend to behaviors I want to continue or to increase?
11. Do I provide alternatives to paper/pencil tasks?
12. Do I pair less-preferred activities with more-preferred activities?

These questions are based on procedures that have been found to be useful in working with many types of students with special needs. As you respond to each of these questions, you should compare your answer to the unique needs of the exceptional student being considered. This will enable you to focus on specific adjustments that can be made in your particular classroom.

Teaching to Different Needs at the Same Time

Grouping for instruction is a widely used procedure in regular classrooms. Grouping arrangements[1] may vary as follows:

1. Monads—individual, student-directed settings, such as cubicles.
2. Dyads—one-to-one teacher-directed settings; includes peer teaching.
3. Personal groups—groups of 3–4 students in a teacher- or student-directed setting.
4. Small groups—5–15 students, in a teacher- or a student-directed setting.
5. Large groups—15–35 students, generally in a teacher-directed setting.

Although monad- and dyad-grouping procedures are recognized as useful for individualized instruction, personal groups, small groups, and large groups are usually considered most practical for additional practice and repetition of newly learned skills, rather than for individualized instruction. However, in a regular classroom it is often necessary to provide instruction to groups of varying size and skill level during the same time period. A procedure that has been successfully used in providing individualized instruction to groups of varying size and skill levels is one known as multilevel teaching.[2] Multilevel teaching is accomplished through one of two ways:

1. Using the same materials to teach different objectives.
2. Using different materials to teach the same objectives.

---

[1] G. R. Alley, "Grouping Secondary Learning Disabled Students," *Academic Therapy*, vol. 13, no. 1 (1977), pp. 37–45.
[2] N. Peterson, *Multilevel Teaching* (Lawrence, KS: Bureau of Child Research, University of Kansas, 1979).

Several students can be working on different levels using the same materials or the same objectives, whichever is more appropriate. The steps that should be used in implementing multilevel teaching are these:

1. Define the objective for each skill and the sequence of steps necessary to teach each of these objectives.
2. Pretest each student to determine his or her entry level for a particular objective.
3. Prepare data sheets for recording performance during the instructional session. These sheets should be prepared prior to the start of the session.
4. Select materials that are easy to manipulate and adapt.
5. Present instructional tasks, record responses and other relevant information.
6. Analyze the data after each session.

Teaching Students Who Do Not Receive Special Services

In addition to those students who are mainstreamed from the special education resource or special day classes, there will be students in the regular class who have special needs but do not qualify for special education services. These students are often referred for special education assessment, and are subsequently determined to be ineligible for these services. Most of these are working significantly below grade level, and continue to fall further and further behind. Often, they have been held back, especially by the time they reach the intermediate grades. Other typical characteristics include inattention, poor listening skills, difficulty following directions, and inconsistent academic performance. The majority of these students are those students who have had chronic middle-ear problems since early development. The language deprivation associated with chronic middle-ear problems during early development may be devastating later, during the school years, even if the middle-ear disorder no longer exists. The regular classroom teacher will usually be solely responsible for providing instruction for this group of students.[1] The best educational approach to be used will depend upon two factors: whether the middle-ear difficulties are still occurring and the current age of the student. In younger students, the goal would be to teach to "fill in the gaps"; in the older student, to catch up. Specific attention should be given to overlearning skills and to developing strategies for learning.

Teaching Slow Learners, Recalcitrant Learners, Gifted Learners, Bilingual Learners, and a Class That Is Mixed

Slower learners in secondary school classes are typically of two different types of students: those students who try to learn but simply need more time to do it; and students who are capable but do not try, who are referred to as underachievers, recalcitrant, or reluctant learners. Teaching strategies that work well with those who do try are not necessarily those that work best with those students who do not or who seem unwilling to try, making it very difficult for a teacher who has a class of 30 students, half who try and half who do not. It is worse still for a teacher who has a

---

[1]R. R. Houchins and M. J. Pearson, "An Inservice Training Program to Assist Regular Classroom Teachers in Serving the Middle Hearing Impaired," *Journal of the Academy of Rehabilitative Audiology,* vol. 12, no. 2 (1979), pp. 86–94.

class of 30 students, some of whom try but have difficulty, perhaps one or two who are gifted learners, and others who seem unwilling to even try.[1] With the material that follows we will offer suggestions for working with each type of student, and then with a class that is a mix.

Guidelines for Teaching the Slow Students Who Indicate Willingness to Try

1. Emphasize basic communication skills, i.e., speaking, listening, reading, and writing.
2. Help these students improve their reading skills, i.e., pronunciation, word meanings, and comprehension.
3. Teach content in small sequential steps with very frequent (at least four during one class period) comprehension checks.
4. Vary your instructional strategies often (about every ten minutes), and use a variety of audiovisual and games materials to engage the visual, verbal, and kinesthetic.
5. Through frequent use of individual positive reinforcement, attend to increasing individual student's sense of personal worth.
6. If you are using a single textbook, be certain that the reading level is adequate for individual student use, or else discard it and rely on materials that you prepare specifically for these students.
7. You probably should not rely upon successful completion of out-of-class time student homework, unless the assignments are carefully made to ensure student success; so, we suggest that you maximize the use of in-class on-task work, the use of cooperative learning, with your close monitoring of individual student progress. You will be moving around the classroom much of the time, and our rule of thumb is that if by the end of the school day your calf muscles do not ache, then you haven't been mobile enough in the classroom.
8. At the beginning of the semester, learn as much about each of the students as you possibly can (refer to the get-acquainted activities presented in Chapter 1).
9. Be less concerned with content coverage than with the students' successful understanding of content that is covered, and with their developing self-concepts. Content knowledge testing, if used at all, is used only as an indicator of progress being made. Grading may be necessary but is largely irrelevant. Check with the school chief administrator about the possibility of using credit/no credit grading or "therapeutic" grading if you think either would be more suitable to your purposes.
10. Use cooperative learning for slow learners who need specific remediation.
11. Individualize the learning as much as possible.

Guidelines for Teaching the Recalcitrant Learners

For working with the recalcitrant learners you can use many of the same guidelines recommended for the slower learners, except that you should understand that

---

[1]Richard D. Kellough, "The humanistic approach: An experiment in the teaching of biology to slow learners in high school—an experiment in classroom experimentation," *Science Education* 54(3):253–262 (1970).

the reasons for their educational behaviors may differ. Slower learners are simply slower to learn, but can learn and are willing to learn. Recalcitrant learners may be slow, or they may even be gifted. Frequently they have inadequate self-concepts about learning, and personal problems that simply distract from their school work, and because of personal problems many have a long history of poor attention to school work habits. Consider the following guidelines.

1. Make clear your classroom behavior rules (CBRs) at the beginning of the semester, and that you intend to enforce them.
2. At the beginning of the semester, learn as much about each of the students as you possibly can (see the get-acquainted activities suggested in Chapter 1), but be cautious in how you do this because many of these students will suspect any indication of a genuine interest in them shown by you or any other adult. Be businesslike, trusting, genuinely interested, and patient.
3. Early in the semester, with the help of adult volunteers, work out an individual educational program (IEP) with each individual student.
4. Help these students improve their studying and learning skills, i.e., concentrating, remembering, and comprehension. Mnemonics, for example, is a device these students positively respond to.
5. Teach content in small, sequential steps with very frequent (at least four during one class period) comprehension checks.
6. Use a variety of audiovisual and simulation materials to engage the visual, verbal, and kinesthetic, especially designed to engage students in active learning as afforded by inquiry and real problem-solving.
7. Through frequent use of individual positive reinforcement, attend to increasing individual student's sense of personal worth. This can be accomplished in a variety of ways, such as special tutoring for individual students by adult volunteers from the community, and by group class meetings designed to diminish individual anxieties, angers, and frustrations.
8. If you are using a single textbook, be certain that the reading level is adequate for individual student use, or else discard it and rely on materials that you have prepared specifically for these students.
9. You should not rely upon successful completion of out-of-class time student homework, unless the assignments are carefully made to ensure student success; so, we suggest that you maximize the use of in-class on-task work, the use of cooperative learning, with your close monitoring of individual student progress.
10. Be less concerned with content coverage than with the students' successful understanding of content that is covered, and with their developing self-concepts. Content knowledge testing, if used at all, is used only as an indicator of progress being made. Grading may be necessary but is largely irrelevant. Check with the school chief administrator about the possibility of using credit/no credit grading or "therapeutic" grading if you think either would be more suitable to your purposes.
11. Forget about trying to use "direct or traditional" teaching techniques, such as lecturing, but rather individualize the learning as often as you possibly can. With the combined use of their IEPs (guideline 3) individual student contracts, and self-instructional packages, you have a sure-fire direction for success with these "at-risk" students, but their programs will take considerable amounts of your time and energy to prepare and implement.

Guidelines for Teaching Gifted and Talented Students

There is no absolute method that is accepted for identification of who these often-neglected students are, although for placement (in special classes or programs for the gifted and talented) in elementary, middle, and junior high school, most school districts use standard IQ testing for identification. By the time these students reach junior high school, other than having been tracked into "college preparatory" type classes, these students generally are expected to, and do, take care of themselves. Guidelines recommended for working with the gifted and talented secondary school student are:

1. Provide reading level and content achievement pretesting so you can better prescribe objectives and activities for each individual student.
2. Provide enrichment activities on an optional and voluntary basis.
3. Provide independent learning opportunities.
4. Emphasize skills in critical thinking, problem solving, and inquiry.
5. Work with individual students in planning their own objectives and activities for learning.
6. Provide in-class seminars for students to discuss topics and problems they are pursuing individually or in small groups.
7. Involve the students in inviting effective guest speakers to class.
8. Involve the students in planning relevant and interesting field trips.
9. Plan assignments and activities that challenge these students to the fullest of their abilities.
10. Become familiar with special off-campus programs specially designed for the gifted and talented[1], and encourage your students to get involved. Although special programs may be expensive, scholarships are usually available.

Guidelines for Teaching Students Who Have Limited English Proficiency

1. Limited proficiency in English (LPE) students are not always proficient in their native languages either; therefore, you may need a teaching aide to help such students make the transition to becoming truly bilingual. In many states Federal grants are available for provision of such classroom assistance. Submersion (placing an LPE student into an ordinary classroom in which English is the language of instruction, and with no special help for the student to overcome his or her language barrier) is unconstitutional.
2. Many secondary schools use a "pull-out" approach where part of the student's school time is spent in special bilingual classes, and the rest of the time he or she is placed in regular classrooms. As a classroom teacher of a regular classroom, you need to know whether your LPE students are in such a program, as you may be expected to work in conjunction with their bilingual program teacher in developing a kind of individualized education program for the LPE students.
3. If you are not bilingual yourself, or do not speak the language(s) of your LPE students, you will need to utilize multisensory approaches when working with these students.

[1]Such as those available for talented junior high and high school students at Johns Hopkins University and at California State University, Sacramento.

4. With LPE students you must use the least abstract forms of instruction (see Chapter 12, Section A).

Working with a Class That Is Mixed

It is not unlikely that as a secondary school teacher you will have a class (or more than one) of students that is mixed; that is, it will include slower learners, reluctant learners, "average" students, perhaps a gifted student, and one or more students who have limited language proficiency. To successfully work with such a class may sound impossible, and although not impossible, it will not be easy. Nobody ever said that teaching was easy. What you *must* do is individualize the instruction, whereby you first establish the interests, needs, and experiences of the students, then develop objectives, lessons, plans, and packages specifically for each individual student.

One type of specific instructional package, which has a track record of having been successfully used with a variety of types of students, is the Self-Instructional Package.

B. MULTICULTURAL EDUCATION AND WHAT A TEACHER CAN DO

Undoubtedly you have heard the term *multicultural education* many times during your professional preparation, but you may yet be unclear as to its real meaning and how, or if, you should implement it in your own teaching. Since the beginning of the Civil Rights Movements of the 1960s there has been a push to make multicultural education an integral part of the public school curriculum. The term *multicultural education* has been used interchangeably with other terms, such as *cross-cultural, interracial, intercultural, multiethnic,* and *global education.*

The term *multicultural education* is defined in various ways, depending upon the paradigms of the definer. For the purposes of this resource guide we define *multicultural education* as "a deliberate educational attempt to help students understand facts, generalizations, attitudes, and behaviors derived from their own ethnic roots as well as others. In this process the students should unlearn racism and biases and recognize the interdependent fabric of our human society, giving due acknowledgement for contributions made by all its members, and realizing the values in our cultural pluralism."

Whether you agree or disagree with our definition, you should know that educators do agree upon the following with respect to characteristics of multicultural education.

- It shows that culture is symbolically represented through language and the interactions of people.
- It teaches that everyone is ethnocentric.
- It points out that children are not born with prejudice or a set of values, but that these are learned primarily through adults and initially through the family.
- It reveals that ethnocentrism, or racism, becomes evil only when superior-inferior distinctions are used to suppress other groups.

- It teaches that we can profit from cultural diversity—the range of knowledge and the vastness of experience.
- It fosters attitudes of openness, tolerance, and acceptance.
- It illustrates that people can live and work together in a pluralistic, or multicultural, society.
- It emphasizes the equal worth and dignity of all people.
- It is interdisciplinary, and cannot be taught in isolation; it must be taught at all levels.
- It rejects the notion that *race* is synonymous with nationality, language, or culture.

Clearly, there are many characteristics to take into consideration when devising a definition of multicultural education. Given the parameters of definition, most teachers can agree that the implementation of multicultural education is important, even crucial, to the well-being of our students and human society. What remains is to determine *where* multicultural education should be implemented. Some teachers feel that such education should be taught only in certain areas: ghettos, ethnic enclaves, poverty pockets, inner cities, etc. These teachers cite the importance of emphasizing pride to those students whom most view as being at risk. However, no matter where you teach, you will have students who are different culturally, religiously, and economically. Therefore, multicultural education can and should be implemented *anywhere* in order to foster the idea that cultural diversity is positive and that we are here together as decent human beings despite our varied backgrounds.

When helping your students toward multicultural education, you must keep the following considerations in mind.

1. To know about your own identity: Who are you (as an individual and as a member of an ethnic group)?
2. To know about other groups in the community/nation: What ethnic group other than your own are in the society?
3. To know about the relationships between ethnic groups: In what way does your ethnic group work or not work together with the others?

What are some of the problems/issues historically and presently? You can design your own course of study covering these considerations through various subjects and including such areas of exploration as mythology, legends, fairy tales, folklore, biography.

In addition to the challenge of setting up a multicultural curriculum, you may also have the additional challenge of encountering some teachers and parents who think very little of multiculturalism in education. They frequently offer remarks like the following:

- "I treat all kids alike. It doesn't matter to me what skin color they have."

- "We have no problem with race or cultural differences. But we may create problems by paying attention to those differences."

- "Your class (school) is not like mine. Multicultural education is really a personal thing—some want to teach it and some don't."

- "Teaching about one's cultural roots belongs at home or possibly in a social studies class—but not in my class."
- "No matter what we teach about cultural literacy or cultural heritage, parents tell students otherwise—so what's the use?"

Despite these discouraging words, you should not give up. Schooling provides for learning about many things in life, and one of the cardinal principles of learning should be to learn about people's different cultural attributes (mores, customs, beliefs, ways and means of making a living, etc.) and to accept and appreciate cultural diversity. Once you make a commitment to multicultural education—and we think it a wise commitment—you will find that there are abundant possibilities and applications to which the subject matter can be readily modified without disturbing the already established course of study or curriculum guides. The following are some suggestions you may wish to adapt to your lesson plans.

Activities for Multicultural Education

We have not designated any subjects/courses nor any grade level for each activity. We leave the decision to the teacher as he or she sees most appropriate and workable.

"WHAT IS MY NAME?"

- Have students write their name in full.
- Does each part of the name have special meaning to it?
- Is any part in non-English? If so, what language is it?
- Can you write in your native language?
- Who gave you that name?
- If you are non-native American, is your name written the same way as in English?
- If you were to change your first and middle name, how would you want to change them?
- Why?
- Have students find the meaning of their first name in a dictionary.

"GETTING TO KNOW YOU!"

- Ask students to choose someone in the class that she or he does not already know.
- Find out the following:
  - Hobbies, things the student loves to do; things the student hates to do.
  - Favorite/least-favorite foods.
  - Place born, places traveled.
  - Any friends of different ethnic backgrounds, and how they are the same as or different from the interviewer.
  - Introduce your partner to the class.
  - Give a short biography.

"BRUSH PAINTING"

- Have students copy the following Chinese characters (calligraphy) for fun. Have them understand the meaning of each character.
- Have native people come to class to give a demonstration.

(people)　　　　(peace)　　　　(mountain)

"FAMILY TREE"

- Have students trace back their family trees four or five generations. A student who is adopted may trace the family tree of the adoptive family. Have them include any interesting tidbits about two or three family members.
- Suggestion: What does your name (first and last) mean? Are there symbols to represent your family name? Does your name change in spelling in different countries, e.g.: Smith, Smithe, Smythe, Schmidt.
- Suggestion: Have students find out why their parents, grandparents, great-grandparents, or earlier ancestors came to the United States.

"ROOTS OF MY FAMILY NAME"

- Ask students to find out what kind of family name one has, e.g., McDonald (Ireland, Scotland), Wong (Chinese).
- Does it have any special meaning? e.g., Peterson: Son of Peter; Chavez: Son of Chav.
- Is your name shorter than others? Put every student's name on butcher paper or on a transparency. See which family names are longest, shortest. Can we make some generalizations about last names in terms of length, e.g., Oriental names vs. European names?
- Are the people having the same last names related to one another? e.g., Brown, Smith, Jones, Kim, Nguyen, Caruso, Rodriguez.

"COLOR BLENDING"

- Give each student a white sheet of paper and, with crayons or watercolors, have them paint colors of the rainbow, beginning with white.

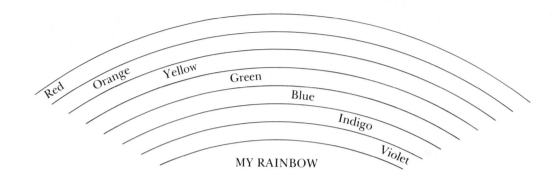

- Have students associate themselves with a color or colors, and each color as a unit of human beings, with all the colors representing society as a whole, as shown in the beginning of the section.
- Have students add some other colors in between for shading differences in color.
- Tell students that white is really the absence of color. So, when we say "white person," "white race," there is no such person, someone who has no color at all. Each person has a shade of color of some sort. Tell students about the inconsistency of labels we use. Ask students to name some adjectives that they associate with different colors. For example: white: pure, clean; red: hot-tempered. Discuss with them how true are these when we call people by such a color label!

"LANGUAGE OF THE DANCES"

- Show students films or videos of dances from various countries, including the United States (square dances, folk dances, social dances, contemporary dances).
- Have students identify something in common or something different between those dances. Does the dance have any special meaning? If so, what is it?
- Is there any particular occasion to use a particular dance? (Dragon dance in China, Hula dance in Hawaii.) Invite dancers to perform in the class or at the school.

Suggested Films

- *Chinese, Korean and Japanese Dance*
- *African Rhythms,* Associated Film, Dallas, Texas
- *Songs and Dances of the Irish,* Everest Music Shop, New York, N.Y.

"NEW AMERICANS"

- Have students look for people who have become naturalized citizens.
- Do you know or does your family know people who are not citizens of this country? What country are they from?
- How can one become a U.S. citizen?
- Invite an immigration lawyer, immigration officer, or someone who has just become a U.S. citizen to the class.

"STUDENT'S BIRTHDAY"

- Find out the birthday of each student.
- You may want to recognize students' birthdays publicly by singing the birthday song or giving a birthday card (impromptu birthday card or a note made in class).
- If you have students from non-Anglo backgrounds, ask them how birthdays are celebrated in their native land. If they have a birthday song in their native language, try singing in that language.
- If all your students come from Anglo backgrounds, have them select a country (perhaps the country from which a relative or friend came) and find out how birthdays are celebrated there.

"PLAYS/POETRY FROM OTHER LANDS"

- When you have a mixture of minority students, have them write a short role-play or skit about their background, as for a puppet show or show-and-tell.
- Have them translate a story or poem from their native language.
- If students are from Anglo backgrounds, have them tell a story or poem from one of their cultures of origin or have them choose from a different culture. How do these stories or poems compare to Anglo stories and poems?

"ROAD MAP"

- On a U.S. road map, have students find the names of places that sound "foreign" (American Indian, Spanish, French, German, etc.).
- Make a list by nationality or culture.

"MASKS OF THE WORLD"

- Locate books/magazines/posters/film/videotapes that show different kinds of masks people wear (including the United States) for various occasions.
- Have students identify what seem to be the similarities or differences in the masks made by people in other countries. Find out if there is any special meaning to each.
- Have students draw out or copy masks. Wear them. Have a class mask party and a contest.
- Local/state museums and foreign embassies may have some good lending information on these.

"SISTER SCHOOL"

- Does our school have a sister school in a sister city?
- What's the name of the school and the town? the meaning of the name(s)?
- If there is no sister school or city, would you like to have one?
- In what city or what other country?
- Write a short letter to the mayor of that town to find out how to establish a relationship with a school or the town itself.
- Have students prepare what to introduce about their own school and the town (include pictures).
- Tasks may be divided among individuals or small groups, or small groups may combine efforts in a group project.

"AMERICAN ENGLISH VS. ENGLISH ENGLISH"

Have students guess the British English words for the following:

American English	British
cookies	biscuits
hood (of car)	bonnet
canned meat	tinned meat
elevator	lift
flashlight	torch
subway	tube
garbage collector	dustman
undershirt	vest
sweater	jumper
gasoline	petrol

Also have students find out different ways of pronunciation and spelling.

"NON-ENGLISH NAMES ON THE MAP"

Use a state or national map to find non-English names on it. e.g.: San Francisco, Utah.

1. Do these names have special meanings? What are they? What language do they represent? What are the places noted for?
2. Write to the chamber of commerce in that town for more information.
3. Suppose you are going to build a new town. What non-English name would you give it? Does it mean anything? What kind of town is it going to be? Will there be different ethnic groups in it? Explain your answer.

"ENGLISH BORROWED"

English comes from many other languages.
Have students recognize some of them:

Ketchup	(Malay)
Alcohol	(Arabic)
Kindergarten	(German)
Menu	(French)
Shampoo	(Hindi)
Bonanza	(Spanish)
Piano	(Italian)
Kosher	(Yiddish)
Smorgasbord	(Swedish)

"DIFFERENT LANGUAGES"

1. What are some of the different languages spoken in the class?
2. Can you say any foreign words of any kind from greetings, asking, etc.?

Once a week:
Learn one or two words for greetings other than English. Make a chart. Use students as teachers.

"FOOD WE LIKE"

Often the foods we like originally came from other countries. Identify the country of origin for the following foods:

- Spaghetti
- Enchiladas
- Fajitas
- Wontons
- Tacos
- Quiches
- Croissants
- Teriyaki
- Fried Rice

Have students list the names and origins of other international foods. Have the students put pictures on the places to which the foods belong on a world map of medium size.

"AMERICAN FOODS—TRUE OR NOT TRUE?"

Ask students where these foods originated from:

Pizza	Chop Suey
Hot Dogs	Ice Cream Cone
Hamburgers	Submarine Sandwich
Noodles	Poor Boy
Tomato	
Chocolate	
Potato	
Hoagy	

Make a scrapbook/collage/bulletin board with the findings from the list above.

"STEREOTYPIC"

- Everyone has heard of or experienced stereotyping, for example: Girls are not as athletic as boys, boys are insensitive, women are better cooks than men, etc. Of course, stereotypes may apply to specific ethnic groups as well.
- List some stereotypes you have heard.[1]
- See if you can find examples in newspapers, magazines, movies, and television shows.
- How do you suppose that these stereotypes came to be?
- Are stereotypes harmful?

[1]For examples, see *Learning 89*, vol. 17, no. 9 (May/June 1989), p. 16.

"LOCAL MURALS"

- There are more and more murals drawn by ethnic minorities near parks, bus stations, railroad stations.
- Have students go to those places when they have time. Photograph or copy those murals. Some murals have been drawn by local artists of ethnic minorities in the community. Invite one of these artists to speak of her or his murals.

"CHOPSTICKS"

- Do you know how to use chopsticks?
- Have some of the Oriental/Asian students demonstrate the proper use of chopsticks (Teacher of the Day).
- Have them help their peers who cannot use chopsticks properly.
- Have students bring different kinds of chopsticks (wood, plastic, silver, etc.). They are not all alike.

"MAY FIFTH"

- May fifth is a special day for children in Korea, Japan, and Mexico. (Children's Day and Cinco de Mayo).
- On this day in Japan you will see pictures (kites, posters) of the carp floating all over. The carp signifies strength, perseverance, and good luck.
- Have students draw carp figures. Put them on a large drawing or bulletin board, or make a float with cloth and hang them in the class.
- What does Cinco de Mayo mean to you? Have students make a personal drawing on how they feel about Cinco de Mayo.

"ETHNIC MONTHS"

Designate different months during the school year for different ethnic groups, e.g., Black (African) month, Mexican/Chicano month, Asian month (Chinese, Vietnamese).

Have students name for the group:

1. Famous persons (both men and women).
2. Famous works of literature.
3. Music and other art forms.
4. Other accomplishments/contributions from that group.

Have a guest speaker for the month from that ethnic group.

C. DEVELOPING THE SELF-INSTRUCTIONAL PACKAGE

Exercise 9.1 will guide you through the process of preparing your first S.I.P.

EXERCISE 9.1: PREPARING A SELF-INSTRUCTIONAL PACKAGE[1]

Instructions: The purpose of this exercise is to guide you through the process of preparing an S.I.P. for use in your own teaching. Beginning here, the exercise continues through the remainder of this chapter; it is important that you follow it step-by-step, beginning with the following boxed-in "cover page."

Self-Instructional Package Number: 1
Instructor's Name: Professor R. D. Kellough
School: California State University, Sacramento
Course: Secondary School Teaching Methods
Intended Students: Middle, Junior, and Senior High Teachers
Topic: How to Write a Self-Instructional Package
Estimated Working Time: Ten hours

For the challenge of today's classroom . . .[2]

---

[1]Pages 204–215 copyright Richard D. Kellough, 1991.
[2]Certain icons copyright Apple Computer, Inc. Used with permission.

INTRODUCTION

You are about to embark upon creating and writing a perfect lesson plan. The result of your hard work will be an instructional module in which you will take a lot of pride, but more importantly, you will have learned a technique of teaching that *absolutely assures* that learning takes place. For what more could you ask?

Let us get to the essence of what the S.I.P. is. This S.I.P. is about "how to write the S.I.P.," and the objective is to gently guide you through the process of preparing and writing your first S.I.P. Let's begin the experience with background about what is the S.I.P.

THE SELF-INSTRUCTIONAL PACKAGE

A History

Research evidence indicates that student achievement in learning is related to time and *quality of attention* being given to the learning task. You knew that already! In 1968, Benjamin Bloom developed a concept of individualized instruction called "mastery learning," based on the idea that students need sufficient time-on-task to master content before moving on to new content. Did you know that? _____. (Please read along with a pencil and fill in the blanks as you go.)

Although Bloom is usually given credit for the concept of "mastery learning," the idea did not originate with him. He reinforced and made popular a model developed earlier by John Carroll. In 1968, Fred Keller developed a similar model (the Keller Plan, or PSI) that quickly became a popular teaching technique in the community and four-year colleges, but especially in community colleges. In about 1972, enter Johnson and Johnson (not the Band-Aid family, but Rita and Stuart Johnson), who developed their model of mastery learning and called it the Self-Instructional Package (S.I.P.). Since 1972 I have been developing a version, which you are now experiencing. As you will learn, *frequent comprehension checks and corrective instruction* are important to the effectiveness of the S.I.P.

One other thing. There are several devices available to individualize instruction, but the S.I.P. has the flexibility to be adaptable for use at all grade and subject levels, from kindergarten through college. Over the years, many graduate students have used this model as the focal point for thesis studies. Let us give you what we believe to be the reasons for the popularity of this strategy.

- The S.I.P. allows the instructor to *create an experience that absolutely assures learning*. Creating makes you feel good; when your students learn, you feel good—two reasons for the S.I.P.'s popularity.
- The S.I.P. is truly *individualized*, because it is a package written for an individual student, with that student in mind as it is written.
- Although it takes time to prepare, the S.I.P. *requires little financial expenditure*, a fact important to today's teacher.
- Once you have prepared your first S.I.P., it is possible that you will see that you have a series begun. Subsequent packages are easier to do, and you may see value in having a series available.

- With today's emphasis on the *basics,* the S.I.P. is particularly helpful for use in remediation.
- When you finish your S.I.P. you will have completed the content that could be used for a *computer program.*
- With today's *large and mixed-ability classes,* teachers need help! Here is time and cost-effective help!
- With emphasis today on competency (performance) based instruction, the S.I.P. makes sense.

How are we doing so far? _____. Are your interest and curiosity aroused? _____. Do you have questions? If so, write them down, then continue.

Questions: _____

_____

_____

What Is the Self-Instructional Package and Why Use It?

The S.I.P. is a learning package designed for an individual student; it is self-instructional (i.e., if you, the instructor, drop dead, heaven forbid, the student can continue to learn) *and requires about 50 minutes of learning time.* The final package can be recorded on tape, on video, on computer disc, written in booklet form, or any combination of these.

Here are ways instructors have found the S.I.P. to be useful.

- As an *enrichment* activity for an accelerated student.
- As a strategy for makeup for a student who has been absent.
- As a strategy for a student in need of *remediation.*
- As a strategy for introducing basic information to an entire class, freeing the instructor to work with individual students, making the act of teaching more *time-efficient,* a particularly significant value of the S.I.P.
- As a learning experience especially coordinated with manipulatives, perhaps in connection with a laboratory experience, or library work, with a computer, tape recording, videotape, videodisc or hands-on materials for an activity, or any combination of these.

One other point before we stop and check your comprehension. *The single most important characteristic of the S.I.P. is that it uses small, sequential steps followed by immediate and corrective feedback to the learner.* In that respect, the S.I.P. resembles "programmed instruction."

Stop the action!
Let's check your learning with the review questions and instructions that follow.

Comprehension Check 1:

Answer the following three questions; then check your responses by reviewing the following Feedback Check 1. If you answer all three questions correctly, continue the package; otherwise, back up and review.

1. How would you define what is an S.I.P.? _____

   _____

2. What is the single most important characteristic of the S.I.P.? _____

   _____

3. What is one way that the S.I.P. could be used in your own teaching, a way that currently stands out in your thinking? _____

   _____

Feedback Check 1:

1. Although we will continue development of the definition, at this point it should resemble this: The S.I.P. is an individualization of learning-teaching strategy that teaches toward mastery learning of one relatively small bit of content by building upon small, sequential steps and providing corrective feedback throughout.

2. It consists of small, sequential steps, followed by immediate and corrective feedback.

3. Your answer is probably related to one of those listed earlier, but could differ.

How Does the S.I.P. Differ From Other Kinds of Learning Packages?

Another characteristic of the S.I.P. is the *amount of learning contained in one package*. Each S.I.P. is designed to teach a relatively small amount of material, but to do it well. *This is a major difference in the S.I.P. from other types of learning activity packages.*

And, in case you have been wondering about what the S.I.P. can be designed to teach, I want to emphasize that it *can be designed*

- For any topic
  - In any discipline
    - For cognitive understanding
      - For psychomotor development
        - For affective learning.

That probably brings to your mind all sorts of thoughts and questions. Hold them for a moment and let's do another comprehension check.

Stop the Action and Check Your Learning

Comprehension Check 2:

Answer the following two questions; then check your responses in the following Feedback Check 2.

---

1. How does the S.I.P. differ from other self-contained learning packages? _____

   _____

2. Although instructors frequently emphasize learning that falls within the cognitive domain, is it possible for the S.I.P. to be written to include learning in the psychomotor and affective domains? Yes or no? _____.

Feedback Check 2:

1. Length of learning time is shorter for the S.I.P., and it is written with an individual student in mind. It is written to teach one thing well, to one student.

2. The S.I.P *can* be written for any domain, although evaluation is trickier for the affective and for the highest-level psychomotor.

Perhaps I should now say a word about what I intend when I use the expression *teach one thing well,* that is, to explain what is meant by "mastery" learning. Theoretically, if the package is being used by an individual student, performance level expectation is 100%. In reality performance level will most likely be between 85–95%, particularly if you are using the S.I.P. for a group of students rather than an individual. That 5–15% difference allows for human errors, as can occur in writing and in reading.

Now that you have learned what is the S.I.P., and how this learning strategy differs from other learning activity packages, it is time to concentrate on development of your S.I.P. Please continue.

S.I.P. DEVELOPMENT

How Do I Develop a Self-Instructional Package?

As with any good lesson plan, it takes time to develop an effective S.I.P. Indeed, preparation of your first S.I.P. will test your imagination and writing skills! Nevertheless, it will be time well spent; you will be proud of your product. *It is important that you continue following this package, step-by-step; do not skip parts, or I will assume no responsibility for your final product! Understand?* _____. Development of your S.I.P. emphasizes the importance of

- Writing the learning objectives clearly, precisely, and in behavioral terms.
- Planning the learning activities in small, sequential steps.
- Providing frequent learning comprehension checks.
- Providing immediate feedback, corrective instruction, and assurance to the learner.
- Preparing evaluative questions that measure against the learning objectives.

As you embark on preparing what may be the most perfect lesson plan you have ever prepared, keep in mind the following two points:

1. Prepare your first S.I.P. so that it will take no more than

---

50 minutes of student time.

---

2. Use a *conversational tone* in your writing. Write in the first person, as though you were talking directly to the student for whom it is intended. For example, when speaking of the learning objectives, use "You will be able to . . . ," rather than "The student will be able to . . ." Keep in mind that you are communicating to one person rather than to an entire class (even though you may be preparing your package for entire class use). It helps to pretend that you are in a one-on-one situation tutoring the student at the chalkboard.

Stop the action, and again check your learning.

Comprehension Check 3:

Answer the following two questions; then check your responses in Feedback Check 3.

---

1. What learning time duration is recommended maximum? _____.

2. What major item of importance has been recommended for you to keep in mind as you write your S.I.P.? _____

_____

_____

Feedback Check 3:

·1. Approximately one hour.

2. Write in the first person, as if you were speaking directly with the student.

Now that I have emphasized the *length of learning time and the personalization of your writing,* here are other important reminders.

3. Make your S.I.P. attractive and stimulating. Consider using cartoons, puns, graphics, scratch-and-sniff stickers, interesting manipulatives. Use your creative imagination! Use both cerebral hemispheres!

 Add sketches, diagrams, models, pictures, magazine clippings, humor, and a conversational tone, as students appreciate a departure from the usual textbooks and worksheets.

4. Use colleagues as resource persons, brainstorming ideas as you proceed through each step of package production.

 During production, use your best cooperative learning skills.

5. The package should *not* be read (or heard) like a lecture. It *must* involve small, sequential steps with frequent practice and corrective feedback instruction (as modeled in this package).

 "... and with the course material broken down into small self-instructional units, students can move through at individual rates."

6. The package should contain a variety of kinds of activities, preferably involving all three learning modalities—*visual, auditory, and kinesthetic.*

7. Vary margins, indentations, fonts, etc.,

so the final package does not have the usual textbook or worksheet appearance with which students are so familiar. Build into your package the "Hawthorne Effect."

Note about the cosmetics of your S.I.P.: My own prejudice about the S.I.P. is that it should be spread out more than the usual textbook page or worksheet. Use double-spaced lines, varied margins, etc. Make cosmetic improvements after finishing your final draft. Write, review, sleep on it, write more, revise, add that final touch. This package that you are using has been "toned down" and modified for practical inclusion in this resource guide.

8. Your S.I.P. does not have to fit the common 8½ by 11 size. You are encouraged to be creative in the design of your S.I.P.'s shape, size, and format.

9. Like all lesson plans, the S.I.P. is subject to revision and improvement after use. *Write, review, sleep on it, write more, revise, test, revise . . .*

Those are nine points to remember as you prepare your package. Perhaps before proceeding, it would be useful to review them. Remember, too, the well-written package *will assure learning*. Your first S.I.P. will take several hours to produce, but it will be worth it!

Proceed with the steps that follow.

Steps for Developing Your S.I.P.

Instructions: It is important that you proceed through the following package development step-by-step. One thing you will notice is that immediately after writing your learning objectives you prepare the evaluative test items; both steps precede the preparation of the learning activities. That is not the usual order followed by a teacher when preparing lessons, but it does help to assure that test items match objectives. Now, here we go! *step-by-step, please.*

Note: From here on, write on separate paper for draft planning.

Step 1. Prepare the cover page. It should include the following items.

- Instructor's name (that is you)
  - School (yours)
    - Class or intended students (who it's for)
      - Topic (specific but not wordy)
        - Estimated working time

For a sample, refer to the beginning of this package (Exercise 9.1). You can vary the design of the cover page according to your needs.

Step 2. *Prepare the instructional objectives.* For now, these should be written in specific behavioral terms (as learned in Chapter 7). Later, when writing these into your package introduction, you can phrase them in more general terms.

Recommended is the inclusion of at least one attitudinal (affective) objective, e.g.: "Upon completion of this package you will tell me your feelings about this kind of learning."

Step 3. Comprehension Check 4:

Share with your colleagues what you have accomplished (with Steps 1 and 2) to solicit their valuable feedback and input.

Step 4. Depending on feedback (from Step 3), *modify items 1 and 2* if necessary. For example, after listing the learning objectives, you may find that you really have more than one package in preparation, and within the list of objectives you may find a natural cutoff between packages 1 and 2. You may discover that you have a *series* of modules begun.

Step 5. *Prepare the pretest.* If the learner does well on the pretest, there may be no need for the student to continue the package. Some packages (like this one) may not include a pretest, although most will, and if this is your first S.I.P. writing experience, I think you *should* include a pretest.

Suggestion: The pretest need not be as long as the posttest, but should include a limited sample of questions to determine whether the student already knows the material and need not continue with the package. A pretest also serves to mentally set the student for the S.I.P.

Step 6. *Prepare the posttest.* The pretest and posttest could be identical, but usually the pretest is shorter. It is important that both pretest and posttest items actually test against the objectives (of Step 2). Try to keep the items objective (e.g., multiple-choice type), avoiding as much as possible the use of subjective test items (e.g., essay type), but do include at least one item measuring an affective objective (see boxed item in Step 2). If you need help in item construction, refer to Chapter 16.

Important reminder: If your package is well written, the student should *achieve 85–100% on the posttest.*

Step 7. Comprehension Check 5.:

Share with colleagues your pretest and posttest items (providing a copy of your objectives) for suggested improvement changes before continuing to the next step.

Use the following space to write notes to yourself about ideas you are having, and regarding any materials you may need to complete your package.

Dear Self.

Good work so far! Before continuing, take a break.

It is time to stop working for a while   and go play!

Step 8. *Okay, enough play, it is time to prepare the text of your S.I.P.* This is the "meat" of your package, what goes between the pretest and the posttest. It is the INSTRUCTION. Reminder: For the S.I.P. to be self-instructional, the learner should be able to work through the package with little or no help from you.

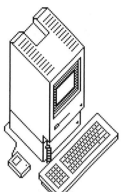

An important ingredient in your package is the *directions*. The package should be self-directed, and self-paced; therefore, each step of the package should be clear to the learner, making you, the instructor, literally unnecessary. *Everything needed by the learner to complete the package should be provided with the package.*

Use small, sequential steps with frequent practice cycles, followed by comprehension checks and corrective feedback. Make it fun and interesting with a variety of activities for the student, activities that provide for learning in several ways, from writing to reading, from viewing a videotape to drawing, from listening to a tape recording to doing a hands-on activity. And, be certain the activities correlate with the learning objectives. The learning cycles should lead to satisfaction of the stated objectives, and the posttest items *must* measure against those objectives.

Step 9. Comprehension Check 6:

Test your package. Try it out on your colleagues as they look for content errors, spelling and grammar errors, clarity, and offer suggestions for improvement. Duplicate and use the Packet Evaluation Form provided (last page of this packet).

Stop the Action
Congratulations on the development of your first S.I.P.!

However, two additional steps need your consideration.

Step 10. *Revision if necessary.* Make appropriate changes to your S.I.P. as a result of the feedback from your colleagues. Then you are ready to give your S.I.P. its first real test—try it out on the student for whom it is intended.

Step 11. *Further revisions.* This comes later, after you have used it with the student for whom it was originally intended. Like any other well-prepared lesson plan, it should always be subject to revision, to improvement, never "set in concrete."

S.I.P. PACKET EVALUATION FORM

1. Packet Identification

      Author:
      Title of S.I.P.:

2. Packet

      Objectives: do they tell the student
      a. what he or she will be able to do?

      b. how he or she will demonstrate this new knowledge or skill?

      Is there a clear statement (overview or introduction) of the importance, telling the learner what will be learned by completing the packet?

3. Pretest

4. Activities (Practice Cycles)

      Are small sequential steps used?
      Are there frequent practice cycles, with comprehension checks and corrective feedback to the learner?

5. Posttest:

      Does it test against the objectives?

6. Clarity and Continuity of Expression

7. Is the Packet Informative, Attractive, and Enjoyable?

8. Additional Comments Useful to the Author of This Packet

QUESTIONS FOR CLASS DISCUSSION

1. For years, but without success, we have attempted to get publishers interested in making available teacher-prepared self-instructional packages to other teachers. In some school districts, the district has duplicated and distributed S.I.P.s to teachers within the district. Do you have any suggestions as to how to better disseminate quality teacher-made materials like the S.I.P.?

2. Do you clearly understand how the S.I.P. differs from other kinds of instructional modules?

3. Learn how in special education the I.E.P. is developed and used, and develop ways you could implement a similar concept for use in your classes.

4. Earlier we stated that the S.I.P. would represent the most perfect lesson plan you would ever write. Now that you have written one, do you agree with our statement? Would you like to develop more? Why or why not?

5. School districts have sponsored in-service workshops for teachers from an entire department to develop a series of instructional modules for use in their teaching. Do you think this would be a worthwhile project that you would like to promote within your own district?

6. How would you go about preparing an instructional module for use by students with limited English proficiency?

7. Today, the use of video recorders is popular in the public schools. Can you think of an imaginative combination of video with the self-instructional package concept?

8. What characteristics would you look for if you believed a student to be gifted and talented?

9. What are the characteristics of an "at-risk" student, and what could the regular classroom teacher do to minimize that student's academic risk?

10. What questions do you have about the content of this chapter? How might answers be found?

SUGGESTED READINGS FOR CHAPTER 9

Baca, L. M., and Cervantes, H. T. *The Bilingual Special Education Interface.* Santa Clara, CA: Times Mirror/Mosby, 1984.

Banks, J. A., and Banks, C. A. M. *Multicultural Education: Issues and Perspectives.* Needham Heights, MA.: Allyn and Bacon, 1989.

Block, J. H., and Anderson, L. W. *Mastery Learning in Classroom Instruction.* New York: Macmillan, 1975.

Bloom, B. S. "The search for methods for group instruction as effective as one-to-one tutoring." *Educational Leadership* 41(8):4–18 (May 1984).

Charles, C. M. *Individualizing Instruction.* St. Louis, MO: C. V. Mosby, 1980.

Gearheart, B. R., and Weishahn, M. W. *The Exceptional Student in the Regular Classroom.* Santa Clara, CA: Times Mirror/Mosby, 1984.

Grant, C. A.; Melnich, S. L.; and Riven, H. N. *In Praise of Diversity: A Resource Book for Multicultural Education.* Washington, D. C.: Association of Teacher Educators, 1977.

Hardman, M.; Drew, C.; and Egan, W. *Human Exceptionality.* 2nd ed. Needham Heights, MA: Allyn & Bacon, 1987.

Horton, L. *Mastery Learning.* Fastback Series Number 154. Bloomington, IN: Phi Delta Kappa, 1981.

Johnson, R. B., and Johnson, S. R. *Toward Individualized Learning: A Developer's Guide to Self-Instruction.* Reading, MA: Addison-Wesley, 1975.

Keller, F. S., and Sherman, J. G. *The PSI Handbook: Essays on Personalized Instruction.* Lawrence, KS: TRI Publications, 1982.

Kulik, J. A. "Individualized systems of instruction." In H. E. Mitzel, ed. *The Encyclopedia of Educational Research.* 5th ed. New York: Macmillan, 1982.

Russell, J. D. *Modular Instruction.* Minneapolis: Burgess, 1974.

Stinard, T. A., and Dolphin, W. D. "Which students benefit from self-paced mastery instruction and why." *Journal of Education Psychology* 73(5):754–753 (Oct. 1981)

Want, M. C., and Wahlberg, H. J., eds. *Adapting Instruction to Individual Differences.* Berkeley, CA: McCutchan, 1985.

PART III

Choosing and Implementing Instructional Strategies in the Secondary Classroom

Part III helps you choose and implement a particular instructional strategy by:

- Providing guidelines for your use of facilitating behaviors.
- Providing skill development exercises for the use of questioning.
- Providing descriptions of the access and delivery modes.
- Providing guidelines for the use of the lecture.
- Providing descriptions of inquiry and discovery methods.
- Providing guidelines for your use of discussions, demonstrations, the textbook, and assignments.
- Providing descriptive educational games and sources of games.
- Providing guidelines for the use of audiovisual aids.
- Providing an annotated list of motivational ideas for various subject fields.
- Identifying professional journals.
- Helping you to begin your resource file.

Tell me, I forget;
show me, I remember;
involve me, I understand.
—Elaine Haglund

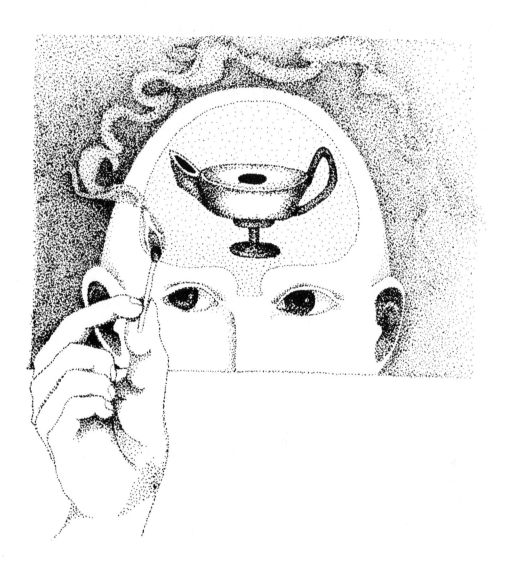

Drawing by Carol Wilson, unpublished material. Reprinted by permission.

10

What Are the Basic Teacher Behaviors That Facilitate Student Learning?

During your career as a teacher you will continue to build your strategy repertoire and to develop your teaching skills. The competent teacher has a large repertoire from which to select a specific strategy for a particular goal. In addition, that teacher has developed skill in using that strategy. This part of our resource guide is designed to assist your building of that repertoire and to begin developing your skill in the use of particular strategies.

It is important that the teacher know why he or she has selected a particular strategy. The unskilled teacher is likely to be inclined to use the strategy that was most commonly used in his or her college classes—the lecture—but, except for 15-minute minilectures, the pure lecture is seldom an effective way to instruct junior and senior high school students, and even then it needs to be supplemented with other important teacher behaviors. As discussed in Chapter 3, today's secondary teacher needs to be eclectic in strategy implementation, choosing the most appropriate combination of strategies to achieve specific goals with particular groups of students.

While there is a seemingly endless list of strategies from which to choose (see next chapter), there are basic teacher behaviors that the secondary teacher uses to facilitate student learning, almost without regard to strategy used. These facilitating teacher behaviors are those that produce the following results:

- The students are actively involved in the learning activities.
- Instructional time is efficiently used—student and teacher times are used to complete quality tasks.
- There is a minimum of classroom interruption.

The effectiveness with which a teacher implements these facilitating behaviors can be measured, and the bottom-line result of effective implementation is that *the students learn*. Let us now describe the specific teacher behaviors that create the basic conditions that enable a student to learn anything, whether that learning be a further understanding of concepts, the internalization of attitudes and values, or the development of cognitive processes and psychomotor skills.

A. FUNDAMENTAL TEACHER CLASSROOM BEHAVIORS

The following teacher behaviors create conditions needed to enable students to learn, whether that learning is a further understanding of concepts, the internalization of attitudes and values, development of cognitive processes, or actuation of the most complex psychomotor behaviors.

1. *Structuring:* The teacher establishes an environment that enables students to productively act and to react. Specific teacher behaviors are:
   - 1.1. Plans detailed lessons that begin each class meeting promptly, and end when the class period is officially ended.
   - 1.2. Learns and uses student names beginning with the first class meeting.
   - 1.3. Delineates tasks, responsibilities, and expectations.
   - 1.4. Establishes, clearing communicates, and maintains classroom rules and procedures.
   - 1.5. Provides clear definitions and instructions.
   - 1.6. Identifies time and resource constraints.
   - 1.7. Helps students organize their learning.
   - 1.8. Clearly communicates objectives.
   - 1.9. Provides reviews.
   - 1.10. Attends to the organization of the classroom so that it provides a positive, safe, and efficient learning environment.

2. *Accountability:* While holding students accountable for their learning, the teacher is willing to be held accountable for the instructional effectiveness. Specific teacher behaviors are:
   - 2.1. Attends to student questions and recitations.
   - 2.2. Requires students to demonstrate their learning.
   - 2.3. Signals to students that they may be called upon to demonstrate their learning.
   - 2.4. Plans activities that engage students in the learning.
   - 2.5. Provides continuous cues for desired learning behaviors.
   - 2.6. Provides incentives contingent upon acceptable performance, such as grades, points, rewards, privileges.
   - 2.7. Communicates to students that accomplishment of course objectives is partly their responsibility.
   - 2.8. Makes active and cooperative efforts to improve instructional effectiveness.
   - 2.9. Communicates clearly to parents, administrators, and colleagues.
   - 2.10. Establishes an understood feedback and monitoring program.

3. *Withitness and Overlapping:* The teacher demonstrates withitness by being able to intervene and redirect potential misbehavior, and overlapping by being able to simultaneously attend to several matters. Specific teacher behaviors are:
   - 3.1. Attends to entire class while working with one student or with a small group, communicating this awareness with gestures, body language, and verbal cues.
   - 3.2. Refocuses or shifts activities when student attention begins to fade.

3.3. Dwells on one topic only as long as necessary for the students' understandings.

3.4. Continually monitors classroom activities to keep students on task.

3.5. Immediately attends to an incessantly disruptive student by asking the student to leave the class and to privately meet later with the teacher.

3.6. Demonstrates an understanding of when comprehension checks are needed.

3.7. Continues monitoring the class even when a visitor comes into the classroom.

4. *Variation and Challenging:* The teacher utilizes a variety of activities that motivate and challenge students to work at the optimum of their abilities, and that reach the learning styles of more of the students more of the time. Specific teacher behaviors are:

4.1. Demonstrates enthusiasm for teaching and learning.

4.2. Demonstrates optimism toward each student's ability.

4.3. Uses interval shifts in kinds of activities and intellectual challenges.

4.4. Plans and effectively implements transition shifts that boost student interest.

4.5. Demonstrates pride in teaching.

4.6. Plans exciting and interesting lessons.

4.7. Moves lessons along with smoothness and briskness.

5. *Modeling:* The teacher's behaviors are consistent with those expected of the students. Specific teacher behaviors are:

5.1. If rational problem solving is a learning goal, the teacher demonstrates problem-solving skills.

5.2. Demonstrates respect for students.

5.3. Uses "I" when "I" is meant, "we" when "we" is meant.

5.4. Readily admits and corrects a mistake made.

5.5. Spells correctly.

5.6. Uses proper grammar.

5.7. Writes clearly and legibly.

5.8. Communicates clearly and directly to the point.

5.9. Arrives promptly to class meetings, and demonstrates on-task behaviors for entire class meeting.

5.10. Is prompt to return homework when promptness is expected of students.

6. *Data Facilitation:* The teacher makes data accessible to the students as input that they can process. Specific teacher behaviors are:

6.1. Provides clear and specific instructions.

6.2. Emphasizes major ideas.

6.3. Creates a responsive classroom environment.

6.4. Provides concrete learning experiences.

6.5. Serves as a resource person.

6.6. Uses cooperative learning, thus regarding students as potential resources.

6.7. Utilizes other faculty as resource persons.

6.8. Assures that sources of information are readily available.

6.9. Utilizes the community as a resource.

6.10. Selects textbook and student materials that facilitate student learning.

7. *Acceptance:* The teacher provides appropriate nonevaluative and nonjudgmental responses that provide a psychologically safe learning environment. Specific teacher behaviors are:
   7.1. Makes limited use of strong praise (i.e., active acceptance).
   7.2. Makes frequent use of minimal reinforcement (i.e., passive acceptance).
   7.3. Praises more frequently for student accomplishment than for effort.
   7.4. Gives paraphrasing and reflective listening.
   7.5. Gives empathic acceptance of a student's mood or expression of feelings.
   7.6. Plans within the lessons positive attendors that indicate respect for the experiences and ideas of individual students.
   7.7. Uses nonverbal cues to demonstrate awareness and acceptance of individual students.
   7.8. Writes reinforcing personalized comments on student papers.
   7.9. Provides positive individual student attention as often as possible.
   7.10. Provides incentives and rewards for student accomplishments.

8. *Clarifying:* The teacher's responding behavior seeks further elaboration from a student about that student's idea or comprehension. Specific teacher behaviors are:
   8.1. Provides step-by-step sequential learning.
   8.2. Does not proceed with the next step until the previous step is learned.
   8.3. Provides frequent review summaries.
   8.4. Assures adequate practice for the content being learned.
   8.5. Invites a student to be more specific.
   8.6. Repeats student responses, allowing the student to correct any teacher misinterpretation.
   8.7. Asks a student to elaborate on or rephrase an idea.
   8.8. Asks a student to provide a concrete illustration of an idea.
   8.9. Provides frequent (at least twice during a single class period) comprehension checks.
   8.10. Relates new content to previously learned content.

9. *Silence:* The teacher effectively uses periods of silence. Specific teacher behaviors are:
   9.1. Uses pauses during lectures.
   9.2. Uses pauses of longer than two seconds after asking a question or posing a problem.
   9.3. Uses teacher silence to stimulate group discussion.
   9.4. Uses teacher silence when students are working quietly.
   9.5. Uses teacher silence and active listening when a student is talking.
   9.6. Uses teacher silence when students are attending to a visual display that demands student concentration.
   9.7. Provides moments for reflection.
   9.8. Uses nonverbal signals and cues to maintain classroom control.

10. *Questioning:* The teacher uses questions to elicit cognitive learning and to stimulate thinking development. Specific teacher behaviors are:
    10.1. Uses a variety of questions, including questions that stimulate divergent thinking as well as those that cause convergent thinking.

10.2. Helps students develop their own questioning skills.
10.3. Plans questioning sequences that elicit a variety of thinking skills, and that move the students into higher levels of cognitive operations.
10.4. Encourages student questioning.
10.5. Is attentive to students' questions, and responds, building upon their content.

Exercises 10.1 and 10.2 are designed to evaluate your current level of competency for each of the ten teacher behaviors, and to facilitate improvement in those behaviors where you need help.

EXERCISE 10.1 FACILITATING BEHAVIORS: MY FIRST SELF-ANALYSIS

Instructions: The purpose of this exercise is for you to evaluate yourself with respect to your perceived ability to perform each of the ten facilitating behaviors described in the preceding section. After doing your self-evaluation, share it with those of your colleagues, then make appropriate revisions to your self-analysis.

Facilitating Behavior	Competent	Need Help
	(place an *X* somewhere on line)	
1. Structuring		
2. Accountability		
3. Withitness and overlapping		
4. Variation and challenging		
5. Modeling		
6. Data facilitation		
7. Acceptance		
8. Clarifying		
9. Silence		
10. Questioning		

EXERCISE 10.2: FACILITATING BEHAVIORS: MY PERSONAL PLAN FOR SKILL DEVELOPMENT

Instructions: From the analysis completed in Exercise 10.1, the purpose of this exercise is for you to develop a personal plan for strengthening of your weaker areas. Use the format that follows:

1. Behaviors needing improvement (identify by name):

2. Specific things I will do to facilitate improvement (separate for each behavior):

3. Identification of resources to facilitate my improvement (separate resources for each behavior):

4. Time line for improvements (separate for each behavior):

5. How I will know improvement has been accomplished (separate for each behavior):

B. ABOUT THE USE OF QUESTIONING

Questioning is an important and frequently used, and abused, instructional facilitating strategy. Teachers use questions for a variety of reasons, including rhetorical questions for the purpose of giving directions, such as "For this discussion, why don't we form a circle?" Questions are posed to gather information, such as "How many of you have finished the laboratory exercise?" Most significant are those questions used to guide student thinking, and that purpose is the focus of the remainder of this chapter, beginning with general guidelines for the use of questioning.

Guidelines for the Use of Questioning

The following general guidelines have been demonstrated as important for the use of questioning.

1. *Write questions in advance.* Include them in your lesson plan, to reduce ambiguity, to assure that wording is clear and specific, and to be certain you use vocabulary understood by the students.
2. *Match questions with their purposes.* Arrange the questions to the levels of cognitive thinking you expect from the students.
3. *Provide students with adequate time to think.* After asking the question, wait in silence for more than two seconds, as long as nine. *Do not answer the question yourself!* After sufficient think-time, the students will probably respond. But, if for some reason students do not respond, ask the question again, pause several seconds (more than two), then call upon a specific student.
4. *Avoid bombarding students with extra verbiage and "shotgun" questioning.* Ask the question, then be quiet.
5. *Practice calling on all the students.* And, be sure you give equal response time to all students.
6. *Use strong praise sparingly, passive acceptance frequently.* If you really want your students to think, you will be stingy with strong praise and active acceptance of responses to your questions, because strong acceptance responses from a teacher tend to cut off further thinking about the question. An example of strong acceptance is "that is absolutely right!" Passive acceptance responses tend to keep the window open for divergent and higher-level thinking. Examples of passive acceptance are "uh-huh" and "okay." Another example of passive acceptance is that, as used in brainstorming sessions, where the teacher says, "After posing the question I will write your ideas on the board." After all ideas have been recorded, the class begins consideration of each. Nonjudgmental acceptance of all ideas generates the greatest amount of thought and the highest levels of cognition.
7. *Encourage students to ask content questions.* There is no such thing as a stupid question. Occasionally students ask questions that easily could just have been looked up, thus consuming valuable class time. For the teacher this can be frustrating, and an initial reaction might be to quickly and mistakenly brush the question off with sarcasm, assuming that the student is too lazy to look it up. Our advice in such cases is for you to think before responding, and to respond kindly and professionally. Be assured, there is a reason for the question; perhaps the student is signaling a need for recognition from you. In large schools espe-

cially, it is easy for a student to feel alone and insignificant, and we believe it is a positive sign when a student initiates an effort to personally interact with the teacher. Gauge carefully your responses to those efforts. If a student question is really off track, off the wall, and out of context with the content of the lesson, consider this response: "That is an interesting question (or comment) and I would very much like to talk with you more about it. Could we meet after school?"

8. *Emphasize asking questions as more important than having right answers.* Knowledge is derived from asking questions. Being able to recognize problems and to formulate questions is the essence of problem solving and critical thinking skill development. One of the most important responsibilities of a teacher is to encourage students to formulate questions, to help them to word their questions in such a way that tentative answers can be sought.

9. *Recognize questioning as the cornerstone to critical thinking and real world problem solving.* In real world problem solving, there are no absolute right answers. The person with the problem (a) recognizes the problem, (b) formulates a question about the problem, (c) collects data, and (d) arrives at a temporarily acceptable answer to the problem, knowing that at some later date new data may force reevaluation of the former conclusion. For example, if an astronomer thinks she has discovered a new planet, there is no textbook (or teacher) to which she may refer to find out if she is correct. On the basis of her self-confidence in problem identification, asking questions, collecting data, and arriving at a tentative answer based on sufficient data, she assumes at this time her conclusion is safe.

10. *Don't bluff an answer to a question for which you do not have an answer.* Nothing will cause you to lose credibility with students any more quickly than when you fake an answer.

11. *Incorporate questions into your lessons.* Questions during a lesson provide welcomed pauses and important comprehension checks.

Cognitive Levels of Questions

Questions posed by a teacher are cues to students for the level of thinking expected, ranging from the lowest level of mental operation, requiring simple recall of knowledge, to the highest, requiring application of divergent thinking.[1] For a secondary school teacher, it is less important that a question be absolutely classified than it is for the teacher to be cognizant of hierarchies of levels of thinking and to understand the importance of attending to student development from low to higher levels of operation. What may be a matter of simple recall for one student may be a higher order mental activity for another. A competent teacher structures questions carefully in a way designed to progress students to higher levels of thinking.

Three levels of questioning are described as follows.[2]

1. *Lowest level: gathering and recalling information.* At this level questions are designed to draw from students concepts, information, feelings, or experiences acquired in the past and stored in memory. Sample key words and desired behaviors are:
   complete; count; define; describe; identify; list; match; name; observe; recall; recite; select.

[1]Arthur L. Costa, *The Enabling Behaviors* (Orangevale, CA: Search Models Unlimited, 1989), p. 2. Copyright by Arthur Costa. By permission.
[2]Costa, pp. 7–9. By permission of Arthur L. Costa.

2. *Intermediate level: processing information.* Questions at this level are designed to draw relationships of cause and effect, to synthesize, analyze, summarize, compare, contrast, or to classify data. Sample key words and desired behaviors are:

analyze; classify; compare; contrast; distinguish; explain; group; infer; make an analogy; organize; plan; synthesize.

3. *Highest level: applying and evaluating in new situations.* Questions at this level invite students to think creatively and hypothetically, to use imagination, to expose a value system, or to make a judgment. Sample key words and desired behaviors are:

apply a principle; build a model; evaluate; extrapolate; forecast; generalize; hypothesize; imagine; judge; predict.

The following exercises are designed to assist your understanding and use of questioning as a valuable instructional strategy.

EXERCISE 10.3: IDENTIFYING THE COGNITIVE LEVELS OF QUESTIONS: A SELF-DIAGNOSTIC TEST

Instructions: The purpose of this exercise is to test your understanding and recognition of the levels of questions. Mark each of the following questions with a

 1 = it is at the lowest level, gathering and recalling data.
 2 = it requires the student to process data.
 3 = it is at the highest level, requiring the student to apply or to evaluate data in a new situation.

  Check your answers with the key that follows. Resolve problems by sharing with your colleagues.

_____ 1. What was the name of the organization represented by our guest speaker?

_____ 2. How are the styles of the two artists similar? different?

_____ 3. Which of the poems do you think to be most interesting?

_____ 4. What other tools could you use to accomplish the same task?

_____ 5. What country lies between China and India?

_____ 6. How might these rocks be logically grouped?

_____ 7. Could you explain how these two types of redwood needles differ?

_____ 8. What do you predict would happen if we mixed equal amounts of 20 percent solutions of calcium chloride and sodium bicarbonate?

_____ 9. With the given notes and key signature, compose a 32-bar ballad.

_____ 10. Describe how this poem makes you feel.

_____ 11. Do you suppose everyone feels the same after reading that poem?

_____ 12. What do you think caused the United States military to pull out of Vietnam?

_____ 13. How would the world be different today had the United States military remained in Vietnam?

_____ 14. Observe what happens when I pour in the second liquid.

_____ 15. Using the formulae you learned for calculating volumes, select the correct formula to determine the volumes for each of these new figures.

Key: 1 = 1 (recall); 2 = 2 (compare); 3 = 3 (judge); 4 = 3 (speculate); 5 = 1 (recall); 6 = 2 (classify); 7 = 2 (contrast); 8 = 3 (hypothesize); 9 = 3 (compose); 10 = 1 (describe); 11 = 3 (predict); 12 = 2 (explain cause and effect); 13 = 3 (speculate); 14 = 1 (observe); 15 = 3 (apply).

EXERCISE 10.4: OBSERVING THE COGNITIVE LEVELS OF CLASSROOM VERBAL INTERACTION

Instructions: The purpose of this exercise is to develop skill in recognizing the levels of classroom questions. Arrange to visit a secondary school class, and in the spaces provided, tally the times you hear questions or statements that cause students to gather or recall information; to process information; and to apply or evaluate in a new situation. In the left hand column you may wish to write in key words to assist your memory. After your observation, compare and discuss with your colleagues.

School and class visited:

Date of observation:

BEHAVIORS OBSERVED	
At recall level. name (etc.)	
At processing level. compare (etc.)	
At application level: predict (etc.)	

EXERCISE 10.5: RAISING QUESTIONS TO HIGHER LEVELS

Instructions: The purpose of this exercise is to further develop your skill in raising questions from one level to the next. Complete the blank squares and share your responses with your colleagues.

Recall Level	Processing Level	Application Level
1. How many of you read a newspaper today?	Why did you read a newspaper?	What do you think would happen if nobody ever read a newspaper again?
2. What was yesterday's newspaper headline?	Why was that so important to be a headline?	Do you think that news item will be in tomorrow's paper?
3. Who is the Vice President of the United States?	How does he or she compare with the previous V.P.?	
4. How many Presidents has the United States had?		
5. (create your own question)		

EXERCISE 10.6: CREATING COGNITIVE QUESTIONS

Instructions: The purpose of this exercise is to provide practice in writing cognitive questions. Read the following passage; then from the passage compose three questions about the passage that cause students to identify, list, and recall; three that cause students to analyze, compare, and explain; and three that cause students to predict, apply, and hypothesize. Share and check responses with your colleagues.

A Short Course in Human Relations

The SIX most important words:
"I admit I made a mistake."
The FIVE most important words:
"You did a good job."
The FOUR most important words:
"What is your opinion?"
The THREE most important words.
"If you please."
The TWO most important words:
"Thank you."
The ONE most important word:
"We"
The LEAST important word:
"I"

—Unknown

Recall Questions:

1. (to identify) _____

_____

_____

2. (to list) _____

_____

_____

3. (to recall) _____

_____

_____

Processing Questions: 1. (to analyze) _____

_____

2. (to compare) _____

_____

3. (to explain) _____

_____

Application Questions: 1. (to predict) _____

_____

2. (to apply) _____

_____

3. (to hypothesize) _____

_____

_____

EXERCISE 10.7: ANALYZING THE LEVEL OF QUESTIONS IN TEXTBOOKS

Instructions: The purpose of this exercise is to examine course materials for the levels of questions presented to students. Examine a textbook for the course you intend to teach, specifically examining questions posed for the students, perhaps at the ends of the chapters. Also examine workbooks, examinations, instructional packages, and any other written materials used by students in the course.

Complete this exercise as follows:

1. Materials examined:

2. Examples of level one (input recall) questions found:

3. Examples of level two (processing) questions found:

4. Examples of level three (application) questions found:

5. Approximate percentages of questions at each level:

     Level one = ____%   Level two = ____%   Level three = ____%

6. Did you find evidence of question-level sequencing? Describe.

EXERCISE 10.8: MICRO PEER TEACHING 1: THE USE OF QUESTIONING

Instructions: The purpose of this exercise is to practice preparing and implementing questions designed to lead student thinking from the lowest level to the highest. Prior to class, prepare a *five-minute lesson* for the purpose of posing questions that will guide the learner from lowest to highest levels of thinking. Teaching will be one-on-one, in groups of four, with each member of the group assuming a particular role—teacher, student, judge, or recorder. Each of the four members of your group will play each of the roles once, five minutes each time. The exercise takes approximately 30 minutes to complete.

Suggested lesson topics:

• About teaching styles
• About evaluation of student achievement
• About some skill or hobby
• About your developing teaching competencies
• About a particular teaching strategy

In class, divide into groups of four:

Teacher: Pose recall, processing, and application-level questions related to one of the topics above, or any topic you choose.

Student: Respond to the questions of the teacher.

Judge: Identify the level of each question of the teacher and the corresponding level of thinking demonstrated by the student.

Recorder: Tally the number of each level of question or statement used by the teacher; tally the level of student response. Record any problems encountered by your group.

TALLY SHEETS FOR EXERCISE 10.8

		Min.	Input	Processing	Output
Sender _____		1			
Receiver _____		2			
		3			
		4			
		5			

	Min.	Input	Processing	Output
Sender —————————————	1			
Receiver ————————————	2			
	3			
	4			
	5			

	Min.	Input	Processing	Output
Sender —————————————	1			
Receiver ————————————	2			
	3			
	4			
	5			

	Min.	Input	Processing	Output
Sender —————————————	1			
Receiver ————————————	2			
	3			
	4			
	5			

EXERCISE 10.9: IDENTIFYING BASIC TEACHER BEHAVIORS IN CLASSROOM INTERACTION[1]

The following is a sample classroom interaction. There are examples of various levels of questions and structuring and response behaviors. See if you can identify them. Your answers should be from this list: structuring; facilitating; acceptance—active; acceptance—passive; clarifying; questioning—input; questioning—processing; questioning—application. Compare your answers with those at the end of the exercise.

	Interaction	Teacher's Behavior
John:	Mr. Brown, here's a picture that shows how a magnet works.	
Teacher:	O.K. John, would you please share this with the rest of the group? Tell us what you think is happening.	1. _____
John:	Well, this boy is in the garage using a magnet to pick up things, and over here it shows all the things a magnet will pick up.	
Teacher:	What kind of things are they, John?	2. _____
John:	Nails, paper clips, spoons, screws, screwdri . . .	
Jim:	It will not pick up spoons, John. I've tried it.	
John:	It will too. It shows right here.	
Bill:	I picked up a spoon with a magnet that my uncle gave me.	
John:	Sure it will!	
Gregory:	No it won't, 'cause . . .	
Teacher:	Just a minute. We'd like to hear everyone's idea, but we can't if we all talk at once. If you'll raise your hand, then I'll know who to call on next.	3. _____
Teacher:	Now, John says a magnet will pick up spoons. Bill says he has picked up one. Jim says that a magnet can't pick it up.	4. _____
Teacher:	Yes, Cathy, what do you think?	5. _____
Cathy:	I'm not sure, but I think it has to be metal.	
Maria:	I think it depends upon the kind of spoon. Some spoons have metal and some are plastic and other stuff.	
Teacher:	That's another possibility.	6. _____
Teacher:	How can we solve this problem as to whether a magnet will pick up the spoons?	7. _____
Jim:	We can get some spoons and try it with our magnet.	
Teacher:	All right. Anybody know where we can get some spoons?	8. _____
Shelly:	There's a spoon in my lunch bag.	

[1]Costa, op. cit., pp. 75–78. Reprinted by permission.

(continued)

Interaction	Teacher's Behavior

Bill: There are some spoons in the cafeteria. Can we go and get them?

Teacher: Yes. Shelly, would you get yours? Bill, would you get some from the cafeteria? John, would you get the magnet?

9. _____

Later

Teacher: Now, because this is Shelly's spoon, what do you think would be the fair thing to do?

10. _____

Cathy: Let her try it on her own spoon.

Teacher: All right, Shelly, what do you think will happen when we touch the magnet to the spoon?

11. _____

Shelly: It probably won't pick it up because it's not the right kind of stuff for a magnet to pick up.

Teacher: What do you mean, "the right kind of stuff?"

12. _____

Gregory: She means the right kind of metal.

Teacher: Shelly, would you try it? Let's all watch.

13. _____

Jim: See, I told you a magnet wouldn't pick up a spoon.

Rick: But it does pick up some spoons.

John: I don't mean all spoons, only those made of metal. The spoon in the book is made of metal.

Maria: Is this pin out of steel?

Teacher: No, Maria, it isn't.

14. _____

Maria: I thought it was steel or stuff like that—like a piece of car.

Teacher: I don't understand what you mean, Maria. What do you mean, "a piece of car?"

15. _____

Maria: When mom banged up our fender, you could see the shining metal under the paint. Dad said it was steel.

Gregory: I think the most powerful magnet in the world might be able to pick it up.

Cathy: An electromagnet, I think, is the strongest magnet that was ever invented by the earliest scientist.

Teacher: Are you saying, Cathy, that you think a stronger magnet would pick up the spoon?

16. _____

Cathy: Um—hm. I think so.

Teacher: What would you want to do to find out?

17. _____

Cathy: We could set up our electromagnet and try it.

Teacher: O.K.

18. _____

Key to Exercise 10.9: Identifying Basic Teacher Behaviors in Classroom Interaction

1. Structuring
2. Question-Input (Listing)
3. Structuring
4. Accepting—Actively
5. Question—Processing (Explaining)
6. Accepting—Passively
7. Question—Processing (Problem solving)
8. Question—Input (Locating)
9. Facilitating Acquisition of Data—Note: This might also be interpreted as a structuring behavior since the teacher directs the students to perform a task.
10. Question—Application (Evaluation)
11. Question—Application (Predicting)
12. Clarifying
13. Facilitating the Acquisition of Data
14. Facilitating the Acquisition of Data
15. Clarifying
16. Clarifying
17. Question—Processing (Planning)
18. Accepting—Passively

QUESTIONS FOR CLASS DISCUSSION

1. Have you noticed that some teachers seem to anticipate a lower-level response to their questions from particular students?
2. While watching a television or radio news or talk-show program, have Exercise 10.4 with you, and identify and analyze the types of questions used.
3. In your field to what extent are teachers expected to teach "critical thinking"? How is it done? How effectively?
4. In your teaching field, to what extent can a teacher assist students in identifying and resolving real life conflicts?
5. With respect to your teaching field, what research can you find about the relationships between task time and learning gains?
6. With respect to your teaching field, what research can you find about the relationships between the type and quality of teacher questions and student learning?
7. Do female secondary school students learn any differently than do male students, or should the question even be asked?
8. When using questioning does a teacher need to be concerned about how students from different cultures might respond to certain types of questions?
9. With respect to your discipline is teaching-learning different from that in other disciplines? Do students in your discipline think differently from those in other disciplines? What research evidence can you find about this?
10. What questions do you have about the content of this chapter? How might answers be found?

SELECTED READINGS FOR CHAPTER 10

Belenky, M., et al. *Women's Ways of Knowing.* New York: Basic Books, 1986.

Brown, G. A., and Edmondson, R. "Asking questions." In E. C. Wragg, ed. *Classroom Teaching Skills.* London: Croom Helm, 97–120 (1984).

Brown, S. I., and Walter, M. I. *The Art of Problem Posing.* Philadelphia: The Franklin Institute Press, 1983.

Costa, Arthur L., *Developing Minds: A Resource Book for Teaching Thinking.* Washington, DC: Association for Supervision and Curriculum Development, 1985.

Dillon, J. T. *Questioning and Teaching: A Manual of Practice.* New York: Teachers College Press, 1988.

Emmer, E. T., et al. *Classroom Management for Secondary Teachers.* Englewood Cliffs, NJ: Prentice Hall, 1989.

Kerry, T. *Effective Questioning.* London: Macmillan, 1982.

Seifert, E. H., and Beck, J. J., Jr. "Relationships between task time and learning gains in secondary schools." *Journal of Educational Research* 78(1):5–10 (September–October 1984).

Smith, H. A. "The marking of transitions by more and less effective teachers." *Theory Into Practice* 24(1):57–62 (Winter 1985).

11

What Are the Guidelines for the Use of Lectures and Other Discretionary Instructional Strategies?

Chapter 10 discussed specific teacher enabling behaviors, including presentation of guidelines for the inevitable use of questioning. In this chapter we focus attention on discretionary instructional strategies.

To achieve a particular goal with a given class, a secondary school teacher has a large repertoire from which to choose a specific instructional strategy. Selection of a particular strategy depends in part upon a teacher's decision whether to directly deliver information to students or to provide students with access to information.

A. FIRST DECISION IN STRATEGY SELECTION: THE DELIVERY OR THE ACCESS MODE?

When selecting an instructional strategy there are two distinct choices from which a decision needs to be made: whether as a teacher you desire to deliver information to the students, or whether you prefer to provide access to information. The traditional mode is to deliver information; that is, knowledge is passed on from those who know (the teacher and the textbook) to those who do not (the students). Within the delivery mode, traditional and time-honored strategies are textbook reading, lecturing, questioning, and discussion.

With the second avenue, the access mode, instead of direct delivery of information, the teacher provides access to information by designing experiences that facilitate students' obtaining new knowledge and skills. Research indicates that student learning may be better when taught by a teacher using this mode. Within this mode an important instructional strategy is inquiry, which most certainly will involve the use of questioning, although the questions likely will come from students. Discussions and lectures, too, may be involved in an inquiry.

It is likely you are more experienced with the delivery mode, and although this chapter provides guidelines for the use of strategies within that mode, you must also become knowledgeable and skillful with the use of access strategies. The intent is *not* to imply that one mode is unquestionably more favorable, but to encourage your skill development with both. Thus, in this chapter you become knowledgeable about use of techniques within each mode so as a teacher you can make intelligent decisions for choosing the best strategy for particular goals and objectives for your own subject and unique classes of students.

DELIVERY MODE: ITS STRENGTHS AND WEAKNESSES

The *strengths* of delivery strategies *are:*

- Much content can be covered within a short span of time, usually by a lecture, which may be followed by an experiential activity.
- The teacher is in control of what content is covered.
- The teacher is in control of time allotted to topic coverage.
- These strategies are consistent with performance-based teaching.
- Student achievement is predictable and manageable.

The *potential weaknesses* of delivery strategies *are:*

- The sources of student motivation are mostly extrinsic.
- Students have little control over pacing of their learning.
- Students make few important decisions about their learning.
- There may be little opportunity for divergent or creative thinking.
- Student self-esteem may be inadequately attended.

ACCESS MODE: ITS STRENGTHS AND WEAKNESSES

The *strengths* of access strategies *are:*

- Students learn content, and in more depth.
- The sources of student motivation are more likely intrinsic.
- Students make important decisions about their learning.
- Students have more control over pacing of their learning.
- Students develop a sense of self worth.

The *potential weaknesses* of access strategies *are:*

- Content coverage is more limited.
- Access strategies are time-consuming.
- The teacher has less control over content and time.
- The outcomes of student learning are less predictable.
- The teacher may have less control over class procedures.

From the preceding you can see that the strengths and weaknesses of one mode are nearly exact opposites of those of the other. Competent teachers should be skillful in the use of strategies from both modes.

As a secondary school teacher you will be pleased to know that there is a wide range of strategies from which to choose (see the list that follows), some of which by their very nature are delivery, while others may more easily be classified as access. For example, as typically used, lecturing is delivery mode, while pure inquiry is access mode. Ideally, a strategy selected in one instance complements the next. For example, a lecture could be used both as a closure to an inquiry investigation, and as a transition to the next topic of study.

A LISTING OF INSTRUCTIONAL STRATEGIES

Assignment	Laser videodisc
Audiovisual equipment	Lecture
Cooperative learning	Library/resource center
Computer-assisted	Mock up
Debate	Panel discussion
Demonstration	Periodicals
Discovery	Problem solving
Discussion	Project, independent study
Drama	Questioning
Drill	Review and practice
Expository	Role play
Field trip	Self-instructional package
Game	Simulation
Group work	Study guide
Guest speaker	Symposium
Homework	Telecommunication
Individualized instruction	Term paper
Inquiry	Textbook
Laboratory investigations	Tutorial

Rule in Planning

An important rule in planning learning activities is to select experiences that are as concrete and as direct as possible (see beginning of next chapter), where the students are actually doing that which they are learning to do. For example, if a chemistry teacher is teaching the students how to bend glass tubing, it is aphoristic that the most effective way to teach that is to actually have the students bend glass tubing. That is referred to as "learning by doing," or "hands-on learning." The least effective would be for the chemistry teacher to lecture about bending glass tubing *without ever* allowing the students to do it. That is analogous to teaching young children the alphabet without ever allowing them to put letters together to make words.

Concrete learning, like that provided by the access mode, is usually the most lasting learning. However, it is not always feasible. So, sometimes the teacher must use learning strategies that are less concrete. Most frequently used is the lecture, but even so, the lecture need not be so abstract.

B. USING THE LECTURE: TWENTY IMPORTANT GUIDELINES

For many secondary school teachers, lecturing is inevitable. For students, a well-planned and executed lecture can be an exciting learning experience. "Effective lecturers combine the talents of scholar, writer, producer, comedian, showman, and teacher."[1] However, a poorly planned and delivered lecture will create more problems than you can imagine!

Careful planning, timing, and practice help to develop lecturing skills. With the following guidelines you can develop your lecturing effectiveness.

1. *Purposes of a lecture.* A lecture can serve for any one, or combination, of the following purposes.
   • Introduce a unit of study.
   • Present a problem.
   • Summarize a problem.
   • Explain an inquiry.
   • Provide "cutting edge" information otherwise unobtainable to students.
   • Share the teacher's experiences.
   • Promote student inquiry or critical thinking.
   • Provide transition from one unit of study to the next.
2. *Objectives of the lecture.* A lecture should center around one major theme, and the learning objectives of the lecture, not too many for one lecture, should be made known to the students; otherwise, the students may never know what it was about.
3. *Short informal lectures.* Although an occasional 45-minute "cutting edge" lecture may, for some classes, be appropriate, spontaneous interactive mini-lectures (10–15 minutes) are preferable over those where there is no teacher–student interaction and that last an entire class meeting. In either case, remember that in today's world students are used to "commercial breaks"; consequently, about 10 minutes into your lecture student attention will begin to drift, at which time you need to have elements planned to recapture their attention, and that will help make the lecture more concrete.

   Elements planned to recapture student attention can be *verbal cues,* such as voice inflections, planned pauses to allow information to sink in, name dropping (discussed later), and humor; or *visual cues,* such as the use of slides, realia, or body gestures; or *sensory cues,* such as moving around the room, casually touching a student without interrupting the lecture, or using an odorous substance to reinforce a topic.

[1]From Wilbert J. McKeachie, *Teaching Tips: A Guidebook for the Beginning College Teacher,* 8th ed. (Lexington, Mass.: D. C. Heath, 1986), p. 69.

4. *Lecture notes for the lecturer.* Preparation of lecture notes is as important and as difficult as is presenting the lecture. Lecture notes should be prepared in narrative form, reduced to an outline of main sections and subsections for the presentation. The lecture is then given from the outline, rather than read from prose.

   In a lecture outline, it is helpful to use color coding with abbreviated visual cues to yourself. Examples of such coding are:
   - Where transitions of ideas occur, mark "pause," or "T," for transition.
   - Where a slide or other visual aid will be demonstrated, mark "AV," for audio-visual.
   - Where to stop and ask a question, mark "Q" or "?."
   - For periodic summaries and comprehension checks, mark "S," or "CS."

5. *Rehearse the lecture.* Rehearse the lecture with a videorecorder, or an audiorecorder, allowing 30 minutes of real class time for a rehearsed lecture that took 20 minutes. In other words, the "live" lecture will take more time than when rehearsed. Some teachers rehearse their lectures in front of mirrors, or with their families. Plan the lecture so it includes a set, lecture body, and a closure. In your lecture outline, including a time plan for each subtopic allows you to gauge your time during lecture implementation.

6. *Don't race through the lecture solely to complete it by class dismissal time.* It is more important that students understand some of the planned content, than that you covered it all and they understood none of it. If you didn't get finished, continue the lecture at the next class meeting, and revise the subsequent class schedule accordingly.

7. *Pacing.* Pacing should be moderate and varied, and interspersed with pauses, verbal (ask questions) and visual (observe student facial gestures and body language) comprehension checks to see if students are understanding the lecture.

8. *Augment the lecture with multisensory stimulation.* This is so the lecture does not rely solely upon verbal communication. When using visuals, such as slides and overhead transparencies, don't think that you must be constantly talking; clearly explain the purpose of the visual, give students time to look at the visual, to think about it, and to ask questions.

9. *Intersperse the lecture with planned attention getters.* This might include student name-dropping, perhaps during comprehension checks. Plan an inclusion of tasteful and appropriate humor.

10. *Content of the lecture.* Rather than to simply repeat or to condense content of the textbook, the lecture material should augment and enhance it. Students are less likely to read the textbook when the teacher's lectures summarize it for them.

11. *Voice.* The lecturer's voice should be pleasant and interesting to listen to, rather than a monotone or a shrieking, irritating, high pitch. Dramatic inflections can be used to emphasize important points.

12. *Vocabulary used.* Words used should be easily understood by the students, while still modeling professionalism. Predict when you are likely to use a word that is foreign to many of the students, stopping to explain its meaning and perhaps its derivation as well. For example, students in biology are more likely to remember the meaning of hermaphroditism when the teacher, after presenting the word, stops to explain its derivation, Hermes (Greek Messenger of the Gods) and Aphrodite (Greek Goddess of Love and Beauty). Plus, the introduction of a bit of Greek mythology is likely to make the biology class a bit more interesting to those students who are only taking the course because it is required.

13. *Lecture only when appropriate.* Do not lecture if a written handout would be better. Many secondary school students can *read and understand faster than they can listen and understand.*

14. *Provide students with a written skeletal outline.* This facilitates their understanding and organization of the lecture material. However, we emphasize the importance of it being a skeletal outline, rather than a complete printed copy of the lecture.

15. *Lecture introduction.* Establishing how you will begin the lecture is probably best done after you have completed your lecture notes. Begin the lecture with a planned and effective entry that captures student attention and sets the preferred mood for the lesson.

    We know of several teachers who play music to set a mood for a lecture. One study reported that students achieved better in calculus when soft background classical music is played during class.

16. *Use familiar examples.* Incorporate ideas and events with which the students are already familiar. A good lecture bridges the gap between what students already know and what they are learning.

17. *Consider students with special needs.* While preparing the lecture, consider the handicapped, the culturally and linguistically different, and other students with special needs, designing the lecture to personalize with the use of special analogies, examples, and appropriate name-dropping. Remember, a real attention getter, the most beautiful sound in the whole world is hearing your own name, of course in a positive manner and in good taste.

    Name-dropping, for example, and as we have used it in this resource guide, involves using a particular student's name in the middle of a sentence during a lecture.

18. *Establish frequent eye contact with students.* With a class of 25 students you can learn to visually scan your audience and *establish* eye contact with each student about once every 45–60 seconds. Frequent eye contact has two major benefits: it provides clues about student attentiveness and comprehension; and helps to establish a rapport between the lecturer and individuals of the audience. Frequent eye contact is easier when using an overhead projector than when using a chalkboard.

19. *Summary and follow-up.* Closure and follow-up experiences should be planned that allow students to question, discuss, and to synthesize the material. Because lecture learning is largely passive learning, a lecture should include or be followed by activities that engage students in active learning.

20. *Obtain feedback about the lecture.* Feedback may be obtained from students so you have an idea how well received and understood was the lecture. For this purpose some teachers early in the semester identify a small group of students who volunteer for the responsibility of periodically reporting to the teacher to give informal feedback about the course and its activities.

    Formal student feedback can be obtained by having the students complete a checklist or brief questionnaire about the lecture. Other ways of obtaining feedback about your lecture are to videotape the lecture, and do a self-evaluation, or have a colleague sit in on your lecture or watch the videotape, and discuss it with you, or collect from a sample of your students their lecture notes and compare their notes with yours.

EXERCISE 11.1: MICRO PEER TEACHING 2: PLANNING AND IMPLEMENTING A LECTURE

Instructions: The purpose of this exercise is for you to plan and implement a 15-minute lecture to your peers (the exact time allotted shall be decided by your course teacher or workshop leader). Your lecture should be videotaped for you to watch and critique. Addressing the previously presented guidelines, prepare your lecture using the following format. Complete items 1–3 on this form and attach to your lecture outline.

1. Purpose of the lecture:

2. Topic of the lecture:

3. Why other strategies were ruled out (why lecturing is the best strategy for this topic):

4. Lecture content outline with a time plan for subtopics:
(Note: Item 4 is to be presented on separate paper with items 5–7 below incorporated in your outline.)

5. Planned set:

6. Planned closure:

7. Planned cues:

Post-implementation analysis instructions: Following the presentation of your lecture, and your review of it on videotape, prepare a summary analysis that indicates the strengths and weaknesses of your lecture, including what specific improvements you would make were you to repeat it. Your analysis should specifically address guidelines 1–9, 11–12, and 14–19, presented immediately prior to this exercise.

C. USING INQUIRY AND DISCOVERY: THE DIFFERENCE

Among teachers there is frequent confusion as to exactly what inquiry teaching is. Sometimes, and understandably so, inquiry is confused with discovery. The following paragraphs provide descriptions of these two important teaching strategies.

Inquiry Versus Discovery

The major reason inquiry and discovery are confused is that in both students are *actively engaged in problem solving*. Provision for practice in problem solving is a major advantage offered by both strategies. To understand the difference between the two strategies it is helpful to study the following chart, identifying *three levels of inquiry, according to what the student does*.

LEVELS OF INQUIRY

	I	*II*	*III*
Problem Identification	Identified by teacher or textbook	Identified by teacher or textbook	Identified by student
Process of Solving the Problem	Decided by teacher or textbook	Decided by student	Decided by student
Identification of Tentative *Solution* to Problem	Resolved by student	Resolved by student	Resolved by student

From the preceding chart, it should be apparent that what is referred to as Level I Inquiry is in fact traditional, didactic, "cookbook" teaching, where a problem is defined for the student, as is the process for working through the problem to the inevitable solution; if the "program" is well designed, the end result is inevitable as the students "discover" that which was intended. This level of inquiry is also referred to as *guided inquiry* or as *discovery*. The students are carefully guided through the process to "discovery."

Level I Inquiry is in reality a strategy within the *delivery mode*, the advantages of which were described at the beginning of this chapter. As it is highly manageable and the learning is predictable, it is probably best for teaching fundamental concepts and principles. However, students who never experience beyond Level I are missing an opportunity to engage their highest mental operations, and do not experience more motivating, real-life problem solving. Furthermore, those students come away with the false notion that problem solving is a linear process, which it is not!

Secondary school students should be provided experiences for true inquiry, which begins with Level II, where students actually design the processes for their inquiry. *True inquiry is cyclic rather than linear!* The cycle is illustrated in the following diagram.

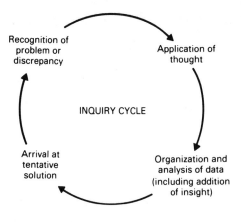

One enters the inquiry cycle whenever a discrepancy is observed, and that can occur at any point in the cycle. In true inquiry we emphasize the tentative nature of conclusions, which makes it more like real-life problem solving, where decisions are based on data, with recognition that those decisions are subject to revision when new data arrive.

In Level III Inquiry, students actually identify the problem as well as decide the processes and reach a conclusion. When using individual projects and independent study as instructional strategies, secondary school teachers are engaging students in this level of inquiry.

The Processes

In inquiry learning the students generate ideas and then design ways to test their ideas. The processes are varied—some are concerned with generating and organizing data, others with building and using ideas. The following diagram illustrates processes in each of these operations.

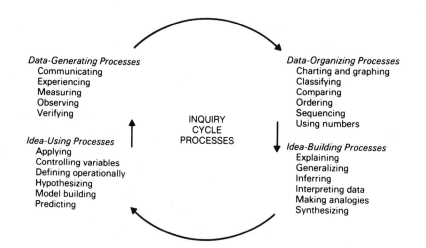

While some processes in the cycle are *discovery,* others are *inquiry.* Inquiry processes are more complex mental operations (all of those in the idea-using category). Children who have reached adolescence are in process of developing formal thought capabilities and should be provided experiences requiring the more complex, higher-level inquiry skills. Such is certainly the case for secondary school students.

Inquiry learning is a higher-level mental operation that introduces the concept of the *discrepant event,*[1] a concept of surprise which helps learners to develop skills in observing and being alert for discrepancies, and provides opportunities for students to investigate their own ideas about explanations. Inquiry, like discovery, is a problem-solving strategy; the difference is in the amount of decision-making responsibility given to the students. Inquiry also helps students understand the nature and importance of suspension of judgment, the tentativeness of "answers" and "solutions," and to better deal with ambiguity.

Promoting Inquiry

Now that you understand the differences between discovery and inquiry, you need to understand the nature of the classroom environment that promotes inquiry. First, let us emphasize that *dogmatic teaching is lethal to true inquiry,* whereas freedom of thought enhances the environment as if it were a think tank, encouraging guessing and intuitive thinking. Healthy skepticism and practice in suspending judgments are behaviors prized in inquiry, and the teacher's modeling of those behaviors counts!

An *open classroom* environment is more conducive to effective inquiry teaching. It requires planning, conviction, self-control, cooperation, and trust, while allowing for serendipity, and places a value on mistakes and on diversity. Openness is not to be confused with permissiveness and ineffective instruction, and it does not imply that there is no content that all students need to learn in a more traditional way.

Retention from inquiry learning is superior to the rate of learning from most other teaching strategies, and the highly personal involvement of the learners is a positive contributor to their feelings of self-worth. However, it takes time and practice for a teacher to develop skills and confidence necessary for effective implementation of inquiry.

Mystery Island: An Inquiry Lesson[2]

One of the most effective ways of stimulating inquiry is to use materials that provoke the students' interest. These materials should be presented in a non-threatening context, such as a game or puzzle, in which students can think, and hypothesize freely. The teacher's role is to encourage the students to form as many hypotheses as possible and to be able to back up these hypotheses with reasons. After the students suggest several ideas, the teacher should begin to move on to higher-order, more abstract questions that involve the development of generalizations and evaluations.

---

[1]Events that seem improbable, and that set the mind into immediate and automatic activity to attempt explanations; in Piaget, referred to as creating "cognitive disequilibrium."
[2]Jack Zevin, "Today's Education," *NEA Journal* (May 1969), pp. 42–43. Reprinted by permission.

Inquiry lessons, such as the Mystery Island geography problem presented here, have a special advantage because they can be used with almost any group of students, regardless of ability. Members of each group approach the problem as an adventure in thinking and apply it to whatever background they can muster. Background experience may enrich a student's approach to the problem but is not crucial to the use or understanding of the evidence presented to him or her.

Mystery Island is presented as it is given to students. They receive information about the island in sequence. Map 1 includes data about rivers, lakes, and size (scale). This map is followed by information about landforms (Map 2), vegetation (Map 3), and climate (Map 4). Other data maps, showing mineral deposits or transportation networks, for example, could easily be added to this series.

All students are asked to solve the same problem after getting each new piece of information. The key problem is to locate "the biggest city." Students are asked, in effect, to accumulate geographic evidence about a place, to form hypotheses, to review these hypotheses in the light of new evidence, and to refine their notions about the reasons underlying the location of cities.

After introducing each new element of Mystery Island, the instructor could ask: "Now that you have this information about Mystery Island, what additional information would be most important to you in understanding the Island? Explain why." Other questions could include: "Where would most people live?" "Where would the least number of people live?" and "What would people do for a living on Mystery Island?"

All student hypotheses or predictions about the location of cities, population distribution, or the economy of Mystery Island should be backed by reasons. These hypotheses can then be analyzed, discussed, and evaluated by the class as a whole.

In addition to analytical problems concerning Mystery Island, value issues may also be proposed for solution. One such issue could center on the clash that occurs when a technologically advanced culture and a technologically undeveloped culture meet on the island. For example, what would happen if Mystery Island were inhabited by a group of hunters and gatherers and was then invaded by people of a different racial or ethnic origin who possessed superior skills?

Students could be asked such questions as: Should the original population be allowed to mix with the new people? What problems will each group face if they live separately? If they live together? What would be best for all concerned parties? Why?

The reader is invited to look at Mystery Island and try to solve the problem posed to the students—locating the biggest city on the island. Take into account all the evidence provided here and make a list of reasons to back up your decision.

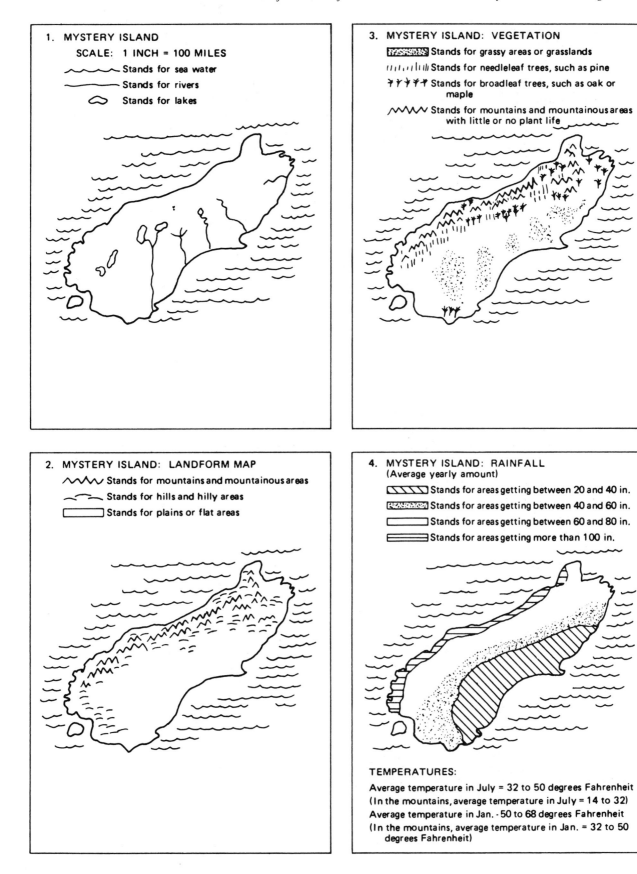

1. MYSTERY ISLAND
   SCALE: 1 INCH = 100 MILES
   —Stands for sea water
   —Stands for rivers
   —Stands for lakes

2. MYSTERY ISLAND: LANDFORM MAP
   —Stands for mountains and mountainous areas
   —Stands for hills and hilly areas
   —Stands for plains or flat areas

3. MYSTERY ISLAND: VEGETATION
   Stands for grassy areas or grasslands
   Stands for needleleaf trees, such as pine
   Stands for broadleaf trees, such as oak or maple
   Stands for mountains and mountainous areas with little or no plant life

4. MYSTERY ISLAND: RAINFALL
   (Average yearly amount)
   Stands for areas getting between 20 and 40 in.
   Stands for areas getting between 40 and 60 in.
   Stands for areas getting between 60 and 80 in.
   Stands for areas getting more than 100 in.

   TEMPERATURES:

   Average temperature in July = 32 to 50 degrees Fahrenheit
   (In the mountains, average temperature in July = 14 to 32)
   Average temperature in Jan. - 50 to 68 degrees Fahrenheit
   (In the mountains, average temperature in Jan. = 32 to 50 degrees Fahrenheit)

D. USING CLASSROOM DISCUSSIONS

Having, for at least 16 years, been a student in formal learning, you are undoubtedly knowledgeable about advantages and disadvantages of this strategy, so we will not bore you with a lengthy discussion of discussion as a strategy, but will "pick your brains" by letting you begin by responding to Exercise 11.2, followed by Exercise 11.3, where discussion guidelines will be generated.

EXERCISE 11.2: DISCUSSION AS A STRATEGY: WHAT DO I ALREADY KNOW?

Please answer these questions, then share your responses with other members of your class, perhaps in subject field discussion groups.

1. My subject field is _____

2. For what reasons would I hold class discussions? _____
   _____

3. How would I arrange the student seating? _____

4. What ground rules would I establish before starting the discussion? _____
   _____
   _____
   _____

5. Should participation be forced? _____
   How would I encourage participation? _____
   How would I discourage one or two students from dominating the discussion? _____
   _____

6. What preparation should the students and I make before the discussion session? _____
   _____

7. How would I handle digression? _____
   _____

8. If I use students as discussion leaders, what training should they receive? _____
   _____

9. What different roles are options for me during class discussions? _____
   _____
   When is each most appropriate? _____
   _____

10. Is a whole-class discussion (20 or more students) ever appropriate or effective? If so, when?
   _____
   How? _____

11. When, if ever, is a "class meeting" appropriate in middle, junior, or senior high school teaching? _____
   _____

12. Can "brainstorming" be a form of discussion? _____

13. What follow-up activities would be appropriate after a discussion session? _____

_____

_____

14. What kinds of activities should precede a discussion? _____

_____

_____

15. Should a discussion be given a set time length? Why or why not? How long? How decided?

_____

_____

_____

16. Should students be graded for participation in class discussions? If so, how? On what basis? By whom? _____

_____

_____

EXERCISE 11.3: GUIDELINES FOR USING DISCUSSIONS

Instructions: Share your group discussion results (from Exercise 11.2) with your colleagues. As a group, generate a list of five general guidelines for the use of discussion as a strategy? Here are questions to guide your discussion:

1. How effective were your small group discussions (Exercise 11.2)?
2. What allowed for or inhibited small group effectiveness?
3. How effective is *this* class discussion? Why?

Guidelines generated:

1.

2.

3.

4.

5.

Equal Time to All Students

As previously emphasized, it is important for a teacher to attend to all students and to attempt to involve all students in class activities, to not fall into the traps of interacting with only the brightest, or the most vocal and assertive, nor to have prejudicial expectations about students based on their gender. In our own teaching we have found it useful to occasionally ask a student to secretly tally classroom interactions between the instructor and students during a class meeting, after which the instructor analyzes the results and arrives at decisions about the instructor's own attending and facilitating behaviors. That is the purpose of Exercise 11.4. The exercise can be modified to include responses and their frequencies according to other student characteristics, such as your calling on *all* students equally, for responses to your questions, to assist you with classroom helping jobs, for misbehavior, and for class leadership roles.

EXERCISE 11.4: TEACHER INTERACTION WITH STUDENTS ACCORDING TO STUDENT GENDER

Instructions: The purpose of this exercise is to provide a tool for your analysis of your own interactions with students according to their gender. The exercise can be modified to include (a) amount of time given for each interaction, (b) response time given by teacher according to student gender, and (c) to include other student characteristics such as ethnicity.

Procedure: Prior to class select a student, or an outside observer, such as a colleague, and ask the volunteer to do the tallying and calculations as follows.

SECRET ASSIGNMENT: During class today, I would like you to secretly tally the interactions between me and individual students. Simply place a tally mark after the name of each student (or if you don't know names, use a seating chart code) that has any verbal interaction with me from this point on. Thank you. Do not count any of your own interactions, nor yourself in the following calculations.

Exact time of start = _____

Time end   = _____

Total time   = _____

1. Total number of students present = ____

2a. Number of female students = ____   2b. Number of male students = ____
    Calculations:

3a. % females in class = _____   3b. % males in class = _____
    = (2a ÷ 1.)   = (2b ÷ 1.)

Tallying:

End of experiment calculations.

4a. Total females interacting = _____   4b. Total males interacting = _____
(how many different students)

5. % of students interacting = _____ = (4a + 4b) ÷ 1.

6a. Total female tallies = _____   6b. Total male tallies = _____

7. Total of all tallies = _____ = (6a + 6b)

8a. % of tallies are females = _____   8b. % of tallies are male = _____
= (6a ÷ 7.)   = (6b ÷ 7.)

9a. Most tallies for any one male = _____ % of total class tallies? _____
= (9a ÷ 7.)

9b. Most tallies for any one female = _____ % of total class tallies? _____
= (9b ÷ 7.)

10. Teacher conclusions as a result of this interaction analysis:

Advice for a Teacher-Led Discussion

We conclude this section with the following advice. For effective discussions, 10–12 feet is the maximum recommended effective distance between participants, so when a discussion is being led by a teacher, it is important to keep the distance between teacher and students within that limitation. The use of teacher mobility and an overhead projector can contribute to maintaining that distance.

With large classes, there are other things a teacher can do to reduce the feeling of distance, and to encourage student interaction, such as personally distributing papers, arriving to class early to chat with early student arrivals, and learning student names early. For the latter, some teachers at the first class meeting request student photographs which are then used to facilitate learning student names, perhaps by pasting the photographs on a seating chart to which, during class, the teacher can readily refer.

E. USING DEMONSTRATIONS

Students like demonstrations, especially when performed by the teacher. They like them because the teacher is actively engaged in a learning activity rather than merely verbalizing about it. Commonly used in science, home economics, physical education, art, and shop classes, the demonstration can be an effectively useful strategy choice in any discipline. A role-playing demonstration is used in a social science course; the mathematics teacher demonstrates steps in using the Pythagorean theorem; the English teacher demonstrates clustering to students ready for a creative writing assignment.

Purposes for a Demonstration

A demonstration can be designed to serve any of the following purposes.

- To illustrate a particular point of content.
- To set up a discrepancy recognition.
- To establish problem recognition.
- To assist in the recognition of a solution to an existing problem.
- To review content already learned.
- As a set for a lesson.
- As an unusual closure to a lesson.
- To give students opportunity for active learning participation.
- To save time and resources (as opposed to entire class doing that which is demonstrated).
- To reduce potential safety hazards (where the teacher demonstrates, using materials too hazardous for student use).

Guidelines for Using a Demonstration

When planning a demonstration, consider the following.

1. Decide which is the *best way* to conduct the demonstration, such as verbal or silent demonstration; by a student or the teacher; to the entire class or to small groups.
2. Ensure that the demonstration is *visible* to all students. The installation of overhead mirrors might be worth the expenditure in classrooms where demonstrations are frequent. For demonstrations some classrooms are now more expensively equipped with videocameras and large television monitors.
3. *Practice* with the materials and procedure prior to demonstrating.
4. Consider the *pacing* of the demonstration, allowing time for wait-see events.
5. At the start of the demonstration explain its *purpose* and the learning objectives.
6. During the demonstration, as in a lecture, *stop and check* (comprehension checks) to ensure that the students are understanding the demonstration.
7. As you plan your demonstration consider *what might go wrong*, because if anything can, it will.
8. Consider the use of a *spotlight* (a slide projector works fine) to highlight the demonstration.
9. Be sure that the *demonstration table and area* are free of unnecessary objects that could distract, be in the way, or pose a safety hazard.
10. With potentially hazardous demonstrations, *model proper safety precautions*: wear safety goggles; have fire-safety equipment at hand; use a protective shield between the demonstration and the student audience.
11. As with any lesson, plan your demonstration *closure,* such as the use of a question and discussion time.

F. USING THE TEXTBOOK
(See also Chapters 6 and 10)

Secondary schools usually go through periodic textbook adoption procedures; then they use the adopted books for a number of years before the next adoption cycle begins. This means for you, the student teacher, or for the beginning first-year teacher, that most likely someone will tell you, "Here are the textbooks you will be using." That is why in Exercise 6.3 we hope that you became familiar with standard textbooks that you are likely to be using in your subject field. After you find out exactly what textbook you are to use comes your decision regarding *how to use it.*

There are many methods from which you may select your use of the student textbook, perhaps the *least* acceptable of which is for you to show a complete dependence on a single textbook and require the students to simply memorize content from that book. That is the lowest level of cognitive learning; furthermore, it implies that the teacher is unaware of other significant reading materials and has nothing more to contribute to the learning of the students.

Another problem brought about by the teacher's reliance upon a single textbook is that for many students that textbook may just not be at the appropriate reading level. In today's secondary school classes the reading range of a class may vary by as much as two-thirds of the chronological age of the students in the class.[1] This means that if the chronological age is 15 years (typical for tenth-grade students) then the reading-level range would be 10 years; that is to say, the class may have some students reading only at the fifth-grade level and others with post-high-school reading ability. And that is one reason why many teacher education programs today require a teaching-of-reading course for secondary credential candidates: teachers in most subject fields will need to devote time to helping students develop their reading skills.

With that introduction to this section, coupled with what you learned about textbooks in Chapter 6, let us now turn your attention to the following general guidelines about the use of the textbook in secondary school teaching.

1. Secondary school students should have a textbook (for most courses) and the textbook *should* be the current edition. If it is not a current edition, then you, the teacher, will need to supplement it with current material. That is not unusual; indeed, it is your professional license!

2. Maintain supplementary reading materials for student use in the classroom; your professional librarian will be most delighted to cooperate in the selection and provision of materials.

3. Some students in your class may benefit from drill, practice, and reinforcement as provided in accompanying workbooks, but this does not mean that all students necessarily benefit from identical activity.

4. Provide vocabulary lists to help your students learn meanings of important words and phrases.

5. Teach your students how to study from their textbook, perhaps by using the S4R method:[2] *surveying* the chapter first, then *reading* the chapter, then *reciting* what was in the chapter, *recording* important items from the chapter in their notebooks, then *reviewing* it all.

6. Encourage students to search in other sources for content that will update the textbook (particularly important in science, social studies, and certain other disciplines).

7. Encourage students to watch for errors in the textbook, errors in content or in publishing—perhaps giving them points when they discover an error. This encourages critical thinking, skill development, and healthy skepticism.

8. In certain classes, particularly in college preparatory studies, the textbook should serve more as a reference; students should be encouraged to utilize a variety of resources to enhance their learning. Going from one cover of the textbook to the other in nine months is not necessarily "teaching."

9. Individualize the learning as much as possible to try to teach students of varying reading and learning abilities. Consider differentiated reading assignments, both in the textbook and in the supplementary resources.

10. Encourage your students to respect their books, perhaps by covering and protecting them and by not marking in them. In many secondary schools this is a rule, and at the end of the semester students are charged for damaged or lost books.

---

[1] See H. Singer and D. Donlan, *Reading and Learning from Texts* (Boston: Little, Brown & Co., 1980), p. 35.
[2] See E. G. Stetson, "Improving Textbook Learning with S4R: A Strategy for Teachers, not Students," *Reading Horizons*, vol. 22, no. 2 (1982), p. 129.

Within the span of your teaching career you may witness and be a part of a revolution in the design of school textbooks. The prediction has been made that with the revolution going on in microcomputer chip technology student textbooks will take on a whole new appearance. Along with this, we are told, will come dramatic changes in the importance and use of student texts, and new problems for the teacher, some of which are predictable. Student "texts" may become credit card size—increasing, of course, the probability of students "losing" their books. On the positive side, it would seem likely that a classroom teacher will have available a variety of "textbooks" to better address the reading levels and interests of individual students in the class. Distribution and maintenance of reading materials might create a new demand on the teacher's time. In any case, we expect that dramatic and exciting events will occur to a teaching tool that has not changed a whole lot throughout the history of education in this country.

G. USING ASSIGNMENTS

Values in Using Assignments

Assignments facilitate student learning in many ways. Consider this list. Assignments help students

- To organize their learning.
- To learn new content.
- To practice what has been learned.
- To develop personal learning.
- By providing a mechanism whereby students receive constructive feedback from the teacher.
- To develop library use skills.
- To develop their study skills.

Guidelines for Using Assignments

Whether completed in class or as homework, assignments help students learn new content, practice what has already been taught, and develop their personal learning. For use of this important teaching strategy, consider the following guidelines.

1. *Plan early* the types of assignments you will give (daily and long-range, minor and major), and prepare assignment specifications. Assignments must *correlate with the specific instructional objectives,* and should never be given as "busy work" or for punishment!
2. Provide *differentiated assignments,* different assignments, or with variations to be selected by the students on the basis of their individual interests and abilities.
3. Determine in advance the *resources* that will be needed by the students in order to complete their assignments; check the availability of those resources. Again, your librarian is an excellent source of help.

4. *Follow-up* of assignments is important. If it is important for the student to do, then it is important for you to give your full attention to the product of the student's efforts. *Read everything that the student writes!*

5. Provide your *written or verbal comments* about the student's work, and try to be *positive* in your comments. Think carefully about your written comments, to be relatively certain that they will convey your meaning to the student.

6. Use *positive reward reinforcers* as frequently as possible, in order to continue to encourage, rather than discourage, the student.

7. *When giving assignments,* it is best to write them on the board or in written form with clear specifications, so that the students understand your expectations.

8. Be prepared when the students' parents complain that you do not assign any homework.

9. *Maintain assignment due dates,* allowing, of course, for legitimate excuses, but also consider allowing students to select their own due dates from teacher-provided options.

10. Allow *time in class* for students to begin work on homework assignments, so you can give individual attention to students who need your help.

11. Also consider asking teacher colleagues to work with students who may benefit from their help on certain assignments.

12. Use *caution* when giving assignments that may be controversial or that may pose a safety hazard to the student. In such cases, before giving the assignment you may wish to talk it over with your departmental chairperson, and/or have students obtain parental permission to do the assignment.

13. One final guideline regarding the use of assignments: when writing your comments on student papers, *use a color other than traditional red.* Red brings with it a host of negative connotations—blood, hurt, danger, stop. We admit that this is our own prejudice, and merely ask that you consider it and form your own opinion about it.

EXERCISE 11.5: PLANNING COURSE ASSIGNMENTS

Instructions: From your unit plan (Exercise 8.5), plan the student assignments, written and oral, using the following format. When completed share this exercise with your colleagues for their suggestions. Reviewers will need a copy of your course syllabus.

1. List all student assignments, and include differentiated assignments.
2. Correlate (by code) all assignments with the stated behavioral objectives.
3. Identify (the best you can) assignment resources.
4. Indicate the relative (grade) weight of each assignment, showing the percent of the assignment to the total course grade.

Let us now take a break from our discussion of particular teaching strategies, and give *you* an assignment where you will gather what you have learned into an analysis of a real teaching episode. That is the nature of Exercise 11.6, which follows.

EXERCISE 11.6: ANALYSIS OF A TEACHING EPISODE

Instructions: The following scenario describes an actual teaching episode. Read it carefully, then answer the questions that follow and prepare to discuss in class.

Background Information: A high school government class
30 students present on this day
A Monday in March
Period 1, 8:30–9:20 a.m.

The Episode:

8:25–8:30 — The students are arriving, teacher is in room chatting with some of the early arriving students.

8:30 — Bell rings, all stand for Pledge of Allegiance.

8:31 — Teacher: "Open your books to p. 49 and read for about 10 minutes the background material for today's lesson, to p. 55."

8:31–8:41 — Students read quietly, one or two arrive (tardy) during this time; teacher takes attendance, places attendance slip on door hook; teacher writes on board a list of words to remember and the word *SAVE*.

8:41 — A quiet buzz session involving three students begins in one area of room, teacher moves there and quietly asks if they are finished reading, students answer yes—the three students quiet now, teacher moves and stands in rear of room.

8:45 — Teacher: "Is everybody finished?" No response tells teacher it is time to begin lecture.
Teacher: "From the reading, what problems faced the organization of labor?" (pause) "Anyone?"
1st Student: "Leadership!"
  Teacher writes *leadership* on board.
2nd Student: "Money!"
  Teacher writes *financial* on board.
3rd Student: "Time!"
  Teacher writes *time* on board.
1st Student again: "Criminal infiltration!"
  Teacher writes *criminal infiltration* on board.

8:58 — Teacher lectures for next 20 minutes on "problems of organizing," mentioning the problems the Indians of South Dakota must be facing today.
Although no student response was solicited, one boy says, "Yeh! Let's go on strike against the school."
Another says, "Yeh, man, let's go sit in the Principal's office."
Another student adds, "Let's get the Principal!"
A fourth student comments, "Right on, man. Teachers' strike!"
The teacher does not respond to these comments, other than with an occasional smile.

9:18 — Teacher completes the lecture and adds, "Tomorrow we will look at the way in which labor solved these problems."

9:19 — Students begin to meander toward exit in anticipation of class change bell.

End of scenario

Questions to Answer for Exercise 11.6

1. *Identify* the teaching strategies used by this teacher. Consider specifically orientation set induction, closure, methods and materials used, and special teacher behaviors such as acceptance, silence, etc.
2. How effective was each strategy during this lesson?
3. What were the good points of the instruction?
4. How might the instruction have been improved?

H. USING TERM PAPERS AND STUDENT ORAL REPORTS

Assigning term papers and student reports can be a frustrating educational experience for both teacher and students unless proper guidance is given by the teacher. The purposes for using this strategy are to (1) provide an opportunity for each student to become especially knowledgeable in one area, and (2) to share that knowledge with the teacher and the other students. But for the experience to be educationally beneficial the teacher should assure the following.

1. Establish guidelines and timelines for the paper and the oral report.
2. Work with each individual student in topic selection and later in the oral reporting technique. Insist that the student use visuals and props during the oral report.
3. Assist each student in the identification of potential resources and in research technique.
4. Insist that each student develop an outline followed by a first draft of the paper, each of which is presented for your review.
5. Maintain a time limit (5–10 minutes is a reasonable maximum) on the oral report with time allowed for discussion and questioning.
6. Provide students with clear descriptions of the evaluation and grading that will be used for the written and oral reports, such as the criteria shown in the following sample form.

FORM FOR EVALUATING WRITTEN AND ORAL REPORT

WRITTEN AND ORAL REPORT EVALUATION _____

Date _____   Topic _____ student _____

Criterion I: Organization of Report	4	3	2	1
A. Research Preparation	very evident	acceptable	needed more	inadequate
B. Content Coverage	super job!	acceptable	needed more	inadequate
C. Bibliography	well done	acceptable	too limited	inadequate

Criterion II: Oral Presentation	2	1	0
A. Enthusiasm	appropriate	okay	lacking
B. Delivery (poise, voice, mannerisms etc.)	excellent	problems	inadequate
C. Use of audiovisuals, materials, etc.	effective	satisfactory	inadequate
D. Use of time allotted	effective	problems	inadequate
E. Overall stimulating presentation	very	okay	inadequate

COMMENTS:

SCORING: Criterion I Possible 12, Mine = _____
Criterion II Possible 10, Mine = _____
20–22 = A   Total   = _____
18–19 = B
15–17 = C
13–14 = D

I. USING GAMES

The use of games in the secondary school classroom can be valuable in enriching the effectiveness of your instruction. As with any other instructional strategy, the use of games should follow a clear educational purpose with careful planning, and must be congruent with the instructional objectives.

Why Are Games Used?

Games can be powerful educational tools, and may have one to several functions, as follows.

• As devices to socialize the class.
• As motivators.

- As devices to add variety and a change of pace.
- As strategies to teach content and/or process.
- To provide opportunity for learning through simulation and role-play.
- As devices to stimulate divergent and creative thinking.
- As devices to stimulate inductive thinking.
- As devices to stimulate critical thinking.
- As devices to evaluate student learning.
- As strategies for achieving affective and psychomotor goals.
- As devices to stimulate interest and skill in computer usage.
- As devices for reviewing content.
- To provide a simple "time out" from the usual rigors of learning.

What Are Games? A Classification

There are seven categories of game types that fall under the general heading of devices referred to as games. Although beyond the scope of this text to discuss advantages and disadvantages for each of the seven types, suffice to say that certain types have greater educational benefits. According to learning psychologists, particularly recommended for academic use are games that do not emphasize the element of competition, that is, that are not "contests."

Characteristics and examples of the seven types are listed in the following chart.

Type	*Characteristics*	*Examples*
1. pure game	promotes laughter, is fun	*New Games*[1] *Cooperation Square Game*
2. pure contest	stimulates competition, built-in inefficiency[2]	political contests, e.g., U.S. presidential race
3. pure simulation	models reality	toddler play
4. contest-game	fun and competition, built-in inefficiency	golf; bowling; *Trivial Pursuit*
5. simulation-game	fun and models reality	*Redwood Controversy*[3] *Stress Survival*
6. contest-simulation	competition and models reality, built-in inefficiency	boxcar derby
7. simulation-game-contest	models reality, fun, competition, built-in inefficiency	*Careers, Life, Monopoly*

[1]A collection of published games popular with teachers of preschool and elementary school.

[2]This means that rules for accomplishing the game objective make accomplishment of that objective less than efficient; e.g., the objective in golf is to get the ball into the hole, but in order to accomplish that, one has to take a peculiarly shaped stick (the club) and hit the ball, go find it, hit it again, continuing until the ball is in the hole.

[3]*Redwood Controversy* is a powerful simulation role-play game patterned from the congressional hearings of the late 1960s which were considering enlarging the Redwood National Parks (still a controversial issue today), and of value to adult classes in English, debate, social studies, and biology. The game is inexpensive and includes rules for play, role cards, transparency, and a wall map, and can be played in approximately two hours, or extended over several class meetings. Houghton Mifflin, 110 Tremont Street, Boston, MA 02107.

SOURCES OF EDUCATIONAL GAMES

Successful games can be invented by ordinary people like you and us. Successful educational games can be invented by any teacher who is motivated to take the time necessary to do it. Indeed, in the history of games inventions, successful games are rarely published by "professionals," but by "ordinary" people. For examples, an accountant, Charles Darrow, invented *Monopoly*. Although he spent the remainder of his life inventing games, and died a millionaire, he never sold another. Ralph Anspach, a professor at San Francisco State University, invented *Anti-Monopoly*. While a student at Oklahoma State University, Gary Gabrel invented *Pente*. His game was rejected by major publishers, so he marketed it himself, and in 1981 had sales of $3 million. The inventor of *Scrabble*, Alfred Butts, was an architect, and that was the only game he invented. Originally invented by him in 1931, it "bombed" when marketed in 1948, and was not successfully marketed until nearly 20 years later, but now outsells most other games. Ann Benson and Robin Landerman spent their own money to develop their first game, *The Yuppie Game*, which sold out its first year in stores. Former journalists, Chris Haney and Scott Abbott, produced *Trivial Pursuit*, originally rejected by major games publishers. The inventor of *Pictionary* marketed his game himself, and only later did major games publishers indicate interest in it.

EXERCISE 11.7: CREATING MY OWN INSTRUCTIONAL GAME

Instructions: The purpose of this exercise is to provide the steps for designing an educational game for use in your teaching. Develop the game and try it out in your class for suggestions for modifications. Follow these steps:

1. Decide the purposes you want the game to serve.
2. Outline what specifically you want the game to teach.
3. Write behavioral objectives for the game.
4. Decide the best format for the game, such as a game board or a simpler, paper-and-pencil format, or a form that hangs on the chalkboard clips.
5. Design materials for the game.
6. Write rules for the game.
7. Develop, test, and revise the game and its rules.

A Sampling of "Homemade" Games

There is no question that teachers can create games useful in their own teaching. Generally, teacher-made games follow one of several formats: board games, paper-and-pencil games, card games, mental games, role-play and simulation games, and materials-manipulation games. Each of these might fit any of the purposes and be of any of the types. Here are a few examples of teacher-made games that can be applied to almost any subject matter:

Game 1: Living Tic Tac Toe

Grade level: any
Type: contest game
Number of players: class
Area: any
Suggested purpose: review of content
Materials: none
Instructions: Place nine chairs in the center of the room to represent the Tic Tac Toe diagram. Divide class into two teams. You ask Side 1 a question; if a student gets the right answer, the student takes a position as desired to represent an "X." If the student answers incorrectly, the teacher then asks Side 2 a question. Alternate sides until one has made three in a row, or until the diagram is filled with student bodies.

Game 2: Oral Communication

Have all students pair off and stand shoulder to shoulder but facing opposite directions. Student 1 is to talk for two minutes *without looking* at Student 2. Student 2 is not to interrupt. Then Student 2 talks for two minutes under the same rules. (All the class does this together.) Then ask the students to write their reactions to the exercise. Collect and discuss these orally. In addition to saying that the exercise is stupid and dumb, students of all ages will usually discover for themselves the need for eye contact, the pleasure of talking uninterrupted, the need for feedback, and so on.

Have each student write a sentence of ten words or so containing an abstract idea, such as, "Love is the most important thing in the world to me." The student then tries to get his or her idea across to others, without words. This exercise helps students discover why we study words and methods of verbal expression. (They have to know and feel comfortable with each other before they will do this one.)

Game 3: Cooperation Square Game[1]

Grade level: any
Type: pure game
Number of players: five or more in multiples of three
Suggested purpose: to learn about cooperation

Materials: Before class, prepare a set of squares and an instruction sheet for each five students. A set consists of five envelopes containing pieces of stiff paper cut into patterns that will form five 6 × 6-inch squares, as shown in the diagram. Several individual combinations will be possible, but only one total combination. Cut each square into parts *a* through *j* and lightly pencil in the letters. Then mark the envelopes *A* through *E* and distribute the pieces thus: Envelope *A*, pieces *i, h, e; B*, pieces *a, a, a, c; C*, pieces *a, j; D*, pieces *d, f;* and *E*, pieces *g, b, f, c.* Erase the small letters from the pieces and write instead the envelope letters *A* through *E*, so that the pieces can be easily returned for reuse.

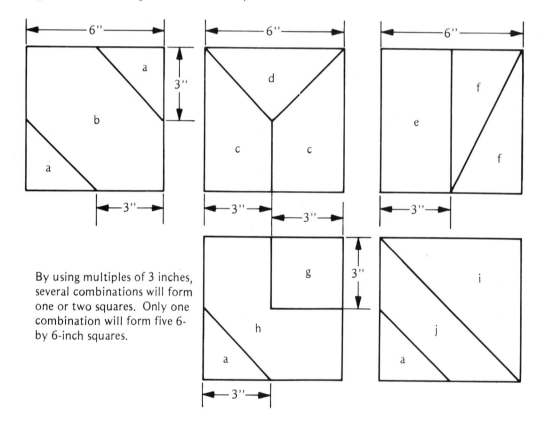

By using multiples of 3 inches, several combinations will form one or two squares. Only one combination will form five 6- by 6-inch squares.

Instructions: Divide the class into groups of five and seat each group at a table equipped with a set of envelopes and an instruction sheet. Ask that the envelopes be opened only on signal. Begin the exercise by asking what *cooperation* means. List on the board the behaviors required in cooperation. For example: Everyone has to understand the problem. Everyone needs to believe that he or she can help. Instructions must be clear. Everyone needs to think of the other person as well as herself or himself.

Describe the experiment as a puzzle that requires cooperation. Read the instructions aloud, point out that each table has a reference copy of them, then give the signal to open

[1]"Today's Education," *NEA Journal* (October 1969), p. 57. Reprinted by permission; also reproduced with permission from *The Handbook of Staff Development and Human Relations Training: Material Developed for Use in Africa,* by D. Nylen, J. R. Mitchell, and A. Stout. Copyright 1967, NTL Institute.

the envelopes. The instructions are as follows: Each person should have an envelope containing pieces for forming squares. At the signal, the task of the group is to form five squares of equal size. The task is not completed until everyone has formed a perfect square and all the squares are of the same size.

These are the rules: No member may speak. No member may ask for a card or in any way signal that he or she wants one. Members may give cards to others.

When all or most of the groups have finished, call "time," then discuss the experience. Ask such questions as: How did you feel when someone held a piece and did not see the solution? What was your reaction when someone finished a square and then sat back without seeing whether his or her solution prevented others from solving the problem?

What were your feelings if you finished your square and then began to realize that you would have to break it up and give away a piece? How did you feel about the person who was slow at seeing the solution? If you were that person, how did you feel? Was there a climate that helped or hindered? If students have helped to monitor, they may have observations to share.

In summarizing the discussion, the teacher may wish to review behaviors listed at the beginning and ask whether the game relates to the way the class works from day to day.

Game 4: Lunar Survival Game

Grade Level: Three and up
Type: simulation game
Number of players: class
Area: science, social studies
Suggested purpose: to encourage inductive reasoning
Materials: paper and pencil
Instructions: The following is placed on a ditto and distributed to class members, perhaps divided into small groups.

You are in a space crew scheduled to rendezvous with a mother ship on the lighted surface of the moon. Mechanical difficulties, however, have forced your ship to crash-land at a spot some two hundreds miles from the rendezvous point. The rough landing damaged much of the equipment aboard. Survival depends on reaching the mother ship, so the most critical items available must be chosen for the two-hundred-mile trip. Below are listed the fifteen items left intact after landing. Your task is to rank them in terms of their importance to your crew, in its attempt to reach the rendezvous point. Place a number *1* by the most important item, a number *2* by the second most important, and so on through number *15*, the least important.

_____ Box of matches
_____ Food concentrate
_____ Fifty feet of nylon rope
_____ Parachute silk
_____ Portable heating unit
_____ Two .45-caliber pistols
_____ One case of dehydrated milk
_____ Two 100-pound tanks of oxygen
_____ Star map of the moon's constellations
_____ Life raft
_____ Magnetic compass
_____ Five gallons of water
_____ Signal flares
_____ First-aid kit containing injection needles
_____ Solar-powered FM receiver-transmitter

SCORING KEY

Listed below are the correct rankings for the items, along with the reasons for the rankings.

_15_ Box of matches (little or no use on the moon)
_4_ Food concentrate (supplies daily food)
_6_ Fifty feet of nylon rope (useful in tying the injured; helps when climbing)
_8_ Parachute silk (shelter against sun's rays)
_13_ Portable heating unit (useful only if party landed on dark side of moon)
_11_ Two .45-caliber pistols (self-propulsion devices could be made from them)
_12_ One case of dehydrated milk (food; mixed with water for drinking)
_1_ Two 100-pound tanks of oxygen (filled respiration requirement)
_3_ Star map of the moon's constellations (one of the principal means of finding directions)
_9_ Life raft (its carbon dioxide bottles could assist in self-propulsion across chasms and the like)
_14_ Magnetic compass (probably no magnetized poles, thus useless)
_2_ Five gallons of water (replenishes water loss, e.g., from sweating)
_10_ Signal flares (distress call within line of sight)
_7_ First-aid kit containing injection needles (oral pills or injection medicine valuable)
_5_ Solar-powered FM receiver-transmitter (distress signal transmitter, possible communication with mother ship)

Game 5: Musical Bingo (Adaptable to Any Subject)

Five categories are chosen. In the sample music game, the categories are: rock groups; solo artists; songs; solo or band artists from the 1950s; and, instruments.

The bingo caller will draw a category with a corresponding column on it and the student will cover the subject that relates to the particular category. For example: the caller would say "G song" and if the student has a song title in the "G" column the student will cover it with his or her marker. The game continues until there is a winner.

Different varieties of bingo may be played, e.g., blackout, four corners, across, up and down, and diagonal.

Blank bingo cards are given to the students before the game begins, and the students fill in the squares with subjects pertaining to the five categories chosen.

B I N G O

B	I	N	G	O
Eagles	piano	tambourine	trumpet	The Four Seasons
Chuck Berry	Fats Domino	America	Cher	guitar
Drums	Paul Simon	Free Spot	Rhinestone Cowboy	Neil Sedaka
Elton John	Let Your Love Flow	Barry Manilow	Chicago	Oh What A Night
Silly Love Song	Spinners	Elvis Presley	Platters	Bill Haley

Additional Sources of Games

There are many sources of commercially available educational games, many of which have come and gone so quickly that in this resource guide it is impossible to maintain a current list of sources and prices. However, the following is a list of sources and selected games that have had staying power.

GAMES SOURCES AND SAMPLE GAMES

Abt Associates, Inc., 14 Concord Lane, Cambridge, MA 02138
  Galapagos, Manchester, Politica, Steam
Carolina Biological Supply Co., 2700 York Road, Burlington, NC 27215.
  Blood Flow, Cell Game, Energy Quest, Pollution, Predator, The Food Chain Game
Denoyer Geppert Co., 5215 N. Ravenswood Ave., Chicago, IL 60640.
Didactic Systems, Inc., P.O. Box 457, Cranford, NJ 07016.
  Principles of Effective Salesmanship
Diversified Educational Enterprises, Inc., 725 Main St., Lafayette, IN 47901.
Educational Research, P.O. Box 4205, Warren, NJ 07060.
  Stress Survival
Edu-Game, P.O. Box 1144, Sun Valley, CA 91352.
Entelek, Inc., 42 Pleasant St., Newburyport, MA 01950.
  Low Bidder
Frey Scientific Co., 905 Hickory Ln., Mansfield, OH 44905.
Houghton-Mifflin, 2 Park Street, Boston, MA 02107.
  Planet Management, Redwood Controversy
Interact Company, P.O. Box 262, Lakeside, CA 92040.
  Blue Wodjet Company
Joint Council on Economic Education, 1212 Avenue of the Americas, New York, NY 10036.
  Marketplace
Krell Software, Flowerfield Bldg., #7 Suite 1D, St. James, NY 11780.
Management Research Systems, Ltd., Suite 201, Executive Center, P.O. Box 1585, Ponte Vedra Beach, FL 32082.
Macmillan Publishing Co., 866 Third Avenue, New York, NY 10022.
  SIMSOC (simulated society game), *Farming; Location of the Metfab Co.; Point Roberts, Portsville, Rutile and the Beach; Section; Solution for ACME Metal; Yes, But Not Here*
Marginal Context Ltd. 35 St. Andrew's Road, Cambridge CB4 1DL, England.
  The Green Revolution Game
New York Zoological Society, Education Dept., Bronx, NY 10460.
Nova Scientific Corp., 111 Tucker St., P.O. Box 500, Burlington, NC 27215.
  Anyone Can, Ecology, Evolution, Environmental Planning, Geologic Time Chart, Food Chains, Metric Bingo
Science Research Associates, Inc., 259 E. Erie St., Chicago, IL 60611
  American History Game
Simile, P.O. Box 1023, La Jolla, CA 92037
  Inner City Planning
Simulations Publications, Inc., 44 East 23d Street, New York, NY 10010.
Social Studies School Service, 10,000 Culver Blvd., Culver City, CA 90230.

Election U.S.A., Propaganda Game, Society Today, Star Power
Stasiuk Enterprises, 3150 NE 30th Ave., P.O. Box 12484, Portland, OR 97212.
Systems Gaming Associates, Triphammer Rd., Ithaca, NY 14850.
  Clug (Community Land Use Game)
Teaching Aids Company, 925 South 300 West, Salt Lake City, UT 84101.
Western Publishing Co., Inc., School and Library Dept., 850 Third Ave., New York, NY 10022.
  Community Disaster
John Wiley & Sons, Inc., 605 Third Avenue, New York, NY 10158.
World Law Fund, 11 West 42nd Street, New York, NY 10036.
  Conflict

QUESTIONS FOR CLASS DISCUSSION

1. Would you like to teach by inquiry? Why or why not?
2. What strategies have you learned about that you are now anxious to try in your teaching?
3. Have you found any good games for teaching in your field, and that you would like to share with your colleagues?
4. What research can you find about the use of cooperation versus competition in the secondary school classroom?
5. What research can you find with respect to strategy choice and achievement in learning with respect to secondary school teaching in your field?
6. With respect to strategy choice, how eclectic can (should) a secondary school teacher be in your field?
7. The term lecture is from the Latin word *lectare,* which means to read aloud. Are lectures ever effective when read verbatim?
8. Discuss how "delivery versus access" (of this chapter) compares with "traditional versus facilitating" (of chapter 3)?
9. Are there cautions teachers need to be aware of in the use of games for teaching?
10. What questions do you have about the content of this chapter? How might answers be found?

SUGGESTED READINGS FOR CHAPTER 11

Bobcock, S. S., and Schild, E. O. *Simulation Games in Learning.* Beverly Hills, CA: Sage, 1968.

Bork, A. *Learning With Computers.* Bedford, MA: Digital Press, 1981.

Bransford, J. D., and Stein, B. S. *The Ideal Problem Solver.* New York: W.H. Freeman, 1984.

Caissy, G. A. "Evaluating educational software: A practitioner's guide." *Phi Delta Kappan* 66(4):249–250 (Dec. 1984).

Cruickshank, D. R., and Tefler, R. "Classroom games and simulations." *Theory Into Practice* 19:75–80 (Winter 1980).

Ellington, H., et al. *A Handbook of Game Design*. New York: Nichols, 1982.

Gall, M. D., and Gall, J. P. "The discussion method." In N. L. Gage, ed. *The Psychology of Teaching Methods—The Seventy-fifth Yearbook of the National Society for the Study of Education, Part 1*. Chicago: The National Society for the Study of Education, 1976.

Greenblat, C. S., and Duke, R. D. *Principles and Practices of Gaming/Simulation*. Beverly Hills, CA: Sage, 1981.

Heinich, R., Molenda, M., and Russell, J. D. *Instructional Media*. 3rd ed. New York: Macmillan, 1989.

Heitzmann, W. R. *Educational Games and Simulations*. Rev. ed. Washington, D. C.: National Education Association, 1987.

Hill, W. F. *Learning Through Discussion*. Beverly Hills, CA: Sage, 1977.

Horn, R. E., and Cleaves, A. *The Guide to Simulation Games for Education and Training*. 4th ed. Beverly Hills, CA: Sage, 1980.

Kahney, H. *Problem Solving: A Cognitive Approach*. Milton Keynes: Open University Press, 1986.

Krupar, K. R. *Communication Games*. New York: Free Press, 1973.

Levin, H. M., and Meister, G. "Is CAI cost-effective?" *Phi Delta Kappan* 67(10):745–749 (June 1986).

Maidment, R. *Simulation Games: Design and Implementation*. Columbus, OH: Merrill, 1973.

McLeish, J. "The lecture method." In N. L. Gage, ed. *The Psychology of Teaching Methods—The Seventy-fifth Yearbook of the National Society for the Study of Education, Part 1*. Chicago: The National Society for the Study of Education, 1976.

Perry, R. P., Abrami, P. C., and Leventhal, L. "Educational seduction: The effect of teacher expressiveness and lecture content on student ratings and achievement." *Journal of Educational Psychology* 71(1):107–116 (Feb. 1979).

Seifert, E. H., and Beck, Jr., J. J. "Relationships between task time and learning gains in secondary schools." *Journal of Educational Research* 78(1):5–10 (September/October 1984).

Sharon, S. "Cooperative learning in small groups: Recent methods and effects on achievement, attitudes, and ethnic relations." *Review of Educational Research* 50(2):241–271 (Summer 1980).

Slavin, R. E. *Cooperative Learning*. Englewood Cliffs, NJ: Prentice Hall, 1990.

Sullivan, D. D. *Games as Learning Tools: A Guide for Effective Use*. New York: McGraw-Hill, 1978.

Wadsworth, B. J. *Piaget's Theory of Cognitive and Affective Development*. 3d ed. White Plains, NY: Longman, 1984.

12

What Other Aids and Resources Are Available to the Secondary-School Teacher?

You will be pleased to know that there is a vast amount of material from which to draw as you plan instructional experiences. You might not be pleased to learn that you will be spending a lot of time sorting and selecting the materials most appropriate for your use. Nobody will know your students better than you, so, although we cannot tell you specifically what you should use, we can provide some guidelines and sources. And someday you may thank us for this recommendation: *Begin your resource file early—now.* Exercise 12.4 will get you started with this project, an activity you will continue throughout your teaching career.

A. GENERAL GUIDELINES FOR SELECTION OF AIDS AND RESOURCES: THE LEARNING EXPERIENCES LADDER[1]

An important general rule in planning is to select learning experiences that are as direct as possible. That is, have them do that which you are teaching them to do. When students are involved in experiences that are direct, they are utilizing all of their senses; and when all of the senses are engaged, learning is the most effective and the longest lasting. This is "learning by doing."

Conversely, at the other end of the spectrum are abstract experiences where students are exposed only to symbolization (i.e., words and numbers) using only one or two senses. Visual and verbal symbolic experiences, although impossible to avoid when teaching, are generally least effective in assuring that planned learning occurs. So, when planning experiences and selecting materials, we urge you to select activities that engage learners in the most direct experiences possible. The triangle that follows depicts this range of experiences from direct to abstract.

---

[1]Earlier versions of this concept can be found in: Charles F. Hoban, Sr., et al., *Visualizing the Curriculum,* New York: Dryden, 1937, p. 39; Edgar Dale, *Audio-Visual Methods in Teaching,* New York: Holt, Rinehart & Winston, 1969, p. 108; and Jerome S. Bruner, *Toward a Theory of Instruction,* Cambridge: Harvard University Press, 1966, p. 49.

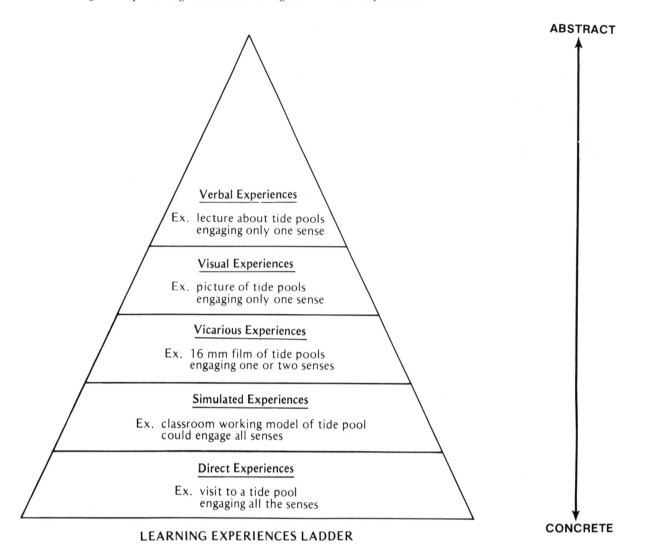

ABSTRACT

Verbal Experiences

Ex. lecture about tide pools
engaging only one sense

Visual Experiences

Ex. picture of tide pools
engaging only one sense

Vicarious Experiences

Ex. 16 mm film of tide pools
engaging one or two senses

Simulated Experiences

Ex. classroom working model of tide pool
could engage all senses

Direct Experiences

Ex. visit to a tide pool
engaging all the senses

CONCRETE

LEARNING EXPERIENCES LADDER

As you can see, when teaching about tide pools, the *most* effective mode is to actually take students to a tide pool (bottom of ladder, most direct experience) where they can see, hear, touch, smell, and perhaps even taste the tide pool. The *least* effective mode is for the teacher to simply lecture (top of ladder, most abstract experience) about the tide pool, engaging only one sense—hearing.

Of course, for various reasons—safety, lack of field-trip money, location of your school—you may not be able to take the students to a tide pool. We cannot, nor should we, always use the most direct experience, so sometimes we settle for an experience higher on the ladder. Self-discovery teaching is *not always best*. Sometimes it is more appropriate to build upon what others have learned. Learners do not need to reinvent the wheel, but the most effective learning *is* that which clearly engages many of their senses.

B. AIDS AND RESOURCES FOR DIRECT AND SIMULATED EXPERIENCES

Among the most likely sources of ideas for direct and simulated experiences related to specific content are the curriculum guides. Textbooks used in secondary school are usually accompanied by a teacher's edition, where you will find many useful ideas. Special methods books used in your teacher education program provide ideas for learning in a particular subject.

Another advantage of direct and simulated experiences is that they are often multidisciplined; that is, they cross subject boundaries. This is more like real life, and therefore provides an important benefit in the students' learning. Simulated experiences include such techniques as role-playing, experimenting, play production, skits, games, and the mock-up (e.g., the in-class tide pool).

C. AIDS AND RESOURCES FOR VICARIOUS EXPERIENCES

Vicarious experiences are those where the learner is indirectly involved in "the doing," where two or three senses usually are involved. Vicarious experiences include still pictures (slides and filmstrips), motion pictures, computer programs, models, maps, and globes. As with all materials, these should be carefully reviewed by the teacher prior to presentation to the class. One of the authors recalls a teaching experience in which he showed a filmstrip that he had not previewed since the year before. In the interim, someone had written an obscene word on one of the frames. How embarrassing!

Computers

As stated earlier in this resource guide, the secondary school teacher of the twenty-first century must be computer literate. It is beyond the scope or intent of this resource guide to be able to detail the countless uses that computers have and will have for the secondary-school teacher, beyond mere mention of some of the current ways that computers have speeded and made more accurate the numerous tasks that used to be done by hand, and to encourage you to become computer literate. For the secondary-school teacher, computers are professionally beneficial far beyond instruction alone: they can be used to manage the instruction (by obtaining information, preparing text materials, maintaining attendance and grade records), to instruct (by use of various instructional software programs), to teach about computers and about thinking (by instruction about computers and through the use of programs about thinking processes).

To learn more about the advantages of computer literacy for secondary-school teachers, you are encouraged to

- Visit and talk with teachers who are using computers in their work.
- Peruse catalogues and periodicals that review software, looking for programs that would be useful in your own teaching field.
- Enroll in a course or workshop to learn about computers.

How will you be able to use a computer in your classroom? You'll be able to use a computer to assist instruction and learning, and to help maintain records, collect data, or project information. A computer will help you create files, store information, compile records of students' progress, devise accounts of your library books, provide audiovisual material, list additional resources, and help you keep an up-to-date inventory. This computer use is referred to as Computer-Assisted Management or CAM. In addition, there are programs for learning enrichment, reinforcement, or supplement. This computer use is labeled Computer-Assisted Learning or CAL. Certain programs instruct your students in a particular skill or in a specific concept and this is labeled Computer-Assisted Instruction or CAI. What can you look for? Look for programs that provide tutoring (remedial instruction material), practice and drill, as well as for simulation programs appropriate to business, social science, mathematics, and science. Other programs give students an opportunity to write original materials as they explore word processing and authoring systems. Still other programs support the individualized needs of your students, and, with your authoring, will produce games, puzzles, or tests, based on your students' interests, the reading material, or other classroom information.

Why Use Computers?

What, in general, can computers do for you and your students?

1. *Computers Can Motivate.* Look for colorful, interesting, and animated programs. Does the program show what is expected of the student before the student is asked to respond? A computer model supports a student's interest, and thus a student's motivation. Does the program provide a response or feedback to the student's responses? Is the correct response displayed? Is there a colorful graphic, such as hands that applaud, a familiar "smiley" face, or a winner's cheer? Or does a personalized statement, with the student's name, appear on the screen?
2. *Computers Can Activate.* Look for a program that can be controlled for rate-of-pacing by the student. Can the student move the program forward for rapidity, move it backward for review purposes, or skip the program and move ahead to the next level of difficulty? Does the program detect and then correct the inaccurate responses by the student? Does the program explain inaccurate responses and then provide a similar item for another learning experience? Does the program summarize the total of correct student responses and then provide an analysis of the errors as a basis for the teacher's diagnosis? The following chart illustrates the various ways that computers are used in teaching.

UTILIZATION OF VARIOUS CAI METHODS[1]

Methods	Description	Role of Teacher	Role of Computer	Role of Student	Applications/ Examples
Drill-and-Practice	Content already taught Review basic facts and terminology Variety of questions in varied formats Question/answer drills repeated as necessary	Arranges for prior instruction Selects material Matches drill to student Checks progress	Asks questions "Evaluates" student response Provides immediate feedback Records student progress	Practices content already taught Responds to questions Receives confirmation and/or correction Chooses content and difficulty level	Parts of a microscope Completing balance sheets Vocabulary building Math facts Product knowledge
Tutorial	Presentation of new information Teaches concepts and principles Provides remedial instruction	Selects material Adapts instruction Monitors	Presents information Asks questions Monitors responses Provides remedial feedback Summarizes key points Keeps records	Interacts with computer Sees results Answers questions Asks questions	Clerical training Bank teller training Science Medical procedures Bible study
Gaming	Competitive Drill-and-practice in a motivational format Individual or small group	Sets limits Directs process Monitors results	Acts as competitor judge scorekeeper	Learns facts/ strategies/skills Evaluates choices Competes with computers	Fraction games Counting games Spelling games Typing (arcade-type) games
Simulation	Approximates real-life situations Based upon realistic models Individual or small group	Introduces subject Presents background Guides "debriefing"	Plays role(s) Delivers results of decisions Maintains the model and its database	Practices decision making Makes choices Receives results of decisions Evaluates decisions	Troubleshooting History Medical diagnosis Simulators (pilot/ driver) Business management Laboratory experiments
Discovery	Inquiry into database Inductive approach Trial and error Tests hypotheses	Presents basic problem Monitors student progress	Presents student with source of information Stores data Permits search procedures	Makes hypotheses Tests guesses Develops principles/rules	Social science Science Food-intake analysis Career choices
Problem Solving	Works with data Systematizes information Performs rapid and accurate calculations	Assigns problems Checks results	Presents problem Manipulates data Maintains database Provides feedback	Defines the problem Sets up the solution Manipulates variables Trial and error	Business Creativity Troubleshooting Mathematics Computer programming

[1]Source: Robert Heinich, Michael Molenda, and James D. Russell. *Instructional Media*. Third Edition. New York: Macmillan Publishing Company, 1989, p. 360. By permission of the Macmillan Publishing Company.

Selecting Computer Software

Computer software available for secondary school instruction is varied and is being developed with ever increasing rapidity. For selection of software programs for your own teaching, your discipline, and for the hardware that you have available, we suggest that you become acquainted with the many courseware reviews, such as

- *Courseware Report Card.* 150 West Carob Street, Compton, CA 90220.
- *EPIE Reports.* EPIE (Educational Product Information Exchange) Institute, P.O. Box 839, Water Mill, NY 11976.
- *Journal of Courseware Review.* Apple Education Foundation, 20525 Mariani Avenue, Cupertino, CA 95014.
- *Microcomputers in Education.* Queue, Inc., 5 Chapel Hill Drive, Fairfield, CT 06432.
- *Micro-Scope.* JEM Research, Discovery Park, University of Victoria, P.O. Box 1700, Victoria, BC V8W 2Y2, Canada.
- *MicroSIFT.* Northwest Regional Educational Lab, 300 SW Sixth Street, Portland, OR 97204.
- *Pipeline.* Conduit Clearinghouse, University of Iowa, Oakdale Campus, Iowa City, IA 55242.
- *Purser's Magazine.* P.O. Box 266, El Dorado, CA 95623.
- *School Microwave Reviews.* Dresden Associates, P.O. Box 246, Dresden, ME 04342.
- *Software Review.* Meckler Publishing, 520 Riverside Avenue, Westport, CT 06880.

In addition to the preceding sources your professional journal (e.g., *The Science Teacher; Science Scope;* etc.) will likely provide reviews of new software issues.

The following Appraisal Checklist is provided for computer courseware evaluation.[1]

[1]Heinich, p. 373, by permission.

Appraisal Checklist: Computer-Based Instruction

Title _____   **Format**

Series title (if applicable) _____   disk size

Source _____

Length (completion time), Range: _____ to _____ minutes, Average _____ minutes

Designed for what system? _____ Memory required? _____

Subject area _____

Intended audience _____

Objectives (stated or implied):

Brief Description:

Entry Capabilities Required:

- Prior subject-matter knowledge/vocabulary
- Reading ability
- Mathematical ability
- Other:

Rating	High		Medium		Low	Comments
Relevance to objectives	☐	☐	☐	☐	☐	
Accuracy of information	☐	☐	☐	☐	☐	
Likely to arouse/maintain interest	☐	☐	☐	☐	☐	
Ease of use ("user friendly")	☐	☐	☐	☐	☐	
Appropriate color, sound, graphics	☐	☐	☐	☐	☐	
Frequent, relevant practice (active participation)	☐	☐	☐	☐	☐	
Feedback provides remedial branches	☐	☐	☐	☐	☐	
Free of technical flaws (e.g., dead ends, infinite loops)	☐	☐	☐	☐	☐	
Clear, complete documentation	☐	☐	☐	☐	☐	
Evidence of effectiveness (e.g., field-test results)	☐	☐	☐	☐	☐	

Strong Points:

Weak Points:

Reviewer _____

Position _____

Recommended action _____   Date _____

The ERIC Information Network

The Educational Resources Information Centers system, established by the United States Office of Education in 1966, is a widely used network providing access to information and research on education. While there are sixteen separate clearinghouses providing information on specific subjects, addresses and phone numbers for those of particular interest to secondary-school teachers are as follows.

- *Adult, Career, and Vocational Education*
    Ohio State University, 1960 Kenny Road, Columbus, OH 43210-1090 (614) 486-3655.
- *Languages and Linguistics*
    Center for Applied Linguistics, 1118 22nd St., N.W., Washington, D.C. 20037-0037. (202) 429-9551.
- *Science, Mathematics, and Environmental Education*
    Ohio State University, 1200 Chambers Road, 3rd Floor, Columbus, OH 43212-1792. (614) 292-6717.
- *Social Studies/Social Science Education*
    Indiana University, Social Studies Development Center, 2805 East 10th St., Bloomington, IN 47405-2373. (812) 335-3838.
- *Tests, Measurements, and Evaluation*
    American Institutes for Research, Washington Research Center, 1055 Thomas Jefferson St., N.W., Washington, D.C. 20007-3893. (202) 342-5060.

EXERCISE 12.1: CONVERSION OF AN ABSTRACT LEARNING EXPERIENCE

Instructions: This exercise may tax your ingenuity. The purpose is for you to select from your course outline a topic that is typically taught by the use of symbolization (at or near the top of the "learning experiences ladder",) and devise a technique whereby, with limited resources, that same content could be taught in a more direct way (at or close to the bottom of the ladder). Upon completion of the exercise share your proposal with your colleagues.

1. Topic selected from course outline:

2. Description of typical way of teaching this topic:

3. Detailed description of way of teaching this topic using direct learning experiences:

4. Statement about why you believe a direct way of teaching this topic is not more common:

5. Ideas resulting from sharing your proposal with others:

D. AIDS AND RESOURCES FOR VISUAL AND VERBAL EXPERIENCES

Materials for visual and verbal experiences include the writing board, graphs and charts, and the inveterate overhead projector. Can you imagine a classroom without a writing board and an overhead projector? Teacher talk has been discussed in previous chapters; here are guidelines for the use of other aids for visual and verbal experiences.

The Writing Board

They used to be slate blackboards. Today, your classroom most likely will have either a board that is painted plywood (chalkboard); a magnetic chalkboard; or a white, multipurpose board on which you write with marking pens. The multipurpose board can be used as a projection screen, to which figures cut from colored transparency film will stick; the board often has a magnetic backing. Whichever the case, here are guidelines for using the classroom writing board.

1. Use colored chalk (or marking pens) to visually highlight your "board talk," particularly beneficial for students with learning difficulties.
2. Start each class with a clean board, and at the end of class don't leave until you have cleaned the board for the teacher who follows you in this classroom—simple professional courtesy.
3. Print neatly, clearly, and orderly, beginning at the far left, and large enough that all can see.
4. Use the board to record student contributions. Print the name of the contributor, as it is a strong, positive reinforcer when that student is recognized thus by the teacher.
5. Rather than giving instructions orally, print them on the board.
6. Above the board you may find clips for hanging posters, maps, etc. Use them.
7. Keep your own personal supply of chalk (or pens) with you at all times.
8. Do not block the view of your board writing, and do not write with your back to your audience.
9. If you have a lot of material to put on the board, do it prior to class, or better yet, put the material on transparencies and use the overhead projector rather than the chalkboard.
10. Plan, practice, and execute your board writing so that it is neat, legible, organized, and visible to all in the class.

The Overhead and Opaque Projectors

While the overhead projector projects light through transparent objects, the opaque projector reflects light from opaque (nontransparent) objects. For the opaque projector, room lights must be out, but an overhead projector works quite well in a fully lit room. Furthermore, while every classroom today is likely to have an overhead projector, you will probably have to scrounge to locate an opaque projector (probably in the art department). While the opaque projector is large and bulky, the overhead is portable. Truly portable overhead projectors are available that can be carried around in their small compact cases.

The opaque projector is useful for showing pages from a book, or for showing realia (objects). But caution: Objects placed in the opaque projector will heat up quickly, pages will begin to brown in no time at all. Some schools are now using new video camera technology that assumes, and improves upon, the function of the opaque projector, focusing on an object, pages of a book, or a demonstration, and transmitting a clear image onto a video monitor large enough for an entire class to see clearly.

The chalkboard and overhead projector have lived longer than or outlived every other teaching aid. Most classrooms are equipped with both. In some respects, the overhead projector is more useful than the chalkboard, particularly for a novice teacher who is nervous: use of the overhead projector rather than the chalkboard helps reduce tension by decreasing the need to pace back and forth to the board. And, by using the overhead projector, rather than the chalkboard, you can better maintain both eye contact and physical proximity with students.

Guidelines for Using the Overhead Projector

1. Ordinary felt-tip pens will not work satisfactorily. Select a transparency marking pen available at an office supply store. The ink of these pens is water soluble, so keep the palm of your hand from resting on the transparency unless you want smudges on your transparency and on your hand. Non–water soluble pens, "permanent markers," can be used, but for reuse, the transparencies must be cleaned with a special compound or a plastic eraser.
2. To highlight your writing and to organize student learning, use pens in a variety of colors. Transparency pens tend to dry out quickly, so the caps must be taken on and off frequently, which is something of a nuisance when working with several colors.
3. Obtain a transparency roll, or a stack of clean transparencies from your department office, or from an office supply store. Some teachers prefer an acetate roll

that can be easily carried around from one class to the next. Transparencies can be cleaned and dried with paper toweling.

4. Some teachers prefer to prepare a lecture outline in advance on transparencies, which allows more careful preparation of the transparencies, and they are then ready for reuse at a later time. For preparation of permanent transparencies, you will probably prefer to use "permanent markers," rather than water soluble marking pens.

5. Find the best place in your classroom to place the projector. If there is no classroom screen, you can hang white paper or a sheet.

6. Turn on the projector, focus the image, locate the projector (stand) so the projected blank image covers the entire screen.

7. When using the projector, face your class. You do not need to turn around to look at the screen. What you write, as you are facing your audience, will show up perfectly (unless out of focus).

8. Practice writing on the transparency, and also practice making overlays. Transparency sheets come in different colors—red, blue, yellow, green, and clear.

9. Rather than using your finger or pointing to the screen, use a pencil to point to material by laying the pencil directly on the transparency.

10. Switch the projector off when you wish student attention to be shifted back to you, or when changing transparencies.

Thermal film processing machines, probably located in your departmental or school office, can be used to make permanent transparencies, and commercially produced thermal transparencies are available. For sources of overhead commercially produced transparencies, check the supply catalogs available in your department office, or at the audiovisual and resources centers in your district. Here is a sample listing of sources.

SOURCES OF OVERHEAD TRANSPARENCIES

Carolina Biological Supply Company, 2700 York Road, Burlington, NC 27215.
Denoyer-Geppert Audiovisuals, 5235 Ravenswood Ave., Chicago, IL 60640.
Educational Media International, 7 Martin St., South Melbourne, Vic. 3206, Australia.
E.M.E., P.O. Box 2805, Danbury, CT 06813-2805.
Films for the Humanities and Sciences, P.O. Box 2053, Princeton, NJ 08543.
Hammond, Inc., 515 Valley Street, Maplewood, NJ 07040.
Media Associates, Inc., 7322 Ohms Lane, Minneapolis, MN 55435.
MMI Corporation, 2950 Wyman Parkway, P.O. Box 19907, Baltimore, MD 21211.
Stasiuk Enterprises, 3150 NE 30th Ave., P.O. Box 12484, Portland, OR 97212.
3M Audio Visual, Building 225-3NE, 3M Center, St. Paul, MN 55144.
United Transparencies, P.O. Box 688, Binghamton, NY 13902.
Ward's Natural Science, 5100 West Henrietta Rd., P.O. Box 92912, Rochester, NY 14692-9012.

---

11. You can use any material that is transparent on the projector, such as rulers, protractors, Petri dishes, and even objects that are opaque if you wish to simply show shapes.

12. To avoid distortion, the projected light should hit the screen at a 90-degree angle.
13. Hand calculators are available specifically for use on the overhead projector, as is a screen that fits onto the stage and is circuited to computers, so that whatever is displayed on the computer monitor is also projected by the overhead projector.
14. The overhead projector can be used as a light source for demonstrations.
15. And, finally, tracing transparent charts or drawings into larger drawings onto paper or the chalkboard is easily done with use of the overhead projector. (Opaque drawings, as from a textbook, may be traced in the same manner with use of an opaque projector.)

EXERCISE 12.2: USING THE OVERHEAD PROJECTOR

Instructions: The purpose of this exercise is to practice writing on the overhead and making transparencies with overlays, including those using colored acetate, until you feel proficient with the overhead projector. For this exercise follow the preceding guidelines.

When you feel competent, the teacher of this course may want to check you out. Some job seekers list on their résumés the teaching tools with which they are competent. Perhaps at the end of the course your instructor will provide you with an audiovisual competency verification certificate.

Charts, Drawings, Globes, Graphs, Maps, and Other Visuals

As discussed in Chapter 2, as a new member of a faculty, one of your first tasks is to discover what visual aids are available and where they are located. Here are general guidelines for their use.

1. As always, ensure visibility for all students.
2. With large charts and maps, use a pointer. If you don't have one, an automobile radio antenna works just fine, or if you can go "first class," purchase a laser pointer.
3. With smaller charts and maps, use either the opaque projector, which has a built-in pointer, or, if you are fortunate to have the equipment, use video transmission as mentioned earlier in the discussion of overhead and opaque projectors.

Objects

Sometimes referred to as realia, objects are props used to enhance your teaching by giving the students visual identification of what is being taught. A teacher of botany may be lecturing about flowers, and use real flowers as props for the lecture. A political science teacher might use a personal collection of campaign buttons when lecturing about presidential races. Visual props enhance student learning, and can help reduce the tension of a beginning teacher who may be inclined toward a heavy reliance on the lecture. Props provide students with something to look at other than the lecturer.

Audio and Video Tapes, Computer Programs, Films, Filmstrips, Laser Videodiscs, and Slides

When using audiovisuals of any kind, *always set up the equipment and have it ready to go* ***before*** *class.*

The VCR is one of the more frequently used pieces of audiovisual equipment in today's secondary school classroom. Videocassettes offer more instructional flexibility and can be checked out by students; and because of their flexibility, lower cost, and greater visual impact, they have literally replaced the earlier popularity of films and filmstrips. The *Encyclopaedia Britannica Educational Corporation,* for example, has transferred its latest and most popular filmstrips onto videocassettes. Like *Concepts of Electricity* (available from *Heathkit/Zenith Educational Systems*), which includes videocassettes and written programmed instructional modules, entire course packages are now available on videocassettes or on computer programs. Your department may have a collection of computer programs and videotapes. Many teachers make their own.

Laser videodiscs and players for classroom use are becoming reasonably priced, with an ever-increasing variety of disc topics for individual disciplines. There are two formats of laser videodisc—freeze frame format (CAV, *Constant Angular Velocity,* or Standard Play) and non–freeze frame format (CLV, *Constant Linear Velocity,* or Extended Play). Both will play on all laser disc players. Discs available at time of this writing are described as visual archives or visual databases, presenting large amounts of information that can be easily retrieved, reorganized, filed, and controlled by the user. Each side of a double-sided disc can store 54,000 separate still-frames of information. Visuals, both still and motion sequences, can be selected and shown on a television monitor or programmed onto a computer floppy disk for an individualized presentation.

Carefully selected programs, tapes, discs, films, and slides enhance sudent learning. For examples, laser videodiscs offer quick, efficient accessibility of thousands of visuals, thus providing an appreciated boost to teachers of students with limited language proficiency. In science, with the use of still-frame control, students can visually observe phenomena they only read about before. In art, students can be taken on a personal guided tour of an entire art museum.

As this book is readied for press, our recommendation is that you stay abreast of developing technologies for use in your field. Laser videodiscs interfaced with computers offer exciting new technologies for educators. New instructional technologies are advancing at an increasingly rapid rate, as also are the costs. It is important that you, the teacher, and your colleagues, maintain vigilance over new developments, constantly looking for those technologies that will not only help make your teaching more effective, but that are cost-effective.

The 1988–89 Edition of the Videodisc Compendium[1] references the titles and sources of more than 400 videodiscs. The following is a sample of titles available.

[1]Published and sold, approximately $8.50, by Emerging Technology Consultants, Inc., P.O. Box 12444, St. Paul, MN 55112. See also: Daynes, R., and Buttler, B., eds., *The Videodisc Book: A Guide and Directory* (New York: Wiley, 1984).

SAMPLE VIDEODISC TITLES AND PUBLISHERS FOR SECONDARY USE

Discipline	Publisher	Title
Art	Videodisc Publishing Inc.	Andrew Wyeth: The Helga Pictures
	Image Entertainment	Ansel Adams, Photographer
	University of Wisconsin–Madison	Helen L. Allen Textile Collection
	Videodisc Publishing, Inc.	National Gallery of Art
	Pioneer Laserdisc Corporation	Vincent Van Gogh: A Portrait in Two Parts
	University of Wisconsin–Madison	Visual History of Residential Interiors
Astronomy (see also "space science")	Optical Data Corporation	Earth Science Sides 3–6: Astronomy and the Sun
Biological Science	Image Entertainment	African Wildlife (National Geographic)
	Image Entertainment	Among the Wild Chimpanzees (National Geographic)
	Pioneer Laserdisc Corporation	Audubon Birds of North America
	Image Entertainment	Australia's Improbable Animals (National Geographic)

SAMPLE VIDEODISC TITLES AND PUBLISHERS FOR SECONDARY USE
(Continued)

Discipline	Publisher	Title
	Videodiscovery	Cell Biology: Motion and Function of the Living Cell
	Image Entertainment	Creatures of the Namib Desert (National Geographic)
	Access Network	ECO-Insights
	Pioneer Laserdisc Corporation	Encyclopedia of Animals (8 volumes)
	Videodiscovery	Live Cycles
	GPN	Life Science Biology I and II
	Optical Data Corporation	Life Science (2 volumes)
	Image Entertainment	Rain Forest (National Geographic)
	Image Entertainment	Realm of the Alligator (National Geographic)
	Videodiscovery	The Bio-Sci Videodisc
	Image Premastering Services, Ltd.	The Birth Disc
	Optical Data Corporation	The Living Textbook—Life Science (3 volumes)
	Waterford Institute, Inc.	Videodisc in Science Education
Business	Edudisc, Inc.	Self Management: Setting Goals
	3M	Scotch Laser VideoDisk
	MGM/UA	The Joy of Stocks
Earth Science	Image Entertainment	Born of Fire
	Systems Impact Inc.	Earth Science
	Optical Data Corporation	Earth Sciences I and II
English	Pioneer Laserdisc Corporation	*David Copperfield*
	Pioneer Laserdisc Corporation	*Hamlet*
	Grolier Electronic Publishing, Inc.	KnowledgeDisc
	Pioneer Laserdisc Corporation	Mark Twain's *A Connecticut Yankee in King Arthur's Court*
	The Voyager Company	*Pygmalion*
	Pioneer Laserdisc Corporation	*Treasure Island*
Foreign Language	Pioneer Laserdisc Corporation	Basic French by Video
	Pioneer Laserdisc Corporation	Basic Spanish by Video
Home Economics	Optical Programming Associates	The Master Cooking Course

SAMPLE VIDEODISC TITLES AND PUBLISHERS FOR SECONDARY USE
(Continued)

Discipline	Publisher	Title
History	Pioneer Laserdisc Corporation	America and the World Since WWII
	Image Entertainment	Atocha: Quest for Treasure (National Geographic)
	Image Entertainment	Egypt: Quest for Eternity (National Geographic)
	Image Entertainment	Jerusalem: Within These Walls (National Geographic)
	Pioneer Laserdisc Corporation	*Mein Kampf*
	Interactive Image Technologies	The Bartletts: An Interactive History
	CEL Educational Resources	The Video Encyclopedia of the 20th Century
	Pioneer Laserdisc Corporation	Vietnam: Ten-Thousand-Day War
Mathematics	Mindscape, Inc.	Adventures in Mathland
	Industrial Training Corporation	Algebra: Using Common Industrial Formulas
	Systems Impact Inc.	Mastering Fractions
	University of Washington	Math in Biology
Music	Pioneer Laserdisc Corporation	*Aida*
	The Voyager Company	*La Strada*
	The Voyager Company	Monterey Pop
	Pioneer Laserdisc Corporation	The Bolshoi Ballet Live
	University of Delaware	The University of Delaware Videodisc Music Series
Physical Education		
	MCA	Jim Fixx on Running
	Optical Programming Associates	Jazz-er-cise
	Pioneer Laserdisc Corporation	World of Martial Arts
Physical Science		
	Image Entertainment	Miniature Miracle: The Computer Chip (National Geographic)
	Optical Data Corporation	Physical Science Sides 1–4
	GPN	Physics I and II
	John Wiley and Sons	Puzzles of Tacoma Narrows Bridge

SAMPLE VIDEODISC TITLES AND PUBLISHERS FOR SECONDARY USE
(Continued)

Discipline	Publisher	Title
Space Science	3M	National Air and Space #1 and #2
	Video Vision	Space Archive: Apollo 17
	Video Vision	Space Archive: Mars
	Optical Data Corporation	Space Archive 6: Encounter
	Vestron Video	The Greatest Adventure

ADDITIONAL SOURCES OF VIDEODISC TITLES

The Complete Interactive Video Courseware Directory. New Hyde Park, NY: Convergent Technologies.
Interactive Video. St. Louis, MO: Applied Video Technology.
Interactive Videodiscs for Education. Ztek Co., P.O. Box 1968, Lexington, KY 40593.
Laser Disc Newsletter. Suite 428, Hudson Street, New York, NY 10014.
LaserVideo, One East Wacker Drive, Chicago, IL 60601.
Media Learning Systems, 1532 Rose Villa St., Pasadena, CA 91106.
MECC—*Videodiscs for Education, A Directory.* Minnesota Educational Computing Corp., 3490 Lexington Ave. North, St. Paul, MN 55126.
MMI Corporation, 2950 Wyman Parkway, P.O. Box 19907, Baltimore, MD 21211.
National Geographic Society, Educational Services, Box 89, Washington, DC 20036.
News, Videodisc Design/Production Group, KUON-TV/University of Nebraska–Lincoln, P.O. Box 83111, Lincoln, NE 68501.
Optical Publishing Directory. Medford, NJ: Learning Information, Inc.
Pioneer Electronics, Laserdisc Corporation of America, 5000 Airport Plaza Drive, Long Beach, CA 90801.
Sony Video Communications, Sony Drive, Park Ridge, NJ 07656.
Systems Impact, 4400 MacArthur Blvd., Suite 203, Washington, DC 20007.
Teaching Technologies, P.O. Box 3808, San Luis Obispo, CA 93403-3808.
Videodiscovery Catalog. Videodiscovery, Inc., 1515 Dexter Ave., #400, Seattle, WA 98109.

For free and inexpensive resource materials check the following sources in your university library.

RESOURCES FOR FREE AND INEXPENSIVE TEACHING MATERIALS

A Guide to Print and Nonprint Materials Available from Organizations, Industry, Governmental Agencies and Specialized Publishers New York: Neal-Schuman.
An Annotated Bibliography of Audiovisual Materials Related to Understanding and Teaching the Culturally Disadvantaged. Washington, DC: National Education Association
Catalog of Audiovisual Materials: A Guide to Government Sources (ED 198 822). Arlington, VA: ERIC Documents Reproduction Service.
Catalog of Free-Loan Educational Films/Video. St. Petersburg, FL: Modern Talking Picture Service.

Educators Progress Service, 214 Center Street, Randolph, WI
Educators Guide to Free Audio and Video Materials
Educator's Guide to Free Films
Educator's Guide to Free Filmstrips
Educator's Guide to Free Health, Physical Education, and Recreation Materials
Educator's Guide to Free Science Materials
Educator's Guide to Free Social Studies Materials
Educators Index of Free Materials
Guide to Free Computer Materials

Community Resources

Valuable resources may be found in the local community. You will want to build your own file of community resources—speakers and field trip locales. Your department, or colleagues within the department, may already have a community resource file for your use.

Copying Machines

Many secondary schools have replaced the spirit duplicator (ditto machine) with modern dry copiers. Whichever type of copying machine is available in your department, here are important guidelines.

1. If the copy machine has broken down, be sure you haven't. Don't cancel class just because the copy machine isn't working.
2. Prepare class copies well in advance of the day intended for use.
3. If permissible at your secondary school, learn to operate the equipment. Some teachers, with home computers and printers, make copies for student distribution, particularly in emergencies and in the absence of the necessary lead time for school duplication. For the purpose of potential income tax deduction, don't forget to maintain records of your professional expenses.
4. When using copyrighted material, cite the source and obtain written or oral permission to copy. There is usually no fee when your purpose is educational, and not for profit. See the guidelines that follow this section.
5. Use varying colors to highlight printed materials for class use. With ditto use, ditto masters come in standard blue, but also in black, red, and green. If not overused, multicolored dittos are interesting and can be meaningful. Don't forget to remove the slip sheet from the ditto master before writing on the white side. A ball point pen is best for preparing a ditto master. The procedure for making a multicolored ditto is as follows: (a) select your base color master, i.e., the color in which the majority of the material will be printed, usually standard blue; (b) remove the brown tissue slip sheet, and begin your writing on the white side; (c) when ready for the second color, remove the carbon sheet from your standard master, replace it with the carbon half of the new color, and (d) continue your writing on the original white page but now with the new color carbon beneath it. Continue the process with each new color.

Dry copy machines are available for color duplication, but the cost is too high for ordinary duplication of sets of class materials. Likewise, for computer printers and computer programs with color commands, the cost of multicolored ribbons is generally prohibitive for more than occasional use of printing class sets of materials.

Guidelines for Use of Copyrighted Materials

You must be aware of the laws regarding use of copyrighted materials, printed and nonprinted. Although space here prohibits full inclusion of United States legal guidelines, your local school district undoubtedly can provide a copy of district policies outlined to insure compliance with all copyright laws. When preparing to make a reproduction you must ascertain whether the copying is permitted by law under the category of "permitted use." If not allowed under "permitted use," then you must obtain written permission to reproduce the material from the copyright holder(s). What follows are basic guidelines. (Other than for broadcast programs and computer software, there are no guidelines for fair use of nonprint materials—e.g., films, filmstrips, and slides.)

Printed Materials[1]

Permitted uses—You may make:[2]

1. Single copies of: a chapter of a book; an article from a periodical, magazine, or newspaper; a short story, short essay, or short poem whether or not from a collected work; a chart, graph, diagram, drawing, cartoon, or an illustration from a book, magazine, or newspaper.
2. Multiple copies for classroom use (not to exceed one copy per student in a course) of: a complete poem if less than 250 words; an excerpt from a longer poem, but not to exceed 250 words; a complete article, story, or essay of less than 2,500 words; an excerpt from a larger printed work not to exceed ten percent of the whole or 1,000 words; one chart, graph, diagram, cartoon, or picture per book or magazine issue.

Prohibited uses—You *may not*:

1. Copy more than one work or two excerpts from a single author during one class term.
2. Copy more than three works from a collective work or periodical volume during one class term.
3. Reproduce more than nine sets of multiple copies for distribution to students in one class term.
4. Copy to create or replace or substitute for anthologies or collective works.
5. Copy "consumable" works, e.g., workbooks, standardized tests, answer sheets.
6. Copy the same work from term to term.

[1]From section 107 of the 1976 Omnibus Copyright Revision Act.
[2]All permitted copying must bear an appropriate reference (i.e., author, title, date, source, publisher.)

Off-air videotaping[1]

Permitted uses—You may:

1. Request your media center to record the program for you if you cannot or if you lack the equipment.
2. Retain a videotaped copy of a broadcast (including cable transmission) for a period of forty-five calendar days, after which the program must be erased.
3. Use the program in class once during the first ten school days of the forty-five calendar days, and a second time if instruction needs to be reinforced.
4. Have professional staff view the program several times for evaluation purposes during the full forty-five day period.
5. Make a limited number of copies to meet legitimate needs, but these copies must be erased when the original videotape is erased.
6. Use only a part of the program if instructional needs warrant (but see the next list).
7. Enter into a licensing agreement with the copyright holder to continue use of the program.

Prohibited uses—You *may not:*

1. Videotape premium cable services such as HBO without express permission.
2. Alter the original content of the program.
3. Exclude the copyright notice on the program.
4. Videorecord in anticipation of a request for use—the request to record must come from an instructor.
5. Retain the program, and any copies, after forty-five days.

Computer software[2]

Permitted use—You may:

1. Make a single back-up or archival copy of the computer program.
2. Adapt the computer program to another language if the program is unavailable in the target language.
3. Add features to make better use of the computer program.

Prohibited use—You *may not:*

1. Make multiple copies.
2. Make replacement copies from an archival or back-up copy.
3. Make copies of copyrighted programs to be sold, leased, loaned, transmitted, or given away.

---

[1]Heinich, p. 431.
[2]From a December, 1980, Congressional amendment to the 1976 Copyright Act.

E. PROFESSIONAL PERIODICALS AND RESOURCES

Professional journals and periodicals provide a splendid source of ideas and resources for teaching. Here is a sample listing.

Art
Art Education
School Arts
Studies in Art Education
The Art Teacher

Bilingual Education
Bilingual Review
TESOL Quarterly

Business Education
American Business Education
Business Education Forum
Business Education World
Business Teacher
Journal of Business Education

Computer Periodicals
Classroom Computer Learning
Collegiate Microcomputer
The Computing Teacher
Education Computing News
Education & Computing
Electronic Education
Interface: the Computer Education Quarterly
Journal of Computer Based Instruction
LOGO & Educational Computing Journal
Microcomputers in Education

English
English
English Journal
English Language Teaching Journal
Educational Theatre Journal
Journal of Reading
Research in the Teaching of English

Industrial Arts
Industrial Arts and Vocational Education
Industrial Arts Teacher
Industrial Education
School Shop

Mathematics
Arithmetic Teacher
Mathematics Teacher
School Science and Mathematics
Journal of Computers in Mathematics and Science Teaching

Music
The American Music Teacher
Educational Music Magazine
Journal of Research in Music Education
Music Educators Journal
The School Musician

Physical Education
Athletic Journal
Journal of Physical Education
Journal of Physical Education and Recreation
Physical Education

Foreign Languages
Classic Journal
Foreign Language Annals
Hispania
Language Learning
Modern Language Forum
Modern Language Journal
The French Review
The German Quarterly

Science
American Journal of Physics
Journal of Chemistry Education
Journal of Geological Education
School Science and Mathematics
Science Education
The American Biology Teacher
The Chemistry Teacher
The Physics Teacher
The Science Teacher
Journal of Secondary School Science Teaching
Journal of Computers in Mathematics and Science Teaching
Journal of Science Teacher Education

Home Economics
Forecast for Home Economics
Journal of Home Economics

Social Studies
Social Education
Social Studies
Holistic Education

EXERCISE 12.3: IDENTIFYING PROFESSIONAL JOURNALS

Your purpose for this exercise is to become familiar with the professional journals applicable to secondary teaching and which are available in your nearest professional library. Visit your college or university library and review the periodical reference book to locate the journals that interest you.

Select one journal and begin browsing through the current issues. Identify the title of the journal, the publication date, and, if available, the professional organization that supports or is affiliated with the journal.

Select one current article that reflects your interest.

Identify the title of the article, the author, and the bibliographical information. Identify which subject area the article has impact on. Take notes on the article and share your notes with others in your class.

Hand your bibliographical information and your notes to your instructor or a class volunteer. If your class members decide they want to develop a current bibliography of interesting journal articles, then the list should be alphabetized by the author's last name: show all of the needed bibliographical information, along with the annotation compiled from each reader's notes.

· ·

Hand to class volunteer for current bibliography.

_____   _____
Author   Article title

_____   _____ _____ _____
Journal title   Volume   Number   Year/pps.

Annotation: _____

_____

_____

_____

_____

_____

_____

_____

_____

_____

_____

_____

EXERCISE 12.4: BEGINNING MY RESOURCE FILE

Instructions: The purpose of this exercise is for you to begin your own aids and resources file, perhaps on your favorite computer data base program, or on file cards. Organize your file in whatever way makes the most sense to you. We suggest the following: (a) name of resource; (b) how, when, and where available; (c) how to use, including name of teaching unit; (d) evaluative comment. This file can build throughout your professional career. You may wish to cross-reference your filing system to accommodate various categories of items, such as follows.

 1. Articles from magazines, newspapers, and periodicals.
 2. Computer programs.
 3. Copies of student worksheets.
 4. Examination question items.
 5. Free and inexpensive materials.
 6. Games and games sources.
 7. Guest speakers and other community resources.
 8. Laser videodisc sources.
 9. Media catalogs.
10. Motivational ideas.
11. Pictures, posters, and other stills.
12. Resources to order.
13. Supply catalogs.
14. Videocassette sources.
15. Miscellaneous.

Using a variety of strategies, resources, and media helps the teacher to effectively and efficiently reach more of the students more of the time. Secondary-school teachers are challenged to meet the needs and to teach content to a variety of students—linguistically and culturally different, poor readers and good readers. We hope the materials in this and in previous chapters are of help. Undoubtedly the future will bring additional technological innovations that are helpful to the classroom teacher; laser videodiscs, computers, and telecommunications equipment mark the beginning of a revolution for teaching the video generation.

QUESTIONS FOR CLASS DISCUSSION

1. What do you predict for the future of computers in the secondary school classroom during your teaching career?
2. What videodiscs have you found for use in your own teaching field?
3. What computer programs have you found as potentially useful in your own teaching?
4. During your visitations to secondary school classrooms, have you seen either computers or videodiscs being used?
5. What ideas can you generate for the use of props in your own teaching?
6. From the discussion of the learning experiences ladder did you get any new ideas for use in your own teaching?
7. From research literature what can you find about the use of telecommunications learning in your field?
8. From laser videodiscs a teacher can select and isolate material onto videocassette or computer disk for use in development of interactive instructional materials. During your school visits, have you observed this use?
9. Historically, changing styles in language and dress frequently caused good 16-mm films and filmstrips to lose their educational impact with students. Will certain videocassette tapes and videodiscs be subject to the same problem?
10. What questions do you have regarding the content of this chapter? How might answers be found?

SUGGESTED READINGS FOR CHAPTER 12

Bitter, G. G., and Camuse, R. A. *Using a Microcomputer in the Classroom.* 2d ed. Englewood Cliffs, NJ: Prentice Hall, 1988.

Caissy, G. A. "Evaluating educational software: A practitioner's guide." *Phi Delta Kappan* 66(4):249–250 (December 1984).

Clark, B., and Creager, A. "Communicating with computer-generated transparencies." *Audio Visual Directions* 3:69–73 (October/November 1981).

Colburn, P., et al. *Practical Guide to Computers in Education.* 2d ed. Reading, MA: Addison-Wesley, 1985.

Copyright Law: What Every School, College and Public Library Should Know. Skokie, Il: Association for Information Media and Equipment, 1987. Videotape.

Crawford, C. *The Art of Computer Game Design.* Berkeley, CA: Osborne/McGraw-Hill, 1984.

Elsdon, G. "Using the laser videodisc to teach biology." *California Science Teacher Journal* 18(4):4–6 (Summer 1988).

Green, L. *501 Ways to Use the Overhead Projector.* Littleton, CO: Libraries Unlimited, 1982.

Gross, B. "Can computer-assisted instruction solve the dropout problem?" *Educational Leadership* 46(5):49–51 (February 1989).

Heinich, R.; Molenda, M.; and Russell, J. D. *Instructional Media.* 3d ed. New York: Macmillan, 1989.

Heitzmann, W. R. *Educational Games and Simulations.* Rev. ed. Washington, DC: National Education Association, 1987.

Horn, R. V. "Laser videodiscs in education: endless possibilities." *Phi Delta Kappan* 68(9):696–700 (May 1987).

Howe, S. *Reading, Writing and Computers: Planning for Integration.* Needham Heights, MA: Allyn & Bacon, 1989.

Johnston, J. *Electronic Learning: From Audiotape to Videodisc.* Hillsdale, NJ: Lawrence Erlbaum, 1987.

Kahn, B. *Computers in Science: Using Computers for Learning and Teaching.* Cambridge: Cambridge University Press, 1986.

Kemp, J. E., and Smellie, D. C. *Planning, Producing, and Using Instructional Media.* 6th ed. New York: Harper & Row, 1989.

Kepner, H. S., Jr., ed. *Computers in the Classroom.* Washington, DC: National Education Association, 1982.

Levin, H. M., and Meister, G. "Is CAI cost-effective?" *Phi Delta Kappan* 67(10):745–749 (June 1986).

Miller, J. K. *Using Copyrighted Videocassettes in Classrooms, Libraries, and Training Centers.* 2d ed. Friday Harbor, WA: Copyright Information Services, 1988.

Reed, M. H. *The Copyright Primer for Librarians and Educators.* Chicago, IL: American Library Association, 1987.

Sinofsky, E. R. *A Copyright Primer for Educational and Industrial Media Producers.* Friday Harbor, WA: Copyright Information Services, 1988.

Talab, R. S. *Copyright and Instructional Technologies: A Guide to Fair Use and Permissions.* 2d ed. Washington, DC: Association for Educational Communications and Technology, 1989.

Turner, S., and Land, M. *Tools for Schools: Applications Software for the Classroom.* Belmont, CA: Wadsworth, 1988.

13

What Are Some Motivational Strategies? An Annotated List of More Than 200 Possibilities— An Idea Bank

What causes you to read this chapter? What makes the "punk-rocks" cut their hair "weird" and dye it with psychedelic colors? What made you "tick" when you were going to junior and senior high school? What forces drive our behavior, what motivates us to behave in a particular way? When we ask questions such as these, we are talking about *d*rives, *i*ncentives, *n*eeds, *m*otivations, and *a*spirations. We shall refer to this as DINMA.

The word *motive* is derived from the Latin *motivus*, meaning moving or impulse, and the psychologist's study of DINMA is analogous to the physicist's study of the phenomenon of motion: What starts the movement, what keeps it going, what stops it, and what decides the direction of the motion?

In this chapter, our intent is to identify salient features of DINMA as they relate to today's secondary school students and to suggest possible applications for secondary school teaching. As teachers, we must be cognizant of the significance of motivation:

- Motivation is a concept of major importance in American society.
- DINMA plays a major role in the success of a student's learning.
- Motivation in the secondary school sets the initial tone for career choices.

The teenagers of today are used to multimillion-dollar productions on television and the movie screen, but when they come into a classroom and are subjected each day to something short of a high-budget production, it is no wonder that they sometimes react in a less than highly motivated fashion. There is no doubt that our youth are growing up in a highly stimulated instant-action society, a society that has learned to expect instant headache relief, instant turn-on television sets, instant dinners, and perhaps even instant high-payment employment. In light of this we are on the side of you, the teacher, who is on the firing line each day, and who is expected to perform, perhaps instantly and entertainingly, but most certainly in a highly competent and professional manner, and in situations not even close to ideal. But in any case,

YOU MUST GAIN YOUR STUDENTS' ATTENTION
BEFORE YOU CAN TEACH!

In this chapter we provide a long list of potential motivators, first those general to all fields, then those more specific to particular subjects. We suggest that you read all of the entries for each field, for although one entry might be identified as specific to one field, it may also be useful in other areas, or it might stimulate a creative idea for your own stock of motivational techniques.

A. GENERAL IDEAS FOR MOTIVATION

1. Your students should clearly understand the objectives of your class activities and assignments.
2. Show enthusiasm and interest in what you have planned and are doing.
3. Present the proper quantity of content at the proper pace.
4. Vary the teaching procedures and the activities. Let students follow the activities of their choice with responsibility for change.
5. Use familiar examples in presenting your materials. Don't just teach definitions, principles, theorems, or rules. Be certain to explicate these with concrete examples that can be understood by students.
6. Use audiovisual materials—but do not assume that the materials have "built-in motivation." Select those that would be relevant and interesting to the students on the topic or subject matter that is under consideration.
7. Use objects for the lesson—foreign stamps, coins, models, antiques, toys, and so on.
8. Plan your orientation set induction (what you do the first few minutes of a class period) with care.
9. Keep students informed of their progress. Don't keep them in the dark as to where they stand.
10. Remember that students need to be recognized by you, by their parents, and by their peers.
11. Remember that students need steady awareness of progress being made, of "How am I doing?", "What can I do better next time?"
12. Talk with individual students about their problems and their interests.
13. Go down your roll book periodically and ask yourself what you know about each individual in the class.
14. Students are sometimes motivated by extrinsic devices such as tests. Use this technique judiciously, not as a weapon for punishment.
15. Give praise or rewards for jobs well done. But in groups, use strong praise sparingly.
16. Utilize a modified version of the elementary show-and-tell activity.
17. Have the students make a movie or slide show of class activities (e.g., a role-playing lesson). Let them plan and write the narration.

18. Word naming in various categories—such as synonyms, same initial letters, various uses of a term—becomes an indicator of ideational fluency.
19. Invite guest speakers when and where appropriate. Perhaps some of the parents can be resource persons. (See also number 22)
20. Hold small-group discussions in class. These often are more beneficial than are large-group or all-class discussions.
21. Utilize Mondays or days following holidays to share with your class an exciting or enjoyable experience.
22. Have students prepare a potential guest speaker resource file.
23. Try playing music in your classroom for mood setting, to relieve anxieties and tensions.
24. Use educational games in your teaching. (Refer to Chapter 11 for sources.)
25. Try role-playing to enhance the reality of material being learned.
26. Try unit contract or contract teaching.
27. Write individual and personalized notes to students on their papers, rather than merely letter grades or point scores.
28. Try videotaping an activity and replaying to the entire class.
29. Invent a useful educational game with class help.
30. Have students plan with you the "open house" and/or "back-to-school-night" activities. This helps in getting parents out, too.
31. Let the class help plan a field trip.
32. Have the students create and design a simulation game for a specific subject area or controversial issue in your field.
33. Create student mailboxes out of ice-cream cartons for distribution of papers. Be sure to have one for yourself. Everyone likes to receive mail. You may wish to limit mail delivery time to the first few minutes of the class period.
34. Recycle old textbooks by removing all text material but leaving pictures and diagrams; then have students create their own texts.
35. Obtain permission from the administration to redecorate your classroom with colorful walls, drapes, and stuffed furniture.
36. Use a mandala to demonstrate the importance of individual experiences, as in interpreting novels (for English), or current events (social studies), or paintings (art).
37. Have students list items related to the subject content, but write with their nondominant hand, as an introduction to brainstorming.
38. Every Friday, provide a "coupon bag" from which students who have behaved and performed well during the week may draw blindly one from a variety of coupons, such as "one free assignment," "5 points extra credit," "teacher's assistant for the day," "one free ice cream cone," "sit where you want for one day."

B. EXPRESSING ENCOURAGEMENT AS A MOTIVATOR

Parents and teachers often express words of encouragement as a motivator. Words and expressions have many different shades and connotations, and therefore it would be very useful for teachers to know what kind of messages the student is receiving: Does the expression truly convey acceptance, trust, confidence, and praise, or does it imply impatience, disappointment, and preaching? Consider the expressions that follow:

39. *"You have improved in . . ."* Improvement may not be where we would like it to be, but if there is progress, there is better chance for success. Students will usually continue to try if they can see some improvement.
40. *"You do a good job of . . ."* Point out some useful act or contribution in each student. Even a comment about something small and insignificant to the teacher may have great importance to a student.
41. *"We like (enjoy) you, but, we don't like what you do."* The student should never think he or she is not liked. It is important to distinguish between the student and the student's behavior, between the act and the actor.
42. *"You can help me (us, the others, etc.) by . . ."* To feel useful and helpful is important to everyone. Students want to be helpful; we have only to give them the opportunity.
43. *"Let's try it together."* Students who think they have to do things perfectly are often afraid to attempt something new for fear of making a mistake or failing.
44. *"You would like us to think you can't do it, but we think you can."* The student says or conveys that something is too difficult for him or her, and hesitates to even try it. If he or she tries and fails, the student has at least had the courage to try.
45. *"I'm sure you can straighten this out [solve this problem] but if you need any help, you know where to find me."* Adults need to express confidence that students are able to and will resolve their own conflicts, if given a chance.
46. *"I can understand how you feel [not sympathy, but empathy] but I'm sure you'll be able to handle it."* Sympathizing with another person seldom helps that person, but understanding the situation and believing in the person's ability to adjust to it is of much greater motivation to the student.

C. MOTIVATIONAL IDEAS SPECIFIC TO SUBJECT AREAS

Art

47. Use lyrics from popular music to influence class work, such as by putting the lyrics into pictures.
48. Bring in examples of the instructor's work, both current and beginning. This would enable students to relate more easily their own beginning frustrations with instructors.
49. Go outside into the schoolyard for free drawing experience. Do a class mural on a piece of quarter-inch plywood.
50. Use a mandala to demonstrate the importance of individual experience, as in interpreting paintings.
51. Arrange a field trip for the class to dig up natural clay. In class, sift and refine, soak in water, and work it into usable clay. Follow with hand-built clay project.

52. As part of a unit on the creative process, have each student draw on a piece of paper, then pass it on to the next person, and that person will make additions to the paper. Instructions could include "improve the drawing," "make the drawing ugly," "add what you think would be necessary to complete the composition."
53. As part of a unit on design or creativity, have students construct, design, and decorate their own kite. When the projects are complete, designate a time to fly them. Make necessary arrangements.
54. Listen to a musical recording and try to illustrate it.
55. Imagine that you're a bird flying over the largest city you have visited. What do you see, hear, smell, feel, taste? Draw a "sensory" map.
56. Assign a different color to each student. Have them arrange themselves into warm and cool colors and explain their decision (why blue is cool, etc.). (Include emotional responses to the color.)
57. Make a class visit to local galleries to observe works of contemporary artists.

Business Education

58. Choose a sentence or paragraph everyone has typed several times already. The instructions are for the students to type until they make an error, whether it be not capitalizing a word, typing a wrong letter, or whatever. The last one typing is the winner.
59. For production work, such as typing letters in a second-semester typing class, you, the teacher, take on the role of the "boss." Therefore, when a letter is typed the "boss" will receive it for signing. In this way the students are not just typing a letter for a grade, but typing it for the "boss," which will mean the letter will be set up according to the boss's instructions.
60. Make a field trip to the front office to observe and talk to the office workers. Those included in the interviews would be the principal's and vice-principal's secretary, the registrar, and attendance clerks. This field trip would interest some students to seek student jobs in the office. In addition, there are other jobs on campus that they can find out about and investigate for possible employment. Back in the classroom, have each student report his or her findings to the rest of the class.
61. Have office (administration) personnel come into class and dictate "real" letters and have students experience office-style dictation.
62. Compose crossword puzzles and newspaper cartoon strips in shorthand.
63. Arrange the students (on a rotational basis) to be "aides" to administration or to free teachers in order to take, transcribe, and type dictation.
64. Flash cards with account titles. Depending on the lesson, students could tell which type of statement the account would be found on, or you could use such cards to reinforce debits and credits. They could be used also as a few-minute drill with the whole class. They are more useful, though, to use as a game between two pupils who need to review. The one who gets most right wins.
65. In typing, on a designated day each week everyone could bring anything they wished to type, e.g., a page from a book, a friendly letter, a magazine article, a term paper, anything they wished.

66. In teaching T-accounts, divide the room into teams, the number on a team depending upon class size. There are four teams usually, so teams will be small. First have one team make up transactions and the other try to answer, then reverse. The team to get the most right out of 20 transactions would win.
67. In typing, by use of letters and following specific directions, students can type pictures.
68. In choosing "practice sets" for accounting, as a teacher try to choose from the sets available several different ones, trying to match student interest.
69. In accounting or shorthand, be specific about amount of work to be done during the week, the work to be collected the following Monday. If the work is all done by Friday at the end of class, there would be no homework over the weekend.
70. Use computer programs, if available, as another activity to stimulate interest.

English (Including ESL, Speech, Drama, Journalism)

71. For a unit such as Elizabethan English, a wall-to-wall mural depicting a village of the times may be a total class project. Students can research customs, costumes, and architecture. Others may paint or draw.
72. For the holidays students can design their own holiday cards, creating their own poems for their cards.
73. To enhance understanding of parts of speech, set up this problem: Provide several boxes containing different parts of speech. Each student is to form one sentence from the fragments chosen from each box, being allowed to discard only at a penalty. The students then nonverbally make trades with other students to make coherent, and perhaps meaningfully amusing sentences. A student may trade a noun for a verb but will have to keep in mind what parts of speech are essential for a sentence. Results may be read aloud as a culmination to this activity.
74. Try this for an exercise in objective versus subjective writing: After a lesson on descriptive writing, bring to the class a nondescript object, such as a potato, and place it before the class. Ask them to write a paragraph either describing the potato in detail, that is, its color, size, markings, and other characteristics, or describing how the potato feels about them.
75. Set up a special communications board somewhere in the room where students may write anonymously or post sealed comments addressed to particular individuals, including the teacher.
76. Read to the class a story without an ending, then ask the students to write their own endings or conclusions.
77. Ask the students to create an advertisement using a propaganda device of their choice.
78. Ask the students to each create and design an invention and then to write a "patent description" for the invention.
79. Establish a "mini-library" in a corner of your room.
80. Ask students to write a physical description of some well-known public figure, such as a movie star, politician, athlete, or musician. Other class members may enjoy trying to identify the "mystery" personality from the written descriptions.

81. A bulletin board may be designated for current events and news in the world of writers. Included may be new books and record releases as well as reviews. News of poets and authors may also be displayed.
82. Start a paperback book library in your classroom. Set aside some time each week for reading. Perhaps one of your students would volunteer to serve as your "librarian."
83. Ask your students to maintain a daily "journal," with emphasis on expressing their feelings and unedited thoughts. Journals should be accepted as personal statements, which are to remain unjudged.
84. Provide students a choice as to which novel they will read next.
85. Design a "game" where students give original names to stories or captions to cartoons.
86. Remove the text from a Sunday newspaper comic strip and have the students create the story line.
87. Use popular recordings to introduce vocabulary words. Use for analysis of antonyms, synonyms, listening, writing, comprehension, and other skill development.
88. Use newspaper want ads to locate jobs as a base for completing job application forms and creating letters of inquiry.
89. Use videotape equipment to record employer-employee role-play situations, interviews for jobs, or child-parent situations, to develop language and listening skills.
90. Have students choose a short story from a text and write it into a play.
91. Use a round robin type of oral exercise to practice different kinds of sentence development.
92. Design an antonym game such as: have one student write a word on the board, then a student who correctly guesses the antonym goes to the board.
93. Have students look in newspapers and magazines for examples of the type of writing being studied in class. Give points for correct examples brought in.
94. When beginning a poetry unit ask students to bring in the words to their favorite songs. Show how these fit into the genre of poetry.
95. Once in a while dress yourself in costume and makeup and role-play the character your class is studying.
96. Have your students look for commercial examples of advertisements that might be classed as "eco-pornographic," i.e., ads that push a product that is potentially damaging to our environment.
97. Change the environment and ask students to write poetry to see if the change in surroundings stimulates or discourages their creativeness. For example, take your class to a large supermarket to write (you are advised to make arrangements first).
98. Bring a television set to class and have your students analyze advertisements for the emotions they appeal to, techniques used, and their integrity. Try the same thing with radio, teen magazines, and other media.
99. Have each student maintain a dream diary from which creative writing develops.
100. Use imagery to stimulate creative writing.
101. Use a mandala to demonstrate the importance of individual experiences, as in interpreting poetry.

Foreign Languages

102. Draw a large outline of the target language country on cardboard and have students fill in the major cities, rivers, and mountains. They can illustrate products of different regions, costumes, and other significant characteristics of the country.
103. Translate the school menu into the target language, perhaps as a daily project of selected groups from within the class.
104. Perhaps your class could earn money and go to a target language restaurant as an end-of-the-year class activity. You could obtain copies of the restaurant menu in advance so that students could select and practice ordering in the target language.
105. Organize a spelling bee in the target language, using the target language alphabet.
106. Play "password" in the target language.
107. Begin a game by saying "I went to (the target country) and took a radio" in the target language. The next student repeats the sentence adding another item, e.g., "I went to (the target country) and took a radio and a raincoat." If a student misses an item he or she is out; this continues until only one student remains.
108. Show the students a tray containing several items they know how to say in the target language. Allow them a few minutes to study it, then remove it and ask them to list all of the items on the tray.
109. Provide puppets in native costume for students to use in practicing dialogue.
110. Invite an exchange student from (the target country) to talk with the class about his or her experiences and culture.
111. Once a month take the class on a "trip" to a city of a country where the target language is spoken, through the use of slides, pictures, realia, native speakers, and music.
112. Establish a pen-pal exchange with a beginning English class in a country where the target language is spoken.
113. Play "fill-in-the-word" game. Each student has a card with one word on it and must find other students with other parts to make a sentence (in the target language).
114. Take your class to a movie spoken in the target language.
115. If you can do it comfortably in the target language, practice opening your class with a *brief* anecdote about a dream, encounter, other event in your life, something in the news, or simply your thoughts about something—spoken at normal-to-rapid speed in the target language. Explain in advance that you will not expect them to understand all that you say, but simply to start getting a "feel" for the language.

Home Economics

116. Take still photos of class members at special events such as dinners, fashion shows, field trips, and special projects. Build a scrapbook or bulletin board with these and display on campus or at Open House.
117. Encourage students to enter their projects in outside contests such as county fairs.

118. Collect cartoons related to food costs, consumer problems, and family relationships.
119. Instruct students on the means of obtaining and completing consumer complaint forms.
120. Set up authentic food-tasting booths; set up campus tasting contests.
121. Establish a play school or nursery in conjunction with a child development class.
122. Use a large box wrapped as a gift to open a lesson on toy safety or toy purchasing.
123. Allow the students to plan and do the shopping for a food lab assignment.
124. Plan a unit on cultural foods, using the traditions, costumes, and music of a particular culture. Have the students decorate the room. Invite the principal for a meal and visit.
125. Take a trip to Small Claims Court. (Plan ahead and obtain permission from the Court.)
126. Plan a color and grooming unit. Ask students to match their personal colors closely to magazine photos. Match to color schemes to determine the most complimentary colors to wear or to use in household furnishings.
127. Try these nutrition-related games:
    a. Bring a bag full of all types of foods. Ask students to group them into the four basic food types. Let them eat the food as a reward for correct classifications.
    b. Pin the name of a food on a student's back. The student must ask another student questions until he or she guesses which food he or she is. Only yes-or-no response questions may be asked.
128. Plan a bulletin board displaying pictures of 100-calorie portions of basic nutritional foods and popular fad foods that contain only empty calories. The display can motivate a discussion on foods with calories and nutrients versus foods with empty calories.
129. Try this for motivation toward a unit on laundry: Pin the names of different garments on the back of students. The students are then to sort themselves into different wash loads. This is a fun game that motivates and involves an entire class.
130. For a clothing unit hold an "idea day." Ask each student to bring in an idea of something that can be done to give clothes a new look, a fun touch, or an extended wearing life. Ideas they may come with include: appliques, embroidery, tie-dye, batik, colorful patches, and restyling old clothes into current or creative fashions.
131. Have the students write, practice, and present skits, perhaps for videotape presentation, on consumer fraud.
132. Take the class on a field trip to the school cafeteria, a nearby supermarket, or a large restaurant. (Make necessary arrangements.)
133. Students should become familiar with shelving practices in stores and supermarkets.

Mathematics

134. Plan an in-class mathematical debate.
135. Try a game of mathematical baseball. Divide the class into two teams. Arrange

the room as a baseball field. The "pitcher" fires content questions to the "hitter." This can be a fun way to review for an examination.

136. Arrange mathematical tournaments with other schools.

137. Do a mathematical survey of your school campus.

138. Plan with your class a role-play unit where members role-play the solar system. Students calculate their weights, set up a proportion system, find a large field, and on the final day actually simulate the solar system, using their own bodies to represent the sun, planets, and moons. Arrange to have it photographed.

139. Have your students build mathematical models. Pyramids can be of special interest to the students.

140. Encourage your students to look for evidence of Fibonacci number series* in nature and in manufactured objects. Here are some examples of where evidence may be found: piano keyboard, petals on flowers, spermatogenesis and oogenesis, and many places in mathematics. Perhaps your students might like to organize a Fibonacci Club.

141. Become familiar with the many games available for teaching mathematics.

142. Divide the class into two teams—the metric team and the nonmetric team. Have each team solve a series of measurement conversion problems. One team would convert nonmetric to metric, the other would convert metric to nonmetric. The team with the most problems correct wins.

143. Join with a physical science class and visit a science museum.

144. Invite an engineer, physical scientist, or computer program writer to speak to the class on how mathematics applies to their profession.

Music

145. Hang a cloth bag on the wall. Buy a sack of potatoes. For every song that students learn to sing, get a potato, write a date and a title of the song learned, and put the potato in the bag. At the end of the semester, buy a MacDonald's certificate for each potato and divide them among the students.

146. Take the class to a concert. They can observe others playing their instruments.

147. Have students find ways in which music is used around them, e.g., for television.

148. Periodically during the school year, after the students are very familiar with a certain piece (have memorized it or can play it perfectly) switch the band or orchestra around by not putting any two of the same instruments together. For example, put no flutes next to each other, put a cello by a trumpet, a violin beside a drummer, or a saxophone next to a viola and bass. This ensures that each person knows his own part and can carry his own weight in terms of performance. This can also be done in chorus, mixing sopranos with altos, tenors, and basses, etc.

149. Find a popular song on the radio that students like. Transpose the melody into unfamiliar keys for each instrument. This makes the student want to learn the song, but in the process the student will have to become more familiar with his or her instrument.

150. Set aside one weekend morning a month and hold small informal recitals (workshops) allowing students to participate/observe the performance situation(s) among their peers and themselves. (Students might be told previously about

---

*Fibonacci numbers are a series of numbers, each of which is the sum of the preceding two, i.e., 1, 1, 2, 3, 5, 8 . . .

these "special days" and encouraged to prepare a selection of their own choosing.)

151. Listen to current popular musical recordings and discuss them as to musical content and performance techniques.

152. As an extra credit project, have students prepare brief oral reports on past composers and give an example of their music by recording, performance. (The student may even enjoy dressing the part of the composer.)

153. Trumpet Clinics: A. With trumpet teachers; B. With trumpet performers (all styles of music); C. With other students from other schools.

154. Plan different money-making projects such as singing telegrams.

155. Play a group-activity rhythm game, one such as the "Dutch Shoe Game" to get students to cooperate, work together, and enjoy themselves using rhythm. If students are willing to sit on the floor, it can be adaptable to any age level. Participants sit in a circle, and as the song is sung, each person passes one of his or her shoes to the person on the right in rhythm to the music. Shoes continue to be passed as long as verses are sung. Those with poor rhythm will end up with a pile of shoes in front of them!

156. Choose a rhythmical, humorous poem or verse to conduct. The students read the poem in chorus, while the teacher stands before them and conducts the poem as if it were a musical work. Students must be sensitive to the intonation, speed, inflection, mood, and dynamics that the teacher wants them to convey in their reading.

157. Play the game "Name that Tune" using works by composers the students have been studying, or take various styles of music and ask them to identify them with composers.

158. Do a series of studies of non-Western music. As a break from studying just Western music, once a week or once every two weeks prepare a program to expose students to the music of a different country, for example, Japan or India or the Polynesian Islands. Records can be used to introduce the sound of the music, slides can be used to view the country and its people, and instruments can be found from different countries. Guest speakers may be available to lecture or perform.

159. A field trip to the opera or a concert can be scheduled. Group rates are usually available, with half price for students as a rule.

160. To motivate a marching band and to let them know how much work goes into making a half-time show, have students form groups and let each group design a portion of a half-time show. For example, one group can put together what tunes should be played and another group could put together the entrance movements of the show.

161. Pick students at random to be the drum major (student band leader) and lead the band in a tune or a given portion of a half-time show; this will not only stimulate interest, but also help students to be able to organize musical patterns.

162. Have the students bring in some of their favorite recordings of popular present-day bands. Play the recordings for the entire class while analyzing each band's style. Give a contest by dividing the class and having the students attempt to classify each band by the style of each recording.

163. To improve marching band skills and to motivate precision marching, let each section of the band (brass, woodwinds, and percussion) demonstrate its marching ability before the rest of the band. At the end of the semester the best marching section can be rewarded.

164. Give students the opportunity to write their own original composition which can be performed in public.

Physical Education

165. Students will choose the famous athlete whom they most admire. A short report will be written about the athlete. The student will then discuss the attributes and/or characteristics that they admire in the athlete, and how they feel they can emulate those qualities.
166. Students will make up an exercise routine to their favorite record and share it with the class.
167. Have the class divide into groups. Given the basic nonlocomotive skills, have each group come up with a "people machine." Each student within the group is hooked up to another demonstrating a nonlocomotive skill and adding some sort of noise to it. Have a contest for the most creative people machine.
168. Have a special talent day—where students may demonstrate an individual talent or group talent, relating it to physical education. (Might have them keep this in mind, practice on rainy days, and present it on a rainy day)
169. Have a mini-Olympic day where students help create the various events to be used, and give honors to winners.
170. Students are given a chance to design a balance beam routine that has two passes on the beam and that must include: front support mount, forward roll, leap, low or high turn, visit, chasse, and cross support dismount. These routines will be posted to show the variety of ways the different maneuvers can be put together.
171. Divide the class into groups. Have them create a new game or activity for the class, using only the equipment they are given. Let the class play these newly created games.
172. Use Friday as a game day—do not introduce anything new. Review what was taught earlier in the week. Have some kind of competitive games or relays related to the skills previously learned.
173. Videotaping is a good device to show student their errors and their improvements in a skill such as batting. It helps them see what they are doing and helps them develop a kinesthetic awareness of their movement.
174. Organize and make available to your students a trip to a professional, collegiate, or any highly skilled team's game. This usually will motivate them if they are at all interested in the sport.
175. Engage a guest speaker, preferably a professional athlete or coach in the sport you are teaching, to talk or demonstrate specific skills.
176. Exercises done to popular music. Let students take turns bringing in music and leading the exercises. The teacher will furnish a general outline to follow.

Science

177. Have your students create microscopes with bamboo rods and drops of water at each end.
178. Have your students make litmus indicators from petals of flowers.

179. Assign themes or problems that require students to predict or hypothesize decision making in a critical incident.
180. Use Polaroid or video cameras for students to record and immediately share observations.
181. Use cassette-tape recorders to record sounds of the environment. Compare day and night sounds. (This can also be helpful in poetry writing.)
182. If you are a life science teacher, make sure your classroom looks like a place for studying life rather than death.
183. The technique of "show and tell" is an excellent motivator and can be modified to be useful to the secondary school teacher. Do not allow students to "rip off" the environment of such things as flowers or beneficial insects or tide-pool life.
184. Encourage students to hypothesize, then to collect data, using their own environment.
185. Use your imagination. If you want, for example, to study predator-prey relationships but you are located in an inner-city school, then your class might use landlord-tenant situations for the study.
186. Have your students make their own cosmetics. Share what you are doing with the Home Economics teachers—perhaps you can combine your efforts.
187. Divide your class into groups and ask each group to create an environment for an imaginary animal, using discarded items from the environment. By asking questions each group will try and learn about other groups' "mystery" animals.
188. Be aware of relevant programs being shown on local television stations. Perhaps you can let students observe one during class time, by pretaping if necessary.
189. If your students have never seen an ocean, a forest, or mountains, and you cannot take them on an appropriate field trip, then do the next best thing and go yourself (perhaps during vacations) and take slides or moving pictures to show them. (Become aware of any income-tax advantages available to you as a teacher.)
190. Become familiar with the many educational games available for teaching science.
191. Students can summarize the steps in a process (for example, setting up a distillation) by *taking photos* of each step to illustrate an instruction book for other students.
192. Let each student "adopt' a chemical element. The student then researches that element and becomes the class expert whenever that particular substance comes up in discussion. There could be a special bulletin board for putting up questions on interesting or little-known facts about the elements.
193. Have the students bring to class current newspaper clippings on environmental problems having to do with chemistry (toxic waste spills, pesticide application, etc.). Have students form discussion groups to try to find practical ways to deal with the problem. This could become a longer-term project, with library research and letter-writing for more information.
194. Milk can be precipitated, separated, and the solid product dried to form a very hard substance that was, in the days before plastic, used to make buttons. Let students make their own buttons from milk.
195. Spray paint molecular models gold. Give the "golden molecule" award for exceptional lab projects, etc. Or give the award for the most disastrous failure (*if the student has a good sense of humor*). The award could be given to a lab group each week to encourage working as a group.

196. Have your students build a model of a molecule using gumdrops and toothpicks. Different colored gumdrops are to represent different elemental atoms. When they show the teacher that they have correctly named and constructed their models, they can eat the gumdrops.

197. Blow a balloon up in class and hold it between your thumb and forefinger. Let it go. Explain that *you* have just demonstrated potential energy and rocket propulsion. Go into the lecture on potential energy.

198. Have your students make their own useful items as related to science, things such as the following:
    a. Library paste: one-half cup cornstarch to three-fourths cup cold water, stir to paste, then add six cups of boiling water and stir until translucent, then cool to room temperature.
    b. Baby oil: two tablespoons of almond oil, eight tablespoons of olive oil, and a few drops of perfume, stir all ingredients together—keep out of reach of children.
    c. Concrete cleaner: dry mix these—sodium metasilicate, three and one-quarter cups; trisodium phosphate, three-quarters cup; soda ash, one-half cup.

Social Science

199. Establish a special "people and things" bulletin board.
200. Have your class play charades to learn geography.
201. Set up a classroom broadcast studio where students prepare and present news broadcasts.
202. Take your class on an imaginary trip around the world. Students can role-play countries.
203. Let your class plan how they would improve their living environment, beginning with the classroom, then moving out to the school, home, and community.
204. Become familiar with the many games available for teaching social studies. Refer to Chapter 11 for sources.
205. Start a pictorial essay on the development and/or changes of a given area in your community, e.g., a major corner or block adjacent to the school. This is a study that would continue for years and that has many social, political, and economic implications.
206. Start a folk hero study. Each year ask "What prominent human being who has lived during the twentieth century do you most admire?" Collect individual responses to the question, tally, and discuss. After you have done this for several years you may wish to share with your class for discussion purposes the results of your surveys of previous years.
207. Play the *Redwood Controversy* game. (See Chapter 11.) Perhaps you and your class can design a simulation game on a controversial social issue.
208. Role-play a simulated family movement West in the 1800s. What items would they take? What would they throw out of the wagon to lighten the load?
209. Have students collect music, art, or athletic records from a particular period of history. Compare with today. Predict the future.
210. Using play money, establish a capitalistic economic system within your classroom. Salaries may be paid for attendance and bonus income for work well

done, taxes may be collected for poor work, and a welfare section established in a corner of the room.

211. Divide your class into small groups and ask that each group make predictions as to what world governments, world geography, world social issues, or some other related topic will be like some time in the future. Let each group give its report, followed by debate and discussion.

212. "Alphabet Geography": A place is given by the teacher, such as a state, city, river, etc. The next person must name a place starting with the same letter as the last in that previously mentioned. Students are eliminated or given points. This game can be used as a drill to acquaint students with place names and where these places are. The class can be divided into groups, or students can stand individually.

213. Use a mandala to demonstrate the importance of individual experiences, as in interpreting current events.

With the preceding suggestions we have only scratched the surface in providing ideas. The total possibilities are limited only by the courage and imagination of the teacher.

A source of valuable information, including ideas for motivation, can be the professional journal(s) for your field.

EXERCISE 13.1. SELECTING AND EXPERIMENTING WITH A MOTIVATIONAL TECHNIQUE

From the list of motivational ideas select one (yes, only one!) and try it out during your student teaching. Yes, you may modify it however you wish. After you have tried it, report back to this class and share the results.

My name _____ My subject field _____

Grade and school _____

The motivational idea I used: _____

_____

_____

_____

_____

The results: _____

_____

_____

_____

_____

Would I use it again? _____

_____

_____

_____

_____

Modifications I would make: _____

_____

_____

_____

_____

QUESTIONS FOR CLASS DISCUSSION

1. Did you find in our list any ideas that were particularly objectionable to you? Which and why?
2. Do you know the difference between extrinsic and intrinsic sources of motivation? Explain.
3. Did you "discover" a professional journal that is of particular interest to you? Which and why does it interest you?
4. What kinds of teaching/learning activities motivate junior high school students today? High school students? Any difference?
5. How long is the attention span of a typical secondary-school student today? Does it differ from that of the past? How do you know?
6. Has student viewing of television been beneficial or detrimental to the efforts of a secondary-school classroom teacher? What evidence can you find to support or reject your opinion?
7. Does the motivation of a secondary-school student vary from one period of the day to the next, simply because of the time of the day? Can you find any research evidence to support your opinion?
8. What effect does the blood sugar level of a secondary-school student have upon his or her motivation level? What research can you find regarding this?
9. Do certain subjects lend themselves to easier student motivation? Which and why? What could a teacher of a "low-motivation course" learn from this?
10. Is there a particular period of the day you would prefer to teach a particular subject to a particular group of students? Why or why not?
11. What other questions do you have regarding the general topic of motivation? How might answers be found?

SUGGESTED READINGS FOR CHAPTER 13

Ames, C., and Ames, R., eds. *Research on Motivation in Education, Vol II: The Classroom Milieu.* Orlando: Academic Press, 1985.

Brophy, J. "Synthesis of research on strategies for motivating students to learn." *Educational Leadership* 45(2):40–48 (October 1987).

Deci, E. L., and Ryan, R. M. *Intrinsic Motivation and Self-Determination in Human Behavior.* New York: Plenum Press, 1985.

Dhority, Lynn. *Acquisition Through Creative Teaching: The Artful Use of Suggestion in Foreign Language Instruction.* Sharon, MA: Center for Continuing Development, 1984.

Galyean, B. *Mind Sight: Learning Through Imaging.* Long Beach, CA: Center for Integrative Learning, 1983.

Good, T. L., and Brophy, J. E. *Looking in Classrooms,* (Chapter 8). 4th ed. New York: Harper and Row, 1987.

Maley, Al, and Grellet, F. *Mind Matters: Activities and Puzzles for Language Learners.* Cambridge, MA: Cambridge University Press, 1981.

Steinhaus, H. *Mathematical Snapshops.* Oxford: Oxford University Press, 1983.

PART IV

Classroom Management, Discipline, and Legal Guidelines

Part IV assists you

- In coping with the daily challenges of teaching.
- With guidelines for beginning the school year.
- In preparing your classroom behavior rules.
- In establishing an effective classroom environment.
- In dealing with the clerical responsibilities.
- In understanding your teaching rights and the rights of the students.
- In understanding effective classroom management procedures.
- In understanding symptoms of drug abuse.
- In understanding how to work with difficult students.

A TEACHERS' CONTRACT IN 1923[1]

Your pay will be $5.00 a month, providing you meet these conditions:

1. Don't get married, and don't keep company with men.
2. Don't be away from home between the hours of 8 p.m. and 6 a.m.
3. Don't loiter in ice cream parlors.
4. Don't smoke cigarettes, don't drink beer, wine, or whiskey.
5. Don't leave town without permission.
6. Don't ride in a carriage or automobile with any man except your father or brother.
7. Don't dress in bright colors, dye your hair, or use face powder, mascara, or lipstick.

[1]Original source unknown, but thought to have been in an Idaho teacher's contract dated 1923.

14

What Do I Need to Know to Cope with the Daily Challenges of Secondary-School Teaching?

Wet spitballs are flying. Some wads are sticking to the classroom ceiling. Aerodynamic paper-shapes spin through the educational sky. Faces are made by creative students. Giggles and whispers are heard. Squirming students are seen. Some students are rude and others refuse to do their lessons as one teacher pleads, "Please be quiet" in Harry Allard's *Miss Nelsen Is Missing* (Houghton, 1977), an imaginative picture story often read aloud to primary and middle grade students. How Miss Nelsen solves her problem of class management (sending in a witchy substitute) may be entirely different from how you plan to solve your problems during the daily challenge of teaching. However, resolving your concerns about classroom management is one step—a giant step—in building your competency as a classroom teacher.

Good classroom management techniques result from careful thought and planning, and should not be left for the student teacher to learn on the job in a sink-or-swim fashion. Consider these general guidelines:

1. Your *voice* should be natural and relaxed. Do not scream and shout at your students, or try to talk over them. If the students are beginning to get too noisy, then change the lesson strategy (e.g., a silent board lesson).
2. Know what to *expect* of each student. Clarify so each student knows what is expected of him or her.

   Remember, in both guidelines, 1 and 2, your own modeling behavior counts!

3. Match the *pacing* of the lessons to the capabilities of your students. Going too fast with slow students will bring trouble just as will going too slow with the more capable students. When you have a class with both slow and fast students, then you will need to vary your strategies frequently and to use cooperative and individual learning strategies.

   A cooperative learning technique that may work for you begins with thinking carefully about individual students in your class and dividing your students into mixed-ability teams of four students per team. You may reward your students on the basis of achievement of all team members.

4. Use *humor* when appropriate. Humor relaxes tension and facilitates learning. Laughing *with* the students is important in making each one feel welcome to the classroom, and the learning environment pleasant and productive.
5. There will be unexpected *class interruptions,* some of which will be out of your control. Prepare so that you can keep your students on task when such interruptions do occur.
6. Teach students the *classroom rules* early (discussed in the next section).

State your classroom behavior rules in positive, rather than in negative, terms. In middle and junior high grades you may wish to post the rules above the writing board. For all students, give positive verbal reinforcers to students who follow the rules. For students who break the rules, the following generalization is appropriate: one break gets a reminder; for the second break, a note or phone call to parents or guardians; for the third break, a trip to the office; for the fourth break, suspension from class.

A. BEGINNING THE SCHOOL YEAR

A major contributor to effective classroom management during the school year is the way you begin the year; a good beginning will make life easier for the entire year. Consider the following guidelines for getting the year started:

1. Spend time at school before the year begins, getting your classroom organized, finding out where equipment and materials are kept, and preparing your teaching plans.
2. During days prior to the beginning of school, think carefully about your classroom behavior rules (CBRs), the rationale for each, and then on the first day of school, state the rules clearly, with their rationales, so that your students understand them. For middle school grades, you might even wish to use a class meeting to discuss situations for rules that need to be made, and then have your students decide on the actual rules. Have no more rules than absolutely necessary, drop or change the rules when appropriate, and involve students in making decisions about rules as much as possible.

ESTABLISHING CLASSROOM BEHAVIOR RULES

When establishing the CBRs, remember this point: the learning time needs to run efficiently (i.e., no dead time), smoothly (i.e., routines are established; transitions between activities are smooth), and with minimum disruption. When stating the classroom rules, try to do so in a positive manner and stress the dos rather than the don'ts. Consider the following things that students need to know:

ESTABLISHING CLASSROOM BEHAVIOR RULES (Continued)

a. *How to correctly obtain your attention and help.* Most teachers who are effective classroom managers ask that students raise their hands and only until the teacher acknowledges (usually by a nod) that he or she has seen the student's hand. With that acknowledgement, the student may lower his or her hand. To prevent that student from becoming bored with waiting, it is important that the teacher attend to that student as quickly as possible.

b. *How to correctly enter and leave the classroom.* When the class (tardy) bell rings, and prior to the final dismissal bell, teachers who are effective classroom managers expect students to be in their seats and to be attentive to the teacher. Students work best when the expectations are clear to them, and when there is an established routine. *Teachers must plan carefully how they will spend the first and final few minutes of each class period or school day. This means establishing and maintaining a regular routine.*

c. *How to correctly store personal belongings.* Students need to know where, when, and how to properly store, retrieve, and care for their coats, books, pencils, medicine, and other items. Classroom control is best when items that students need for class activities are neatly arranged and located in places that require minimum foot traffic.[1]

d. *How to correctly go to the drinking fountain and to the bathroom.* Once again, we emphasize the importance of establishing a regular routine, and at the same time we should point out that teachers who are effective class managers avoid having the entire class line up at the same time to do something—*whenever the entire class is forced into off-task time (e.g., standing in line), problems are most certain to occur.*

e. *How to behave during a class interruption.* Unfortunately, class interruptions do occur: For some important reason, the principal or some other person from the office may need to interrupt the class to see the teacher or a student or to make an announcement to the entire class. Students need to know what behavior is expected of them during such interruptions.

f. *How to correctly obtain and to use papers, books, the pencil sharpener, and other materials, supplies, and equipment available for their use in the classroom.* As stated earlier, classroom management is easiest to maintain when there is the least amount of foot traffic, when there are established routines that students clearly expect and understand, when there is the least amount of student off-task time, and when items that students need for class activities are neatly arranged and located in nearby places. Therefore, plan the room arrangement, equipment and materials storage, preparation of equipment, materials, and transitions between activities so that you avoid needless delays and confusion.[2]

g. *What to do when they are late to school, or when they will be leaving school early.* Understand the school policies regarding early dismissals and tardy students, and follow them. With regard to school policies, routinize your own procedures so that students clearly understand what they are to do if they must leave school early (e.g., a medical appointment), or are tardy.

[1]Thomas L. Good and Jere E. Brophy, *Looking in Classrooms*, 4th ed. (New York: Harper & Row, 1987) p. 232.
[2]Good and Brophy, p. 232.

3. It is important that you constantly monitor student behavior and respond quickly and appropriately to both "good" and "bad" behaviors, establish early your expectations and the consequences students may expect. Consider the following.

TEACHER RESPONSES TO APPROPRIATE STUDENT BEHAVIORS

It is clear that behaviors that are reinforced are most likely to reoccur. Knowing that, then, emphasizes the importance of reinforcing appropriate student behaviors, and of *not* reinforcing their not-wanted behaviors. Teacher reinforcement of good student behaviors usually comes in some form of praise. For positive reinforcement of student behaviors, the form of that praise is important. As discussed earlier, to be effective the praise from the teacher should be

a. Private, low-keyed, and specific to the behavior.
b. Spontaneous, sincere, verbal *and* nonverbal, and individualized.

TEACHER RESPONSES TO INAPPROPRIATE STUDENT BEHAVIORS

Even though you follow the guidelines for effective teaching that have been established in this resource guide, there still will be misbehaviors by students. Infrequent and minor disruptions resulting from the behaviors of students can and should be ignored by the teacher (e.g., when a student is slow to close his workbook after the teacher has asked the class to put their workbooks away and get ready for another activity). Too-frequent interventions by a teacher can cause more problems than they cure. Sometimes you and the student have a better relationship when you ignore some minor infractions.

Too many times teachers attempt to reprimand misbehaviors with verbal commands (*direct intervention*), when nonverbal gestures (*indirect intervention*) such as eye contact, touch, and teacher body language can be less disruptive and more effective in quieting a disruptive student.

Direct intervention (verbal reminders or direct verbal commands to the students) should be reserved for only the most serious misbehaviors. When using direct intervention, the teacher should give a direct statement either reminding the student of what he or she is supposed to be doing, or telling the student what to do. Do *not* intervene by asking a question (e.g., "John, why are you doing that?").

When giving students directions about what they are supposed to be doing, you may be asked by the student "Why?". You may give a brief educational reason but to *not* get defensive about it or make threats. And, rather than spending an inordinate amount of time on the misbehavior, try and focus the student's attention on a desired behavior.

Most classroom problems will be prevented or resolved by guidelines that have been presented in this resource guide. When students reach middle and junior high school, peer pressure and resentment of authority by certain students can result in classroom management becoming a major concern of teachers at those grade levels. Major problems in classroom control may call for extra effort on the part of the teacher in understanding and in dealing with them (see the next chapter). There are no short-term solutions for the teacher when trying to resolve a conflict with a student who causes major problems for that teacher. Although punishment (e.g., suspension) may offer short-term relief to the situation, long-term counseling is probably called for, but as stated by Good and Brophy:

There has been much debate, but little research and certainly no conclusive evidence, about how to handle the most serious problems: racial and other group tensions; severe withdrawal and refusal to communicate; hostile, antisocial act-ing-out, truancy; refusal to work or obey; vandalism; and severe behavioral disorders or criminality. Psychotherapists have not achieved much success in dealing with behavior disorders, and neither they nor correctional institutions have achieved even modest success in dealing with severe delinquency and crimi-nality. Yet teachers typically are asked to cope with such problems . . .[1]

An increasing number of effective middle schools are those that have recognized that students in their early adolescent years need a special educational experience to nurture them through an unstable interval of their development, providing these students with interdisciplinary teaching teams and supportive guidance activities. *To be academically effective and to minimize teachers' classroom management problems, schools and teachers that teach students in their early adolescent years must be responsive to the energy levels and special needs of children of that developmental stage.* Simply making minor changes in grade-level representation and changing the name of a school from "jun-ior high" to "middle school" is ineffective. To be effective, techniques for teaching these students must be distinguishable from those that are commonly used in high school teaching.[2]

4. Use strong communication skills, such as giving directions clearly, listening care-fully and actively, and smiling when appropriate.

To cope with the daily challenges of secondary-school teaching, you should be able to maintain the physical environment of your classroom; be efficient in your routines, clerical responsibilities, and class management (see Chapter 13); and realize the legal guidelines that exist for you in your state's education code to protect and ensure your teaching rights and the rights of your students.

B. SURVEYING THE PHYSICAL ENVIRONMENT OF THE CLASSROOM

Consider your omnipresent challenge of maintaining the physical environment of your classroom. Check yourself on each item in Exercise 14.1 and share your responses with your classmates.

---

[1]Good and Brophy, p. 274.

[2]For a powerful report that makes strong recommendations for the education of this age group, see the 1989 task force report, "Turning Points: Preparing American Youth for the 21st Century," available from the Carnegie Council on Adolescent Development, 11 Dupont Circle, N.W., Washington, DC 20036.

EXERCISE 14.1: WHAT SHOULD I DO TO MAINTAIN THE PHYSICAL ENVIRONMENT OF MY CLASSROOM?

Instructions: The following provides a self-check list of items to consider to maintain the physical environment of your classroom. After you have completed your self-check, use the questions as a focus for a class discussion about the importance of the physical environment of classrooms.

	Needs Attention	Satisfactory
1. Am I always aware of the physical environment of my classroom?	_____	_____
2. Do I take the time to check the room temperature each day?	_____	_____
3. Do I assure that there is adequate ventilation?	_____	_____
4. Do I adjust the window shades to control any glare or bright light that enters the room as the sun changes position during the school day?	_____	_____
5. Am I concerned with the room's overall appearance?	_____	_____
6. Is my classroom neat and well organized?	_____	_____
7. Do the bulletin boards contribute to the appearance of the classroom?	_____	_____
8. Have I included classroom decorations about approaching events, holidays, students' art work, or information about units, topics, or themes the students are studying?	_____	_____
9. Are classroom storage spaces well organized?	_____	_____
10. Are shelves arranged in a neat and orderly manner?	_____	_____
11. Are materials stored in a safe manner, e.g., no heavy objects placed high on shelving?	_____	_____
12. Is classroom equipment accessible but out of student traffic patterns?	_____	_____
13. Have I considered a functional seating arrangement for the students and provided space for such activities as independent work, construction projects, and computer-assisted instruction?	_____	_____
14. Will this functional arrangement allow the students to quickly rearrange the seating if needed for such activities as cooperative learning activities, or for a skit?	_____	_____
15. Have I considered the seating arrangements to meet individual needs of students (such as for left-handed students, or for those with hearing or vision difficulties)?	_____	_____
16. Do I need to provide a "time-out" area for a student whose behavior interrupts the learning of other students?	_____	_____

17. Have I carefully planned the ways I will organize the materials I need for the lessons each day?   _____ _____

18. Have I systematically prepared, collected, and stored all of the supplies I will need, and placed or stored them in a convenient location?   _____ _____

19. Have I considered the most efficient way to distribute these materials and/or supplies to the students? For example, consider having one student from each group, or row, as a teacher helper in distributing materials.   _____ _____

20. Have I considered an effective collection method?   _____ _____

Review your responses. What are some items that need your careful attention? Share your responses with your peers.

Now, turn your attention to the following information about maintenance and clerical responsibilities.

C. ACHIEVING ROUTINE MAINTENANCE

Consider the routine maintenance procedures that you have observed in a middle school, junior high school, or high school classroom. Did the teacher have a routine procedure for the start of the school day? What were the attendance procedures? The lunch-count procedures? Record your observations here and discuss with your peers.

_____

_____

_____

_____

The normal routines of the classroom may be interrupted on certain days or at certain times during a day. For instance, not all days are equal in terms of the energy level of the students in the classroom. Your anticipation and careful planning for days of higher energy levels will undoubtedly help preserve your own mental health. Times of high energy level for some students are:

• At the beginning of each school day.
• Toward the ending of each school day.
• Toward the ending of each Friday afternoon.
• Just before lunch.
• In anticipation of a holiday.
• In anticipation of a field trip.
• In anticipation of a special event, e.g., being photographed for the annual school picture, or a school assembly.
• The day a substitute teacher arrives.
• The day of report cards.

What experiences have interrupted your classroom routines? What specifically could you plan to help avert some of these potentially interrupting days?

_____

_____

_____

_____

_____

_____

_____

_____

_____

After the beginning of a school day, teachers demonstrate their abilities in making smooth transitions from the opening exercises into a following lesson. What transition statements have you heard during your classroom observations? Were these transitions clear and concise? Did the teacher state his or her expectations? From your point of view, which transition statements seem to be most effective? Write your selected statements below and discuss them with your classmates, then turn your attention to Exercise 14.2.

EXERCISE 14.2: HOW CAN I MAINTAIN EFFICIENCY IN RESPONDING TO ROUTINES AND CLERICAL RESPONSIBILITIES?

Instructions: The following provides a self-check list of items to consider in responding to routines and clerical responsibilities. After you have completed your self-check, use the statements as a focus for a class discussion about classroom routines and clerical responsibilities. These statements and the discussion will promote your efficiency and help you to use your time more productively.

	I Can Do This!	Not Yet!
1. I can develop a quick and accurate procedure for taking attendance, and for reporting students who are tardy.	_____	_____
2. I understand the value of beginning the academic day with a sharing time, opening exercises and activities, or with a lesson—instead of requiring students to wait quietly and idly while I take attendance, lunch counts, etc.—and realize I can accomplish those tasks five or ten minutes later, when the students are busy.	_____	_____
3. I understand the importance of *my* reading information from the school bulletin to the students.	_____	_____
4. I can organize the distribution and collection of materials, supplies, equipment, and furniture in my classroom.	_____	_____
5. I can keep a current accounting of the materials, supplies, equipment, and furniture in my room.	_____	_____
6. I can provide accurate information about materials that are loaned.	_____	_____
7. I can enforce school and district policies when books, equipment, or furniture are damaged.	_____	_____
8. I understand that my gradebook is a legal document that should be a current and accurate record of each student's educational progress.	_____	_____
9. I can evaluate all student assignments in an efficient manner and return their evaluated work promptly.	_____	_____
10. I can maintain due dates for homework and other special assignments, remembering to acknowledge illnesses, emergencies, and other special reasons for absences or lateness of work turned in.	_____	_____
11. I understand that a student's improvement may be a signal for a phone call from me to interested parents, just as much as a student's difficulties may be.	_____	_____
12. I understand that notes to parents can convey positive messages more often than negative ones.	_____	_____

EXERCISE 14.3: WRITING A POSITIVE NOTE TO A PARENT/GUARDIAN

Instructions: Indeed, a note to the parents (or guardian) of one of your students can convey a positive message. Consider one example of a positive message from you to a parent. Practice writing one example of a positive message below. Ask another teacher candidate to react to your message. Does your message convey what you intend for it to say?

Situation: _____

_____

Practice note to parent: _____

_____

_____

_____

_____

Reaction comments:

Review your responses. What are areas you want to focus on for class discussion? Talk about them with others, then turn your attention to the next section on legal guidelines that support your teaching rights and the rights of secondary-school students.

D. LEGAL GUIDELINES THAT SUPPORT YOUR TEACHING RIGHTS AND THE RIGHTS OF SECONDARY-SCHOOL STUDENTS

You need to know that **Federal Law Title IX** prohibits the schools from discriminating on the basis of sex. Girls and boys must be treated the same in classes that they take, in the ways they are treated in course work, in counseling sessions, and in extracurricular activities. Further, no teacher, administrator, other school employee, or student can make sexual advances toward a student (touching or speaking in a sexual manner). Students should be informed of their rights under this law and may report any suspected violations of their rights to the school principal. Each district or school will have further steps to follow in this process of protecting a student's rights.

You probably have a multitude of questions regarding that which you as a teacher can and cannot do, and about what you must and must not do. Without reading ahead, write down some of those questions that you have.

_____

_____

_____

_____

_____

_____

_____

_____

_____

_____

_____

_____

The topic of teacher and student rights often generates many concerned questions. Teacher candidates ask about the legal status of a teacher, about the legal status of the secondary-school student, and about the legal status of the teaching contract with the school district. Other teacher candidates are interested in tenure laws, retirement laws, and teacher's organizations. Still others are concerned about the collective bargaining framework, the legal requirements concerning student discipline, teaching liability, and teaching negligence. Almost all teacher candidates want to know something about their legal status during the student teaching experience.

Of course, you have certain rights that cannot be overlooked, and your school administration carries the responsibility to safeguard these rights. What are your rights? Turn your attention to Exercise 14.4.

EXERCISE 14.4: WHAT LEGAL GUIDELINES ARE AVAILABLE TO ME?

Instructions: Consider the following questions about your teaching rights and respond. Discuss with your classmates, and check your responses against the education code and other existing laws for your state.

	Yes!	No!
1. Do you have the right to expect your classroom to be free from disruption by students, parents, and others?	_____	_____
2. Do you have the right to expect each student to come to class with the materials necessary to accomplish the educational activities?	_____	_____
3. Do you have the right to pertinent information about any student placed in your classroom?	_____	_____
4. For specified reasons, do you have the right to request that a particular student be transferred out of your classroom?	_____	_____
5. If you are the teacher responsible for an extracurricular activity, do you have the right to exclude a particular student from that activity?	_____	_____
6. According to your state's education code, do you have the right to suspend a student from your class?	_____	_____
7. Do you have the right to use reasonable physical restraint to protect yourself or other students?	_____	_____
8. Do you have the right to expect support from your school administrator?	_____	_____

Your secondary school students have rights, too.

	Yes!	No!
1. Do students have the right to due process?	_____	_____
2. In your state, does due process include a school hearing, knowledge of the charges, and the student's opportunity to defend?	_____	_____
3. Do your students have the right to know what behavior is expected of them?	_____	_____
4. Do your students have the right to know what consequences will occur for noncompliance of rules and regulations?	_____	_____
5. Do your students have the right to be treated in a courteous and respectful manner?	_____	_____
6. Do your students have the right to expect that their constitutional rights will be respected?	_____	_____
7. Providing that students meet the qualifications of a sponsoring organization, do students have the right to participate in school activities?	_____	_____

Key to Exercise 14.4:

Although the state education code varies from state to state, we predict that for your state, all answers to these questions above will be yes. Check with the instructor for your course. If you scored

_____ 10–15 correct. You are not going to be thrown into confusion by legal terms or by school situations that arise. Your knowledge of teachers' rights and students' rights will help you feel in control in a variety of educationally related situations.

_____ 6–9 correct. You have a fair knowledge of teachers' rights and students' rights but could use some additional information.

_____ 0–5 correct. To increase your knowledge in this area, try investing time to review the pertinent education code entries from your state and local districts.

Now that you have considered the rights of teachers and of students, what else do you need to know about student conduct and certain standards of student behavior? Sometimes a student is expelled or suspended for misbehavior. What does a student do to cause one of these actions, and how is the action carried out in your state or local district? For these actions we encourage you to research the approaches used in local districts in your state.

EXERCISE 14.5: WHAT DO I KNOW ABOUT LEGAL GUIDELINES IN MY STATE FOR THE SECONDARY-SCHOOL TEACHER?

Instructions: Respond to each of the following questions; then research the answers according to the education code of your state and compare your state's code with the answer key that follows, which is based mostly on California state codes and legal decisions.

	Yes	No
1. As a certificated female teacher, will I receive less salary than a certificated male teacher when we both perform similar teaching services?	___	___
2. Has teacher tenure been abolished in my state?	___	___
3. Will my substitute teaching, summer-school teaching, or adult education teaching be included in the computation toward my permanent teaching status?	___	___
4. Can I be assigned supervision duties outside of my regular classroom teaching assignments?	___	___
5. Can I be dismissed for not following the prescribed course of study?	___	___
6. Must I maintain student attendance records?	___	___
7. Can I administer a consequence if a student refuses to stand and salute the flag of the United States of America?	___	___
8. May I require that my students purchase a weekly news supplement if I provide free copies to any students who cannot afford to purchase it?	___	___
9. Can I receive royalties for a textbook I have written and published?	___	___
10. Can I administer a survey, a questionnaire, or a test asking about a student's sexual beliefs or practices without parental (or legal guardian's) written permission?	___	___
11. May I search a student or a student's locker at random?	___	___
12. Can I be considered negligent if I am present in the classroom when a physical injury occurs to one of my students?	___	___
13. Is a student guilty of a felony if he or she places permabond glue in the lock of the classroom door?	___	___
14. Can I suspend a student from my classroom?	___	___
15. Can I arrest a student?	___	___
16. Can I arrest a student for taunting and challenging another student to fight?	___	___
17. If I am attacked, assaulted, or menaced by a student, is someone in the administration obligated to report the incident to local law-enforcement authorities?	___	___
18. If a student resists my arrest with force, will the local authorities charge that student with assault and battery?	___	___
19. Can one student arrest another student?	___	___
20. Do I have the option of not reporting any witnessed student assault on a teaching colleague?	___	___

	Yes	No

21. Do I have a professional obligation to break up a seemingly friendly altercation? _____ _____

22. Do I have the professional and legal obligation to administer disciplinary consequences for disciplinary offenses? _____ _____

23. Can I suspend any student from my class for one week or longer? _____ _____

24. Can I call the school principal or another teacher an abusive name in the faculty lounge while arguing over school policy? _____ _____

25. Am I obligated to give students the right to be heard so long as that process does not substantially disrupt the orderly operation of the school? _____ _____

26. Must I tolerate student statements or actions that degrade others? _____ _____

27. Can a student be expelled if a student sells or furnishes narcotics or other substances represented to be controlled substances? _____ _____

28. Can a student be expelled for assault and battery on me or other school personnel? _____ _____

29. Can a student be expelled for the use of weapons or instruments or substances designed for or capable of doing bodily harm to me? _____ _____

30. As a teacher, must I report an instance of child abuse which I know exists? _____ _____

31. Must a student be given a *Miranda* warning before being questioned by school authorities? _____ _____

32. Can I, or the school principal, administer corporal punishment to a student for his or her misbehavior? _____ _____

Key to Exercise 14.5

This key to the previous questions is based on Education and Penal Codes, mostly from California, and on certain legal decisions that have affected public schools. You are encouraged to become familiar with and compare with legal codes from your own state.

1. No   California Education Code 13501
2. No
3. No   California Education Code 1332, 1333
4. Yes   California Education Code 13557
5. Yes   California Education Code 13556
6. Yes   California Education Code 10951
7. No   Court decision in West Virginia v. State Board of Education 319 U.S. 624.
8. No   California Education Code 9552, 9851
9. Yes   California Education Code 9256
10. No   California Education Code 10901
11. No
12. Yes   Biggers v. Sacramento City Unified School District 25, Cal APP 3d 269.
13. No

14. Yes California Education Code 10601
15. Yes California Penal Code 837. However, in some areas, the term *taken into custody* is preferred over *arrest* when the situation involves a juvenile. Check out the meaning of these two terms with your local authorities.
16. Yes California Penal Code 415
17. Yes California Education Code 12916. Supervisor who does not report it may be guilty of a misdemeanor and subject to a fine.
18. Yes In most cases, the juvenile will be "taken into custody."
19. Yes California Penal Code 837
20. No California Education Code 12912. Guilty of misdemeanor if you do not report assault.
21. Yes California Education Code 741, 747. Daily vs. Los Angeles Unified School District Ca.
22. Yes California Education Code 13357.
23. No California Education Code 10601. Teacher may suspend student from class for that day and the day following; immediately reports suspension to principal.
24. Do not! Connck v. Myers, Supreme Court Decision (1983) maintains that the dismissal of a public employee who protests internal policy in a manner that disrupts office harmony, undermines authority, and damages worker collegiality, does not offend the first amendment (free speech). Also, Amburgery v. Cassady, 370 F. Supp. 571, E.D. Ky. 1974.
25. Yes California Education Code 48916.
26. No California Education Code 32051.
27. Yes California Education Code 32051, California Health and Safety Code Section 11351–11368.
28. Yes California Education Code Section 48903.
29. Yes California Education Code Section 48909; California Penal Code Sections 245 and 626.9.
30. Yes California A.B. 518 Penal Code Section 11172 (b) reads: "Any person who fails to report an instance of child abuse which he or she knows to exist or reasonably should know to exist, as required by this article, is guilty of misdemeanor and is punishable by confinement in the county jail for a term not to exceed six months or by a fine of not more than five hundred dollars ($500) or by both."
31. No Boynton v. Casey, 543 F. Supp. 995, D. Me. 1982.
32. Not in California, as of 1987.

YOUR TEACHING CONTRACT AND TENURE

What will it mean to you when you sign your first teaching contract? Consider the following:

1. Your contract is a legal agreement between you and the governing school board in the district.
2. Your contract guarantees you employment, a teaching assignment, a salary, and your expected length of service, provided that there are students in need of your service.
3. Your length of service is identified, i.e., service for one year, or that of continuing service to the district.
4. You are legally required to perform your assigned duties as specified in your teaching contract.
5. Before a tenure contract is offered to you, there is a probationary period of employment (that varies from state to state, but usually is one to three years).
6. Although school district tenure laws vary from state to state, the tenure law is regarded as due process for you, the teacher. It ensures you against any unfair assignment charge, unjust transfer, demotion, reduction in salary, and other unfair changes.
7. A district's tenure law is not regarded as a safeguard against reduction in force policies or a protection against job loss. Tenure is *not* a guarantee that your job will continue regardless of what events or financial situations arise in the district.

Liability Insurance

Although teachers of public schools are usually protected by their districts against litigation, you may decide that the district liability coverage is insufficient. Our recommendation is that both *student teachers and employed teachers* investigate carefully the extent of their own coverages in the schools where they work. They should talk with teacher's association representatives about additional coverage that may be available through professional organizations, and with insurance agents, then decide what is best for their particular and individual situations.

QUESTIONS FOR CLASS DISCUSSION

1. What are some of the tasks you will perform to maintain the physical environment of your classroom? If you arranged these tasks in a time-ordered sequence, what tasks would you do first each morning upon your arrival?
2. Would some of the tasks (in number 1) vary day to day? Give an example.
3. What are some ways you can increase your efficiency in performing routine and clerical tasks?
4. On what grounds may middle school, junior high school, and high school students in your local districts be suspended or expelled?
5. What changes in your state's legal guidelines do you think need to be made?

6. Have teacher's unions made it easier or more difficult for teachers to teach? Explain.
7. Is it okay for the teacher to touch a student? Why or why not?
8. Find research to indicate what relation there is between classroom management and class size.
9. What safety precautions should you make for teaching in your subject?
10. When confronting an unpopular principal who appears to be incompetent, should teachers distribute a flyer describing their concerns and the strife at their school to other teachers in the district? One administrator's response is that this is an unprofessional and unjust action. By sending out unproven charges in writing, the teachers have exposed themselves to charges of slander, defamation of character, and unprofessional conduct. Do you agree? Why or why not?
11. The Supreme Court has affirmed its ban on organized prayer in public schools and outlawed daily moments of silence if students are told they may pray during that time (1985). Do you understand this to mean that every state law for providing daily moments of silence is invalid? Does it seem that if the state legislature did not intend to endorse school prayer, the state law is still valid? What is your opinion on this?
12. What questions do you have regarding the content of this chapter? How might answers be found?

SUGGESTED READINGS FOR CHAPTER 14

Baker, K. "Research Evidence of a School Discipline Problem." *Phi Delta Kappan* 66(7):482–488 (March 1985).

Cangelosi, J. S. *Classroom Management Strategies.* White Plains, NY: Longman, 1988.

Carducci, K. J., and Carducci, J. B. *The Caring Classroom.* Palo Alto, CA: Bull Publishing Company, 1984.

Curran, D. K. *Adolescent Suicidal Behavior.* New York: Hemisphere Publishing Corporation, 1987.

Emmer, E. T., et al. *Classroom Management for Secondary Teachers.* 3d ed. Englewood Cliffs, NJ: Prentice Hall, 1989.

Good, T. L., and Brophy, J. E. *Looking in Classrooms.* New York: Harper & Row, 1987.

Lemlech, J. K. *Classroom Management: Methods and Techniques for Elementary and Secondary Teachers.* 2d ed. White Plains, NY: Longman, 1988.

Ogden, E., and Germinario, V. *The At-Risk Student: Answers for Educators.* Lancaster, PA: Technomic Publishing Company, 1988.

Rinne, C. H. *Attention: The Fundamentals of Classroom Control.* Columbus, OH: Charles E. Merrill, 1984.

Sanford J. P., and Emmer, E. T. *Understanding Classroom Management: An Observation Guide.* Englewood Cliffs, NJ: Prentice Hall, 1988.

Sprick, R. S. *Discipline in the Secondary Classroom: A Problem-by-Problem Survival Guide.* West Nyack, NY: The Center for Applied Research in Education, 1989.

15

What Do Some Authorities Suggest as Approaches to Classroom Control?

In Chapter 14 you learned about the legal guidelines within which the classroom teacher must work and about certain guidelines for effective classroom management. In this chapter, we address the ever-important topic of classroom control and offer more guiding statements.

Classroom control has always been a topic of concern to teachers and for which volumes of literature are available. Let us review for you what the term *classroom control* meant in the past and what it means today.

A. THE MEANING OF CLASSROOM CONTROL

In the 1800s, instead of classroom control, educators spoke of "classroom discipline," and that meant punishment, an interpretation that was consistent with the then-popular learning theory that assumed children were essentially bad and that misbehavior could be prevented by strictness, or treated with punishment.[1] Schools in the middle of that century have been described as being "wild and unruly places," and "full of idleness and disorder."[2]

By the early 1900s, educators were asking "Why are the children still misbehaving?" Their answer indicated that the children were misbehaving *because* of the rigid punitive system.[3] On this point began the progressive education era that provided students the opportunity (freedom) to decide for themselves what (if anything) they would learn. The teacher's job then became one of providing a rich classroom of resources and materials to stimulate the students' natural curiosity. And since the system no longer would be causing misbehavior, punishment would be unnecessary. However, "a completely permissive class appears to be more anxiety producing than a traditional class"[4] (traditional as in the practice of the 1800s).

---

[1] Robert R. Reilly and Ernest L. Lewis, *Educational Psychology* (New York: Macmillan, 1983), p. 557.
[2] Irwin A. Hyman and John D'Allessandro. "Oversimplifying the Discipline Problem," *Education Week*, vol. 3, no. 29 (April 11, 1984), p. 24.
[3] Reilly, op. cit., p. 558.
[4] Reilly, op. cit., p. 559.

Today, rather than classroom "discipline," we talk of classroom "control," and are referring to *the process of controlling student behavior in the classroom.* Classroom control is an important aspect of the broader area of classroom management procedures. Classroom control involves

1. steps in *preventing student misbehavior,* and
2. ideas for *handling student misbehavior.*

Today's secondary-school teacher is probably eclectic in his or her approach to classroom control, perhaps leaning slightly toward a traditional approach. A teacher's behavior (in-control procedures) does reflect that teacher's philosophy about how students learn, and those behaviors represent the teacher's concept of effective management.

B. STUDENT RESPONSES TO QUESTIONS ABOUT MANAGEMENT AND DISCIPLINE

Perhaps a reflection of a school's concept of effective discipline can appear from students' responses to questions about discipline. Here are some replies we received by talking with young people.

When asked what she thought of when she heard the words "class management and discipline," one junior high school student said: "If you break a rule, you get suspended or expelled. You can't goof off. You can't get into drugs like marijuana or coke. It means no fighting. You get suspended for five days. It means no cheating on tests because you get a referral to the principal. Then the principal tells you not to cheat anymore or he might give you a work-study assignment. That's when you report after school for a certain number of hours. If you are late to class three times, you could get a work-study assignment. If you are late to class more than three times, you get suspended for a couple of days. It means no food fighting. If you fight with food in the cafeteria, you can't go to any school activities for the rest of the year. It means no talking in class because your citizenship grade drops. If you swear, you get a behavioral referral (a message to the principal, who gives you a warning before calling your parents). If you steal or break into someone's locker, you get suspension for three days."

A tenth-grade student replied: "Well, first of all, I want to know what degrees of discipline you are talking about. In P.E. we are disciplined for coming in late to class. That means doing a lap around the field. We are disciplined for not dressing down. That means either running laps or picking up garbage on the field during P.E. class. In other classes, if we come in late, the teacher takes something off our citizenship grade. For cheating, fighting, and swearing, they send you down to the office. They don't waste any time with you. One class I have is a kickback class. We're not required to do all that much. All the kids are cool and the teacher is cool. We all get along with the teacher. In one class the biggest deal is you have to have a certain materials card turned in to the teacher or something comes off your citizenship grade. In another class the teacher never controls the class, so there are no problems with discipline. Stuff goes on all the time, but she is powerless to do anything about it. In another one, when we talk the teacher moves you. Talking is the biggest offense in that class. Drugs will get you kicked out of the district. Stealing is usually dealt with by expelling you from school. Your parents are called and you have this 'way-hanging-big' conversation with everybody. They'll call the cops if you nabbed something from the teacher. If you steal something from another student, they'll call your parents. See, they figure that's the toughest thing they can do to you. Nine-tenths of the time they are right. Fighting? If you started it, planned it, they'd expel you from the district. They consider who started the fight, how bad the fight was, and what each fighter's intention was. It usually means five days suspension. Weapons? If you've got any sort of weapon, they'll call the police. And alcohol or drugs? If they catch you with either on the school grounds, it's an instant call to the police."

As this previous student brought up the topic of drugs, perhaps this is a good place to emphasize the importance for teachers to be aware of and on the watch for symptoms of potential drug abuse. *If you suspect drug abuse, you should notify the appropriate person at your school* (be aware of specific district or school policies regarding this; usually the person to be notified is the principal or school nurse). You may want to attend an educator's workshop on drug abuse where symptoms of abuse, such as those that follow in the chart, are discussed.

When asked to discuss "the best teacher she has met," one seventh-grade girl selects a male teacher. "He would stand outside the classroom as we came to class. When we went inside he went to his desk. He stood in the front of the room. Each day, he told us what we would learn. Then he'd help us out and explain everything. After that he'd tell us a story. He would tell jokes. Then he let us go to work. He gave us homework every night and we would correct it the next day. It took me (from) one and one-half hours to two hours every night. What I liked best about him was that he was helpful."

An eighth-grade boy mentions a particular female teacher as "best": "It's hard to pin down what she did do and what she didn't do. She would wait until we got quiet. She explained what was going to be, how far we'd get, and how short we'd fall from getting there. She handed us a slip of paper with the rules on it. Usually, she was at her desk. She always had everything ready and organized. She got upset (but in a joking way) if we weren't ready and organized. She explained things as we went along. Then she moved around the room a lot. Mostly, she moved around in front of the room because there were usually a lot of things going on in the front of the room. Once in a while she would review things, especially if we were doing something in a series, something she was quite fond of. She was interesting. Businesslike. Had humor. But she also had a theory of 'get it done.' Sometimes we had homework every day. It would take me from an hour to an hour and one-half to do. I liked her."

It seems clear that these young people's reflections demonstrate an emphasis on *rules, control, and punishment.* More subtly perhaps, they also indicate the teacher's *understanding.* The eclectic approach we mentioned earlier sees classroom control as involving

1. *Control* from within the learner and also from outside factors.
2. *Understanding* the learner and the learner's perceptions of his or her own behaviors.
3. *Referral* to "specialists" when appropriate.
4. *Prevention* through the application of effective teaching strategies.
5. *Individualized* instruction because of the unique needs of each individual student.

SYMPTOMS OF DRUG ABUSE[1]				
Group	*Symptoms*	*Drugs*	*Slang Terms*	*Dangers From Overdose*
cannabis	relaxed inhibitions disoriented behavior euphoria increased appetite	marijuana hashish	reefer, pot, joint, weed, Thai stick, sinsemilla, grass hash	fatigue possible psychosis paranoia
depressants	slurred speech disorientation drunken behavior	chloral hydrate barbiturates tranquilizer	joy juice, mickey yellow jackets, goof balls red devils, downers	shallow respiration clammy skin dilated pupils weak, rapid pulse coma, possible death
hallucinogens	illusions hallucinations poor time and distance perception	LSD mescaline PCP	acid, microdot, sunshine cactus, mexc, buttons angel dust, hog	intense "trips" episodes psychosis possible death
narcotics	euphoria drowsiness constricted pupils respiratory depression nausea	opium morphine codeine heroin	paregoric, cube Dover's powder miss anna, school boy school boy snow, junk, horse smack	shallow breathing clammy skin convulsions coma possible death
stimulants	increased alertness excitation dilated pupils increased pulse rate insomnia euphoria loss of appetite	cocaine amphetamines	coke, gold dust, snow, smack, flake speed, uppers, bennies	agitation hallucinations increased body temperature convulsions possible death

C. TODAY'S EFFECTIVE CLASSROOM MANAGEMENT SYSTEMS

Our intention in this chapter is to provide background information that may guide you toward the development of your own successful classroom management system, one that is consistent with your own beliefs. Today's effective classroom management systems have evolved from the works of leading authorities. Let's now look at what those leading authorities have provided.

[1]Adapted from: U.S. Department of Justice, Drug Enforcement Administration, *Drugs of Abuse*, Washington, DC: U.S. Government Printing Office, 1988, p. 30–31.

Lee and Marlene Canter emphasize that: (1) you have professional rights in your classroom and should expect appropriate student behavior; (2) your students have rights to choose how to behave in your classroom, and you should plan limits for inappropriate student behavior; (3) your assertive discipline approach means you clearly state your expectations in a firm voice and explain the boundaries for behavior; and (4) you establish consequences for student misbehavior and you follow through in a consistent way.

Dr. Rudolf Dreikurs emphasizes six points to consider in determining if you are an effective teacher. You are effective if you: (1) are a democratic teacher, fair, firm, and friendly, and involve your students in developing and implementing class rules; (2) arrange your classroom so that students know the rules and the consequences for misbehavior; (3) allow the students to be responsible not only for their own actions but for influencing others to maintain appropriate behavior in your classroom; (4) encourage students to show respect for themselves and for others and you provide each student with a sense of belonging to the class; (5) recognize and encourage student goals of belonging, acquiring status, and recognition; and (6) recognize but do not reinforce correlated student goals of getting attention, seeking power, taking revenge, and asking to be left alone.

William Glasser moves his idea of "reality therapy" (i.e., the condition of the present contributes to inappropriate behavior) into the classroom. He emphasizes that: (1) students have a responsibility to learn at school and to maintain appropriate behavior while there; (2) with your help, the students can make better choices about their behavior in school; and (3) classroom meetings can be devoted to establishing class rules, student behavior, matters of misbehavior, and the consequences.

Haim G. Ginott emphasizes ways for you and a student to communicate: (1) by sending a clear message (or messages) regarding a situation instead of to the student's character; and, (2) by your modeling of the behavior you expect from your students. Ginott's suggested messages are those that express feelings appropriately, acknowledge student's feelings, give appropriate direction, and invite cooperation.

Jacob S. Kounin is well known for his identification of the "ripple effect" (i.e., the effect of your response to one student's misbehavior on students whose behavior was appropriate), and of "withitness" (i.e., correcting misbehavior as soon as it has occurred, and correcting the right student). Kounin challenges you to: (1) realize the influence the ripple effect has on students; (2) exhibit "withitness" by remaining alert to all students in your classroom at all times; (3) keep the teaching-learning momentum going during educational activities (i.e., avoid dead time during class); (4) plan smooth transitions from one activity to the next; and (5) see that each student is responsible for learning the lesson's content.

In addition to the approaches to classroom management presented by the Canters, Dreikurs, Glasser, Ginott, and Kounin, you are probably familiar with the term "behavior modification"—a number of popular techniques effective in changing the behavior of others in an observable and predictable way—and with B. F. Skinner's ideas about how students learn, how behavior can be modified by reinforcements (rewards), and how his principles of behavior shaping have been extended by others.

Behavior modification begins with four steps: (1) identifying the problem behavior that you wish to modify; (2) recording how often and under what conditions that particular behavior occurs; (3) arranging a change to occur by reinforcing a behavior you want repeated by following the behavior with a rewarding consequence (a positive reinforcer); and (4) considering the different types of positive reinforcers to award—auditory (music), edibles (food and drink), manipulatives (toys), social reinforcers (attention, praise), tactile (clay), and visual (pictures).

As you review these classic contributions to today's approaches to effective classroom management, you read of expert opinion as well as research evidence that point out the importance of

- Concentrating your attention on desirable student behaviors,
- Quickly attending to misbehavior,
- Being aware of all that is happening in your classroom,
- Providing smooth transitions,
- Maintaining group alertness,
- Preventing "dead" time,
- Involving students by providing challenges, class meetings, ways of establishing rules and consequences, opportunities to receive and to return compliments, and to build self-esteem.

Using the criteria of your own philosophy, your feelings, your values, and your perceptions, you are encouraged to devise a classroom management system that is effective for you. Remember: you must have the attention of the students before you can teach them. Here are specific guidelines for your consideration in the development of your own effective management system.

D. GUIDELINES FOR ESTABLISHING AN EFFECTIVE CLASSROOM MANAGEMENT SYSTEM

The following guidelines to classroom management can help you build a strong foundation for your classroom-control techniques.[1]

1. Establish your classroom control during the first few days of the school year, and in the best way possible for you.
2. Have as few rules and regulations as absolutely necessary, and enforce them.
3. Involve students in making and in enforcing classroom rules and regulations.
4. Learn the names of your students quickly, and use them.
5. Establish and maintain classroom routines.
6. Use caution in making any threats, and when you do threaten, make it clear, understandable, and one that you can carry out.
7. Maintain a sense of humor about misbehaviors, trying to be firm, fair, but friendly.
8. Learn about the policies, attitudes, and practices of your colleagues and of the chief administrator.
9. Use your eyes, voice, feet, and body posture to effectively communicate nonverbal cues.
10. Discuss misbehavior in private with the student whenever feasible.

---

[1]Adapted from Reilly, op.cit., numbers 1–20, pp 579–593. Used by permission.

11. Be yourself, as only the real you can succeed in the classroom.
12. Use reason and logic in your behavioral requests and in your consequences.
13. Vary classroom activities, with occasional breaks and changes in pace.
14. When you use consequences, make them as immediate and as appropriate as possible.
15. Avoid using the process of writing as a consequence for misbehavior.
16. Avoid punishing the entire class for the misbehavior of a few.
17. Be cautious with the use of sarcasm in the classroom.
18. Be a model for your students; behave as you want them to behave.
19. Be aware of personality conflicts (between you and individual students) and don't feel guilty about them. You can handle it.
20. Spend time outside of class time diagnosing problems and planning strategies.
21. Be aware of your own mood levels, and personal high-stress days, and anticipate that your own tolerance levels on those days may be low.
22. Be aware of individual student problems that may be sources of high stress for those students. Through individual talks, you may be able to help those students to cope.

One source of stress for many students is that caused by the breakup of the family—a divorce. Teachers who are interested in learning more about how to help those students cope may be interested in the number of resources designed to do just that.

RESOURCES FOR TEACHERS WORKING WITH CHILDREN AFFECTED BY DIVORCE

Banana Splits: A School-Based Program for the Survivors of the Divorce Wars. Contact Elizabeth McGonagle, Wood Road Elementary School, Ballston Spa Central Schools, Ballston Spa, N.Y. 12020, (518) 885-5361.

Rainbows for All Children. Contact 1111 Tower Road, Schaumburg, IL 60173, (312) 310-1880.

Shapes: Families of Today: A Curriculum Guide on Today's Changing Families for Children Ages Eight to Eighteen. Contact Families in Transition Education Project, Stepfamily Association of America, Santa Barbara Chapter, P. O. Box 91233, Santa Barbara, CA 93190-1233, (805) 687-4983.

Support for Stepfamilies: Suggestions for Schools. Contact Emily and John Visher, 599 Sky Hy Circle, Lafayette, CA 94549, (415) 284-1524.

The National Council for Children's Rights. Contact N.C.C.R., 2001 O St., N.W., Washington, D.C. 20036, (202) 223-6227.

The Pittsburgh Center for Stepfamilies. Contact Judith L. Bauersfield, 4815 Liberty Ave., Suite 422, Pittsburgh, PA 15224, (412) 362-7837.

Now, on the basis of what you have learned in this and in previous chapters, try the exercises that follow.

EXERCISE 15.1: CASE STUDIES FOR CLASS DISCUSSION

The cases that follow have been provided for analysis and discussion in your class. Study the cases and decide what you would do in similar situations. For your convenience, here is a brief statement of what each case is about:

1. A slow learner in junior high school, a boy who hangs around the teacher.
2. A bully in the tenth grade, an active-destructive type.
3. A lonely, unhappy, disinterested girl in Grade 10, a potentially passive-destructive type.
4,5. Accidents at school.
6. "Please stop baiting and harrying me."
7. "Five points deducted for your name!"

We hope that use of these case studies will add depth to your perceptions and insight about the day-by-day events that occur in teaching.

CASE 1: THE BOY WHO HANGS AROUND

Background

Bill is male, age 13, in general science. He is tall and awkward. He has a poor skin condition. He is considered "crazy" by his classmates. He has minor police offenses and is in apparent conflict with his father. He has taken an apparent liking to the general science teacher and spends many extra hours in the classroom. He is energetic and displays an inquisitive nature. He is quick to get interested in projects but almost as quick to lose interest. He likes to run the film projector for the teacher, but he does not like to participate in discussions with the rest of the class. He likes personal chats with the teacher but feels that the other students laugh at him.

The Situation

Bill's IQ is 95. The teacher attempted to work with Bill in improving his apparent feelings of inadequacy. The teacher had frank talks with Bill about his gangliness and his acne. What follows is actual material as written by Bill during the course of the first semester of school.

September: "I want to make the best out of the time I am on earth. I want to be somebody, not just exist either. . . . The members of this class influence me and what I think of doing. . . . They also make me feel real low. Their teasing me has changed me. . . . The teacher of my science class has helped me very much. . . . My greatest problem is in holding my head up and fighting for myself. . . .

October: "I have made a lot of headway in the past weeks. . . . I think I have done a good choice in the subject I am studying. . . . I also thank my teacher's actions toward me, that we may get to be very good friends, and learn a lot to know that teachers are human too, that they also have problems to solve and goals to head for.

November: "I don't have to fear anybody or anything on the idea of getting up and saying what I feel I have accomplished in this class and I have learned to make my own dissisions on what I will study or maybe do when I get out of school.

December: "I have learned that I have confidence in others only when I have confidence in myself.

January: "I have my report on the afect of geabriilic acid on plants. . . . I told (the class) about all my failures and they were quite interested. I told them that I had failed four times . . . that my science teacher told me I should not give up at this point and that a seintice (scientist) does not give up. I had no longer stated that fact and they all seemed like they could help in some way. I think the report went over well."

So the student developed courage to stand in front of his peers, holding his head high, and confidently reporting to the class how he kept at his plant experiment, even after four failures. He was proud of what he had learned about the work of the scientist. And he was even more proud that the students no longer teased and laughed at him.

QUESTIONS FOR CLASS DISCUSSION

1. How did you feel after reading this case?
2. Did Bill learn anything that semester? What?
3. Did he learn science?
4. What did the teacher do to facilitate Bill's learning?
5. What is ahead for Bill in school?

CASE 2: THE CASE OF THE BULLY

Background

Tony is considered by his peers as one of the "tough guys." He is 15 and in the tenth grade at Green High. Tony is prone to bullying, frequently quarreling with his fellow students and teachers; is considered by his parents to be disobedient. He has a record of minor offenses that range from truancy to destructiveness of property to drunkenness and offensive behavior. In general, Tony gets his satisfactions in ways that are damaging and unfair to others.

It is obvious to school officials that Tony is beyond parental control. He is frequently beaten by his father. Tony's mother has no apparent ability to control Tony's behavior.

Tony is not a member of any school organization of an extracurricular nature. His midquarter progress shows that he is failing in three subjects.

The Situation

One of the subjects Tony is failing is tenth-grade English. Tony is a discipline problem in your class and although it makes you feel guilty, you cannot help but be pleased when Tony is absent from class.

QUESTIONS FOR CLASS DISCUSSION

1. Where is the problem?
2. Where is Tony heading?
3. What can and should be done, if anything? By whom?
4. What is the role for Tony? His teachers? His peers? The school administration? His parents? Society in general?
5. Is it too late for Tony?

CASE 3: THE CASE OF MARY

Background

Mary has been characterized by her peers and by her teachers as being lonely, indifferent, and generally unhappy. She avoids both students and teachers. She will lie and cheat to avoid attention. Her "close" friends describe her as thoughtless and unkind. She often uses damaging remarks about members of her class, calling them conceited, teacher's pets, and so on. She considers members of her class as thoughtless, unkind, and uninterested in her.

Mary will do what she has to do in order to achieve average success in her studies. Her association with adults, her parents, and her teachers would be described as one of "merely getting along," doing what "I have to do in order not to get too much attention."

The Situation

One of Mary's friends is another 15-year-old girl, Jane. Jane is an above-average student in school, seemingly well adjusted, interested in people, and has gotten to know Mary because they are neighbors and walk together to school. Because of Jane's interest in other people and her closeness to Mary, she has become interested in "trying to bring Mary out of her shell."

Mary has told Jane that she feels her teachers are unreasonably severe. Mary said, "The teachers are only interested in the popular kids." Jane disagreed. Mary said, "You only disagree because you are pretty and popular." At this point, the conversation was broken by a boy running up and saying, "Hey, Jane, you're late for the council meeting."

QUESTIONS FOR CLASS DISCUSSION

1. Where is the problem?
2. What if you were Mary's teacher?
3. How did you feel after reading this case?

CASE 4: THE CASE OF THE STABBING VICTIM

Ron King, 16, who claims he was stabbed in the back during an English class, wants $100,000 in damages from North High School, Central Union High School District, and student Richard Decarlo.

According to the action, filed by King's mother, Lee, of 460 Bowman Avenue, the incident occurred last February. King says he was stabbed by Decarlo and lost his spleen as a result.

The suit says there was no teacher in the classroom when the stabbing took place and that the school was negligent in not providing supervision.

The action also contends that school officials knew that Decarlo secretly carried deadly weapons with him on the school grounds.

CASE 5: "MY STUDENTS ARE NICE YOUNGSTERS, BUT . . . . "

I have a feeling that my tenth-grade class sees through my youth and inexperience to my hidden fears and insecurity. I often feel that they are giggling while my back is turned. I catch glimpses of quickly hidden notes. Little things go on that I sense but do not see. My students are nice youngsters, really, but these minor annoyances are making me a nervous wreck. How can I stop these actions without alienating the children?

CASE 6: "PLEASE STOP BAITING AND HARRYING ME!"

I was fortunate enough to get an appealing and able seventh-grade class as my first teaching assignment. However, one boy is ruining my progress with them and my happiness in my work. He is a constant noise maker and trouble instigator. No special incident or difficulty precipitated his attitude, but he seems to take an actual delight in baiting and harrying me. I don't know how to change his attitude. What would you do?

CASE 7: "FIVE POINTS DEDUCTED FOR YOUR NAME!"

I was having difficulty explaining the solution of a problem because of continual talking among the students. I announced to the class, "I have reminded you students several times about our earlier discussion on courtesy in the classroom. Apparently it hasn't meant much to you, so from now on I shall write on the board the names of anyone talking out of place, and those individuals will have five points subtracted from their next examination grade—yes, five points for each time their names appear on the board."

EXERCISE 15.2: HOW TO WORK WITH A DIFFICULT STUDENT: BRAINSTORMING IDEAS

Instructions: The purpose of this exercise is to show you how to generate ideas about what you might do when you have a difficult student. You can use this exercise alone, or in groups, whenever you have a student that is giving you problems. Whichever the case, completion of the exercise is most certain to generate new ideas about what you can do when you have a special problem with a specific student.

Step 1: *Statement of the problem.* State as clearly as you can what the problem is, e.g., the student is disruptive to classroom learning; the student just sits and does nothing; the student is constantly made fun of by other students.

Step 2: *Identification of what you have observed about or that is related to this student.* List *everything* you know and have observed about the student, whether you believe it to be relevant or not. Include student behaviors, physical characteristics, grade level, subject, grades, attendance, punctuality, age of student, time of day, whether student has brothers or sisters, parents, hobbies, special talents, disabilities, how the student is getting along with other teachers, etc.

Step 3: *List of things tried.* List *everything* you have tried with this student and their results, e.g., isolation in the classroom, referrals, talk with parent, rewards, discussions with the student in or out of class, discussions with the student's other teachers.

Step 4: *New things to try with this student.* As you complete the previous steps you will most certainly generate ideas about new ways to work with this student. As those ideas are generated write them down.

Step 5: *Follow-up report of what was tried and the results.* At some later date, perhaps in a week or two, list here (and perhaps report to your group) what you tried and describe the results.

1. Statement of problem:

2. Observations about the student:

3. Things I have tried: Their results:

4. New ideas: 5: Their results:

QUESTIONS FOR CLASS DISCUSSIONS

1. It has been said that the teacher should practice the "three Fs": be firm, be fair, be friendly. Do you think this is sound advice? Why or why not?
2. It has been said that "hostility begets hostility." How do you feel about that? Does it have meaning for the classroom teacher and that teacher's behaviors?
3. It has been said that teachers should attend to desirable student behaviors. Do you believe some teachers tend to spend too much time reacting to student misbehaviors?
4. It has been said that the professional responsibility of the teacher is to diagnose and to prescribe, not to label. Discuss the meaning this has for you.
5. Choose a grade level and subject that you teach or plan to teach and list the specific classroom rules you will establish. How will you communicate those rules to the students?
6. How specifically can students help establish and enforce classroom rules?
7. What "threats" are permissible for the teacher to make?
8. Can teacher's nonverbal cues ever miscommunicate? Give an example.
9. Is there ever a time when punishment can or should be delayed?
10. Do you need to "like" all the students? Can you accept a student but not particularly like that individual? How can a teacher effectively teach a student he or she does not like?
11. Have any schools you have visited used the concept of a "holding area"?
12. When, if ever, is it appropriate for a teacher to temporarily remove a student from the classroom?
13. Using flour for cocaine, oregano for marijuana, candy as uppers and downers, and *Monopoly* money, fifth- and sixth-graders used the bogus drugs to buy property while playing the board game, *Monopoly*. The students played it until a teacher intervened. What would you have done and said if you were the teacher who intervened?
14. Middle school teachers will have an interest in current laws affecting teens and their use of alcohol and drugs. Some states now have laws affecting the driving privileges of teenagers (ages 13–21) convicted of drug- or alcohol-related offenses. One law (California, 1989) states that teens ages 13–16 convicted of drug- or alcohol-related offenses will face a one-year delay in obtaining their licenses once they reach 16, and that the courts will suspend for one year the driver's license of anyone between 16 and 21 years of age who is convicted of buying, attempting to buy, possessing, or being under the influence of drugs or alcohol. Do you agree that the prospect of losing a driver's license will persuade a teenager from using alcohol or drugs? Why or why not?
15. What questions do you have regarding the content of this chapter? How might answers be found?

SUGGESTED READINGS FOR CHAPTER 15

Baker, K. "Research Evidence of a School Discipline Problem." *Phi Delta Kappan* 66(7):482–488 (March 1985).

Cangelosi, J. S. *Classroom Management Strategies*. White Plains, NY: Longman, 1988.

Canter, L. "Assertive Discipline—More Than Names on the Board and Marbles in the Jar." *Phi Delta Kappan* 71(1):57–61 (September 1989).

Carducci, K. J., and Carducci, J. B. *The Caring Classroom*. Palo Alto, CA: Bull Publishing Company, 1984.

Charles, C. M. *Building Classroom Discipline*. 3rd ed. White Plains, NY: Longman, 1989.

Curran, D. K. *Adolescent Suicidal Behavior*. New York: Hemisphere Publishing Corporation, 1987.

Dreikurs, R. et al. *Maintaining Sanity in the Classroom: Classroom Management Techniques*. 2d ed. New York: Harper & Row, 1982.

Englander, M. *Strategies for Classroom Discipline*. New York: Praeger Publishing, 1987.

Good, T. L., and Brophy, J. E. *Looking in Classrooms*. 4th ed. New York: Harper & Row, 1987.

Lemlech, J. K. *Classroom Management: Methods and Techniques for Elementary and Secondary Teachers*. 2d ed. White Plains, NY: Longman, 1988.

McDaniel, T. R. "A Primer on Classroom Discipline: Principles Old and New." *Phi Delta Kappan* 68(1):63–67 (Sept. 1986).

Ogden, E., and Germinario, V. *The At-Risk Student: Answers for Educators*. Lancaster, PA: Technomic Publishing Company, 1988.

Reilly, R. R., and Lewis, E. L. *Educational Psychology: Applications for Classroom Learning and Instruction*. New York: Macmillan, 1983.

Rinne, C. H. *Attention: The Fundamentals of Classroom Control*. Columbus, OH: Charles E. Merrill, 1984.

Sanford, J. P., and Emmer, E. T. *Understanding Classroom Management: An Observation Guide*. Englewood Cliffs, NJ: Prentice Hall, 1988.

Vogel, J. *A Stress Test for Children—Is Your "Problem Child's" Problem Nutrition? Here's How To Find Out*. New Canaan, CT: Keats Publishing Company, 1983.

Wolfgang, C. H., and Glickman, C. D. *Solving Discipline Problems: Strategies for Classroom Teachers*. 2d ed. Needham Heights, MA: Allyn & Bacon, Longwood Division, 1987.

PART V

Evaluation of Teacher Performance and Student Achievement

Part V assists you with

- Tools of evaluation.
- Methods of grading.
- Dealing with an angry student.
- Self-evaluation through micro-teaching.
- Methods of evaluating teacher performance.
- Knowledge of evaluation forms used by educators.
- Knowledge of your growth in competency development.
- Guidelines for meeting and conferencing with parents.

You, therefore, who teach another, do you not teach yourself?
—Romans 2:21

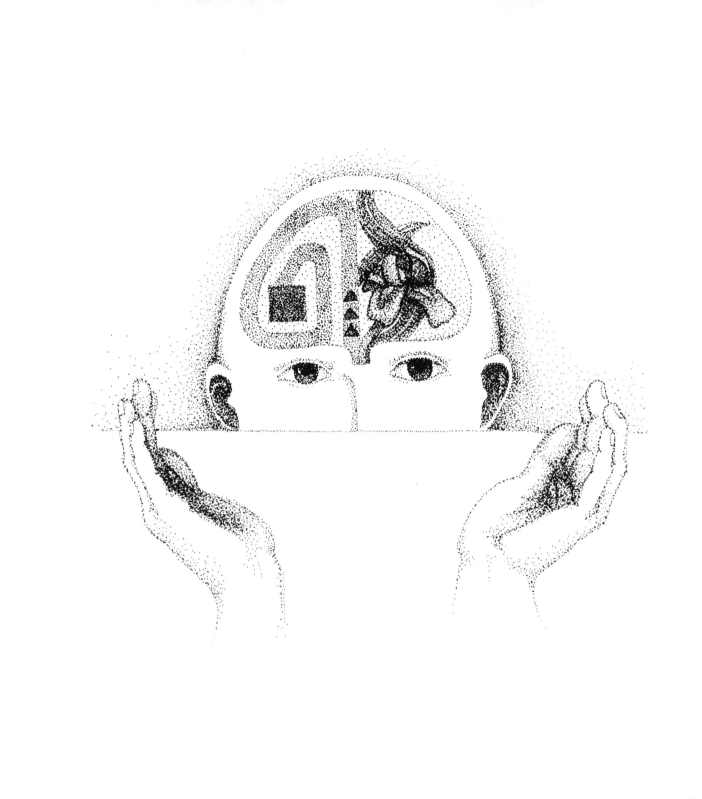

Drawing by Carol Wilson, unpublished material. Reprinted by permission.

16

How Do I Evaluate and Report Student Achievement?

While preceding parts of this text addressed the *why, what,* and *how* of secondary-school teaching, this part focuses on the fourth and final component of the teaching-learning reciprocal process—the *how well* component. Together, those four components comprise the essentials of competent instruction.

A. PURPOSES OF THE ASSESSMENT COMPONENT

The *how well* component is the assessment element and serves the following functions.

1. *To evaluate and improve student learning.* This is perhaps the function first thought of when speaking of evaluation, and is the primary focus of this chapter.
2. *To identify student strengths and weaknesses.* Assessment of student strengths and weaknesses is necessary for two reasons: to restructure the learning activities, and to restructure the program. With respect to the first, data about student strengths and weaknesses are important to the teacher for redesigning course structure and activities. For the second purpose, data about student strengths and weaknesses are useful for making appropriate modifications in the curriculum program of which one course is a part. Knowledge of student strengths and weaknesses is necessary for establishment of program goals, objectives, and prerequisites.
3. *To assess the effectiveness of a particular instructional strategy.* It is important for a teacher to know how well a particular strategy helped accomplish a particular goal or objective. Competent teachers constantly evaluate their strategy choices, on the basis of student achievement as measured by tests, and from their own intuitions.
4. *To evaluate and improve program effectiveness.* Although an on-going process, program effectiveness is formally evaluated by faculty committees when preparing self-study reports for accreditation reviews.
5. *To initiate and evaluate program change.* Program changes—which must undergo periodic assessment for continuation or modification—are usually an outgrowth of self-study reports and formal accreditation reports.

6. *To evaluate and improve teacher effectiveness.* Teacher effectiveness is formally addressed during administrative reviews.
7. To communicate to parents their children's progress.

B. GUIDELINES THAT PERMEATE THE ASSESSMENT COMPONENT

Because the careers, livelihood, and futures of so many people depend upon the outcomes, it is impossible to overemphasize the importance of this component. Here are threads that should imbue the assessment process.

1. Teachers need to know how well they are doing.
2. Students need to know how well they are doing.
3. Evidence, feedback, and input for knowing how well the teacher and students are doing should come from a variety of sources.
4. Although feedback and evaluation are separate but related processes, both important to the assessment component, feedback is more likely to lead to adjustments in performance.
5. Evaluation is an ongoing process.
6. Self-evaluation is an important component of the assessment program.
7. Much of the evaluation process can and should be systematized. Recent upon the educational scene are computer-managed instructional systems (CMI), where learning objectives are set and programmed into a computer system; then, specific evaluative items are established that reveal when a student has learned those particular skills.
8. The evaluation process should facilitate teaching effectiveness and contribute to the academic and personal growth of students.
9. Evaluation is a reciprocal process, including evaluation of teacher performance as well as evaluation of student achievement.
10. A teacher's professional responsibility is to teach and to assess student progress, and the teacher is held accountable for that responsibility.

This chapter is about techniques for evaluating student achievement, as critical as any of the other components of planning. When used inappropriately, evaluation can have damaging consequences. Evaluating student achievement can consume a large portion of your time, as it involves selecting and designing items and instruments, implementation, checking and analyzing results, recording, reporting, and arranging and conducting postevaluation conferences with students and parents. Perhaps this chapter will make the job for you a little easier, although no less significant.

Teaching-learning is a complex human activity, and when evaluating that activity we can never be absolutely sure of the *validity* and *reliability* of our measures. *Validity is the degree to which the technique measures that which is intended to be measured. Reliability is the accuracy with which a technique consistently measures that which it does measure.* A technique must have reliability before it can have validity. However, although a technique may have reliability (that is, if used again, it would produce similar results), it may not be valid (because of poor design, it is not measuring what it is supposed to measure).

In the next chapter we address the strategies for teacher-centered evaluation, that is, those designed for the evaluation and improvement of teaching. Included are samples of instruments used by supervisory personnel for evaluation of student teaching, and those of school districts for their evaluation of teachers: instruments that illustrate the criteria by which the beginning teacher is likely to be evaluated.

C. EVALUATING STUDENT ACHIEVEMENT

There are three avenues for assessing student achievement: (1) what the learner *says,* as in a student's contributions to class activities; (2) what the learner *does,* as in a student's personal course project, which could indicate how well the student has internalized the learning; and, (3) what the learner *writes,* as indicated by written tests and homework assignments. Your own personal philosophy (Chapter 3) will dictate the levels of importance and weights you give to each.

Evaluation of student achievement is a three-step process, involving: (1) diagnostic evaluation, which is pretesting of student knowledge and skills; (2) formative evaluation, which is an assessment of learning in progress; and, (3) summative evaluation, which is the final phase that is usually represented by the student's final semester grade.

Evaluating a Student's Verbal and Nonverbal Behaviors

When evaluating what the learner says, you should:

1. Listen to the student's questions, responses, and interactions with other students.
2. Observe the student's attentiveness, involvement in class activities, and his or her responses to challenges.

Notice that the teacher should listen and observe. While listening to what the student is saying, you should, simultaneously, be observing the student's nonverbal behaviors. For this you may use checklists and rating scales, behavioral-growth record forms, observations of the student's performance of classroom activities, and periodic conferences with the student.

We remind you that, with each technique used, you will operate from an awareness of anticipated learning outcomes, and will evaluate the learner's progress toward meeting these objectives. Here are guidelines to follow when evaluating the student's verbal and nonverbal behaviors in the classroom.

Guidelines for Evaluating What the Learner Does and Says

1. *Make a list* of desirable behaviors.
2. *Check the list* against the specific instructional objectives.
3. *Record your observations* of the student as quickly as possible following your obser-

vation. Tape or video recordings can assist you in checking your memory accuracy, but if this is inconvenient, we recommend that you spend some time during school, immediately after, or later that evening, recording your observations, while they are still fresh in your mind.

4. *Record your professional judgment* regarding the learner's progress toward the desired behavior (see form that follows), but think it through before writing it down (see Section D of this chapter).

5. *Write comments* that are reminders to yourself, such as:
   "Check validity by further testing."
   "Discuss my observations with student's parents."
   "Discuss my observations with the student's counselor."

EVALUATING AND RECORDING STUDENT VERBAL AND NONVERBAL BEHAVIORS: SAMPLE FORM

**Verbal and Nonverbal Behaviors
Observation Form**

Student	*Grade*	*School*

Observer	*Period or Subject Observed*

Date

Objective for Time Period or Subject:	*Desired Behavior*	*What Student Did, Said, or Wrote*

Your professional comments: _____

_____

_____

_____

_____

_____

_____

_____

_____

_____

_____

_____

_____

_____

_____

_____

_____

_____

_____

_____

_____

_____

_____

_____

_____

_____

_____

_____

_____

Evaluating a Student's Written Behaviors

To follow this avenue of evaluation you will use worksheets, written homework, and tests. Worksheets and homework assignments are most often used for the formative evaluation of a learner's progress. Tests, too, should be a part of this ongoing evaluation, but are also used for summative evaluation at the end of a unit or period of learning, and for diagnostic testing. Your summative evaluation of a student's achievement, and any other final judgments that you make about a student, can have enormous impact upon the development of that student; we give special attention to that subject in the next section.

Guidelines for Evaluating What the Student Writes

1. Worksheets, homework and test items should *correlate with the specific* instructional objectives.
2. *Read everything* the learner writes. If it is important enough for the student to do, then it is important that you give your professional attention to the product of the learner's efforts.
3. *Provide* written or verbal *comments* about the student's work, and be *positive* in your comments.
4. Use *positive reward reinforcers* as frequently as possible.
5. When writing your comments on student papers, use *a color other than red*. Red brings a host of negative connotations, such as blood, hurt, and danger. (We admit this is our own prejudice, and merely ask that you consider it and form your own opinion as to its psychological merit.)
6. *Think through your comments before writing on the student's paper,* asking yourself, "How will this comment be interpreted by the student and by the parents?"

Guideline six is related to guideline four of the guidelines for evaluating what a learner says and does. Because what a teacher writes can have an enormous impact upon a student's development, we give this topic special consideration in the next section of this chapter.

Regardless of avenues chosen, and their relative weights given by the teacher, *the teacher must evaluate against the instructional objectives!* Any given objective may be checked by using more than one avenue, and by using more than one instrument. Indeed, whereas evaluation of cognitive objectives lends itself to traditional written tests of achievement, evaluation of affective and psychomotor domains may require using performance checklists where student behaviors are observed in action, and for the teacher who may never see a student again after a one-semester course, the effects of the course on a student's values and attitudes may never be observed at all. Subjectivity, inherent in the evaluation process, may be reduced as the teacher checks for validity, comparing results of one measuring technique against those of another.

D. RECORDING MY OBSERVATIONS AND JUDGMENTS: A WORD OF CAUTION ABOUT THE ANECDOTES I WRITE

It is important that you consider carefully the written comments you make regarding a student. We have seen anecdotal comments in a pupil's permanent school record that said more about the teacher who made the comment than we learned about the pupil. Sometimes comments that go into a student's permanent record can be quite detrimental to the student's welfare and progress, in school and beyond. Teacher comments must be professional, that is, *diagnostically useful to the further development of the student.* This is true for any comment you write, whether on a student paper, a note to the student's parents, or one that becomes a permanent comment on the student's school record.

Here is an example of an *unprofessional comment* observed in one student's school record: "John is lazy." Describing a student as "lazy" could be done by anyone! It is nonproductive, and is certainly not a professional diagnosis. Moreover, it could be detrimental to the future of the student by causing prejudicial behaviors from the student's future teachers and/or employers. Saying that a student is lazy merely *describes* behavior as observed by the teacher who wrote the comment. More important, and productive, would have been an attempt by the teacher to analyze *why* the student was behaving that way, then *prescribing* activities that would have been more likely to activate the student to behave in a more acceptable way.

Teachers' comments should be useful, productive, analytical, diagnostic, and prescriptive, for the continued development of the learner. The professional teacher performs diagnoses and prepares prescriptions; the teacher *does not label* students as "lazy," "vulgar," "slow," "dumb," or "unmotivated"—no matter how great the temptation to do so. The competent teacher sees the behavior of students as being goal-directed; perhaps the "lazy" student has developed that behavioral pattern in order to gain attention. That student's goal, then, is attention (we all like and need attention), and that student has assumed negative, perhaps even destructive, behavioral patterns to accomplish that goal. The task of the professional teacher is to facilitate the student's understanding (perception) of his or her goal, and then to identify acceptable behaviors positively designed to reach it.

That which separates the professional teacher from "anyone off the street" is the teacher's skill in going beyond the mere description of student behavior. Always keep this fact in mind as you write comments that will be read by the student, the student's parents or guardians, other teachers, and by future employers of the student. Let us now reinforce this concept with Exercise 16.1.

EXERCISE 16.1: AN EVALUATION OF WRITTEN TEACHER COMMENTS

Instructions: Here are some written teacher comments as drawn from student records. Check those you consider to be professionally useful, then compare your responses against the key. Discuss your results with your classmates.

Professionally Useful

	Yes	No
1. This year, I have observed that Patty performs her math assignments much better when done in class than when they are given as homework.	( )	( )
2. Anthony has been consistently disruptive this year in my class.	( )	( )
3. Dick has a lot of difficulty staying in his seat.	( )	( )
4. Sue seems most responsive in "hands-on" learning activities.	( )	( )
5. Stanley seems to have an excess of nervous energy which may be affected by his eating habits.	( )	( )
6. Emily did very well this year in science laboratory activities but seems to have reading difficulties.	( )	( )
7. Mark does not get along well with the other students.	( )	( )
8. Gretchen seems unable to understand my verbal directions.	( )	( )
9. I am recommending special remediation in mathematics for Noreen, perhaps through private tutoring, before she is promoted.	( )	( )
10. I do not appreciate Eugene's use of slang expressions in the classroom.	( )	( )

Key to Exercise 16.1

1. This is useful information.
2. Not useful, as there are no helpful specifics. It could provide a bias to the student's next teacher. "Disruptive" is merely descriptive, not prescriptive.
3. Could be useful to the next teacher.
4. Useful.
5. Useful.
6. Useful, although more specifics would help.
7. Not useful; could bias the next teacher.
8. Not useful. Tells more about the teacher than about Gretchen.
9. Useful.
10. Not useful.

E. MAINTAINING RECORDS OF STUDENT ACHIEVEMENT

The record book should include tardies and absences as well as all records for scores on exams, quizzes, homework, and other assignments. Complete and current records of student achievment are absolutely essential and should be carefully maintained in a record book that is convenient to carry with you, or on a computer disk (an "electronic gradebook") with a weekly updated backup disk. When maintained on a computer program we suggest that the record for each student include not only that student's name but also the student's social security number, or at least the first five digits of that number. Using that number as a student identification number, periodic current grade printouts may be posted so that students know their current standings in the course, and can check to see that scores are properly recorded. Catching recording errors early can prevent end-of-semester problems.

F. GRADING STUDENT ACHIEVEMENT

If conditions were ideal, and if teachers did their job perfectly well, then all students would receive top grades (the ultimate in mastery learning), and there would be less of a need here to address the topic of grading. Mastery learning, however, indicates that there is some final end point of learning that is attainable, but there probably isn't. In any case, conditions are never ideal, so let's continue with this topic of extreme interest to you and to your students.

What is *achievement*? Is it achievement of the objectives against a preset standard, or is it simply achievement alone? Most teachers choose the former, where each teacher subjectively establishes a standard that must be met in order for a student to receive a certain grade for the assignment, test, or course. Preset standards are usually expressed in percentages needed for grades of "A," "B," "C," etc. If no student achieves the standard required for an "A" grade, then no student receives that grade. If all students of a class meet the preset standards for an "A" grade, then all receive that grade (and the teacher, prior to teaching the course again, may need to reconsider his or her standards). That is *criterion-referenced measurement.*

Criterion-referenced Versus Norm-referenced Grading

As stated in the preceding paragraph, criterion-referenced grading is based on present standards. Norm-referenced grading is based on relative achievement within the group, comparing and ranking students within the group, and is commonly known as "grading on the curve." Because it encourages competition, and discourages cooperative learning, for determination of course grades norm-referenced grading is *not* recommended. Each student is an individual and should not be converted to a statistic on a frequency-distribution curve. You can periodically produce frequency-distribution studies of grades for your own information, but *do not grade secondary-school students on a curve.* Achievement grades should be tied to performance levels.

Arriving at Grades

Arriving at course grades for students is serious business because, once entered onto transcripts, grades have significant impacts upon the futures of students. With respect to grading, several decisions must be made by you. Consider the following guidelines.

1. *Criteria* for "A," "B," "C," etc. grades. Select a percentage standard, such as 90 percent (or higher) for an "A," 80 percent (or higher) for a "B," etc.
2. *Sources of data* for determination of the final grade. First, we recommend using a point system for grading, where everything the students write, say, and do is given points, then the possible point total is the factor for grade determination. For example, if 90 percent is the cut off for an "A," and 500 points are possible, then any student with 450 points (500 × .90) has achieved an "A." Likewise for an exam or any other assignment, if the exam value is 100 points, the cut off for an "A" is 90. With a point system and preset standards, the teacher and students always know the current points possible and current grade standings. Students know always exactly where they stand in the course.

   Second, you must determine point values for various things students write, say, and do. Some teachers negotiate certain of these values with their students at the beginning of the semester. We are not certain there is any value in doing that. Some teachers base student grades solely on exam scores, whereas others use a variety of factors that include assignments and class participation. We think your decision on this policy must rest with your own philosophy, and by the nature of the subject, the course, and the students with whom you work. Some teachers give points for mere attendance, and there is justification for doing that if, by simply being present, students gain something that cannot be achieved in any other way. That is a personal judgment about your own course that you must make.
3. About *makeup* work. Students will be absent and will miss assignments and examinations, and it is best that you decide beforehand your policy regarding makeups. With respect to assignments our recommendation is that you strictly adhere to due dates, making allowances in only a few instances and preferably when prearranged between you and the individual student. In any case, there should be a brief time limit during which late assignments are acceptable, perhaps no more than a week from original due dates. If assignments are clearly listed on the course syllabus, students have plenty of time to plan and prepare them, and in only rare instances should late assignments be accepted.

   Occasionally students will be absent during major examinations. It is important that your policy of missed examinations be clearly stated on your syllabus. Some teachers allow students to miss or discount one exam. Another technique used by some teachers is to allow each student to substitute a formal paper for any one examination. A student absent from an examination would then be required to write a term paper for that missed examination content, but of course this resolves nothing if the same student misses another examination. Another possibility is to give the absent student the choice of either taking a makeup exam or having the next exam count double. We advise against makeup examinations, but if they are given, then *the makeup exam should be taken within a week of the regular examination.*

4. The first- and third-quarter grades are in fact *progress reports.* It is the final semester grade that counts the most—the one that ends up on student transcripts, and that is used in determining high school graduation, college entrance, and the awarding of scholarships. Keep this important concept in mind as you work with students through each grading period.

5. The items used in determining the students' final quarter and semester grades should be a *good balance of homework, classwork, quizzes, major tests, and exams.* In many classes, the number of major tests (including exams) should be a minimum of six for an entire semester. The number of quizzes would be much greater. The total grade should be determined by approximately 50 percent test (including quiz) scores, and 50 percent classwork and homework. This is a general guideline only; just be cautious if you develop a system that counts too heavily on students' scores on major tests.

6. Especially when you grade using a point system, you will encounter students who will ask for *extra-credit* assignments, and this will occur with increased frequency as the grading period draws to a close. Our recommendation: *do not burden yourself with having to devise extra assignments for students who did not do the regular assignments.* Extra assignments may have a reasonable place for students who *need* extra work because of legitimate absences or who are above and beyond where the rest of the class is, or who have special needs (see Chapter 1), but in most cases those will be discerned much earlier during the grading period.

7. A special hint that will perhaps make your job a bit easier is to *consider giving your quarter exams* (first and third) *a week before the end of the grading period.* This is not the norm for secondary-school teachers, but if it is possible, it will give you an extra week to read the exams, score them, make final grade determinations, and mark the computer printout grade report forms. Doing so might help preserve your home life!

8. *Grading procedures in performance classes,* such as art and music, will vary from many of the previous guidelines, particularly those dealing with the administration of tests that can be measured objectively. In these courses the teacher will perhaps rely more heavily on subjective items, such as classroom participation. Is the student demonstrating a positive attitude toward trying? Does the student respect other students and the correct use of materials, instruments, and supplies? Are assignments neat and turned in on time? Does the student's performance (see acceptable verbs in Section D of Chapter 7) satisfy the concept of the task? A point scoring system can still be utilized for the final determination of student grades.

9. A final guideline concerns the fact that you will also be arriving at a mark that represents the student's social behavior in your class—commonly referred to as the "citizenship grade." Although the student's social behavior will likely affect his or her academic achievement, the two marks are separated on reporting forms (see Section J). Our advice to you: *Do not deduct academic accomplishment points from the student's total points just because his or her citizenship is less than satisfactory to you!* Unless you are teaching in a particular area of social studies where you can safely combine the grades, they should be kept separate, and reported separately. You might have a student in your class who is a real "smart alec" and whose behavior you abhor but who still achieves well academically. The academic grade reflects his or her academic achievement, not necessarily his or her immature behavior in your classroom.

G. TESTING FOR STUDENT ACHIEVEMENT

Competent planning, preparing, administering, and scoring of tests is an important professional skill. Here are helpful guidelines.

Purposes for Testing

Tests can be designed for several purposes, and a variety of kinds of test can keep your testing program interesting and reliable. Purposes for which tests are used include:

1. To provide review and drill to enhance teaching and learning.
2. To serve as motivational devices.
3. To assist in decision-making regarding promotion and classification.
4. To provide information for planning for individualization.
5. To help determine teaching effectiveness.
6. To serve as a source of information for student counseling and guidance.
7. To assess and aid in curriculum planning.
8. To measure student achievement.

As a college student, perhaps you are most experienced with testing for the purpose of measuring achievement (purpose no. 8), but as a secondary-school teacher you will use testing in a number of different ways.

After determining the purpose for which you are designing a test, you should identify the specific instructional objectives the test is being designed to measure. Your written instructional objectives are specific so that you can write test items to measure against those objectives. So, the first step in test construction is identification of the test purpose. The second step is to identify the objectives to be measured, and the third step is to prepare the test items.

When and How Often to Test

We believe that in most secondary-school courses, major tests should be cumulative and frequent, and by frequent we mean at least every four weeks. Advantages of giving tests that are cumulative include review, reinforcement, and articulation of "old material" with the more recent. Frequent testing has several advantages, including reduction of test anxiety and increasing the validity of final grade determinations.

Administering Tests

For many students test-taking is a high anxiety time, and to more accurately measure student achievement the teacher should take steps to reduce test anxiety. Consider the following guidelines.

1. Be sure *the classroom* is well ventilated, temperature is ideal, and seats are well spaced.

2. Prior to test time be certain that you have a *sufficient quantity of complete copies* of the test.
3. When the class bell rings, don't drag it out, but *distribute* tests quickly.
4. Before starting the test, explain to the students what they are to do upon *completion* of the test, such as a homework assignment for the next day.
5. If you plan to *post grades* later, then do so by test numbers or the first five digits of student Social Security numbers, rather than by student names.
6. Once testing has begun, *do not interrupt* students. Items of important information can be written on the board.
7. During testing, *remain in the room* (bring work to do).
8. If the test is not going to take an entire class period, give it at the beginning of class.

About Cheating

Cheating on tests does occur but there are ways of discouraging it or of reducing the opportunity and pressure to cheat. Consider the following options.

1. *Space student seating* during testing, thereby reducing the opportunity to cheat.
2. Use *alternate forms* of the test, and distribute them so that adjacent students have different forms.
3. *Frequent testing* tends to reduce test anxiety and the pressure that can cause cheating.
4. Write exam questions that are *unambiguous,* thereby reducing student frustration with the test.
5. Keep exams in a *safe location,* and if kept on a computer disk, be sure you have a current backup copy.

If and when you do suspect cheating *is* occurring, simply moving and standing in the area of the suspect will probably stop it. When you suspect cheating *has* occurred you are faced with a serious dilemma. Unless your suspicion is backed by absolute proof, you are best advised to forget it. If you do have absolute proof, then you are professionally obligated to proceed with school policies regarding student cheating on examinations. This may result in disciplinary action or counseling for the student.

Time Needed for a Test

The amount of time needed for a test is determined by the type of test items. The following chart is a general guide.

Type of Test Item	*Time Needed Per Item*
matching	1 minute per match
multiple-choice	1 minute
completion	1 minute
completion drawing	2–3 minutes, or more

arrangement	2–3 minutes
identification	2–3 minutes
short explanation	2–3 minutes, or more
essay and performance	15 or more minutes

H. PREPARING TEST ITEMS: TWELVE TYPES

General Guidelines for Test Item Preparation

1. Use several kinds of test items.
2. Be sure that content coverage is complete, that all relevant objectives are being measured.
3. Each item of the test should be reliable, that is, it should measure the intended objective. One way to check item reliability is to have more than one test item measuring for the same objective.
4. Each test item is clear and unambiguous.
5. The test is difficult enough for the poorly prepared student, but easy enough for the student who has learned.
6. Prepare your test, put it aside and think about it, then work it over again. The test should represent your very best professional efforts. A quickly and poorly prepared test is likely to be more damaging than beneficial to the learning of the students.

A good testing program uses a variety of test item types to provide validity checks and for individual differences among students. This section provides a review of advantages and disadvantages, and guidelines for use of twelve types of test items, some of which may be more useful in certain subjects than in others.[1] Consider each.

[1]Ready-made test item banks are available on computer disks, and also usually accompany school textbooks, but if you plan to use these be certain that the items match your course objectives, and are well written.

---

1. ARRANGEMENT TYPE

Description: Terms are to be arranged in a specific order.
Sample 1: (From a listing of the planets in the solar system), arrange them in order beginning with the planet that is closest to the sun.
Sample 2: Arrange the following list of fabrics according to their wear durability, beginning with that which is most durable.
Advantages: This type of item tests for knowledge of sequence and order, and is good for review and for initiating discussions.
Disadvantage: Scoring may be difficult, so be cautious about using this type for grading purposes.
Guideline for use: Include instructions to students to include the rationale for their arrangement, making it a combined arrangement and short explanation type (being sure to allow adequate spacing for explanations).

2. COMPLETION DRAWING TYPE

Description: An incomplete drawing is presented and the student is to complete it.
Sample 1: Complete the following partially diagrammed sentences.
Sample 2: In the following food web, draw arrows indicating which organisms are consumers and which are producers.
Advantages: This type requires less time than is required for a complete drawing as may be required in an essay item. Scoring is relatively simple.
Disadvantage: Care needs to be exercised in the instructions so that students do not misinterpret the expectation. If students have prior practice with this item type, then there should be less of a problem in their accomplishing it.
Guideline for use: Use occasionally for diversion from the more usual item types, but use care in preparing. Consider making the item a combined completion-drawing, short-explanation type by having students include rationales for their drawings, being sure to allow spacing for explanations.

3. COMPLETION STATEMENT TYPE

Description: An incomplete sentence is given and the student is to complete it by filling in the blank(s).
Sample 1: The great earthquakes of the San Francisco bay area were in 1906 and ___.
Sample 2: The states that bound California are Oregon, Nevada, and ___.
Advantages: Usually this test item measures for recall, and is easy to devise, to take, and to score.
Disadvantages: It is difficult to write this kind of item for measuring higher levels of cognition, and the teacher must be alert for a correct student response different from the expected answer.
Guideline for use: Use occasionally for review, but, except for problems involving mathematical calculations, never for grading purposes.

4. CORRECTION TYPE

Description: Similar to "completion" type, except that sentences or paragraphs are complete but with italicized words that must be changed to make the sentence correct.
Sample: Photosynthesis in *purple animals* is the breakdown of *dirt* into hydrogen and oxygen, the release of the *minerals,* then the combining of the *argon* with carbon dioxide to make *clay.*
Advantages: Like the completion type, the correction type usually measures recall. Students may enjoy occasional use of this type for the tension relief afforded by the incorrect absurdities.
Guideline for use: Use occasionally for diversion from the usual test item types. Consider making it a combined correction, short-explanation type, being sure to allow spacing for explanations.

5. ESSAY TYPE

Description: A question or problem is presented and the student composes a response in the form of sustained prose, using the student's own words, phrases, and ideas, and within the limits of the question or problem.

Sample: Describe an experiment you would design to determine how much energy could be saved by using storm doors in a home.

Advantages: Measures higher mental processes, such as ability to synthesize material and to express ideas in clear and precise written language.

Disadvantages: Essay items require a great deal of time to read and to score. They tend to provide an unreliable sampling of achievement, and are vulnerable to teacher subjectivity and unreliable scoring. Furthermore, they tend to punish a student who writes slowly and laboriously, but nevertheless may have achieved as well as a student who writes faster.

Guidelines for use:

1. When preparing an essay-only test, a large number of questions, each requiring a relatively short prose response, is preferable to a smaller number of questions requiring long prose responses. Briefer answers tend to be more precise, and a larger number of items provides a more reliable sampling of achievement.
2. Be certain students have adequate time to fully respond to the questions.
3. Different qualities of achievement are more likely comparable when all students must answer the same questions, although providing a list of 12 questions of which each student selects any 10 is not unreasonable.
4. After preparing the essay items, you need to make a tentative scoring key, deciding the key themes you expect students to accurately identify, and how many points will be allotted to each.
5. Students should be informed about the relative test value for each essay question. If point values differ for each item, they can be listed in the margin of the test adjacent to each item.
6. When reading student essays, read all student papers for one item at a time and, while doing that, make notes to yourself; then return and while reading that item again, score each student paper for that item. Repeat the process for the next item.
7. In order to nullify the "halo effect," rather than having students write their names on their essay papers some teachers use a numbering code so while reading the papers the teacher is unaware of whose paper is being read. If you do this, use extra caution to not misplace or confuse student exam identification codes.
8. The level of the following student performances is commonly measured by means of the essay item:
   a. Comparison of two (or more) things on a given basis.
   b. Comparison of two (or more) things in general.
   c. Decision for or against.
   d. Statement of causes or effects.
   e. Explanation of meanings, use of words, phrases, or longer portions of given passages.
   f. Summary.
   g. Analysis.
   h. Statement of relationships.
   i. Original illustration or exemplification of rules, principles, procedures, usages, etc.
   j. Classification.
   k. Applications of rules, laws, and principles to a new situation.
   l. Statement of aims of author in selection or organization of material.
   m. Criticism as to adequacy, correctness, or relevance of words, phrases, or statements.
   n. Outlining.
   o. Reorganization of facts previously encountered in different arrangements.
   p. Formulation of new questions and problems.
   q. Suggestion of new methods of procedure.

SUGGESTIONS FOR THE USE OF KEY WORDS IN ESSAY ITEMS

In our observations secondary-school teachers are inclined to use subjective tests (essay tests) more frequently than objective tests for various reasons. It must be noted here that there are a number of key words for essay questions that the tester could use; however, the connotation and/or the meaning of each key word may be different. Please note the following:

"Compare"—asks for analysis of similarity and difference, with greater emphasis on *similarities* or *likenesses.*

"Contrast"—asks more for *differences* than for *similarities.*

"Criticize"—asks for the "goods" and "bads" of an idea or a situation.

"Define"—asks student to express clearly and concisely the meaning of a term (as in the dictionary, or in the writer's own words).

"Describe"—asks student, writing sequentially, to give an account of or to sketch a specified topic.

"Diagram"—asks student to put quantities or numerical values into the form of a chart, a graph, or drawings.

"Discuss"—asks student to explain or argue, presenting various sides of events, ideas, or situations.

"Enumerate"—asks student to count over or list one after another; different from "Explain briefly" or "Tell in 2–3 words."

"Evaluate"—asks student to express worth, value, judgment.

"Explain"—asks student to describe with emphasis on cause and effect, in an open manner.

"Illustrate"—asks student to describe by means of examples, figures, pictures, and/or diagrams.

"Interpret"—asks student to describe or explain a given fact, theory, principle, or doctrine in a specific context.

"Justify"—asks student to show reasons, with emphasis on "right," "positive," and "advantageous."

"List"—asks student to simply name items in a category or to include them in a list, without much description.

"Outline"—asks student to give a short summary with headings and subheadings.

"Relate"—asks student to tell how specified things are connected or brought into some kind of relationships.

"Summarize"—asks student to recapitulate the main points without examples or illustrations.

"Trace"—asks student to follow a history or series of events step-by-step by going backward over the evidence.

"Prove"—asks student to present materials as witnesses, proof, and evidence.

6. GROUPING TYPE

Description: A list of several items is presented and the student is to select and group those that are related.

Sample 1: Separate the following list of fabrics into two groups, those that are natural fibers and those that are synthetic.

Sample 2: Draw a line through the one figure that is least like the others: triangle, circle, square, rectangle.

Advantages: This type of item tests knowledge of groupings, and can be used to measure for higher levels of cognition. Students seem to like this type of question, and it can stimulate discussion. Like in sample 2, it can be similar to a multiple-choice type item.

Disadvantages: A student may have a valid alternative rationale for grouping.

Guideline for use: To allow for an alternative correct response consider making the item a combination grouping, short-explanation type, being certain to allow spacing for explanations.

7. IDENTIFICATION TYPE

Description: Unknown specimens are to be identified by name or some other criterion.

Sample 1: Identify by names the fabrics as shown.

Sample 2: Identify by name the authors of each of the three poems.

Advantages: Students can be working with real materials. Verbalization (use of abstract symbols) is less significant, and the item can test for procedural understanding.

Disadvantages: To be fair, specimens should be equally familiar or unfamiliar to all students. Adequate materials must be provided.

Guideline for use: Consider this item type as it is useful in all disciplines, although more common to the arts, mathematics, sciences, home economics, and shop courses. If photocopies or pictures are used, rather than actual materials, they must be clear and not confusing to students.

8. MATCHING TYPE

Description: Match related items from a list of numbered items to a list of lettered choices.

Sample: Identify by using the associated letter the name of the person who accomplished each of the following:

Stem Column	*Answer Column*
___ 1. first President of the U.S.	A. Thomas Jefferson
___ 2. current President of the U.S.	B. George Washington
___ 3. (etc.)	C. (etc.)

Advantages:

- Can measure for ability to judge relationships between similar ideas, facts, definitions, and concepts.
- Easy to score.
- Can test a broad range of content.
- Reduces guessing, especially if one column contains more items.

Disadvantages:

- Not easily adapted to measuring for higher cognition.
- Because all parts must be homogeneous it is possible that clues will be given, thus reducing item validity.
- A student might have a legitimate rationale for an "incorrect" response.

Guidelines for use:

1. The number of items in the "answer" column should exceed the number in the stem column.
2. The number of items to be matched should not exceed twelve.
3. Matching sets should have high homogeneity; that is, items in both columns should be of the same general category.
4. If "answers" can be used more than once, the directions should so state.
5. Be prepared for the student who can legitimately defend an "incorrect" response.

9. MULTIPLE-CHOICE TYPE

Description: Similar to a completion item in that statements are presented, sometimes in incomplete form, but with several options, requiring recognition, or even higher cognitive processes, rather than mere recall.

Sample: For this sample examination question, "Design an experiment to determine how much energy could be saved by using storm doors in a home," the highest level of cognition required for answering the question, is: (a) application, (b) comprehension, (c) evaluation, (d) knowledge, (e) synthesis.

Advantages: Items can be answered and machine-scored quickly. A wide range of content, and higher levels of cognition can be tested in a relatively short time. For example, the sample question is intended to measure the student's ability to synthesize, a higher level of cognition than simple recall of knowledge. Excellent for all testing purposes—motivation, review, and assessment of learning.

Disadvantages: Because multiple-choice questions are relatively easy to write, there is a tendency to write items that measure only for low levels of cognition. Multiple-choice items are excellent for major testing, but it takes time to write good questions that measure higher levels of learning. When scoring is too mechanical, assessment of student learning could be missed.

Guidelines for use:

1. If the item is in the form of an incomplete statement, it should be meaningful in itself and imply a direct question rather than merely lead into a collection of unrelated true and false statements. For example:

    Faulty: The United States of America
    a. has more than 200,000 people.
    b. grows large amounts of rubber.
    c. has few good harbors.
    d. is comprised of people of varied nationalities.

Improved: The population of the United States is characterized by its:
   a. zero-population birthrate.
   b. people of varied national backgrounds.
   c. even geographical distribution.
   d. increasing proportion of young people.

2. Use a level of language that is easy enough for even the poorest readers to understand, and avoid unnecessary wordiness. For example:

   Too wordy: Which of the following metals is characterized by extensive utilization in the aircraft industry?

   Improved: Which of the following metals is most used in manufacturing airplanes?

3. If there is much variation in the length of alternatives, arrange the alternatives in order from shortest to longest; i.e., first alternative is the shortest, last alternative the longest.

4. For single-word alternatives, consistent alphabetical arrangement of alternatives, as in the sample given for this type, is recommended (see guideline number 18).

5. Incorrect responses (distractors) should be plausible, and related to the same concept as the correct alternative. Although an occasional humorous distractor helps to relieve test anxiety, along with absurd distractors they should generally be avoided as they offer no measuring value.

6. Arrangement of alternatives should be uniform throughout the test, and listed in column form rather than in paragraph form.

7. Every item should be grammatically consistent; e.g., if the stem is in the form of an incomplete sentence, it should be possible to complete the sentence by attaching any of the alternatives to it.

8. It is not necessary to maintain a fixed number of alternatives for every item, but the use of less than three is not recommended, and the use of four or five reduces chance responses and guessing, thereby increasing the reliability of the item.

9. The stem should be expressed in positive form, as a negative stem presents a psychological disadvantage to the student. Negative items are those that ask what is *not* characteristic of something, what is the *least* useful, etc. Discard the item if you cannot express it in positive terminology.

10. Responses such as "all of these," or "one of these," should be used *only* when they will contribute more than another plausible distractor. Care must be taken that such responses answer or complete the stem. "All of the above" is a poorer response than "none of the above" because items that use it have four or five correct answers; also, if it is the right answer, knowledge of any two of the distractors will cue it.

11. There must be only one correct or best response. However, this is easier said than done (refer to guideline number 19).

12. The stem must mean the same thing to everyone.

13. Measuring for understanding of definitions is better tested by furnishing the name or word and requiring choice between alternative definitions than by presenting the definition and requiring choice between alternative words.

14. The stem should state a single and specific thing.

15. The stem must not include clues which would indicate the correct alternative. For example:

    Faulty: A four-sided figure whose opposite sides are parallel is called:
    a. a trapezoid.
    b. a parallelogram.
    c. an octagon.
    d. a triangle.

16. Avoid using alternatives that include absolute terms such as *never* and *always*.

17. Multiple-choice items need not be entirely verbal. Consider the use of charts, diagrams, and other visuals, as they will make the test more interesting, especially for students with lower verbal abilities.

18. Once you have composed your multiple-choice test, tally the position of answers to be sure they are evenly distributed, to avoid a common psychological mistake of having the correct response in the third option position. Also, *occasionally* have the same correct option position in consecutive questions.

19. Consider providing space between test items for students to include rationales for their response selections, thus making the test a combination multiple-choice and short-explanation item type. This allows for the student who can rationalize a response that you had not considered plausible, and for measurement of higher levels of cognition.

20. While scoring, on a blank copy of your test, for each item tally "wrong" responses. Analyze student "wrong" responses to each item to discover potential errors in your original keying.

21. Start a multiple-choice item data bank, analyzing and improving items after each testing use.

10. PERFORMANCE TYPE

Description: Provided certain conditions or materials, the student solves a problem or accomplishes some other action.

Sample 1: Given a class of ten students the student will prepare and teach an effective 15-minute inquiry lesson.

Sample 2: Demonstrate your understanding of diffusion by designing and completing a laboratory experiment utilizing the chemicals and equipment located on the table.

Advantages: Performance tests come closer to measuring certain expected outcomes of a course than do most other types. Little or no verbalization may be necessary. Psychomotor skills are tested. Learning that is difficult to verbalize can be assessed. Students who do poorly on verbal tests may do well on performance tests.

Disadvantages: Difficult and time-consuming to administer to large groups. Scoring tends to be subjective.

Guidelines for use: Use your creativity to design and utilize performance tests, as they tend to measure the most important course objectives. The use of colleagues or student assistants may be helpful for implementation. To reduce subjectivity in scoring, provide distinct scoring guidelines.

11. SHORT EXPLANATION TYPE

Description: An essay-type question that requires a shorter answer.

Sample 1: Explain in a brief paragraph why piano wires are not equal in length.

Sample 2: Explain in one sentence why neon is unlikely to form compounds with other elements.

Advantages: Like with an essay question, the student's understanding is measured, but takes less time for the teacher to read and to score. By using several questions of this type, a greater amount of content can be covered than with a fewer number of essay questions. This type of question is good practice for students to learn to express themselves succinctly.

Disadvantages: Many students have difficulty expressing themselves in such a limited fashion.

Guidelines for use: Perhaps most useful for occasional reviews and quizzes. For scoring, follow the guidelines as outlined for the essay type.

12. TRUE-FALSE TYPE

Description: A statement is given that the student is to judge to be accurate or not.
Sample: Write the word *true* or *false* in the blank for each statement.

_____ 1. Photosynthesis is the opposite of respiration.
_____ 2. Photosynthesis can be represented by $CO_2 + H_2O \rightarrow C_6H_{12}O_6$

Advantages: A great number of items can be answered in a brief time, making broad content coverage possible. Scoring is quick and simple. A test made up entirely of this item type can be machine-scored. True-false tests are good for initiating discussions, review, and for diagnostic evaluation.

Disadvantages: As in the samples, it is difficult to write true-false items that are strictly true or false without qualifying them in such a way that clues the answer. Much of the content that lends itself to this type of test item is relatively unimportant. Students have a 50-percent chance of guessing the correct answer, thus giving this item type poor validity and reliability. Scoring and grading give no indication as to why the student missed an item. *True-false items should not be used for grade determination purposes.* See guidelines that follow, particularly number 11.

Guidelines for preparing true-false statements:

1. First write out the statement as a true statement, then make it false by changing a word or phrase.
2. Avoid negative statements.
3. A true-false statement should include only one idea.
4. Use approximately an equal number of true and false items on a true-false test or section of a test.
5. Avoid specific determiners, which often clue that the statement is false, e.g., *always, all,* or *none.*
6. Avoid words that may clue that the statement is true, such as *often, probably,* and *sometimes.*
7. Avoid words that may have different meanings for different students.
8. Avoid using exact language from the textbook or a lecture.
9. Avoid trick items.
10. Avoid taking sentences directly from the textbook or lecture.
11. For grading purposes, you may use modified true-false items, where space is provided between items and students *must* write in explanations, thus making the item a combined true-false, short-explanation type.
12. "Sometimes-always-never" is another modified form of true-false. Although introduction of the third alternative, "sometimes," reduces chances for guessing, this item is only cautiously recommended for grade determination purposes.

EXERCISE 16.2: PREPARING TEST ITEMS

Instructions: The purpose of this exercise is to develop your skill in preparing the twelve different types of test items as discussed previously. From your course syllabus select one specific instructional objective and write test items for it. When completed share this exercise with your colleagues for their feedback.

The objective:

1. Arrangement item:

2. Completion drawing item:

3. Completion statement item:

4. Correction item:

5. Essay item:

6. Grouping item:

7. Identification item:

8. Matching item:

9. Multiple-choice item:

10. Performance item:

11. Short explanation item:

12. True-false item:

EXERCISE 16.3: MY GRADE DETERMINATION PROCEDURE

Instructions: The purpose of this exercise is to initiate your thinking about how you will determine grades for a course you intend to teach. Outline and prepare to defend your grade determination procedure. Use separate paper and share the completed exercise with your colleagues for their feedback.

Example:

Quarter Grading for ―――――――― Using a point system with 90% = A, 80% = B, 70% = C, and 60% = D.

Quarter Points Possible = 875   **Distribution as follows:**

A = 787.5–875	Attendance: 5 points/day × 45 days = 225 points (25%)
B = 700–787	Quizzes: 10 best of 12 @ 10 points = 100 points (11%)
C = 612.5–699	Unit Tests: 3 best of 4 @ 100 points = 300 points (34%)
D = 525–612	Assignments: 25 @ 10 points = 250 points (29%)

I. CONFERENCING WITH AN ANGRY STUDENT

How should you react when an irate student complains to you about a grade received? This will inevitably happen, and if it happens often, then you will need to evaluate your grading procedures. If it happens only once or twice a semester, we offer the following guidelines.

1. Unfortunately, too many students try to solve their disputes with you during class time, or immediately following class. That is not the time for individual conferences of this sort, and you should make that clear in your course syllabus. In our own course syllabi, we have found this statement helpful: "When of general course content and procedures, please feel free to ask questions at any time; however, when with respect to a problem specific to you, please seek individual guidance and assistance during my regular or special office hours."

2. When the student has followed your advice and meets privately with you in your office, remain calm in your discussion with the student, allowing the student time to explain his or her position.

3. Do not allow yourself to be positioned into having to defend yourself or your policies. If you have followed guidelines established in this resource guide, then your grading policies are clearly set forth in your syllabus.

4. If the student's complaint is about a score that you gave on an essay test item or a term paper, then simply tell the student you will gladly take the paper and read and score it again. And do so. One technique that seems to work well is to ask students who have complaints about their grades to write a paragraph describing their complaint or point of view, declaring your willingness to review the paper of anyone who brings in such a paragraph, and that you may change the grade either positively or negatively.

5. Scoring of tests of factual knowledge will cause fewer complaints than will that of the scoring of items that require students to operate at higher levels of cognition—perhaps the reason so many teachers measure only achievement at the lowest cognitive domain—but measuring only for recall of factual knowledge is not a professionally defensible posture. You must try to raise the level of student thinking, and be prepared for a potential deluge of student complaints about the obscurity of your expectations.

6. When you and a student are alone together in your office or classroom, always leave the door open.

J. REPORTING A STUDENT'S ACHIEVEMENT

One of the teacher's responsibilities is to report student achievement. In most secondary-school districts this is done in either of two ways: some junior high schools and even some senior high schools continue to use the traditional "report card," which is marked and sent home either with the student or by mail; but many high schools today use the more modern method of reporting by computer printouts, which are often sent by mail directly to the student's home address. Such printouts might include all of the courses taken by the student while enrolled in that high school, as well as the student's current accumulation of units and grade point average to date.

Whichever reporting form is used, it will separate the social from the academic behaviors of the student. In high schools, the academic achievement is usually indicated by a letter grade (A through F) and the social behavior (citizenship) simply by a "satisfactory" or an "unsatisfactory." Junior high and middle school reporting forms may be more specific regarding social behavior items.

In either case, please note the following.

SUGGESTIONS FOR PREPARING REPORT CARDS

1. Study the Report Card/Progress Report/Quarterly Report used in your school. Be familiar with the policies/regulations governing the report card.
2. If you have to grade "Citizenship," be extra careful to guard against teacher subjectivity (biases and prejudices).
3. You should always make separate assessments for achievement and citizenship.
4. If you are not satisfied with the report card established by the school, create your own for your students or a more detailed one for parents. Let your administrators know you are doing this.
5. Invite students and parents to talk about the report card with you.

K. CONFERENCING WITH A PARENT

As a secondary-school teacher you are likely to be meeting many of the parents early in the school year during "Back to School Night" and throughout the year in individual parent conferences. Frequently these are anxious times for the beginning teacher. Here are guidelines to help you with those experiences.

Guidelines for Parent–Teacher Meetings

1. When discussing your method of operation during "Back to School Night," remember the parents are anxious to learn about their child's new teacher. Tell them about yourself and then make some straightforward remarks about your expectations of the students in your class. The parents will be glad to learn that you (1) have your program well planned, (2) are a "task master," (3) will communicate with them frequently. The parents will be delighted to find that you are from the school of the three F's—firm, friendly, and fair.

Parents will expect to learn about your curriculum, about any long-term projects, and about your grading procedures. They will need to know what you expect of them: Will there be homework, and if so, should they help their children? Try to anticipate questions there are likely to be—such as how they can contact you. Your principal may be of assistance in helping you anticipate and prepare for these questions. But of course you can never prepare for the question that comes from left field. Just stay calm and don't get flustered. Parents will be reassured to know you are an in-control person.

2. Later in the year, when meeting parents in individual conferences, our advice is for you to be as specific as possible when explaining to the parent the progress of his or her child. Be helpful to their understanding, and don't bombard the parent with more information than necessary. As a group, teachers tend to talk too much. Resist that tendency and allow time for the parent to ask questions. Keep your answers succinct. Never compare one child with another, or even with the entire class. If the parent asks a question for which you do not have an answer, tell the parent you will try to find the answer and phone him or her as quickly as you can. And do it! Have the student's work with you during parent conferences so you can *show* the parent examples of what is being discussed.

3. When a parent asks how he or she may help at home, here are suggestions for *consideration:*

   a. Limit television viewing.

   b. Save all of the student's papers, digging them out once in a while to review progress with the student.

   c. Establish a regular time each evening for a family discussion about school.

   d. Ask your child to share with you each evening one specific thing learned that day in school.

   e. As needed, plan short family meetings *after* dinner, but while you are still seated at the table. Ask for a "tableside" report of "What's happening in your school life?" Ask, "How can I help?" When your child expresses a concern, emphasize ways to solve problems that occur, e.g., problems with classes, teacher, peers, homework, and social interaction.

4. When a parent is angry and hostile toward you or the school, use the following guidelines:

   a. Remain calm in your discussion with the parent, allowing the parent to talk about his or her hostility while you say little. The parent may just need to vent frustrations that might have very little to do with you.

   b. Do not allow yourself to be backed into a corner. If the parent tries to do so by attacking you personally, do not press your defense at this point. Perhaps the parent has made a point that you would like some time to consider, and now is a good time to arrange for another conference with this parent in about a week.

   c. Generally, the less you say the better off you probably will be, and what you do say must be objective and to the point of the student's work in the classroom.

   d. It is important that you not talk about other students in the class; keep the conversation about this parent's child's progress. Have objective data at hand that you can refer to during the conversation.

   e. The parent does not really need to hear about how busy you are and about how many other students you are dealing with simultaneously, unless he or she asks.

   f. This parent is not your rival, or should not be. You both are interested in the education of the child. Try and establish an adult conversation with the parent with a focus on a mutual diagnosis of the problem, with mutually agreed upon steps you both will undertake to resolve the problem. To this end you may need to solicit help from the principal or another third party. Do not hesitate to take that step when it appears necessary.

QUESTIONS FOR CLASS DISCUSSION

1. Can a teacher be too objective in evaluating student achivement? Explain.
2. The best evidence for evaluating student achievement is a variety of evidence. Explain the importance of this statement to you as related to your discipline.
3. Why do you suppose so much is written about the "slower learner," the "special needs learner," and about the "gifted and talented learner," but so little about the "average learner"? In school, which were you?
4. Do you believe in the use of "therapeutic" grading? Why or why not?
5. Assume that you are a secondary teacher and are preparing to meet the parents of your students for the first time (perhaps at a "Back to School Night"). What will you say to them? Try it out on your classmates.
6. What standardized tests are administered to the secondary school students at the schools you have visited? What are their purposes? How are their results used?
7. Do you believe that students should be failed or held back in grades? When, if ever, should their parents be involved in such decisions?
8. Are competency tests administered in the secondary schools of your state? For all subjects? In your field? To what grades? How are their results used? What are the arguments for and against such statewide testing?
9. Do you believe that teacher licensing should be based on teacher's and/or teacher-candidate's scores on standardized examinations of their knowledge about pedagogy? Why or why not?
10. What question do you have about the content of this chapter? How might answers be found?

SUGGESTED READINGS FOR CHAPTER 16

Cangelosi, J. S. *Designing Tests for Evaluating Student Achievement*. White Plains, NY: Longman, 1989.

Cunningham, G. K. *Educational and Psychological Measurement*. New York: Macmillan, 1986.

Cirn, J. T. "True/false versus short answer questions." *College Teaching* 34(1):34–37 (Winter 1986).

Gronlund, N. F., and Linn, R. L. *Measurement and Evaluation in Teaching*. 6th ed. New York: Macmillan, 1990.

Gronlund, N. F. *Constructing Achievement Tests*. 3d ed. Englewood Cliffs, NJ: Prentice-Hall, 1982.

17

How Can I Continue to Evaluate My Developing Competency?

The evaluation of your instructional effectiveness is an ongoing process that will continue throughout your teaching career. The content of this chapter should be helpful toward the continued improvement of your teaching competency.

A. A LOOK AT MY PRE-EMPLOYMENT COMPETENCY DEVELOPMENT: MICRO PEER TEACHING 3

Micro peer teaching (MPT) is a useful skill-development strategy: with Exercises 10.6 (questioning) and 11.1 (lecturing), you have completed two already. Micro peer teaching is a scaled-down teaching experience involving the following.

- A limited objective.
- A brief period of time for teaching the lesson.
- A lesson taught to a limited number of peer students (8–10).

Research indicates that micro peer teaching can be an excellent predictor of subsequent teacher effectiveness in a regular classroom, but more important, it provides opportunity to develop and improve specific teaching behaviors. A videotaped MPT allows the "teacher" to observe himself or herself in action for self-evaluation and diagnosis.

Evaluation of MPT is related to the following criteria:

1. What was the quality of "teacher" preparation and lesson implementation?
2. What was the quality of the planned and implemented "student" involvement?
3. Were the instructional objectives reached?
4. Was the cognitive level of the lesson appropriate?

For the micro peer teaching exercise that follows, the completed MPT has three ingredients:

a. Preparation and implementation of the demonstration lesson.
b. A packet turned in to the teacher by each "teacher" upon completion, which is in

effect a summative peer and self-evaluation, including statements of what the teacher would change were the lesson to be repeated.

c. The course teacher's evaluation of the teacher's participation in the total MPT exercise, in these four roles: *teaching, playback, student, and evaluator of other's MPTs.*

You will now put together the best that you have learned about teaching, in a final MPT exercise, Exercise 17.1 that follows.

EXERCISE 17.1: MICRO PEER TEACHING 3: PUTTING IT ALL TOGETHER

Instructions: The purpose of this exercise is for you to prepare and implement a 30-minute lesson to a group of peers (exact time to be established by your instructor or workshop leader). (No fair showing a 30-minute film!) While some members of your class will be your *students*, others will be evaluators of your teaching. You will be videotaped for your self-evaluation. See forms that follow.

After your presentation you will collect your peer evaluations (Form B), then review your playback. After that, you will prepare an MPT Packet that will be given to the course teacher no later than one week after your presentation. The packet should include, in this order, the following items:

1. Form A.
2. Lesson plan.
3. Raw peer evaluations.
4. Your tabulated summary of the peer evaluations.
5. A self-evaluation based on your analysis of the peer evaluations, your feelings after having completed the MPT, and viewing the tape.
6. A one-page summary analysis that includes your selection and description of strengths and weaknesses, and how you would improve were you to repeat the presentation.
7. Form C for teacher's completion.

Upon receipt of the packet, using Form C, your course instructor will provide final evaluation of your MPT.

EXERCISE 17.1: MICRO PEER TEACHING 3 FORM A: MPT PREPARATION

Instructions: Use this form for initial preparation of your lesson. (Study Form B.) After completing this form and receiving approval from your instructor, you prepare a lesson plan for your MPT. *A copy of your lesson plan must be presented to the evaluators at the time of implementation.*

1. Lesson I will teach:

2. Specific instructional objectives for the lesson:

3. Strategies to be used:
    set:

    transitions:

    others:

    closure:

4. Student experiences to be provided:

5. Materials, equipment and resources needed:

6. Approved by instructor: _____ Date _____

EXERCISE 17.1: MPT 3 FORM B: PEER EVALUATION

Instructions: Peer evaluators use this form, making their marks anywhere between *5* and *1*. Completed forms are collected by the "teacher" upon completion of the MPT, and reviewed *prior* to viewing tape.

To evaluators: Comments as well as marks are very useful to "teacher."

To "teacher": Give one copy of your lesson plan to evaluators at the start of MPT.

Teacher: _____ Date: _____

Topic: _____

I. Organization of lesson:	—5—	—4—	—3—	—2—	—1—
A. Lesson preparation	very evident		somewhat evident		not evident
B. Lesson beginning	effective set		somewhat effective		poor start
C. Subject-matter knowledge	well informed and much to offer		somewhat evident		not well-informed
D. Strategy choices	effective		somewhat effective		poor
E. Closure	effective ending		rough		abrupt

Comments:

II. Lesson Implementation

F. Eye contact	excellent eye contact		needs better contact somewhat fleeting		relies too much on notes; fleeting
G. Enthusiasm	enthusiastic		somewhat evident		lacking
H. Speech delivery	articulate		minor problems		monotone, boring
I. Voice inflection, cueing	effective		minor problems		poor

J.	Use of vocabulary	well chosen	minor problems	inappropriate
K.	Aids, props & materials	effectively used	somewhat effective	none, but needed
L.	Examples and analogies	excellent and logical	need more	none, but needed
M.	Involvement of audience	excellent and tactful	somewhat passive	none, but needed
N.	Overlapping	effective	some avoidance	poor
O.	Nonverbal communication	effectively used	somewhat confusing	distracting
P.	Active listening	effective demonstrated	somewhat demonstrated	poor
Q.	Responses to audience	personal and accepting	passive or indifferent	impersonal
R.	Use of questions	fluent, well-selected	somewhat effective	poor
S.	Use of student names	effectively used	somewhat effective	not used, needed
T.	Use of humor	effectively used	somewhat effective	none, but needed
U.	Directions and refocusing	clear and to the points	somewhat vague	confusing
V.	Teacher mobility	effectively used	somewhat effective	none, but needed
W.	Transitions	smooth and clear	somewhat disjointed	abrupt, unclear
X.	Motivating presentation	very	somewhat	not at all
Y.	Momentum of lesson	smooth and brisk	pacing mostly okay	too slow; too fast

Comments:

What to Look for in Video Playback Session for Your Self-Evaluation

Upon collection of your peer evaluations, you will move to another room where you will view the playback of your teaching demonstration. During the playback, there are specifics you should look for. These are:

1. Effective use of verbal responses.
2. Effective use of nonverbal responses (gestures).
3. Fluency in use of questioning.
4. Use of voice inflection and nonverbal cueing.
5. Use of set induction.
6. Stimulus variation (variety of materials and experiences).
7. Use of time and closure.
8. Examples and analogies.
9. Eye contact.
10. Peripheral awareness (overlapping).
11. Acceptance.
12. Listening.
13. Use of names.
14. Sense of humor.
15. Pertinence of MPT (nonfrivolous).
16. Keeps you relaxed but interested.
17. Overall creativity.
18. Effective use of body, hands.
19. Mobility.
20. Listen to your questions—clear and understood?

During the playback, you may stop the tape at various times, and backwind to see certain things a second time. Also, you should be reviewing the peer evaluations for any characteristics frequently mentioned and which you can see during the playback. Later you may wish to do a frequency-distribution analysis on the peer evaluations. A single comment from one evaluator may not be as informative as one mentioned by many of the evaluators.

EXERCISE 17.1: MPT 3 FORM C: INSTRUCTOR'S EVALUATION

Instructions: This form is to be included at end of your MPT Packet for your instructor's completion.

_____
student

Packet due _____ Packet received _____

Criterion I: the Presentation

Lesson Objective: _____
1. Implementation (items A,C,X,Y)   10 9 8 7 6 5 4 3 2 1 0
2. Personal (items F,G,M,N,O,P,Q,S,T)   10 9 8 7 6 5 4 3 2 1 0
3. Voice (items H,I,J)   10 9 8 7 6 5 4 3 2 1 0
4. Materials (item K)   10 9 8 7 6 5 4 3 2 1 0
5. Strategies (items B,D,E,L,R,U,V,W)   10 9 8 7 6 5 4 3 2 1 0

Subtotal criterion I _____

Criterion II: the Packet

6. Tabulation and summary analysis   10 9 8 7 6 5 4 3 2 1 0
7. Selection and description   10 9 8 7 6 5 4 3 2 1 0

Subtotal criterion II _____

Criterion III: Participation during MPTs

8. Lesson plan effectively prepared   10 9 8 7 6 5 4 3 2 1 0
9. Participation as student   10 9 8 7 6 5 4 3 2 1 0
10. Participation as evaluator   10 9 8 7 6 5 4 3 2 1 0

Subtotal criterion III _____

Grand Total Criteria I, II, and III = _____

Final MPT grade _____

Reteach: YES   NO

Instructor's Comments:

EXERCISE 17.2: HOW CAN I FURTHER ANALYZE MY VERBAL INTERACTIONS WITH STUDENTS?

Instructions: Analyze your verbal interactions. There are two ways that observations may be made—by you as you listen to a recording (audio or audio-video) made during your teaching, or by another observer who sits in your room during class. While observing, tallies are made of those behaviors observed. Observations and their corresponding tallies could be made at regular intervals of 15 seconds, or each time there is a new teacher or student behavior.

An analysis of tallies can provide a picture of the percentages of class time spent in:

Teacher-initiated talk
Student-initiated talk
Teacher-response talk
Student-response talk
Silence
Confusion

and of the cognitive levels of those activities.

An analysis of tallies of praises or compliments you express to your students can also provide a picture as to what kind of and how frequently you use the said expressions in the classroom. From recording and analyzing your teacher talk and your interaction with the secondary students, you will be able to determine:

- If you are accepting and clarifying the positive or negative feelings and attitudes of students.
- If you are praising and encouraging students, and using humor.
- If you are criticizing, directing, commanding, ordering, and lecturing.
- If students have the freedom to express their ideas, and to share their opinions and thoughts.
- If there are periods of confusion, of planned or unplanned silence, and of pausing.

Knowledge gained from an interaction analysis of your classroom gives you teaching power, power that will help you examine the effects of your verbal teaching behavior on the student's verbal behavior.

B. ANOTHER LOOK: MY SECONDARY TEACHALOGUE, WITH TWENTY TEACHING SUGGESTIONS

What additional advice can we give you as a beginning teacher? Can this advice be compacted into some special hints, ideas, or secrets? We have summarized them in this "teachalogue," containing twenty teaching suggestions for secondary teachers to help you further evaluate yourself.

SECONDARY TEACHALOGUE CHECKLIST

Before the Lesson

1. Did you write specific, concrete goals, aims, and objectives, and will you share them with your students?
2. Did you refer to the established course of study for your subject and grade level, and review state framework documents, teacher's manuals, and scope and sequence charts?
3. Is your motivation relevant to your lesson? Do you know the difference between a topic that is interesting to students and a topic that needs additional motivation?
4. Are you taking secondary students' interest in a topic for granted, or does your motivational component of the lesson meet the needs and interests of your students?
5. Did you order audiovisual materials pertinent to your lesson, and did you preview the material?
6. Did you prepare demonstration materials and display them so that all students can see?
7. Have you planned very carefully your lesson transitions from one topic/activity to another, and from one lesson to the next, and do you have the required supplies and materials ready and available for each lesson?
8. Have you established efficient, orderly routines and procedures for your class management tasks, such as collecting homework, taking roll, sharpening pencils, distributing and collecting books and materials, using the wastebasket, and dismissal at the end of the period?

During the Lesson

9. Are you beginning each period with a clean chalkboard?
10. Are you remembering that sometimes the material is clearer to students when they can see it than when they hear it?
11. Are you remembering to write legibly and boldly, and orderly, so all can read your writing on the chalkboard?
12. Are you being empathic to your students, indicating that you know that they *can* learn?
13. Are you allowing your students to participate in discussions (to talk), and be heard, and are you giving each one the quiet praise that he or she deserves?
14. Are you setting the mental stage, varying your class activities, and, when possible, building upon each student's contributions during the lesson?

15. Are you making clear all relationships between main ideas and details for your students, and presenting examples of abstract concepts in a simple, concrete way?
16. Are you explaining, discussing, and commenting on audiovisual materials you use in your lesson?
17. When asking questions of students, are you giving students time to review the topic; to hear your frame of reference for your questions; to recognize that your question is on their level of understanding; and to participate in "think-time" or "brainstorming time" before they respond to your questions? Are you remembering never to answer your own questions?
18. Are you introducing materials to the students *before* they are needed in the lesson?
19. Are you evincing enthusiasm in your speech, keeping a moderate pace in your delivery, and insisting that all students give you their attention when you begin the lesson?
20. Are you properly attending to the needs of special students in your class, attempting to individualize their learning according to their individual needs, interests, and abilities?

C. STILL ANOTHER LOOK: SECONDARY STUDENT-TEACHING EVALUATION FORM AND COMPETENCY DESCRIPTIONS

EVALUATION FOR MIDTERM _____ FINAL _____

_____   _____   _____
Student Teacher   Grade   School

_____
Cooperating Teacher

_____
Date

_____
College or University Supervisor

Place a check __✓__ in one of the categories for each evaluative competency.*

1. The teacher candidate exhibits professional traits such as showing enthusiasm for learning and teaching, for self-evaluation, and for correcting behaviors that affect teaching.

   Needs Improvement _____ Progressing Satisfactorily _____ Toward Competency _____

2. The teacher candidate plans lessons ahead, identifies objectives, and selects a variety of appropriate activities to develop objectives.

   Needs Improvement _____ Progressing Satisfactorily _____ Toward Competency _____

3. The teacher candidate demonstrates a knowledge of the subject matter that is taught in the secondary school.

   Needs Improvement _____ Progressing Satisfactorily _____ Toward Competency _____

4. The teacher candidate successfully carries out a variety of instructional techniques.

   Needs Improvement _____ Progressing Satisfactorily _____ Toward Competency _____

5. The teacher candidate has an effective classroom management style that is consistent with his or her behavioral expectations of students.

   Needs Improvement _____ Progressing Satisfactorily _____ Toward Competency _____

6. The teacher candidate constructs a variety of teacher-made instructional materials that are clear and appropriate and function as good models.

   Needs Improvement _____ Progressing Satisfactorily _____ Toward Competency _____

*At the end of the term, a teacher candidate whose teaching competency receives an "inadequate" rating in one or more of the competency areas is not ready to be recommended for a teaching credential.

Competency Descriptions for Each Evaluative Criterion

1. The teacher candidate exhibits professional traits, such as showing enthusiasm for learning and teaching, for self-evaluation, and for correcting behaviors that affect teaching negatively.

   ___ *Needs Improvement:* Has a poor attendance record; gives excuses when evaluated; does not attempt to correct behaviors that affect teaching-learning environment; does not seek help and suggestions; has ineffective voice control; is dependent upon others to plan and prescribe lessons.

   ___ *Progressing Satisfactorily:* Has an average attendance record; responds to constructive evaluation; attempts to correct behaviors that affect teaching negatively; often seeks help and suggestions; has effective voice control; plans independently.

   ___ *Toward Competency:* Is responsive to evaluations of the candidate's work; self-evaluates; has a good attendance record; is a good model for students; seeks suggestions and help; plans independently; shows enthusiasm for teaching and learning; always corrects any habits or manners that may negatively affect teaching.

2. The teacher candidate plans lessons ahead, identifies objectives, and selects a variety of appropriate activities to achieve objectives.

   ___ *Needs Improvement:* Uses only one instructional activity; is reluctant to plan; has difficulty in identifying objective; is not interested in varying activities.

   ___ *Progressive Satisfactorily:* Is aware of the value of varying the learning activities; maintains lesson plans ahead; knows objectives.

   ___ *Toward Competency:* Always plans lessons ahead; identifies objectives for students' as well as teacher's goal; stimulates learning environment by offering a variety of activities; can change instruction, using different approaches and procedures.

3. The teacher candidate demonstrates a knowledge of the content that is taught in the subject discipline.

   ___ *Needs Improvement:* Knowledge is somewhat superficial; sometimes makes errors or gives misinformation in statements; relies on the school textbook, teacher's guides, or courses of study alone for information and ideas.

   ___ *Progressing Satisfactorily:* Has reliable information; shows an awareness of recent developments or materials in subject area; has broad knowledge.

   ___ *Toward Competency:* Introduces reliable, pertinent information; has a wide background of experience; is accurate; resourceful; has a command of content taught at the secondary-school level.

4. The teacher candidate successfully carries out a variety of instructional techniques.

____ *Needs Improvement:* Seems to follow the same teaching technique regardless of topic, students, or classroom conditions.

____ *Progressing Satisfactorily:* Usually selects an instructional technique that is appropriate for a lesson; recognizes that different instructional techniques help or hinder a teacher's effectiveness under differing classroom conditions.

____ *Toward Competency:* Consistently selects an instructional technique that is effective for the topic, the students, and the classroom condition; is ready to change the technique quickly if necessary; can successfully implement directed reading lessons, lectures and demonstrations, guided discovery, experiments, and informal group discussions; is able to give individual help.

5. The teacher candidate has an effective classroom management style that is consistent with his or her behavioral expectations of students.

____ *Needs Improvement:* Often lacks group control; allows disruptive noise and other conditions to interfere with learning; seems unaware of school and district policies and procedures about student conduct; teacher behavior often results in student hostility, resentment, or lack of respect.

____ *Progressing Satisfactorily:* Manages group so that learning continues; understands and accepts district and school policies and procedures about student conduct; shows an improvement in teacher-student relationships during the student teaching assignment.

____ *Toward Competency:* Strong group management is evident with friendly and cooperative teacher-student relationships; students work toward educational goals; teacher accepts students' individual differences and needs; group and individual respect is evident; is comfortable with this age group; gives precise directions, does not overreact, uses eye contact, gestures, uses appropriate pacing, always has activities for emergency situations; can teach a small group while being aware of the rest of the class; is fair.

6. The teacher candidate constructs a variety of teacher-made instructional materials that are clear, appropriate, and function as good models.

____ *Needs Improvement:* Is unconcerned about preparing instructional aids (or is unaware of the need to prepare them).

____ *Progressing Satisfactorily:* Occasionally prepares an instructional aid with urging from the cooperating teacher and/or supervisor; appears hesitant to prepare any materials independently.

____ *Toward Competency:* Identifies lessons where instructional aids are appropriate; consistently selects and prepares a matching aid that will provide an effective learning experience; relates difficulty level of the material to the level of the students.

EXERCISE 17.3: SECONDARY STUDENT-TEACHING: WHAT DOES MY SECOND SELF-EVALUATION TELL ME?

Turn back to the "Secondary Student-Teaching Evaluation Form" immediately preceding. Read the descriptions of the competencies that follow it, then complete your own competency self-evaluation check. What does this second self-evaluation tell you?

Now compare your evaluation with the earlier evaluation done in Exercise 4.1. Can you identify progress that has been made in your own competencies development? Discuss your comparisons with your classmates.

D. LOOKING AHEAD: SAMPLE FORMS USED TO EVALUATE TEACHER EFFECTIVENESS

Secondary school teachers periodically are reviewed for purposes of self-improvement and for personnel decisions about retention and tenure. For these purposes, data from several sources are collected, and although from school to school, even within the same district, forms vary in wording and in format, there remains a common set of addressed competencies as have been discussed in this resource guide.

Data about a teacher's effectiveness are collected from two sources—*teacher self-evaluation* and *administrative evaluations*.

Teacher Self-evaluation

Data for self-evaluation come from a variety of sources, and one of those sources can result from the use of a form such as follows. The teacher's completion of this or of a similar form is often required as part of a larger review process that includes administrative evaluations. As a trial experience evaluate yourself using the following "teacher self-evaluation" form.

TEACHER SELF-EVALUATION: SAMPLE FORM[1]

Teacher's name _____ Date _____

Course number _____ Subject _____

Instructions: Rate yourself from 1–5 for each of the following statements.
5 = excellent; 4 = above average; 3 = average; 2 = below average; 1 = poor

Subject Area

_____ I have thorough training in the subject matter.

_____ I have adequate knowledge of subject matter in the courses I teach.

_____ I have enough knowledge of subject matter in other fields of learning to integrate with related areas.

_____ I have had sufficient practical experience to furnish me with the understanding I need for proper teaching of the subject.

_____ I find the subject matter interesting, exciting, and absorbing.

_____ I read current literature on the subject and keep myself mentally alert, informed, and able to supplement my course material with interesting examples.

_____ I attend meetings of appropriate organizations and participate in discussions of subject matter with my colleagues.

_____ I have sufficient interest in the subject to engage in some type of research to further my knowledge of subject matter or methods of teaching my subject.

---

[1]Adapted by the authors from an unknown original source.

TEACHER SELF-EVALUATION: SAMPLE FORM (Continued)

_____ I am willing to devote time and energy to work cooperatively with others on projects.

_____ I try to keep informed about the field in order to point out to my students the interrelationships of the subject matter with more general areas.

_____ I am qualified to evaluate texts and other materials for my course, in terms of learning objectives rather than in terms of ease for myself.

_____ My greatest professional interest is that of teaching the subject of the course.

_____ I am growing in my understanding of the subject matter.

Personal Characteristics

_____ I possess the self-reliance and confidence necessary to meet my students and to conduct my classes with calmness and poise.

_____ I speak distinctly and present my ideas in clear understandable language.

_____ I organize and present ideas in a logical sequence and manner.

_____ I am able to develop interest and to motivate effort from my students.

_____ I possess a manner that creates a favorable impression on those with whom I work.

_____ I maintain a neat and clean personal appearance.

_____ I attempt to identify and eliminate any of my annoying mannerisms.

_____ I work industriously and conscientiously to learn and to teach my subject.

_____ I readily admit any error and seek to correct it.

_____ I have a sense of humor.

_____ My health is such that I can apply my efforts energetically and enthusiastically in assisting my students in their learning.

_____ I respect the ideas of others and I express a willingness to learn from them.

_____ I control the class adequately to foster learning.

_____ I am prompt at opening and closing classes according to schedule.

_____ I use a level of vocabulary that is appropriate to the class.

Attitude Towards Students

_____ I regard teaching as an opportunity to be of service to learners.

_____ I am sympathetic with students who have difficulty learning the subject.

_____ I maintain a courteous and respectful approach when meeting and conferencing with students.

_____ I am willing to devote considerable time to assist individual students who seek my advice.

_____ I put aside other matters readily when a student wishes to confer with me.

_____ I welcome student questions and expressions of opinion.

_____ I treat all students honestly and fairly and without effort to attain popularity by underworking, overgrading, or otherwise lowering standards.

_____ I encourage students to seek my advice and give courteous consideration to their personal problems.

_____ I do not "pick on" certain students, or resort to sarcasm to make a point.

TEACHER SELF-EVALUATION: SAMPLE FORM (Continued)

Assignments

_____ My assignments are given after full consideration of my course objectives and the abilities of my students.

_____ Each assignment is carefully planned for its significance, its degree of difficulty, and its time requirement.

_____ I choose test and problem assignments to meet the learning needs of the students rather than for the ease with which I can handle them.

_____ I explain the purpose of each assignment and inspire my students to put forth effort in preparation for class discussions.

_____ I provide clear directions with sufficient explanations to enable students to relate new material to old but without destroying the values that come from the student's own efforts to learn.

_____ The materials related to the assignments are readily available to the students.

_____ I endeavor to clarify the minimum standards of quality of work expected from my students.

_____ I insist upon promptness by students in submitting written evidence of their daily preparations.

_____ My assignments are designed to develop written expression as well as knowledge of content.

_____ My assignments are occasionally modified to meet the learning needs of the students as the course progresses.

Methods and Procedures

_____ My teaching methods are selected to meet specific learning objectives rather than to serve my own convenience.

_____ I plan classroom time to explain and to discuss the principles covered by assignments.

_____ I attempt to achieve an effective balance between theory and procedural applications.

_____ I encourage student participation in class discussion at every opportunity.

_____ My teaching efforts are directed towards stimulating thought and expression by my students.

_____ My class presentations are clearly, forcefully, and interestingly presented.

_____ My presentations always include or are followed by periods of discussion to clarify ideas.

_____ I recognize the student's primary responsibility for learning and encourage students to think for themselves.

_____ Through frequent use of survey and review I assist my students in seeing meaning and purpose in their study.

_____ I effectively vary class procedure to maintain student attention and interest, and to attempt to reach students' varying learning styles.

_____ I incorporate into my lessons the latest in relevant visual aids and other materials.

Examinations and Grades

_____ I use care in the construction of written examinations to ensure that they best serve my testing purposes.

TEACHER SELF-EVALUATION: SAMPLE FORM (Continued)

_____ My examinations are always at a level that achievement and completion by a majority of the students is accomplished during the allotted time.

_____ My examinations are directly related to the subject matter assignment and discussed.

_____ I explain to students the basis for my grading.

_____ I adequately explain solutions to examination questions, either by presenting them orally or having them duplicated for distribution.

_____ I am fair and impartial in grading papers.

_____ I grade and return all papers promptly.

_____ I always discuss examination results with the students.

_____ I am willing to correct grading errors.

_____ I grade all judgment-type examinations myself, and allow others to grade only those papers in which no alternative answers are possible.

_____ I provide a sufficient number of examinations to provide a fair sample for appraising student progress and achievement in the course.

_____ I avoid justifying the suspicion that I will change any grade if a student exerts enough pressure.

_____ My students understand that my grades express my opinion about their learning achievements.

_____ I make it clear that grades are earned, not given.

General

_____ I cooperate with the administration in working toward meeting the objectives of the school and the department.

_____ I conscientiously perform my share of the noninstructional duties required for successful operation of the school.

_____ I participate in community affairs.

_____ I cultivate interests outside the field of study to broaden my knowledge and to make possible more meaningful teaching of my subject.

_____ I constantly work toward improvement of myself, and of my courses.

_____ I engage in additional study leading to an advanced degree or another credential.

_____ I take an interest in and participate in student planned events.

Please Circle any of the Following Statements that Apply to You.

In order to improve this class, I will devote time and effort to the following items:

1. Presenting material more rapidly. Presenting material less rapidly.
2. Giving more examinations. Giving fewer examinations.
3. Using more outside readings. Using fewer outside readings.
4. Using more visual aids. Using fewer visual aids.
5. Using more guest speakers. Using fewer guest speakers.
6. Using more field trips. Using fewer field trips.
7. Using a greater variety of evaluative devices to arrive at final grades.
8. Being more prompt in returning student papers.
9. Providing more comprehensive coverage of content in examinations.
10. Providing more challenge in examinations.

TEACHER SELF-EVALUATION: SAMPLE FORM (Continued)

11. Making examination questions clearer.
12. Speaking more clearly.
13. Using better grammar.
14. Demonstrating more confidence and poise. Demonstrating less pomposity.
15. Starting and/or dismissing classes more efficiently and/or promptly.
16. Making the nature and purpose of each assignment more clear.
17. Distributing the student work loads more evenly over the semester.
18. Demonstrating more of a sense of humor.
19. Writing more legibly on the writing board and overhead projector.
20. Better relating the course material to student interests, experiences, and problems.
21. Showing more courtesy toward students.
22. Being less frivolous.

EXERCISE 17.4: SELF-IMPROVEMENT PLAN

Instructions: The purpose of this exercise is for you to formulate your own plan for competency improvement.

Step 1: From what you have learned about secondary-school teacher competencies, identify no less than 10 of your own specific competency strengths and no less than 10 areas where you need continued growth. You may need to return to previous sections of this resource guide (consult the index for "competencies") as well as to your self-ratings on the immediately preceding form.

Strengths:

1.
2.
3.
4.
5.
6.
7.
8.
9.
10.

Weaknesses:

1.
2.
3.
4.
5.
6.
7.
8.
9.
10.

Step 2: Now, prioritize your list of "weaknesses," share with your colleagues and instructor, and identify specific resources for strengthening each of those areas, and a time plan for assessing progress.

	Weakness	Resources	Progress Assessment Date
1.			
2.			
3.			
4.			
5.			
6.			
7.			
8.			
9.			
10.			

TEACHER EVALUATION BY CLASSROOM VISITATION: SAMPLE LONG FORM

Course Number and Title _____

Date of Observation _____   Class size _____

Teacher's Name _____ Observer's Name _____

Date of follow-up conference _____

SECTION I: General Evaluation
Following are several sets of statements concerning specific aspects of the class that you just observed.
Please indicate the extent to which you agree or disagree with each statement concerning the teacher.
1 = strongly agree; 2 = agree; 3 = disagree; 4 = strongly disagree; 5 = uncertain or not applicable.

A. Structure and Goals

_____ 1. The teacher clearly conveyed the purpose for each activity of the class period.
_____ 2. The stated purposes were consistently followed throughout the class period.
_____ 3. The class presentation seemed carefully planned and organized.
_____ 4. Various elements of the class period were effectively integrated.
_____ 5. The class presentation built toward one or more basic principles or conclusions that students seemed to understand clearly.

B. Teacher-Student Rapport

_____ 6. The teacher demonstrated fair and equal concern for all students.
_____ 7. The teacher answered student questions in a straightforward and understandable manner.
_____ 8. The teacher encouraged and facilitated interaction among the students.
_____ 9. The teacher appeared open to all ideas, suggestions, and criticisms displayed by students.
_____ 10. The students seemed genuinely receptive to the ideas of the teacher.

C. Subject Matter and Instruction

_____ 11. The teacher conveyed enthusiasm about the course and the subject matter.
_____ 12. The teacher presented material that was appropriate for the level of the course and for the level of preparation of the students.
_____ 13. Biases of the teacher were clearly and consistently conveyed during this period.
_____ 14. The teacher demonstrated adequate knowledge of the subject matter.
_____ 15. The teacher introduced topic(s) of this class period in a manner that was stimulating and relevant.
_____ 16. Transitions between topics were conducted in an effective manner.
_____ 17. Major points of this class period were reviewed by the teacher.
_____ 18. The teacher asked questions requiring opinion, previous knowledge, or thought.
_____ 19. The teacher used student answers and comments to encourage or to bring other students into the discussion.

TEACHER EVALUATION BY CLASSROOM VISITATION: SAMPLE LONG FORM
(Continued)

_____ 20. Questions were interspersed throughout the class period.
_____ 21. Students were generally attentive throughout the class period.
_____ 22. Special aids or supplementary materials were effectively managed by the teacher.

D. General

_____ 23. I would recommend this class to students.
_____ 24. I personally found this class period to be interesting and informative.
_____ 25. I believe that I was able to fairly judge the nature and tenor of the teaching-learning process during this class observation.

Comments: (to clarify or expand on any of the preceding ratings)

SECTION II: The Teacher

Indicate for each word or phrase listed below the extent to which you think it accurately describes the teacher as you observed his or her performance in this class. Use the following key:

1 = this word or phrase does *not* describe this teacher
2 = this word or phrase partially decribes this teacher
3 = this word or phrase accurately describes this teacher

___ Effective use of gestures
___ Varies pitch and tone of voice
___ Sufficient eye contact with students
___ Flexible in responses to students
___ Effective use of mobility

___ Effective use of pauses
___ Uses understandable vocabulary
___ Clear presentations

Comments:

SECTION III: Teaching Strategies

Several teaching strategies have been found to be effective means of increasing student involvement, as well as student learning, in a variety of disciplines. Please read the brief descriptions of each strategy, then indicate the extent to which you observed the strategy being employed during this class period. If possible, also provide concrete examples of each strategy as it was used during this class period.

1. *Setting the Stage:*   the preparation of a class for the learning which is to follow, often through an analogy, a demonstration, or a leading or provoking question; providing a common frame of reference between the teacher and the students and increasing the interest of the students in the topic to be covered.

___ I did not observe stage setting.
___ I observed stage setting being used in a relatively unsuccessful manner.
___ I observed stage setting being successfully used.

TEACHER EVALUATION BY CLASSROOM VISITATION: SAMPLE LONG FORM
(Continued)

Evidence:

2. *Varying the Presentation:* verbal and/or nonverbal techniques for varying the mode of presentation to the students—e.g., variations in interaction styles, movement, planned repetition, audiovisual materials, use of examples.

__ I observed no variation in presentation of materials.
__ I observed very little variation.
__ I observed a proper amount of variation.

Evidence:

3. *Encouraging the Students:* the teacher encourages participation by means of a smile, nod of the head, eye contact, etc.

__ I observed no encouragement of students.
__ I observed a moderate amount of encouragement.
__ I observed an effective amount of encouragement.

Evidence:

4. *Awareness of Student Attention:* an overlapping awareness of student behaviors, e.g., facial expressions showing boredom or interest, comprehension or puzzlement, involvement or withdrawal.

__ The teacher did not demonstrate awareness of student attention.
__ The teacher seemed moderately aware.
__ The teacher was effectively aware of student attention.

Evidence:

TEACHER EVALUATION BY CLASSROOM VISITATION: SAMPLE LONG FORM
(Continued)

5. *Clarifying Questions:*   the response of the teacher to superficial or preliminary answers or statements made by students. Asking for clarification requires the students to go beyond a one word response. Skillful probing techniques help the teacher both to bring more out of a student and to keep a classroom discussion interesting.

— I did not observe any clarifying questioning.
— I observed only moderate use of clarifying questions.
— I observed effective use of clarifying questions.

Evidence:

6. *Processing questions:*   questions that require a student to make sense out of what has been learned, to draw relationships of cause and effect, to synthesize, analyze, compare new information with old.

— I did not observe process questioning.
— I observed only moderate use of processing questions.
— I observed effective use of output-level questions.

Evidence:

7. *Applying and Evaluating Questions:*   output-level questions, ones without "right" answers, requiring students to use both concrete and abstract thinking, and to determine for themselves appropriate responses. Students are urged to explore a problem in whatever direction they prefer, and to think creatively and hypothetically, to use imagination, to expose a value system, or to make a judgment.

— I observed no use of output-level questions.
— I observed only moderate use of output-level questions.
— I observed effective use of output-level questions.

Evidence:

TEACHER EVALUATION BY CLASSROOM VISITATION: SAMPLE LONG FORM
(Continued)

8. *Closure:* integrating the major points of a presentation, providing a link between the familiar and the new parts of the presentation, providing the students with a needed sense of achievement at the end of the presentation (or of subsections of the presentation).

— I observed no closure being used.
— I observed moderate use of closure.
— I observed effective use of closure.

Evidence:

SECTION IV: Final Comments
Please answer the following open-ended questions. Try to be as specific as possible.

1. What part(s) of the class period seemed to particularly enhance the learning process?

2. What specific suggestions do you have concerning how this particular class could have been improved?

TEACHER EVALUATION BY CLASSROOM VISITATION: SAMPLE SHORT FORM 1

Course _____

Date of Observation _____ Class size _____

Teacher's Name _____ Observer's Name _____

Date of follow-up conference _____

A. A checklist for evaluating some key points. (5 = highest level of performance; 1 = lowest)

	Unsatisfactory	Minimal	Satisfactory	Highly Satisfactory	Exceptional	NA
	1	2	3	4	5	NA
Personal Characteristics						
1. Enthusiasm for the subject						
2. Imagination						
3. Vocabulary and grammar usage						
4. Presence, Voice						
Teaching Characteristics						
1. Mastery of subject matter						
2. Organization of class (including use of objectives)						
3. Effective use of class time						
4. Utilization of teaching aids available						
5. Responsiveness to needs and interests of students						
6. Poise in handling student challenges						
7. Rapport with students						
8. Holding student interest						
9. Guiding discussion						
10. Obtaining student cooperation						

TEACHER EVALUATION BY CLASSROOM VISITATION: SAMPLE SHORT FORM 1
(Continued)

11. Using questions effectively						
12. Relating learning to students' experiences						
13. Responsiveness to individual differences in how students learn						
14. Responsiveness to individual differences in learning rate						

B. Answer the following questions as they apply to your evaluation.
　1. In what ways does the teacher need to improve?
　2. What strong points characterize this teacher's teaching?
　3. Is the method of instruction the best for this learning situation?

C. Evaluation of general teaching effectiveness (check one)
　1. Unsatisfactory ＿＿＿　　　4. Highly satisfactory ＿＿＿
　2. Minimal ＿＿＿　　　5. Exceptional ＿＿＿
　3. Satisfactory ＿＿＿

D. Additional Comments (Observer should include specific recommendations to assist teacher in improving teaching effectiveness. If possible, this section should be cooperatively developed by the observer and observed teacher.)

TEACHER EVALUATION BY CLASSROOM VISITATION: SAMPLE SHORT FORM 2

Teacher _____ Grade _____ Students _____ Minutes _____

Observer _____ Date _____

Unit or Lesson

A. LEARNING ENVIRONMENT	COMMENTS
1. Presence a. The teacher displays a sense of self-confidence in the classroom. b. The teacher is businesslike and authoritative in the conduct of the class. c. The teacher consistently monitors the progress of the students.	
2. Organization a. The teacher presents a lesson that has a clear, logical structure. b. The teacher is well organized throughout the lesson. c. The teacher has available well-prepared or well-chosen materials for students.	
3. Clarity a. The teacher speaks in a clear, easily understood voice. b. The teacher tells the students what is expected of them. c. The teacher gives clear, easily understood feedback to students. d. The teacher's directions to students are clear and easily understood.	
4. Enthusiasm a. The teacher makes the lesson interesting. b. The teacher seems to enjoy the lesson. c. The teacher displays a personal interest in the lesson. d. The teacher displays a sense of humor in a positive manner.	
5. Student Dignity a. The teacher provides good support of student dignity.	
6. Academic Learning Time a. The majority of the students are actively engaged in learning tasks which are related to goals and objectives from the curriculum.	

TEACHER EVALUATION BY CLASSROOM VISITATION: SAMPLE SHORT FORM 2
(Continued)

7. Discipline
   a. The majority of the students are responsible for their behavior.
   b. The teacher's management of the students is clearly established.
   c. The teacher consistently monitors the behavior of the students.

8. Other

QUESTIONS FOR CLASS DISCUSSION

1. Define effective instruction. Effective schools.
2. Can teaching effectiveness be measured? If so, how?
3. Why don't some teachers teach as well as they might or should?
4. Can evaluation of teachers improve instruction? Why or why not?
5. To what extent should the entire faculty be involved in the teacher evaluation process? To what extent is it?
6. Has collective bargaining affected the teacher evaluation process? If so, how?
7. Describe the ways a secondary teacher can grow professionlly.
8. Can you find any studies correlating teacher effectiveness with the number of years of teaching experience?
9. Can you find any studies correlating teacher effectiveness with class size?
10. What questions do you have about the content of this chapter, and how might answers be found?

SELECTED READINGS FOR CHAPTER 17

Braskamp, L. A.; Brandenburg, D. C.; and Ory, J. C. *Evaluating Teacher Effectiveness: A Practical Guide.* Beverly Hills, CA: Sage, 1984.

Doyle, K. O., Jr. *Evaluating Teaching.* Lexington, MA: Lexington Books, 1983.

Leith, G. O. M. "The influence of personality on learning to teach: Effects and delayed effects of microteaching." *Educational Review* 34(3):195–204 (November 1982).

Medley, D. M.; Coker, H.; and Soar, R. S. *Measurement Based Evaluation of Teacher Performance.* New York: Longman, 1984.

Millman, J., ed. *Handbook of Teacher Evaluation.* Beverly Hills, CA: Sage, 1981.

Newton, R. R. "Teacher evaluation: Focus on outcomes." *Peabody Journal of Education* 58(1):45–54 (October 1980).

Patton, M. Q. "Truth or consequences in evaluation." *Education and Urban Society* 13(1):97–104 (November–December 1980).

Wickert, D. M. "Using teacher evaluation for improving instruction." *The Clearing House* 61:23–24 (September 1987).

PART VI

What Should I Know About the Student-Teaching Experience and Beyond?

Part VI provides information about

- The paraprofessional experience.
- The student teaching experience.
- Getting a teaching job.
- Writing a résumé.
- Interviewing for a job.
- Credential requirement information sources.
- Educational associations related to secondary-school teaching.

Too many people quit looking for work when they find a job.
—Hillsborough (*Illinois*) Rotarian

18

What Should I Know About the Student-Teaching Experience?

You are excited about the prospect of being assigned as a student teacher to your first high school, junior high, or middle school classroom, but you are also very concerned. Will your host (cooperating) teacher like you? Will the two of you get along? Will the students like you? Will you be assigned to the grade level you want? What will the students be like? Will there be many behavioral problems? What about mainstreamed youngsters? If in a middle school, will there be a combination of fifth- and sixth-grade students? Will the class be all self-contained instruction, or will students move to another classroom for various subjects? Will your responsibilities be different from those you had as a paraprofessional?

Indeed, you should be excited and concerned, for this experience—the experience of student teaching—is one of the most significant and important facets of your teacher education program. In some programs, the practical teaching experience is planned as a coexperience with your college or university theory classes. In other programs, your student-teaching is a culminating experience. Different sequences are represented in different programs. For example, at one college or university you may have a field teaching experience that extends over a two-semester or a three-semester time period. In other colleges or universities, you may take part in a theory-class-first arrangement, followed by a full semester of student-teaching. Regardless of when and how your student-teaching occurs, the experience is a bright and shining opportunity to improve your teaching skills in a real classroom environment. You will be supported by an experienced college or university supervisor and by carefully selected cooperating teachers, who will share their years of classroom experience with you. Teacher education programs refer to these fine cooperating teachers in various ways—cooperating teachers, host teachers, master teachers, or mentors.

Everyone concerned in the teacher education program—your cooperating teacher, your university instructors, and your university supervisor—realizes that, for you, this is practice in learning how to teach. During your student-teaching, you will, no doubt, create some teaching errors, and you will benefit and learn from those errors. Sometimes your fresh approach to motivation, your creative ideas for learning activities that support the concept being taught, and your energy and enthusiasm make it possible for the cooperating teacher to learn from you! What is of value to both of you on this educational team is that students who are involved with you in the teaching-learning process will benefit from your role as the teacher-candidate in the classroom.

The following guidelines are offered to you and to your cooperating teacher to help make these classroom experiences beneficial to everyone involved.

A. THE PARAPROFESSIONAL EXPERIENCE

Have You Had Prior Classroom Experience as a Paraprofessional?

We believe that the teacher-candidate should, if possible, bring a background of some sort of secondary-school classroom experience into his or her student teaching. Some teacher training programs require paraprofessional classroom experience *as a prerequisite* to acceptance into their programs. Others require such experience during the program but as a prerequisite to the student-teaching phase.

Read the following list and check off the kinds of experiences you have had. If, however, you have had no experience, Exercise 18.1 will increase your awareness of the basic duties you will be expected to perform as you participate in the daily activities of the secondary-school classroom.

EXERCISE 18.1: CLASSROOM PARAPROFESSIONAL DUTIES: SELF-EVALUATION

Instructions: Many of these items are things that student teachers do during their first fews days in the classroom, or that paraprofessionals do prior to the student-teaching experience. Check items in this list according to your experience and skill in being able to do each.

	Definitely	Somewhat	No
1. I know how to order free and inexpensive class materials.	____	____	____
2. I can keep attendance records.	____	____	____
3. I can enter evaluation records in the teacher's paper grade book.	____	____	____
4. I can enter evaluation records onto the teacher's computer grade book.	____	____	____
5. I can average academic scores and prepare grade reports.	____	____	____
6. I can keep records of class schedules.	____	____	____
7. I can keep a written inventory of class equipment, books, and other instructional supplies.	____	____	____
8. I can maintain a computer inventory of class equipment, books, and other instructional supplies.	____	____	____
9. I can manage a classroom library.	____	____	____
10. I can maintain a seating chart for the entire class and for various groups.	____	____	____
11. I can type, duplicate, collate, and staple needed materials.	____	____	____
12. I can word process, duplicate, collate, and staple needed materials.	____	____	____
13. I can duplicate (photocopy) students' work if requested.	____	____	____
14. I can prepare and duplicate original scripts for student skits.	____	____	____
15. I can locate resource materials for teaching units.	____	____	____
16. I can compile information for required reports.	____	____	____
17. I can prepare bulletins and/or memos for parents to explain class rules, events, and programs.	____	____	____
18. I can manage instructional supplies so they are readily available when needed.	____	____	____
19. I can keep the bulletin boards current, neat, and eye-catching.	____	____	____
20. I can assemble supplementary materials needed for instructional purposes.	____	____	____
21. I can distribute students' books and supplies efficiently.	____	____	____
22. I can collect homework and test papers efficiently.	____	____	____
23. I am familiar with the procedures for checking out books in the school and/or city library for student and for teacher use.	____	____	____

	Definitely	Somewhat	No
24. I have participated on committees involved in educational projects.	___	___	___
25. I can help students settle their quarrels and disputes.	___	___	___
26. I can organize special exhibits in the classroom or in the school hallway display cases.	___	___	___
27. I know the procedures for accompanying a student to the nurse's room, or to the principal's office.	___	___	___
28. I feel comfortable when I am assigned a supervision task.	___	___	___
29. I have helped a teacher supervise students on a field trip.	___	___	___
30. I can accomplish errands that are related to classroom work.	___	___	___
31. I recognize the importance of reading school bulletins to the students, and I take the time to do this myself.	___	___	___
32. I know the procedure for ordering and returning films, filmstrips, cassettes, video discs, computer programs, and other media.	___	___	___
33. I know where in the building to reserve, procure, and return audiovisual equipment.	___	___	___
34. I can set up and operate the overhead projector, slide projector, laser disc player, and other instructional equipment.	___	___	___
35. I can turn on, insert programs in, and operate the classroom computer(s).	___	___	___
36. I take the time to preview filmstrips, cassettes, video discs, computer programs, and other audiovisual materials that are shared with the students.	___	___	___
37. When introducing the students to each media presentation, I take the time to plan an effective educational introduction.	___	___	___
38. With the cooperating teacher's direction, I can correct standardized and informal tests and can prepare student profiles.	___	___	___
39. With the cooperating teacher's direction, I can evaluate students' homework and workbooks, always recognizing and reporting a student's strengths and/ or weaknesses to the credentialed teacher.	___	___	___
40. With the cooperating teacher's direction, I feel comfortable interviewing a student who has an identified learning problem.	___	___	___
41. I am alert and can observe the students' behaviors and can prepare anecdotal reports.	___	___	___
42. I can prepare an informal test and other instruments for evaluation of student achievement.	___	___	___

	Definitely	Somewhat	No

43. I can prepare the needed instructional materials, such as flash cards, charts, overhead transparencies, masters for duplicating, puppets, and game boards. ____ ____ ____

44. I can prepare a demonstration or a display for a lesson. ____ ____ ____

45. I can prepare any learning materials needed to meet a student's individual differences, such as read-along tapes to assist reluctant readers; use primary-print typewriter for students with reduced vision capacity; and use tactile cards for students who need tactile learning experiences. ____ ____ ____

46. I can teach a small group of students who are concentrating on a specific skill, understanding, or attitude. ____ ____ ____

47. I feel comfortable tutoring students in a one-to-one setting—the GATE (Gifted and Talented students) *and* the reluctant learners. ____ ____ ____

48. I can supervise and help students with library assignments: know where to find biographies, autobiographies, informational books, and fiction. ____ ____ ____

49. I can teach students who missed needed instruction. ____ ____ ____

50. I can prepare and teach a brief lesson to the entire class. ____ ____ ____

51. I can reteach a lesson for reluctant learners. ____ ____ ____

52. I take time to listen to the "reading-out-loud" performed by a student. ____ ____ ____

53. I help students with their writing, and who have problems with punctuation, verb tense, possessive, capitalization, spelling, or sentence structure. ____ ____ ____

54. I take time to instruct students in careful and safe use of classroom equipment, tools, and materials. ____ ____ ____

55. I realize the importance of taking time to emphasize good manners, proper health habits, and etiquette during lunchtime, and during other classroom and school activities. ____ ____ ____

56. I can assist the teacher in classroom demonstrations. ____ ____ ____

57. I can help students find needed reference materials— dictionaries, encyclopedias, atlas, and special information books. ____ ____ ____

58. I can prepare vocabulary lists for spelling, for reading, and for subject content areas. ____ ____ ____

59. I can supervise laboratory work for science or mathematics. ____ ____ ____

60. I have clear, legible printing and handwriting and write needed written work on the writing board. ____ ____ ____

	Definitely	Somewhat	No
61. I can assist in related practice and drill activities with time tests.	____	____	____
62. I can help students as they complete their work at their desks and quickly check their progress.	____	____	____
63. I am familiar with the school building and have visited the offices of the counselor, the chief administrator, the nurse, the school psychologist, the reading specialist, the media center, and the librarian.	____	____	____
64. I can work with students who have limited English proficiency.	____	____	____

During this initial experience with all of these important educational responsibilities, we maintain that, as a paraprofessional, you should **not** be expected to

1. Be left alone with the class.
2. Be a free substitute if the teacher has to leave the school grounds for a meeting, a workshop, a conference, or a district event, or for any other reason.
3. Do the entire routine for regular teachers, which includes all of the filing, typing dittos, preparing duplicated copies, collating, stapling, preparing written work, and tests.
4. Bring coffee or lunch to the teacher.
5. Take classroom-related work home each evening, such as a stack of students' papers to grade for the next day.
6. Do any work unrelated to your classroom assignment, such as run a personal errand for the classroom teacher.

AS A STUDENT-TEACHER, WHAT DO I NEED TO KNOW?

B. THE STUDENT-TEACHING EXPERIENCE

Will My Student-Teaching Be the "Real Thing?"

Of course student-teaching will be the "real thing," but then, it won't be—quite! Your student-teaching experience will be real because you will be teaching responsive young people, and you will have a classroom as the setting for improving your teaching skills with real students. On the other hand, your student-teaching can't be considered real because your credentialed cooperating teacher is the one who has the ultimate responsibility for the classroom.

How Can I Best Get Ready for My Student-Teaching?

To prepare yourself for student-teaching, study, plan, and practice. Be knowledgeable about your students and their developmental backgrounds. In your theory classes you learned a great deal about students. Go back and review your class notes and textbooks from those courses, or select some readings from those suggested for Chapters 1 and 3 of this resource guide. Perhaps some of the topics will have more meaning for you now.

Be knowledgeable about your assigned school and the community that surrounds it. Review the subject areas you will be teaching and the content in those areas. Carefully discuss with your cooperating teacher and your university supervisor all of the responsibilities that you will be expected to assume. One student teacher we know verbally runs through each lesson in front of the bathroom mirror the night before teaching her lesson. Another reads through each lesson, audiotapes the readings, plays it back, and then evaluates whether her directions are clear, the sequence is logical, and the lesson closure is concise. Still another student teacher always has a "Plan B" in mind if "Plan A" turns out to be inappropriate.

C. THE STUDENT-TEACHING EXPERIENCE FROM THE COOPERATING TEACHER'S POINT OF VIEW

For your consideration, here are questions and answers about student teaching from the cooperating teacher's point of view. You may wish to share this section with your cooperating teacher.

1. What Is My Role?

As the cooperating teacher, your role is to assist when necessary: to provide guidance, to review lesson plans before presented, to facilitate the learning and skill development of your student teacher, and to help your student teacher become and feel like a member of the profession.

2. How Can I Prepare for It?

Get to know your student teacher prior to the beginning of the experience. Develop a collegial rapport with the student teacher.

3. Who Is My Student Teacher?

One who is making the transition from a career change, or from being a college student, to a professional teacher. He or she may be your age, or even older, and making a career change, or in his or her mid-twenties and fresh out of college; in either case, the student teacher may be scared to death, anxious, knowledgeable, and somewhere between being a romantic idealist and a pragmatic realist. Don't destroy the idealism—help the student teacher with understanding and dealing with the realism of everyday school teaching.

Students in teacher preparation today have likely had much better training and much more pre-student-teaching classroom experience than you did when you went through your training. For example, many teacher education programs today require more than one semester of field experience, perhaps as many as three, including one semester of student teaching in one school, then another semester in another school in another grade level. Learn from your student teacher what kinds of experiences she or he has had prior to this assignment.

4. What Kind of Support, Criticism, and Supervision Should I Give?

You may have to decide this yourself. On the other hand, some teacher education programs include seminars for the cooperating teachers, seminars that train them in supervisory techniques in working with their student teachers. Today many teacher education programs select cooperating teachers because of their effectiveness as teachers and in working with other adults. It is possible that you will be working as a member of a team—you, the student teacher, and the university supervisor—in a clinical supervision model (as discussed in Chapter 4).

Generally speaking, your student teacher will need lots of support, helpful criticisms, and supervision. Student teachers deserve more than to be placed into total "sink-or-swim" situations.

5. What Dangers Should I Look For?

Your student teacher may be very different from you in both appearance and in teaching style, but may be potentially just as effective a teacher. Judge his or her effectiveness slowly and cautiously. Offer suggestions, but do not make demands. A student teacher who is not preparing well is likely heading for trouble. So too is one who seems to show no interest in the school outside of the classroom. The student teacher should be prompt, anxious to spend extra time with you, and aware of the necessity of school clerical tasks. If you feel that there is a lurking problem, then let the student teacher or the university supervisor know your feelings. Poor communication between members of the team is a danger signal.

6. What Else Should I Know?

Your student teacher may be partially employed elsewhere and have other demands on his or her time. Become aware of his or her situation, keeping in mind the educational welfare of your students.

Be sure that your student teacher becomes a total member of the faculty, is invited to faculty functions, has his or her mailbox (or is allowed to share yours), and has total awareness of school policies, procedures, curriculum documents, and so on.

Once your student teacher is well grounded, then he or she should be ready to be gradually left alone with the class for increasingly longer periods of time. For a specified period of time, a student teacher's goal is to work toward a competency level that enables him or her to begin the class, teach the entire period, and close the class period—with an increasing responsibility for everything. This means that you are nearby and on call in case of an emergency but out of sight of the students.

D. THE STUDENT-TEACHING EXPERIENCE FROM THE PRINCIPAL'S POINT OF VIEW

For your consideration, here are questions and answers about student teaching from the school principal's point of view. You may wish to share these with your cooperating school principal.

1. What Is My Role?

As chief administrator of the school, it is your obligation to meet the student teacher when he or she arrives for the first time; give a brief verbal orientation about the school, the community, and important policies; and to arrange an introductory tour of the school plant. Introduce the cooperating teacher to the student teacher. And, encourage the student teacher to fully participate in various school meetings, activities, and events. Many busy secondary school principals, after initially meeting the student teacher, delegate these preceding functions to a vice principal.

2. How Can I Prepare for Hosting a Student Teacher?

Block out some time for the day the student teacher arrives for the first time on your campus. It is advisable that you have current knowledge about the college or university teacher education program of experiences from which this student teacher is coming, knowledge that can be provided by the university supervisor.

3. Who Is the Student Teacher?

The student teacher is a person making the transition from a career change, or from being a college student, to a professional teacher. He or she may be your age, or even older, and making a career change, or in his or her mid-twenties and fresh out of college; in either case, the student teacher may be scared to death, anxious, knowledgeable, and somewhere between being a romantic idealist and a pragmatic realist. Don't destroy the idealism—help the student teacher with understanding and dealing with the realism of everyday secondary school teaching.

Students in teacher education today have likely had much better training and much more pre-student-teaching classroom experience than you did when you went through your training. For example, many teacher education programs today require more than one semester of field experience, perhaps as many as three, including one semester of student teaching in one school, then another semester in another school in another grade level. Learn from the student teacher what kinds of experiences she or he has had prior to being invited to student teach at your school.

4. Should I Give Constructive Evaluations?

We don't need to remind you that you are responsible for everything that goes on at your school, and in that role of responsibility we suggest that you make every effort to visit the student teacher and observe his or her teaching during the assignment at your school. This gives you firsthand information about the competency of this beginning teacher and gives the student teacher some insight about the beginning years when evaluation takes place by the chief school administrator.

If your busy schedule permits a follow-up conference with the student teacher, then it is of value to arrange a brief discussion time with him or her soon after your classroom observation. Some principals share their district's credentialed-employees evaluation form with the student teacher. Others mention the strengths they observed and gently indicate any areas of teaching that seem to need attention. Remember, the student teacher may be terrified about all this because it is likely a "first" for him or her. Your talents can help ease the stress that the student teacher may feel about being evaluated by the school principal.

5. What Dangers Should I Look For?

Keep in close contact with the cooperating teacher. Listen to what cooperating teachers are saying when they discuss their student teachers. Is the student teacher showing an interest in your school? Is he or she arriving on time each day? If you read the verbal and nonverbal signals of your cooperating teachers in such a way that you believe there is a problem looming, then let the student teacher, cooperating teacher, or university supervisor know your feelings. Keep the channels of communication open between those persons and yourself.

6. What Else Should I Know?

Does the student teacher commute from a great distance? Does he or she have heavy family responsibilities? Is there a financial problem? Is he or she working elsewhere part-time? What is the additional college or university workload? Has there been a severe illness or recent death in the family? A divorce? Or an engagement called off? As you know, any and all of these situations can affect a student teacher's effectiveness in the classroom. Know what is going on. When the cooperating teacher indicates to you that the student teacher is ready because he or she appears competent in planning and implementing lessons and in maintaining classroom control, then the student teacher may, with your approval, begin to be left alone with the students for ever-increasing periods of time.

For a specified period of time, a student teacher's goal is to work toward a competency level that enables him or her to gradually take responsibility for entire class periods. This means the cooperating teacher is nearby and on call in case of an emergency but out of sight of the students.

EXERCISE 18.2: THE STUDENT-TEACHING EXPERIENCE FROM THE STUDENT TEACHER'S POINT OF VIEW: HOW CAN I CONTINUE MY SELF-EVALUATION AS A SECONDARY-SCHOOL TEACHER?

1. Repeat Exercise 17.3.
2. Repeat Exercise 4.1.
3. Share and discuss the results of the above with your cooperating teacher and with your university supervisor.
4. Record your thoughts about your discussion.

QUESTION FOR CLASS DISCUSSION

1. You must have many questions related to the content of this chapter. Identify them, pool yours with those of other members of the class, and arrange to have them all answered reasonably well prior to the beginning of your student-teaching experience.

SUGGESTED READINGS FOR CHAPTER 18

Acheson, K. A., and Gall, M. D. *Techniques in the Clinical Supervision of Teachers.* White Plains, NY: Longman, 1987.

Austin-Martin, G. G. "Effects of Student Teaching and Pretesting on Student Teacher's Attitudes." *Journal of Experimental Education* 49(1):36–38 (Fall 1979).

Scherer, C. "Effects of Early Experience on Student Teachers, Self-Concepts and Performance." *Journal of Experimental Education* 47(3):208–214 (Spring 1979).

19

What Do I Need to Know That May Help Me in Getting a Teaching Job?

You have spent four or five years in a college or university preparing yourself for a teaching credential. Now that you have that credential, or are about to receive it, you are ready to embark upon finding your first paid teaching job. The following guidelines are provided to help you accomplish that goal.

A. GUIDELINES TO HELP ME GET A TEACHING JOB

Resources for Locating a Teaching Position

In order to locate teaching vacancies you can establish contact with any of the following:

1. *College or university placement office.* Establishing a confidential placement file with your local college or university placement service is an excellent way to begin the process of locating your first teaching position. Placement services usually provide information about school districts that are hiring teachers, and, upon your request, will prepare and mail your completed file to whomever you request.
2. *Local school or district personnel office.* You can contact school personnel offices to obtain information about teaching vacancies and job interview schedules.
3. *County educational agency.* Contact your local county education office for information about teaching vacancies.
4. *State department of education.* Some state departments of education maintain information about job openings.
5. *Private schools.* You can contact private schools that interest you, either directly or through private educational placement services such as:

    IES (Independent Educational Services), 20 Nassau Street, Princeton, NJ 08542, (800) 257-5102 or (609) 921-6195. IES is a large, nonprofit, school services organization that recruits both experienced and new teachers for over 900 independent schools nationwide. Certification is not required, and there is no fee from the candidate.

6. *Commercial placement agencies.* Nationwide job listings and placement services are available from:

> National Education Services Center, P. O. Box 1279, Dept. FA, Riverton, WY 8251, (307) 856-0170.
>
> Carney, Sandoe & Associates, 136 Boylston St., Boston, MA 02116, (617) 542-0160 or (800) 225-7986.

7. *Out-of-country teaching opportunities.* Information regarding out-of-United States teaching can be obtained from:

> Department of Defense Dependent Schools, 2461 Eisenhower Ave., Room 120, Alexandria, VA 22331, (202) 325-0885.
>
> International Schools Service, P. O. Box 5910, Princeton, NJ 08543, (609) 452-0990. ISS operates an annual February ISS International Recruitment Center program.

8. *Professional educational journals and other publications.* Professional teaching journals often run advertisements of teaching vacancies, as do education newspapers such as *Education Week.*

The Professional Résumé and Its Accompanying Application Letter

How-to books are written about it, computer programs are available for it, and commercial services provide assistance for résumé preparation, but a résumé for a teaching position is specific. Although no one can tell you for sure what résumé will work best for you, as we have learned there are a few general guidelines that are especially helpful for educators. Consider the following:

1. The résumé should be no more than *two pages* in length.
2. It should look attractive and *uncluttered.*
3. *Size* should be standard 8½" × 11".
4. Stationery *color* can be off-white, cream, light gray, or beige. Since copies may be made for committee member use, we caution about using bright colored stationery that photocopies poorly.
5. Do *not* include personal data, such as age, height, weight, marital status, or a photograph.
6. Sentences must be *concise,* avoiding educational jargon, awkward phrases, abbreviations, and unfamiliar words.
7. *Organize the information carefully.* Put your name, address, and telephone number first, followed by your education, professional experiences, credential status, location of confidential placement papers, professional affiliations, and honors.
8. Identify your *experiences*—academic, teaching, and relevant life experiences—in reverse chronological order, first listing your current position and moving back chronologically.
9. Take time to develop your first résumé, then keep it current. Rather than making hundreds of copies, *clean-type it each time you apply for a job.*
10. Prepare a *cover letter* to accompany your résumé. Write the cover letter specifically for the position you are applying for. Address the letter personally but formally to the personnel director. Keep the letter to a maximum of two pages; emphasize yourself, your educational interests, and why you feel qualified for the position. In your letter, indicate your familiarity with that school or district.

11. Have the résumé and cover letter *edited* by someone familiar with résumé preparation and editing. A poorly written and poorly typed résumé, fraught with errors in spelling and grammar, will guarantee failure to reach the personal interview stage.

12. Be sure your application reaches the personnel director by the announced *due date*. If for some reason it will be late, then telephone the director, explain the circumstances, and ask permission to submit your application late.

EXERCISE 19.1: PREPARING A RÉSUMÉ AND APPLICATION COVER LETTER

Instructions: The purposes of this exercise are to begin preparing your résumé and to practice writing an application cover letter. Other than for the provision of the guidelines above, this exercise is left open to your imagination and for the critique of your product by your instructor and peers. After preparing the two items, share them with your colleagues for their feedback.

Step 1: Prepare your professional résumé as complete and as accurately as possible.

Step 2: Prepare a cover letter for a real or fictional teaching position.

Step 3: Share the two items with your colleagues and instructor for feedback.

The Personal Interview

If your application and résumé are attractive to the hiring personnel director or to the add-staff committee during paper screening, then you will be notified and scheduled for a personal interview. *In many school districts, the hiring interview precedes their request for your personnel papers.* Whichever the case, congratulations to you for having made it this far in the hiring process, as many do not. For this important step in obtaining a full-time teaching position, we offer the following advice.

1. When notified, you will be given a specific time, date, and place for the interview. Regardless of your other activities, *accept the time, date, and interview location suggested,* rather than trying to manipulate the interviewing person or committee around your own preferred schedule.
2. Be prompt for the interview, certainly not late, and possibly arrive a little early to familiarize yourself with the surroundings.
3. Prior to the interview, you will be told whether the interviewing committee will expect a formal teaching demonstration from you as a part of the interview. If so, we need not remind you of the importance of carefully planning it. Sometimes hiring committees request a videotape of the applicant actually teaching. Preparation of a demonstration videotape is something you may wish to do just to have on hand in case of such a request. For that purpose our own students frequently have used their MPT tapes.
4. Dress appropriately. Regardless of what else you may presently do for a living, take the necessary time to make a professional appearance before the interview person or committee.
5. Do not arrive at the interview with small children.
6. Arrive promptly at the assigned location, shake hands firmly, initiate conversation with a friendly comment about some personal knowledge you have about the school or district to which you are applying.
7. Hiring committees will sometimes send the *questions* that will be asked so you can prepare for them; other times the list of questions is handed to you upon arrival at the interview. In either case, you need to know that the questions asked are usually identical for each candidate interviewed. Questions likely to be asked will be about your
   a. experiences with young people
   b. hobbies and travels
   c. extracurricular interests and experiences
   d. attitudes toward classroom management
   e. knowledge of the subject for which you are being considered to teach
   f. "academic mobility," i.e., can you, and would you, teach in more than one subject or discipline
   g. educational philosophy
8. Throughout the interview demonstrate interest, enthusiasm, and confidence.
9. When the opportunity arises, ask one or two professional questions that you have planned ahead of time, legitimate questions that demonstrate your knowledge and interest in the position.
10. When the interview has obviously been brought to a close by the chair, that is your signal to leave. Don't hang around as if lacking confidence.

11. You may wish to follow the interview with a thank-you letter addressed to the committee.

When you are offered a contract, and you sign it, then you should inform any other district that has offered you a contract that you are no longer available.

B. INFORMATION SOURCES ABOUT CREDENTIAL REQUIREMENTS STATE BY STATE

Alabama
Teacher Education and
    Certification Section
State Department of
    Education
349 State Office Building
Montgomery 36130, 205/
    261-5060

Alaska
Coordinator of Teacher
    Education and
    Certification
State Department of
    Education
Pouch F, Alaska Office
    Building
Juneau 99811, 907/465-
    2810

Arizona
Arizona Department of
    Education
Teacher Certification
    Unit
1535 West Jefferson
P.O. Box 25609
Phoenix 85007, 602/255-
    4367

Arkansas
Teacher Certification
Room 106-107-B
Arkansas Department of
    Education
Little Rock 72201, 501/
    371-1474

California
Commission on Teacher
    Credentialing
1020 "O" Street
Sacramento 94244-2700,
    916/445-7254

Colorado
Director, Teacher
    Certification
State Office Building
201 East Colfax, 5th
    Floor
Denver 80203, 303/866-
    6749

Connecticut
Chief, Bureau of School
    Services
State Department of
    Education
P.O. Box 2219
Hartford 06145, 203/566-
    5541

Delaware
Supervisor of
    Certification and
    Personnel
Department of Public
    Instruction
Townsend Building
Dover 19903, 302/736-
    4688

District of Columbia
Director of Certification
    and Accreditation
District of Columbia
    Public Schools, Room
    1004
415 12th Street, N.W.
Washington, D.C. 20004,
    202/724-4230

Florida
Administrator, Teacher
    Certification
Department of Education
Knott Building
Tallahassee 32301, 904/
    488-2317

Georgia
Director of Certification
Georgia Department of
    Education
1452 Twin Towers East
Atlanta 30334, 404/656-
    2406

Hawaii
Administrator
    (Certification)
Office of Personnel
    Services
State Department of
    Education
P.O. Box 2360
Honolulu 96804, 808/
    548-5217

Idaho
Director of Teacher
Education and
Certification
State Department of
Education
Len B. Jordan Office
Building
Boise 83720, 208/334-
3475

Illinois
Manager, Teacher
Certification and
Placement
Illinois State Board of
Education
100 North First Street
Springfield 62777, 217/
782-2805

Indiana
Director, Division of
Teacher Education and
Certification
State Department of
Public Instruction
Room 229, State House
Indianapolis 46204, 317/
232-6636

Iowa
Director, Division of
Teacher Education and
Certification
State Department of
Public Instruction
Grimes State Office
Building
Des Moines 50319, 515/
281-3245

Kansas
Director, Certification
Section
State Department of
Education
120 East 10th Street
Topeka 66612, 913/296-
2288

Kentucky
Director, Division of
Teacher Education and
Certification
State Department of
Education
18th Floor, Capital Plaza
Tower
Frankfort 40601, 502/
564-4752

Louisiana
Director, Higher
Education and Teacher
Certification
State Department of
Education
Baton Rouge 70804, 504/
342-3490

Maine
Director, Teacher
Certification and
Placement
Division of Certification,
Placement and Teacher
Education
State House Station 23
Augusta 04333, 207/289-
5944

Maryland
Assistant Superintendent
in Certification and
Accreditation
State Department of
Education
200 West Baltimore
Street
Baltimore 21201, 301/
659-2141

Massachusetts
Director, Bureau of
Teacher Preparation,
Certification and
Placement
Quincy Center Plaza
1385 Hancock Street
Quincy 02169, 617/770-
7517

Michigan
Director, Division of
Teacher Preparation
and Certification
Services
State Department of
Education
Ottawa Street Office
Building
South Tower, Second
Floor
Lansing 48909, 517/373-
1924

Minnesota
Manager, Personnel
Licensing and
Placement
State Department of
Education
616 Capitol Square
Building
550 Cedar Street
St. Paul 55101, 612/296-
2046

Mississippi
Supervisor of Teacher
Certification
State Department of
Education
P.O. Box 771
Jackson 39205, 601/359-
3483

Missouri
Director of Teacher
Education and
Certification
State Department of
Education
Jefferson Building, 7th
Floor
P.O. Box 480
Jefferson City 65102, 314/
751-3486

Montana
Director of Teacher
  Certification
Office of Public
  Instruction
Department of Basic
  Instructional Services
1300 Eleventh Avenue
Helena 59620, 406/444-
  3150

Nebraska
Director of Certification
  and Teacher Education
State Department of
  Education
301 Centennial Mall
  South
Box 94987
Lincoln 68509, 402/471-
  2496

Nevada
Supervisor of Teacher
  Certification
State Department of
  Education
400 West King Street
Carson City 89710, 702/
  885-3116

New Hampshire
Director of Teacher
  Education and
  Professional Standards
State Department of
  Education
101 Pleasant Street
Concord 03301-3860,
  603/271-2407

New Jersey
Director, Bureau of
  Teacher Preparation
  and Certification
State Department of
  Education
225 West State Street, CN
  500
Trenton 08625-0503,
  609/984-1216

New Mexico
Certification Director
Division of Teacher
  Education and
  Certification
State Department of
  Education
DeVargas and Don
  Gasper Street
State Capitol Complex,
  Room 105
Santa Fe 87501-2786,
  505/827-6581

New York
Division of Teacher
  Certification
Cultural Education
  Center Room 5A 11
Madison Avenue
Albany 12230, 518/474-
  3901

North Carolina
Director, Division of
  Certification
State Department of
  Public Instruction
116 West Edenton Street
Raleigh 27603-1712, 919/
  733-4125

North Dakota
Director of Teacher
  Certification
State Department of
  Public Instruction
State Capitol, 9th Floor
Bismarck 58505, 701/224-
  2264

Ohio
Director, Division of
  Teacher Education and
  Certification
State Department of
  Education
Ohio Department
  Building, Room 1012
Columbus 43215, 614/
  466-3593

Oklahoma
Administrator, Teacher
  Certification
State Department of
  Education
Hodge Education
  Building
2500 North Lincoln
  Boulevard
Oklahoma City 73105-
  4599, 405/521-3337

Oregon
Teachers Standards and
  Practices Commission
730—12th Street, S.E.
Salem 97310, 503/378-
  3586

Pennsylvania
Bureau of Teacher
  Preparation and
  Certification
Department of Education
333 Market Street, 3rd
  Floor
Harrisburg 17126-0333,
  717/787-2967

Puerto Rico
Certification Officer
Department of Education
Hato Rey 00900, 809/764-
  1100

Rhode Island
Coordinator for Teacher
  Education, Certification
  and Placement
State Department of
  Education
Roger Williams Building
22 Hayes Street
Providence 02908, 401/
  277-2675

South Carolina
Director of Teacher
  Education and
  Certification
State Department of
  Education
1015 Rutledge, Room
  1004
Columbia 29201, 803/
  758-8527

South Dakota
Director, Office of
  Teacher Education and
  Certification
Division of Elementary
  and Secondary
  Education
Kneip Office Building
700 North Illinois
Pierre 57501, 605/773-
  3553

Tennessee
Director, Teacher
  Education and
  Certification
State Department of
  Education
125 Cordell Hull Building
Nashville 37219, 615/741-
  1644

Texas
Director, Division of
  Teacher Certification
Texas Education Agency
William B. Travis State
  Office Building
1701 North Congress
  Avenue
Austin 78701, 512/463-
  8976

Utah
Supervisor of Teacher
  Certification
Instruction and Support
  Section
Utah State Office of
  Education
250 East 500 South
Salt Lake City 84111,
  801/533-5965

Vermont
Director, Certification
  Division
State Department of
  Education
Montpelier 05602, 802/
  828-2445

Virginia
Director of Teacher
  Certification
Division of Teacher
  Education and
  Certification
State Department of
  Education
Box 6Q, James Monroe
  Building
Richmond 23216, 804/
  225-2907

Washington
Director of Certification
  and Licensing
Office of the
  Superintendent of
  Public Instruction
Old Capitol Building
Olympia 98504, 206/753-
  6773

West Virginia
Director, Office of
  Educational Personnel
  Development
State Department of
  Education
Capitol Complex, Room
  B304, Building 6
Charleston 25305, 304/
  348-2696

Wisconsin
Administrator, Teacher
  Certification
Bureau of Teacher
  Education and
  Certification
State Department of
  Public Instruction
125 South Webster Street
P.O. Box 7841
Madison 53707, 608/266-
  1027

Wyoming
Director, Certification and
  Licensing Unit
State Department of
  Education
Hathaway Building
Cheyenne 82002-0050,
  307/777-6261

C. PROFESSIONAL ASSOCIATIONS IN THE UNITED STATES OF INTEREST TO SECONDARY-SCHOOL TEACHERS

AAAS   American Association for the Advancement of Science, 1333 H
        Street, NW, Washington, DC 20005.

AAHPER	American Alliance for Health, Physical Education and Recreation, 1201 Sixteenth Street, N.W., Washington, DC 20036.
AAPT	American Association of Physics Teachers, 5110 Roanoke Place, Suite 101, College Park, MD 20740.
AASL	American Association of School Librarians, 50 E. Huron Street, Chicago, IL 60611.
ACMST	Association for Computers in Mathematics and Science Teaching, P. O. Box 4455, Austin, TX 78765.
AECT	Association for Educational Communications Technology, 1201 Sixteenth Street, N.W., Washington, DC 20036.
AHEA	American Home Economics Association, 2010 Massachusetts Avenue, N.W., Washington, DC 20036.
AIAA	American Industrial Arts Association, 1201 Sixteenth Street, N.W., Washington, DC 20036.
AVA	American Vocational Association, 1510 H Street, N.W., Washington, DC 20005.
CLR	Council for Library Resources, Inc., One Dupont Circle, Washington, DC 20036.
IRA	International Reading Association, 800 Barksdale Road, Newark, DE 19711.
JCEE	Joint Council on Economic Education, 1212 Avenue of the Americas, New York, NY 10036.
MENC	Music Educators National Conference, 1902 Association Drive, Reston, VA 22091.
NABT	National Association of Biology Teachers, 11250 Roger Bacon Drive, Reston, VA 22090.
NAEA	National Arts Education Association, 1916 Association Drive, Reston, VA 22091.
NAGT	National Association of Geology Teachers, P. O. Box 368, Lawrence, KS 66044.
NAPE	National Association of Professional Educators, 412 First St., SE, Washington, DC 20003.
NBEA	National Business Education Association, 1906 Association Drive, Reston, VA 22091.
NCSS	National Council for the Social Studies, 1515 Wilson Blvd., Suite 101, Arlington, VA 22209.
NCTE	National Council of Teachers of English, 1111 Kenyon Road, Urbana, IL 61801.
NCTM	National Council of Teachers of Mathematics, 1906 Association Drive, Reston, VA 22091.
NSTA	National Science Teachers Association, 1742 Connecticut Avenue, NW, Washington, DC 20009.

What associations or corrections do you recommend adding to the preceding list?

EXERCISE 19.2: MY FINAL SELF-EVALUATION OF COMPETENCIES AS REVIEWED THROUGH
A RESOURCE GUIDE FOR SECONDARY SCHOOL TEACHING: PLANNING
FOR COMPETENCE

Instructions: Now that you have completed this resource guide, check yourself on this final 53-item competency list. In the appropriate square to the right of each item, write in

> *3* if you have definite readiness or awareness.
> *2* if you have comfortable readiness or awareness.
> *1* if you are still weak and uncomfortable, and need more work.
> *0* if you didn't do it and have no awareness or knowledge about it.

Share the results with your instructor.

	3 Definite Yes	2 Comfortable	1 Still Weak	0 Zip
1. I am aware of secondary school programs, purposes, goals, and can recall information about students, instructors, and administrators. (Chapter 1)				
2. I am aware of the instructional and noninstructional responsibilities I will have as a teacher. (Chapter 2)				
3. I am knowledgeable about things I must do prior to the beginning of school. (Chapter 2)				
4. I am skillful in the use of the facilitating behaviors. (Chapter 10)				
5. I have identified my emerging teaching style. (Chapter 3)				
6. I am aware of the characteristics of an effective learning environment. (Chapter 14)				

	3 Definite Yes	2 Comfortable	1 Still Weak	0 Zip
7. I have identified my teaching skills. (Chapters 4, 10, 17, 19)				
8. I have learned about the characteristics of a competent teacher. (Chapters 4, 17)				
9. I am aware of the characteristics of effective instructional delivery. (Chapters 4, 10, 11, 17)				
10. I am aware of the importance of providing frequent learning comprehension checks. (Chapters 4, 7, 8, 9)				
11. I feel confident about working with students who have special needs. (Chapters 1, 9)				
12. I can be a competent student advisor. (Chapters 2, 9)				
13. I have prepared a complete instructional plan. (Chapters 8, 9)				
14. I have prepared my first self-instructional package. (Chapter 9)				
15. I have prepared an effective course syllabus. (Chapter 8)				
16. I am aware of the importance of being constantly vigilant over the safety and welfare of my students. (Chapters 4, 14)				

	3 Definite Yes	2 Comfortable	1 Still Weak	0 Zip
17. I know what to do when a supervisor or an administrator visits my class to evaluate my teaching. (Chapters 4, 17)				
18. I am aware of ways of making evaluations of my teaching professionally rewarding experiences for me. (Chapters 4, 17)				
19. I am aware of the importance of careful planning. (Chapters 5–9)				
20. I have examined courses of study, teacher's plans, and textbooks. (Chapter 6)				
21. I know how to determine textbook readability. (Chapter 6)				
22. I can write instructional objectives in behavioral terms. (Chapter 7)				
23. I can prepare effective daily lessons. (Chapter 8)				
24. I can individualize the learning experiences for students. (Chapter 9)				
25. I can effectively select and implement a variety of instructional strategies. (Chapters 10–11)				

	3 Definite Yes	2 Comfortable	1 Still Weak	0 Zip
26. I have developed my knowledge about where to locate resources and aids that will enhance my teaching. (Chapter 12)				
27. I can effectively use the chalkboard. (Chapter 12)				
28. I am aware of the importance of maintaining the physical environment of my classroom. (Chapters 4, 14)				
29. I am efficient in handling routine clerical matters, e.g., attendance and record keeping. (Chapter 14)				
30. I am knowledgeable about classroom management techniques. (Chapters 14–15)				
31. I am prepared to deal with disruptive students. (Chapter 15)				
32. I can evaluate student achievement. (Chapter 16)				
33. I can write a variety of kinds of test items. (Chapter 16)				
34. I am aware of the necessity that I promptly read, mark, grade, and return student papers. (Chapter 16)				

	3 Definite Yes	2 Comfortable	1 Still Weak	0 Zip
35. I have effectively prepared and implemented micro peer teaching lessons. (Chapters 10, 11, 17)				
36. I am aware of the value of grading using a point system, and can do it. (Chapter 16)				
37. I can discuss the growth I have made in my teaching skills. (Chapters 4, 10, 17, 19)				
38. I am aware of the importance of evaluating according to course objectives. (Chapters 4, 7, 8, 16)				
39. I am aware of the nature of evaluation forms used to evaluate teachers. (Chapter 17)				
40. I am familiar with the expectations of me as a teacher. (Chapters 2, 17)				
41. I am aware of the importance of establishing collegial relationships with clerical and custodial staffs, administrators, and other teachers. (Chapter 4)				
42. I am familiar with techniques for locating a teaching position. (Chapter 19)				

	3 Definite Yes	2 Comfortable	1 Still Weak	0 Zip
43. I am familiar with techniques for preparing a job application. (Chapter 19)				
44. I have prepared my professional résumé and a sample cover letter. (Chapter 19)				
45. I am aware of how best to prepare for an employment interview. (Chapter 19)				
46. I know where I can contact professional associations of interest to me. (Chapter 19)				
47. I am knowledgeable about professional journals and associations for my discipline. (Chapters 12, 19)				
48. I have performed several self-evaluations and am fully aware of my own current teaching strengths and weaknesses. (Chapters 4, 10, 17, 19)				
49. I am knowledgeable about the Professional Code of Ethics and legal guidelines for the classroom teacher. (Chapters 2, 14)				
50. I am confident that I will be an effective teacher. (Chapter 19)				

	3 Definite Yes	2 Comfortable	1 Still Weak	0 Zip
51. I am aware of the cultural diversity of our public schools today and am prepared to effectively work with students of varying cultural backgrounds. (Chapters 1, 9)				
52. I am academically prepared to teach my subject.				
53. I am ready and eager to teach in a secondary school, whether it is a middle school, a junior high school, or a senior high school.				
Totals (159 = perfect)				

This resource guide began by providing input data about secondary school teaching, then proceeded to guide you through additional data collection and sharing of those data, processing of those data into your own plans for teaching, to where you are now ready for the highest level of application—a full-time teaching position. From your self-evaluation (Exercise 19.2), are you ready?

We wish you the very best in your exciting career choice and for continued professional development. Occasionally you may wish to revisit this resource guide.

QUESTIONS FOR CLASS DISCUSSION

1. Share with others in the class information you can obtain regarding teacher retirement plans, sick-leave benefits, insurance programs, and related fringe benefits now available in your state for public and private school teachers.
2. What merit or incentive plans for classroom teachers are in existence, or in planning stages, for your local or state schools?
3. Before applying for a teaching position, you may want to refer to a recent edition of *Estimates of School Statistics* (Washington, DC: National Education Association).

The 1986–87 edition shows that teachers working in the following locations received the highest annual salaries: Alaska, $43,970; The District of Columbia, $33,797; New York, $32,620; Michigan, $31,500; and California, $31,170. As you look toward beginning your teaching career and identifying school districts that interest you, have you taken the time to collect information (including salary range and benefits) about the districts?

4. Some predictions indicate that education will be different in the twenty-first century: education will continue to be viewed as a lifelong process (the early years will remain critically important in human development), with experimental education increasing. More technologies (voice-recognition systems, videos, discs, computer programs) will be used, and more individualization will be planned, with some students doing school work at home (called distance learning). Further, the next century may see some public schools going private, other schools facing lawsuits when graduates fail to meet minimum competency standards, and still others increasing the length of summer sessions or changing to year-round schedules. Further, there is the possibility of a technology gap as well-to-do parents purchase computers and other educational equipment for their children. These girls and boys may have a technological edge and develop much faster than children in poorer homes. What meaning do these predictions have for you as you consider teaching students in the twenty-first century?

5. Congratulations! You have reached the end of this resource guide, but there may be questions remaining in your mind. As before, identify them, with ways you may find answers.

SUGGESTED READINGS FOR CHAPTER 19

Litt, M. D., and Turk, D. C. "Sources of stress and dissatisfaction in experienced high school teachers." *Journal of Educational Research* 78(3):178–185 (January-February 1985).

Swick, K. J., and Hanley, P. E. *Stress and the Classroom Teacher.* Washington, DC: National Education Association, 1980.

Epilogue

THE CLASSROOM TEACHER IS LIKE A SYMPHONY CONDUCTOR. You are the person ultimately accountable for the quality of the performance. You must understand the potential of the contribution of each section of the orchestra, of each individual member. You must work at getting each member to perform to full potential. You must comprehend the origin of the score, its history, the mood of the composer, and you must be able to "hear" the finished piece before it is played.

During performances you must not only be in control of the orchestra every moment, but simultaneously be several bars ahead in your thinking. There is no time to belabor the sour notes, nor fret over an occasional missed beat. You have planned and rehearsed the orchestra so well that you have confidence in its overall ability and in the quality of the anticipated performance.

You are aware of the limitations and constraints placed on you by equipment or surrounding resources and outside influences. You perceive these as providing challenges, and as evidence of a need for improved community understanding of the value of the orchestra. You respect the community support, but know of the need for improved instruments, more rehearsal time, new scores, better pay, and incentives for good performance.

Concomitant with these responsibilities is the potential for stress and professional "burn-out." Aware of this you have developed a plan for coping with stress and that plan includes:

1. taking good care of yourself physically by eating well and exercising regularly.
2. taking good care of yourself mentally by planning days of relaxation away from the orchestra and from thinking about its performances, by being aware of when you need some time off, and rewarding yourself accordingly.
3. by developing support groups that will include colleagues and other peer relationships where you can vent your feelings, discuss your work, and develop your own skills; by developing a supportive relationship with your staff and administrators.

Have a good career, the best of performances!

E. C. K.
R. D. K.

Glossary

accountability. Reference to the concept that an individual is responsible for his or her own behaviors and should be able to document the value and effectiveness of activities carried out.

advance organizer. Preinstructional cues used to enhance retention of materials to be taught.

affective domain. An area of learning related to appreciations, interests, attitudes, feelings, and values development.

AFT. The American Federation of Teachers, a national professional organization for teachers.

at-risk. General term given to students who show a high potential for dropping out of formal education.

behavioral objective. A statement describing what the learner should be able to do upon completion of the instruction. It contains four ingredients: the audience (learner), the behavior, the conditions, and the degree (performance level).

brainstorming. A teaching strategy where judgments of the ideas of others is forbidden. It is used to create a stream of new ideas.

classroom management. The teacher's system of establishing a climate for learning, including techniques for preventing and handling student misbehavior.

clinical supervision. In education, a nonevaluative collegial process of facilitating teaching effectiveness by involving a triad of individuals: in teacher education, the triad consists of the student teacher, the cooperating teacher, and the college or university supervisor. Clinical supervision (sometimes known as "effective supervision") will involve: (1) a preobservation conference between the supervisor and the supervisee to specify and agree upon the specific objectives for the observation visit; (2) a data collection observation; and (3) a postobservation conference to analyze the data collected during the observation, and to set goals for future observations.

cognitive domain. The area of learning related to intellectual skills, such as retention and assimilation of knowledge.

competency-based instruction. See *performance-based instruction.*

comprehension. A level of cognition that refers to the skill of "understanding."

computer-assisted instruction (CAI). Instruction received by a student when interacting with lessons programmed into a computer system.

computer-based instruction (CBI). Used for any reference to the use of computers for instruction.

computer literacy. The ability at some level on a continuum to understand and to be able to use computers.

computer-managed instruction (CMI). The use of a computer system to manage information about learner performance and learning-resources options in order to prescribe and control individual lessons.

convergent thinking. Thinking that is directed to a preset conclusion.

cooperative learning. An instructional strategy that uses small groups of students working together and helping each other on learning tasks, stressing support for one another rather than competition.

criterion. A standard by which behavioral performance is judged.

criterion-referenced. Standards that are established and behaviors that are judged against the preset standards, rather than against behaviors of others.

critical thinking. The ability to recognize and identify problems and discrepancies, to propose and to test solutions, and to arrive at tentative conclusions.

curriculum. Originally derived from a Latin term referring to a race course for the chariots, there still is not a widely accepted definition of the term *curriculum* as used in education today. For this resource guide we define *curriculum* as all of the planned experiences students have in a program of education.

deductive learning. Learning that proceeds from the general to the specific.

direct intervention. Teacher use of verbal reminders or verbal commands to redirect student misbehavior, as opposed to the use of nonverbal gestures or cues (indirect intervention).

discipline. In teaching, the process of controlling student behavior in the classroom. An archaic term that has been largely replaced by the term *classroom control* or *classroom management*.

discovery learning. Learning that proceeds from identification of a problem, development of hypotheses, testing of hypotheses, and arrival at conclusion.

discretionary strategies. Teaching techniques, not necessarily required for student learning, but which represent choices from which a teacher may select techniques appropriate for her or his own unique class of students and subject.

divergent thinking. Thinking that expands beyond an initial thought.

eclectic. Utilizing the best from a variety of sources.

educational goal. A desired instructional outcome that is broad in scope.

effective school. A school where students master basic skills, seek academic excellence in all subjects, demonstrate achievement, and display improved behavior and attendance.

empathy. The ability to understand the feelings of another person.

evaluation. The process of judging the value of results by considering evidence in light of preset standards.

exceptional child. A child who deviates from the average or normal child in any of the following ways: mental characteristics, sensory ability, neuromotor or physical characteristics, social behavior, communication ability, or in multiple handicaps.

facilitating behaviors. Teacher behaviors that make it possible for students to learn.

feedback. In interpersonal communication, information sent from the receiver to the originator that provides disclosure about the reception of the intended message.

goal, course. A broad, generalized statement telling about the course.

goal, instructor. A statement telling what the instructor intends to do.

high school. See *secondary school*.

holistic learning. Learning that incorporates emotions with thinking.

individualized learning. The self-paced process whereby individual students assume their own responsibility for learning through study, practice, feedback, and reinforcement, with appropriately designed instructional packages.

inductive learning. Learning that proceeds from the specific to the general.

inquiry learning. Like discovery learning except that the learner designs the processes to be used in resolving a problem. Inquiry learning typically demands higher levels of mental operation than does discovery learning.

instructional module. Like the self-instructional package (S.I.P.), any free-standing instructional unit that includes these components: rationale, objectives, pretest, learning activities, comprehension checks, posttest.

internalization. The extent to which an attitude or value becomes a part of the learner.

junior high school. See *secondary school*.

learning. A change in behavior resulting from experience.

mainstreaming. Placing an "exceptional child" in a regular classroom for all or part of his or her learning.

mandala. A visual geometric pattern that stimulates right-brain functions.

mastery learning. The concept that a student should master the content of one lesson before moving on to the content of the next lesson.

measurement. The process of collecting and interpreting data.

metacognition. The ability to think about, understand, and develop one's own thinking and learning.

micro peer teaching. A clinical technique of preparing, implementing, and evaluating a teaching demonstration to a small group of peers.

middle school. A school that has been planned for students ranging in age from 9 through 14. Middle schools generally have grades five through eight (with grades six through eight being the most popular organization), although many varied patterns exist. For example, a school might include grades seven and eight and still be called a middle school. Although middle schools vary considerably in organization, generally the fifth and sixth grades are each self-contained (each class has one teacher for all or most of the day), while seventh and eighth grades are departmentalized, i.e., students in these grades may meet each day for a home-base class, then go to other rooms and teachers for other subjects.

multicultural education. A deliberate educational attempt to help students understand facts, generalizations, attitudes, and behaviors derived from their own ethnic roots as well as those of others. In this process the students should unlearn racism and biases and recognize the interdependent fabric of our human society, giving due acknowledgment for contributions made by all its members, and realizing the values in our cultural pluralism.

NEA. The National Education Association, a national professional organization of teachers.

norm-referenced. Individual performance that is judged relative to overall performance of the group.

opaque projector. A projector that projects enlarged images of reflected light from pages of a book or any other nontransparent object.

overhead projector. A projector that transmits light through transparent materials and projects an enlarged image on the screen.

overlapping. The teacher's ability to attend to several matters at once.

performance-based instruction. Instruction designed around evaluating student achievement against specified and predetermined behavioral objectives.

performance objective. See *behavioral objective*.

positive reinforcement. Encouraging desired student behaviors by awarding those behaviors when they occur.

probationary teacher. An untenured teacher. (After a designated number of years teaching in the same district, upon rehire the probationary teacher receives a tenure contract.)

psychomotor domain. An area of learning related to development of locomotor behaviors and skills.

realia. Real objects used as visual props in teaching, such as political campaign buttons, plants, memorabilia, etc.

reliability. In measurement, the consistency with which an item is measured over time.

secondary school. Traditionally, any school that has students from grades seven through twelve. Those secondary schools with grades seven, eight, and sometimes nine, are termed junior high schools; schools with grades twelve, eleven, ten, and sometimes nine are termed high schools.

simulation. An abstraction or simplification of a real-life situation.

SQ3R. A study strategy where students survey the reading, create questions, read to answer the questions, recite the answers, and review the original material.

student teaching. The field experience component of teacher education where the teacher candidate practices teaching students under the direct supervision of a credentialed teacher and a college or university supervisor.

teaching style. The way a teacher teaches: that teacher's distinctive mannerisms complemented by his or her choices of teaching behaviors and strategies.

tenured teacher. After serving a designated number of years in the same district as a probationary teacher, upon rehire the teacher receives a tenure contract. This means that the teacher is automatically rehired each year thereafter, unless the contract is revoked by either the district or the teacher for specific and legal reasons.

terminal behavior. That which has been learned as a direct result of instruction.

think-time. See *wait time*.

validity. In measurement, the degree to which an item measures that which it is intended to measure.

wait time. In the use of questioning, the period of silence between the time a question is asked and the inquirer does something, such as repeats the question, or calls upon a particular student, or answers the question himself or herself.

withitness. The teacher's ability to spot quickly and prevent by redirecting potential student misbehavior.

Index

Abbott, S., 280
Abstract learning experiences, 291, 292, 299
Academic freedom, the teacher and, 111–112
Acceptance, use of, 224, 228
Access mode, 245, 246
Accountability, 66, 222, 388
Accreditation, school, 93, 93n, 387
Acheson, K. A., 74n
Achievement
    evaluating student, 389, 395
    reporting student, 413
    testing for, 388
Adler, M. J., 15
Administrative review, 388, 434
Administrative support, 14
Administrator, school, 13, 22, 33, 73, 414, 461
Advance organizer, 61
Affective domain, classification of, 125
Affective objectives and evaluation, 392
Ahrendt, K., viii
AIDS, 37
Aids and resources, 291
Allard, H., 345
Alley, G. R., 189
Anecdotal records, 393, 394
Angry parent, 415
Angry student, 413
Anspach, R., 280
Apple Computer, Inc., 204n
Arrangement test item, 400
Art, 163, 308, 315, 326
Articulation, scope and sequence, 81
Assertive discipline, 373
Assessment of learning, 67, 136, 387
Assessment, purposes of, 387
Assignments
    controversial, 271
    use of, 191, 270–273, 396, 436
Associations, professional, 476
At-risk students, 192, 195
Attention getter, 249, 250
Attention, student, 141, 393
Attitudes, teacher, 435, 441
Audiovisual, see Aids and resources
Awareness, teacher, 443

Back-to-School Night, 25, 414
Baldwin, D., viii
Ball, O. E., 53
Barbe, W. B., 52, 53
Beginning the class period, 141, 142, 355
Beginning teacher, 4–5
Beginning the year, 9, 346
Behavior
    goal directed, 393

student, 66, 255, 348–349, 393
    teacher, 51, 59, 66, 222–225, 241–243, 255, 293
Behavior modification, 373
Behavioral objectives, 117
    classification of, 121, 123
    recognition of, 120
Behavioral objectives diagnostic test (BODT),
    126
Behaviorism, 50
Benson, A., 280
Berquist, W. H., 55n
Bilingual education, 315
Bilingual learners, 190, 193
Biology, 165, 183, 308
Blackboard, see Chalkboard
Bloom, B., 122, 187, 187n, 205
Body language, teacher use of, 185
Boyer, E. L., 15
Brain research, learning and, 52
Briggs, K. C., 53
Briggs, L., 123n
Briggs-Myers, I., 53
Brophy, J. E., 347n, 348, 349n
Bruner, J., 50, 291n
Bulletin, reading the school, 355
Business education, 170, 309, 315, 327
Buttler, B., 308n
Butts, A., 280

California State University, Sacramento, 193n
California, State of, 95, 363
Campus, the school, 5
Canfield, A. A., 53
Canfield, J. S., 53
Canter, L., 373
Canter, M., 373
Carroll, J., 187, 187n, 205
Case studies, use of, 376
Certification, teacher, 469. See also Credential
Chalkboard, 301
Cheating, student, 399
Chiarelott, L., viii
Churchill, W., 1
Citizenship grading, 397, 414
Clarifying, use of, 224, 443
Class interruptions, 221, 246, 347, 353
Class meeting, 373
Class time, use of, 142, 346–347
Classroom
    behavior rules, 9, 346–349, 374
    control, 81, 345, 369–370
    environment, 51, 255, 349
    interaction, 241, 263
    management, 9, 345, 369–370, 372, 374
    observations, 74–75, 441, 446, 448

Classroom (*Continued*)
 as a stage, 185
 visitation, 19, 441, 446, 448
Claus, C. K., 128*n*
Clerical responsibilities, 355
Clinical supervision, 74
Closure
 lesson, 142, 444
 sample of, 146
Code of Ethics of the Education Profession, 39
Codes, lesson plan, 168–169, 249
Cognitive disequilibrium, *see* Discrepant event
Cognitive domain, 121, 122, 392, 413
 classification of, 122
Cognitive-experimentalism, 50
Combs, A. W., 50
Comments, teacher written, 393, 394
Communication
 classroom, 9
 skills, 9
 teacher and, 22, 349, 373, 374
Competencies, teacher, 65, 73, 479
Competency based instruction, 119
Competency development, resources for, 73
Competent instruction, components of, 387
Completion test item, 401
Comprehension checks, 153, 191, 205, 224
Computer, 293, 308
 periodicals, 296, 315
 software, 296–297, 314
Computer assisted instruction (CAI), 294, 295
Computer assisted learning (CAL), 294
Computer assisted management (CAM), 294
Concrete learning, 248
Conferencing
 with parents, 415
 with supervisor, 75
Consequences, behavior and, 375
Content coverage, 191, 192
Content, selecting course, 93
Contract, teacher's, 366
Contract unit plan, 183
Control, classroom, 81, 345, 369–370
Controversial issues, teaching, 111, 113
Cooperating teacher, the, 4, 453, 459
Cooperation Square Game, the, 284
Cooperative learning, using, 345
Copy machine, using a, 312
Copyright laws, the, 313
Correction test item, 401
Corrective feedback, 206
Costa, A. L., 229*n*, 241*n*
Course
 content, 93, 109, 191
 goals, 117, 135
 outline, 109
 schedule, 135, 137
 of study, 93, 97
 syllabus, 136, 139
Credential information, sources for, 475
Credential, the teaching, 8
Criterion-referenced evaluation, 395
Critical thinking, teaching, 229
Cross-cultural education, *see* Multicultural education
Cuing, use of, 248
Cultural diversity, 8, 195
Curriculum
 documents for, 93
 frameworks for, 95
 textbooks and the, 99

Curriculum articulation, 81
Curriculum guides, 93, 97, 107

D'Allessandro, J., 369*n*
Dale, E., 291*n*
Darrow, C., 280
Data facilitation, use of, 223
Daynes, R., 308*n*
Dead time during class, 373–374
Defense Dependent schools, 470
Delivery mode, 245, 246, 253
Demonstration, use of, 267
Dewey, J., 50
Direct experiencing, 293
Direct intervention, use of, 348
Direct teaching, *see* Traditional teaching behaviors
Disciplinary action, 346
Discipline, 348, 369–370
 assertive, 373
Discovery, use of, 253, 295
Discrepant event, use of the, 255
Discussion, use of, 258–267
Disruptive student, 383
Ditto, making a, 312
Divorce, students of, 375
Donlan, D., 269*n*
Donovan, J. F., 89*n*
Dreikurs, R., 373
Drill and practice, computer, 295
Dropout, rate of student, 16
Drug and alcohol abuse, 371, 372, 383
Dunn, K. J., 52, 53
Dunn, R. S., 52, 53
Duplication of class materials, law regarding the, 313
Duplicator, the spirit, 312

Eclectic teaching style, 49, 50, 63, 221
Education for All Handicapped Children Act, 7
Educational Policies Commission, 90
Educational reports, year of, 14
Emotionally handicapped (EH) students, 8
Encouragement, use of, 228, 325, 443
Ending the class period, 142
English, 173, 309, 315, 328
Entwistle, N., 53
Environment, the classroom, 51, 255, 349
ERIC, 298
Essay test, 401
Ethnocentrism, 194
Evaluation, 388, 392
 final self-, 479
 formative, 389
 forms for teacher, 434, 441, 448
 student teacher, 430
 summative, 389, 392
Evaluation and subjectivity, 392
Evers, N., viii
Examinations, 396, 436
Exceptional child, 7. *See also* Special needs students
Exceptional students, 188
Exceptionality, areas of, 7
Expectations of a teacher, 39
Extra-credit, using, 397
Eye contact, use of, 9, 250

Facilitating behaviors, teacher, 49, 59, 221, 222–225, 245
Federal Law Title IX, 359
Feedback
 from administrators, 73
 evaluation and, 388

Feedback (*Continued*)
  strategies, sample use of, 168–169
  from students, 73
  from university supervisor, 73
Feeney, T., 179n
Feistritzer, E., 15
Films and filmstrips, sample use of, 307
First day, the, 9, 267
Focusing, use of, 146
FORECAST formula, 105n
Foreign language, 181, 309, 316, 330
Formative evaluation, use of, 389
Framework, curriculum, 95
Free materials, sources of, 311
Free period, 5, 6
Freedom of expression, 111
Freud, S., 50
Futrell, M. H., 6n

Gabrel, G., 280
Gagné, R. M., 123n
Gall, M. D., 74n
Gallup Poll, 15
Games
  classification of, 279
  samples of, 283, 288
  sources of, 280, 288
  use of, 278
Gaming, computers and, 295
GATE students, 457
Gender, interaction and, 66, 263, 265, 359
Geometry lesson plan, model, 145
Gerken, M., 53
Get-acquainted activities, 9–11
Gifted students, 190, 193, 457
Ginot, H. G., 373
Glasser, W., 373
Goals, course, 117, 135
Goals and objectives, 117
Good, T. L., 347n, 348, 349n
Goodlad, J. I., 15
Grade reporting, 413
Grade
  the academic, 397
  arriving at a, 396, 411
  the citizenship, 397, 411
Gradebook, the, 355, 395
Grades, posting, 399
Grading, 395, 436
  criteria for, 396
  point system, 396–397
Grading on the curve, 395
Grading performance classes, 397
Grant, C., 8n
Graubard, S. R., 15
Green, R. P., viii
Gregorc, A. F., 53
Grobman, D., 165n
Grouping for instruction, 189
Grouping test item, 403

Haglund, E., 219
Hands-on learning, 247
Haney, C., 280
Health and safety, student, 66, 268
Heinich, R., 295n, 296n, 297n, 314n
Hemisphere, brain, 52
Heron, J., 59
Hill, Joseph, 52
History, 310

Hoban, C. F., 291n
Hoeltke, G., 53
Home economics, 171, 309, 316, 330
Homework, 192, 414. *See also* Assignments
Houchings, R. R., 190n
Hoyle, J. V., viii
Humor, use of, 67, 346, 374
Hunt, J. B., Jr., 15
Hunter, M., 89
Hyman, I. A., 369n

Identification test item, 404
Incentives, use of, 222
Independent schools, 469
Indirect intervention, teacher, 348
Individual differences, dealing with, 7, 81, 153, 159, 187
Individualized Education Plan (IEP), 188
Individualizing for instruction, 188, 189
Industrial arts, 315
Inquiry lesson, sample, 255
Inquiry teaching
  learning from, 255
  use of, 253–257
Inservice teacher, 111
Instant-action society, 323
Instructional objectives, 117
Instructional responsibilities, 41
Instructional strategies
  listing of, 247
  selecting, 245
Instructional Theory Into Practice (ITIP), 89
Instructional units, purpose of, 157
Instructor goals, 117
Interaction
  classroom, 232, 241, 263, 265
  evaluation of classroom, 427
  and gender, 66, 263, 265, 359
  maximum distance for, 267
Interruptions, class, 221, 346–347, 353
Intervention, teacher, 348
Interview
  of administrators, 33
  the job, 472
  of students, 21, 23
  of teacher candidates, 29
  of teachers, 31
Issues in schools today, 16
ITIP, 89

Jenkins, E. S., viii
Job getting, 469
Job interview, 472
Johns Hopkins University, 193n
Johnson, R., 187, 187n, 205
Johnson, S., 187, 187n, 205

Kagan, N., 52
Keller, F., 187, 205
Keller Plan, 187, 205
Kellough, N., ix
Kellough, R. D., 191n, 204, 204n
Kim, S., ix
Kinesic variation, example of, 146
Kolb, D. A., 52
Kounin, J., 373
Krathwohl, D. R., 52

Landerman, R., 280
Language barrier, 193
Laser videodisc, use and sources of, 307

Learner
  bilingual, 190, 193
  disabled, 8
  gifted and talented, 190, 193, 457
  recalcitrant, 190–192
  slow, 190, 191
Learners, 52
Learning
  abstract, 291
  concrete, 248
  definition of, 117
  effective, 121
  hands-on, 247
  mastery, 187, 205, 208
  motivation for, 133, 323
  philosophies of, 50
  processes of, 65
Learning by doing, 247, 291
Learning disabled (LD) student, 8
Learning experiences, 291
Learning experiences ladder, 291, 299
Learning modality, 52, 210
Learning style assessment, sources for, 52–53
Lecture, use of, 221, 248
Lee, H. C., 74n, 76n
Legal guidelines, 359
Lesson
  body of, 142, 146
  that failed, analysis of, 143
Lesson body, components of, 153
Lesson plan
  analysis of, 143, 275
  evaluation of, 155
  format for, 153
  model, 145
  preparation of, 87, 141, 153
Lesson plan format, generic, 153
Lesson planning variables, 51
Lesson plans, sample, 143, 145
Levels of thinking, 229
Lewis, E. L., 369n
Liability insurance, teacher, 366
Limited Proficiency in English (LPE), 193
Lindsay, Jr., T., 183n
Locke, J., 50
Lutz, N., 53

Mainstreaming, 7, 188
Makeup work, use of, 396
Malcom, P., 53
Management, classroom, 345
Mastery learning, 187, 205, 208, 395
Matching test item, 404
Mathematics, 145, 310, 315, 331
McKeachie, W. J., 248n
Meeks, J., 163n
Meeting, orientation, 4
Mentor teacher, 14
Micro peer teaching, 239, 251, 417, 472
Middle ear problems, 190
Middle school, 3n, 349
Miller, A. R., viii
Miller, P. W., 52n
Misbehavior, student, 348–349
Mitchell, J. R., 284n
Mobility in the classroom, teacher, 9, 191
Modality preference, 52
Modeling, teacher use of, 66, 223, 255, 345, 375
Modular scheduling, 5
Molenda, M., 295n

Morgan, S., 173n
Motivation, student, 133, 323, 339
Multicultural education, 7, 8, 194, 196
  activities for, 196–203
  goals of, 8
Multilevel teaching, 189
Multiple-choice test item, 405
Multipurpose board, 301
Multisensory stimulation, 249
Music, 175, 310, 315, 331
Mystery island inquiry, 255, 257

Names, learning student, 9, 267, 374
Napa, CA, 89
National Education Association, 39n, 40, 90
Noninstructional responsibilities, 42
Nonverbal communication, use of, 52, 185, 224, 374
Norm-referenced grading, use of, 395
Nylen, D., 284n

Objectives
  classification of learning, 123
  instructional, 117. See also *Behavioral objectives*
  performance, see Behavioral objectives
Objectives and evaluation, 389, 392
Objectives and selection of verbs, 119, 128–130
Objects, *see* Realia
Observation conference, classroom, 75
Observations, classroom, 74
Office, the teacher's, 413
Off-task time, 347. *See also* Dead time during class
Opaque projector, 301–302
Open classroom, 255
Open house, 25
Oral report, use of, 277–278
Organizations, professional, 476
Organizers, use of advance, 61
Orientation meeting, 4
Outcome-based instruction, *see* Performance-based instruction
Overhead projector, 301–305
Overlapping, teacher's use of, 222, 443
Overobjectivity, danger in, 133

Pacing of lessons, 223, 249, 345
Paraprofessional experiences, 454
Parent, communication with, 355, 357, 414
Parent–teacher organization, 27
Pause, use of, 224
Pearson, M. J., 189n
Performance classes, grading in, 397
Performance expectations, *see* Performance level
Performance level, 119
Performance objectives, 117
Performance test item, 407
Performance-based instruction, 119, 133
Period
  beginning the class, 141, 142, 355
  ending the class, 142
  teacher preparation, 5, 6
Periodicals, professional, 315
Periods, class, 5
Personality conflicts, 375
Personalized System of Instruction (PSI), 187, 205
PET, 89
Peterson, N., 189n
Phillips, S. R., 55n
Philosophy of teaching, 57
Physical education, 177, 310, 315, 334

Piaget, J., 50, 255*n*
Placement, job, 469, 470
Plan, the seven-step, 135
Planning lesson, rule for, 247
Planning
  first step in instructional, 107
  instructional, 51, 81, 87, 107, 135, 141
  long-range, 81
  reasons for instructional, 81
Plans, evaluation of, 15, 161
Policies, school, 4, 13
Praise, use of, 52, 224, 228, 348
Prayer in the classroom, 367
Preparation period, teacher, 5
Price, G. E., 52
Principal, the school, 13, 414, 461
Printed material, use of, 313
Private school, 469
Problem solving, use of, 229, 253, 295
Processes, inquiry, 254
Profession, commitment to, 40
Professional associations, 476
Professional commitment to students, 40
Professional growth, 13
Professional periodicals, 315–317
Professional responsibilities, 40–43
Professionalism, 39
Program for Effective Teaching (PET), 89
Progress reports, 397
Progressive education era, 369
Props, *see* Realia
Psychomotor domain, 121, 392
  classification of, 124
Public Law 94-142, 7
Pull-out approach, 193
Punishment, use of, 375

Questioning, use of, 51, 224, 225, 228, 443, 444
Questions
  applying and evaluating, 444
  clarifying, 443
  classification of, 229–230
  classroom interaction and, 241
  cognitive level of, 229, 231, 232, 233, 235
  praise and, 228
  processing, 444
  rhetorical, 228
  textbook, 237
Questions and use of think-time, 228
Questions used in job interviews, 472

Readability formula, textbook, 105
Reading level, range of, 268–269
Realia, 307
Reality therapy, 373
Records, class, 13, 395
Reilly, R. R., 369*n*, 374*n*
Reinforcement, positive, use of, 192, 373
Reliability, teacher's, 68
Reliability in testing, 388
Report card, 413–414
Resource file, 319
Resource unit, 107
Responses, student behavior and teacher, 229, 348–349
Responsibilities, teacher, 39–46, 355
Résumé preparation, professional, 470
Rewards, use of, 373
Reynolds, C. R., 53
Riechmann, S. W., 53
Riegel, T. R., 53

Rights
  student, 40, 361, 375
  teacher, 361
Ripple effect, 373
Risk taking, teacher, 66
Rodriquez, G., 181*n*
Romanticism–maturationism, 50
Ross, N. M., 105*n*
Rousseau, J. J., 50
Rules, classroom behavior, 9, 346–349, 374
Russell, J. D., 295*n*

Safety, student, 66, 268
Salaries, teacher, 486
Schedule
  course, 135, 137
  modular, 5
  school, 4–6
School campus, the, 5
School day, the, 5
School organization, 3
School policies, 4, 13
School year, the, 5
School, year-round, the, 5
Schools
  Defense Dependent, 470
  private, 469
Science, 308–311, 316, 334
Scofield, C., 170*n*
Scope and sequence, curriculum, 81, 97
Self-discovery learning, 292
Self-evaluation, teacher, 68–71, 82, 226, 434, 479
Self-instructional package (SIP), 187, 204
Set, use of, 141, 442
Shifting interaction, example of, 146
Shipp, D., 177*n*
Short explanation test item, 407
Silence, use of teacher, 146, 224, 228
Simulated experiences, 293
Simulation, use of computer, 295
Singer, H., 269*n*
Sizer, T. R., 15
Skinner, B. F., 50, 373
Skorich, J., 175*n*
Slavin, R. E., 89*n*
Sleeter, C., 8*n*
Slow learners, teaching, 190, 191
Social science, *see* Social studies
Social studies, 179, 316, 336
Sousa, D. A., 89*n*
South Carolina, 89
Spanish, 181
Special needs students, 7
Stallings, J., 89*n*
Stimulus variation, use of, 142, 146
Stout, A., 284*n*
Strategies, list of teaching, 247
Strategy, selection of teaching, 245
Stress
  student under, 375
  teacher under, 375
Structuring, 222
Student
  angry, 413
  difficult, 381
  disruptive, 381
  learning disabled (LD), 8
Student attention, 141
Student cheating, 399
Student disagreement, 111

Student feedback, 73
Student motivation, 133, 323
Student opinions, using, 73
Student records, 393
Student rights, 40, 361, 375
Student teacher and academic freedom, 112
Student teacher, controversy and the, 111
Student teaching
   competencies for, 430
   description of, 453
   experiences before, 454
   experiences during, 459
Students
   emotionally handicapped (EH), 8
   exceptional, 8, 188
   female, 66
   handicapped, 7
   health and safety of, 66, 268
   individual differences of, 81
   interviewing, 21, 23
   LPE, 193
   meeting your, 9
   secondary, 6
   special needs, 8, 66
Students at-risk, 192
Students and sense of personal worth, 192
Style
   eclectic teaching, 50
   facilitating teaching, 49
   origins of teaching, 50
   teaching, 49, 55, 59
   traditional teaching, 49
Subject knowledge, teacher's, 65, 434, 441
Subjectivity and evaluation, 392
Submersion, language, 193
Summative evaluation, use of, 389
Supervision, clinical, 74
Supervisor, university or college, 73, 75, 75*n*, 453
Swassing, R., 53
Syllabus, course, 136, 139, 386, 413

Teachalogue, 428
Teacher
   the cooperating, 4, 453, 459
   the inservice, 111
   interviewing a, 31
   the student, 111, 430, 453, 454
   typical week of a, 45
Teacher arrival time, 6
Teacher behaviors, 51, 59, 222–225, 241–243
Teacher biases and prejudices, 66
Teacher candidate, 29
Teacher as communicator, 66
Teacher competencies, 65, 431, 479
Teacher as facilitator, 49, 59, 221, 222–225, 245
Teacher interests, 67
Teacher liability, 366
Teacher observation forms, 441
Teacher and other adults, 67
Teacher reliability, 68
Teacher responsibilities, 39, 41, 67, 355, 393
Teacher rights, 361
Teacher and risk taking, 66
Teacher schedule, 5
Teacher self-evaluation, 68–71, 82, 226, 434, 479
Teacher sign in, use of, 6
Teacher stress, 375
Teacher and subject knowledge, 65, 66, 434, 441
Teacher tenure, 366

Teacher written comments, use of, 392–394
Teacher's attitude toward students, 435, 441
Teacher's body position, 185
Teacher's confidence in students, 67
Teacher's contract, 366
Teacher's duty time, 6
Teacher's location in classroom, 185
Teacher's mobility in classroom, 9, 191
Teacher's office, 413
Teacher's optimism, 67
Teacher's salaries, 486
Teacher's voice, 249, 345
Teachers
   characteristics of secondary, 13, 435
   shortage of, 16
Teaching behaviors
   facilitating, 49, 59
   traditional, 49, 59
Teaching credential, 8
Teaching evaluation forms, 434, 441
Teaching methods, 436
Teaching, philosophy of, 57
Teaching style, 49, 55
Teaching unit, 107
   evaluation of, 161
   preparation of a, 157, 159
   purpose of the, 157
Tenure, teacher and, 366
Term papers, use of, 277
Test, administering a, 398
Test anxiety, 398
Test construction, 400
Test items, types of, 400
Testing, 398, 436
   frequency of, 398
   purposes of, 398
   time needed for, 399
Textbook, 99, 103, 237, 268
   adoption of, 99, 268
   examination of, 101–105
   questions in, 237
   selection of, 103
   use of, 268–270
Textbooks, readability of, 105
Think time, 228
Thinking
   critical, 229
   levels of, 229
Thinking style, 52
Thorndike, A. H., 50
Time-on-task, 205
Title IX, 359
Torrance, E. P., 53
Traditional teaching behaviors, 49, 59, 192, 245
Transitions, use of, 155, 354
Transparencies, 302–303
True-false test item, 408
Truth, values, and morality, teaching about, 112
Tudor, J. D., 89*n*

Unit
   contract, 183
   purposes of an instructional, 157
   resource, 91
   teaching, 157, 159
Unit plan
   components of, 159
   evaluation of, 161

Unit Plan (*Continued*)
   format for, 157, 159
   time duration of, 157
Unit plans, sample, 163–184

Validity in testing, 388
Van Doren, M., 79
Variables that affect learning, 50
Variation in interaction, 443
VCR, use of, 307
Verebal cues, use of, 248
Verbal experiences, 292, 301
Vicarious experiences, 293
Videodisc, use of, 307
Videodisc Compendium, 308
Videodiscs, sources of, 308–311
Videotaping, off-air, 314
Visitation, school, 19, 21, 25, 27
Visual cues, use of, 248

Visual experiences, 292, 301
Vocabulary used, 249
Voice, teacher's, 249, 345

Wager, W., 123n
Walberg, H. J., 89n
Watson, J., 50
Week, teacher's, 45
West Orange, NJ, 89
Wilson, C., 2n, 220n, 386n
Withitness, 222, 373
Wong, J., 145n
Writing board, use of, 301

Year, beginning the school, 9, 346
Year of educational reports, 14
Year-round school, 5

Zevin, J., 255n

Notes